COMMEMORATION IN AMERICA

COMMEMORATION IN AMERICA

ESSAYS ON MONUMENTS, MEMORIALIZATION, AND MEMORY

EDITED BY DAVID GOBEL AND DAVES ROSSELL

University of Virginia Press | Charlottesville and London

University of Virginia Press

Printed in the United States of America on acid-free paper
First published 2013
1 3 5 7 9 8 6 4 2

Library of Congress Cataloging-in-Publication Data
Commemoration in America : essays on monuments, memorialization, and memory / edited by David Gobel and Daves Rossell.
pages cm
Includes bibliographical references and index.
ISBN 978-0-8139-3372-6 (cloth : alk. paper)
ISBN 978-0-8139-3373-3 (pbk. : alk. paper)
ISBN 978-0-8139-3433-4 (e-book)
1. Monuments — United States. 2. Memorialization — United States. 3. Nationalism and collective memory — United States. 4. Art and society — United States. I. Gobel, David Walter, editor of compilation. II. Rossell, Daves, 1960– editor of compilation.
NA9347.C66 2013
725'.940973 — dc23
2013004143

Contents

Acknowledgments

NEARLY TEN YEARS AGO more than eighty scholars from nine countries gathered in Savannah, Georgia, to consider the manifold ways in which commemorative acts have been and continue to be manifested in architectural and urban form. It was at this Third Savannah Symposium on Commemoration and the City that the present volume was conceived. The stimulating presentations given at the symposium and the fruitful conversations that followed led us to focus that theme further in this collection of essays on the perplexing issues that surround commemorative acts specifically in America. We are grateful, therefore, to the Savannah College of Art and Design, the Department of Architectural History and all those who participated in that symposium for paving the path that led to this volume of essays. We are particularly indebted to Robin Williams, chair of the Department of Architectural History, and to Paula Wallace, president of the Savannah College of Art and Design. The Georgia Humanities Council also contributed by generously supporting the symposium. Above all, Boyd Zenner, architecture and environmental editor at the University of Virginia Press, has patiently nurtured this project through a long maturation period, exhorting and encouraging as only she can. Also at UVaP, Mark Mones, assistant managing editor, and Angie Hogan, assistant to the director, deserve much credit for seeing this through. Finally, Dell Upton and Catherine Bishir are to be specifically thanked for their wise council and encouragement.

COMMEMORATION IN AMERICA

DAVID GOBEL AND DAVES ROSSELL

Introduction

Democracy has no monuments. It strikes no medallions.
It does not bear the head of a man on its coins.
—John Quincy Adams

ONCE A WILDERNESS bearing witness only to the authoritative cycles of nature, America has become a landscape littered with monuments, memorials, and memories. Heedless of the admonitions of anti-memorialists such as John Quincy Adams, Americans have sought for centuries to satisfy their insatiable appetite for commemorating by building monuments, preserving buildings, performing rituals, renaming streets, planting trees, and thinking of ever-new ways to remember. As the results of this habit, commemorative acts and objects shape our lives in fundamental ways, but their meaning is always multivalent and conflicted. Our monuments and commemorative acts attest to both triumphs and tragedies, but each of us remembers different acts and achievements from different perspectives and for different reasons. Constituting a vital part of both our individual and national identity, commemoration is also inherently complicated and contentious. Its contradictions strike at the core of our identity and speak to the importance of commemoration in the construction of our cultural landscape. Clearly we have much to learn regarding the nature and meaning of commemorative acts.

The premise of this collection of essays is that memories are ineffable connections with the past that are processed and stored by the brain and that memorials are the particular placement of material form, structure, and words to commemorate such memories. The often complicated negotiations involved — including the event, its interpretation, its editing, and the subsequent proposal and creation — are the stuff of history.

Paradoxically, a need or desire for change is imbedded in every expression of remembrance, as the essays in this volume attest. A multiuse public building is rediscovered and transformed into Independence Hall, which then becomes the centerpiece of a multi-acre project transforming blocks of downtown Philadelphia into an extensive green mall. A fifty-four-mile stretch of highway named in honor of both the president of the Confederacy and a 1950s white supremacist becomes a National Historic Trail dedicated to the civil rights movement. Commemoration is rarely just about concretizing past conceptions or ideals; it also valorizes new ones. Every commemorative act translates an ideal into a new language.

Commemoration, inevitably, also involves dialogue. Just as every commemorative site or cause or figure has multiple facets, so too are the interested interpreters diverse in their insights and aspirations. Even the civil rights movement, dedicated to the seemingly immutable ideals of tolerance and equality, employed many narratives to achieve multiple commemorative ends. With so many competing interests involved in whatever is to be commemorated, it is amazing that any single monument ever gets built. Commemoration is a multimedia spectacle with respectful orations intoned amid parades, fireworks, beauty contests, hip-hop competitions, text panels, and sometimes even traditional monuments. With such a broadly orchestrated range of materials and events involved, spatial placement and dynamics of movement are critical. The fixity of monuments is largely a fiction, as many acts of commemoration begin and end as celebrations, while the physical monuments are inevitably retouched, restored, or otherwise renewed as time goes on. At least a part of their identity is thus always expressed in contemporary terms.

This volume addresses specific historical events and their reception by diverse audiences at varying times. As editors, we have tried to provide a spectrum of time frames and geographic settings. There is much in the following essays to be learned about critical moments in the nation's past and the long-standing processes that have defined space and place in America. Four sections highlight different perspectives. The first section of essays is explanatory, leading us through the nuances of meaning within a range of monuments. The second addresses the ascendancy of form and expression in traditional forms of commemoration. The third explores the ambivalence of commemorative expressions that flow from disturbing or even horrific events — trampling, internment, and prejudice. And the final essay addresses the historical lack of commemoration.

Discovering the Monumental Theme

If we acknowledge that understanding a monument is always more than simply knowing what a particular figure symbolizes, what then is the process of uncovering fuller meanings? What materials should we look at? What questions should we ask? What if the commemoration is not explicitly a monument? Dell Upton addresses these questions in "Why Do Contemporary Monuments Talk So Much?" Identifying two great monumentalizing periods — the 1880s to the 1930s and the 1980s to the present — he provides a series of guidelines for interpreting them. Any monument's identity can be gauged by locating it on three axes or sliding scales. One must first assess a memorial's relative public-to-private character (i.e., differentiating between commemoration that is intended to be public from that which is private or personal); then consider the work's specificity versus its abstraction (referring not only to the inherent ambiguity of meaning in figural representation but also to its trajectory from specific commemorative function to larger didactic goals); and, finally, we must address how broadly representative a particular monument is. Stripped to these essentials, monuments float somewhere within a theoretical triangle described by literalism, allegory, and formalism, with literalism being the purported facts related to the commemoration, allegory its higher ideals, and formalism the technique of expression. Upton tells us that all monuments have a message; they always say more about the people, times, and places of their creation than they do about the people, times, and places they honor, and they are always promoted by interested parties.

Catherine W. Bishir's "Memorial Observances" offers a case study of two Southern monuments. Connecting the works with her own history, she urges us to be mindful of the backstories of monuments, to consider them carefully and let their message or messages sink in. All history, she reminds us, is personal, and the story we tell is always our own story. Bishir helps us understand a single pair of monuments in Lexington, Kentucky, and Raleigh, North Carolina, but in doing so she also tells us a surprising amount about Southern history, and about her own historical process of discovery.

The physical commemoration of events is the subject of Mark A. Peterson's "Stone Witnesses, Dumb Pictures, and Voices from the Grave: Objects, Images, and Collective Memory in Early Boston." Peterson charts what he calls "memory preservation" in the Puritan use of biographies (literary memorials), portraits (visual memorials), and gravestones in the colonial era. He notes the sometimes subtle, sometimes dramatic transition to what were called "ebenezers," or stones of help, and more traditional stone monuments in the post-Revolutionary age. Complementing the creation of these memorial forms are the later traditions echoing — commemorating — the Puritan age in works of Hawthorne, Emerson, and Longfellow. These forms are successful because they "[fold] together the literary and the spiritual with the monumental and the particular."

The Triumphal Marker

Several case studies in this section demonstrate the ways in which powerful segments of society use commemoration to assert their authority, and how they are sometimes thwarted. Fusing hallowed models of the past and urgent needs of the present, proponents embrace a variety of markers from parades and holidays to changes in the urban fabric, individual pledges, and trees. Each commemoration celebrates an ideal and a cause, one directly related to an audience and setting.

Jhennifer A. Amundson explores such compelling circumstances in her essay, "Staging a Triumph, Raising a Temple: Philadelphia's 'Welcoming Parade' for Lafayette, 1824." Philadelphia was the premier destination in Lafayette's unparalleled thirteen-month tour through each of America's then twenty-four states, but it was also a diverse city with discrete neighborhoods and classes and occupations. At least ten triumphal arches lined a three-mile, thirty-block-long route through the city for a parade celebrating Lafayette's support of American independence. Some hundred thousand spectators lined streets enhanced by the monument-building of several decades — what Amundson calls "a three-dimensional architectural history chronicling the city's growth from foundation to revolution and independence." She does not, however, allow the triumphalism of the moment to obscure her observation of the remarkably diverse group of citizens who creatively adapted classical ideals for the service of the present.

Ellen M. Litwicki's essay, "'Liberty Regulated by Law': Civic Instruction on the George Washington Inaugural Centennial in Chicago," goes to the heart of big-city industrial America in the late nineteenth century by showing how carefully crafted and contentious a national holiday can be. Though intangible, holidays are reverential emblems of time, diversely expressed. Litwicki explores how officials used city celebrations as a calculated attempt "to legitimize their position as the civic leaders of Gilded Age society" and promote national law and order.

In "The Democratic Monument: The Reframing of History as Heritage," Richard M. Sommer and Glenn Forley also discuss how commemoration of something in the past can be a response to the needs of the present. In charting the dramatic development of Independence Mall in Philadelphia in 1949, Sommer and Forley show how a new bridge, fulfilling a century-long goal of spanning the Delaware, can inadvertently create traffic jams and offer particularly embarrassing vistas of a dilapidated area. A nineteenth-century reinvention of a state building can lead to early-twentieth-century appropriation of the building form but in a new context. Sommer and Forley's interests, however, go beyond the analysis of historic site creation, and address the larger question of "heritage" versus "history," as seen, for instance, in the 1947 tour of the Freedom Train. Expanding the discussion of patriotism that Litwicki introduced with Chicago, Sommer and Forley take on national interests in business-government cooperation to combat global threats and promote freedom and liberty.

If history can be recast as heritage, so a prominent tree can become a monument. As hallowed as Elm Streets are in the American cityscape, they were little studied as cultural icons before Thomas J. Campanella revealed their particularly monumental function. His essay, "'As a Witness upon the Field of History:' The American Elm as Commemorative Vessel in Nineteenth-Century New England," demonstrates that in settings largely without monuments, the majestic elm became a natural marker. Although the trees' actual roles in historic events were often found to be fabricated, they were nevertheless imbued with historical associations.

The Weight of History

Some events are so horrific or hotly contested that many wish they could be erased and forgotten. How does one commemorate the loss of seventy-three lives in an uncharged but probably criminal act? How does one do justice to a brilliant legal mind that essentially legalized murder for slave masters? How does one commemorate the struggle for civil rights one hundred years after the end of slavery?

At times, emotions are so raw that memorialization is not an option. So some monuments are incomplete; some are inconclusive. Compromised commemoration has its own story to tell, often as rich as it is contentious. America's history of industrial violence provides many such challenging opportunities for commemoration. In "Unresolved: The Italian Hall Memorial in Calumet, Michigan," Alison K. Hoagland dissects the troubled memorialization of the deaths in December 1913 of seventy-three people, most of them children, trapped at the bottom of a stairway while trying to flee a building they thought was burning. The question of who yelled "Fire!" and why the doors were closed grew even more troubling in the context of a miners' strike that began five months earlier, taking fifteen thousand workers away from their jobs in the single most productive copper-mining year to date. The facts that no one was ever charged, that there was lingering divisiveness between workers and the company, and that the building itself was ultimately condemned some seventy years after the tragedy added to the poignancy. The meager memorial that ultimately was created left only clues about a complex story of conflicting interpretations: outsiders versus locals, unions versus the company, and strikers versus non-strikers.

And what of Judge Thomas Ruffin, famed for his ruling in *State v. Mann* in 1829 allowing for a slave master to kill a slave in the name of property? Sally Greene, in her essay, "Judge Thomas Ruffin and the Shadows of Southern History," tracks the ambivalent support that gradually turned to outrage over the decision. What was once called the Ruffin Building is no longer so named, and nowadays Ruffin's statue sits in an inconspicuous alcove away from easy public view. The placement speaks to a more enlightened age's embarrassment at what is now seen as an overzealous reading of the law. Aesthetics and iconography secure an aura of dignity, but the actual historical circumstances render the visage disreputable.

Glenn T. Eskew, in his "Commemorating the Civil Rights Movement with Monuments in the Urban South," analyzes a broad range of memorials and identifies what he calls a "new civic religion"— a narrative of triumphant toleration, led by Martin Luther King Jr., that rose above many individual localized stories. Looking closely at Atlanta, Birmingham, Memphis, and Montgomery, Eskew describes the creation of a new collective memory fostered by scholars, veterans of the movement, and "heritage tourism," and underwritten by government funds. A second theme is the regular tension between different parties with an interest in the design, whether it is the King family criticizing the federal government in

Atlanta or the local Civil Rights Institute Task Force refusing to cede leadership to the architects in Birmingham.

In "Inventing Homelands in Japanese American Concentration Camps," Lynne Horiuchi narrates the forced relocation of more than one hundred thousand Japanese Americans. Whether Issei (Japanese immigrants to America), or Nisei (their American-born children), suspected insurgents were dragged from their homes, businesses, and schools, and cast into barren stockades, literally no-man's-land. What could they commemorate? Choosing an American identity, they were still incarcerated and denied rights as citizens in their country of choice, potentially deported and declared traitors in their native land. Choosing to remain culturally Japanese, they ran the risk of inflaming their captors' suspicions of treason. In such a complex situation, there were many ironies. Bonds between Issei and Nisei generations, which were prone to separate in America, may actually have been strengthened in incarceration through community events and Buddhist festivals aimed at boosting ethnic pride.

Forgoing Memory

The volume's final section, "Forgoing Memory," includes a single essay. David Lowenthal's "Adorning Damnable Cities: *Pro Urbis Amore* and *Damnatio Memoriae*" serves as a brilliant, if sobering, counterpoint to the commemorative elements addressed in previous essays. Perhaps more directly than any other work in the volume, Lowenthal's essay addresses the theme of commemoration and the city, which he finds a historic oxymoron. "Commemoration and the city — what an unlikely conjunction, especially in America!" he writes. Lowenthal investigates what he sees as the long-standing abnegation of commemoration in urban locales brought about by headlong development, halfhearted preservation efforts, and the continuous allure of more rustic settings. But even Lowenthal grudgingly notes that urban commemorative activities do exist, and, not surprisingly, his litany touches on the diverse activities addressed by other contributors: preservation, restoration, nomenclature, imagery, pictorial display, and storytelling.

In all, this volume encompasses a notably broad spectrum of places and the events associated with them. We can see them for what they are: hard-won, unusual, and singular in each case. Just as important as that grand bronze statue high on a plinth was the struggle to place even the wooden marker that preceded the stone on Bunker Hill.

What matters most is the ever-shifting and deeply personal nature of historical commemoration, the fact that remembrance in any form is contingent on place and time and circumstance. As the author Eudora Welty once said in *One Writer's Beginnings,* "The memory is a living thing—it too is in transit. But during its moment, all that is remembered joins, and lives—the old and the young, the past and the present, the living and the dead" (14).

DISCOVERING THE MONUMENTAL THEME

12

DELL UPTON

Why Do Contemporary Monuments Talk So Much?

WE LIVE IN AN AGE of monuments. Over the past quarter century, familiar statues of soldiers, presidents, and businessmen have been joined by memorials to events, people, places, and even animals that would never have been honored before, among them San Francisco, California's Summer of Love; Shenandoah, Pennsylvania's anthracite miners; Union City, Alabama's great bird dogs and their masters; Santa Cruz, California's pioneering surfers; a gray whale who strayed into California's Sacramento Delta; and the victims of a freeway bridge collapse in Webbers Falls, Oklahoma (fig. 1).[1]

After more than two decades of such energetic commemoration, the process of creating a monument in the United States has become highly ritualized. Like the monument builders of earlier ages, contemporary memorialists tend to be closely connected with the honored people or events, to pay close attention to the manner in which the subjects are represented, and to do so in a way that sacralizes the subject and translates specific people, places, and events into lofty abstractions.

At the same time there is something novel about contemporary American public monuments. Not only do they depict a wider variety of subjects than those of the past, but they seem to be erected more rapidly than their predecessors. While monuments to the Civil War were not constructed until after the war was over and most were not built until the end of the nineteenth century (except in cemeteries), a memorial to those killed in the 2002 collapse of the Webbers Falls freeway bridge was completed within a year of the accident.[2] The monument to the victims of the 1995 Oklahoma City bombing was undertaken almost as quickly. And plans for a memorial to the victims of the September 11, 2001, World Trade Center attacks seem to have been under way by September 12.

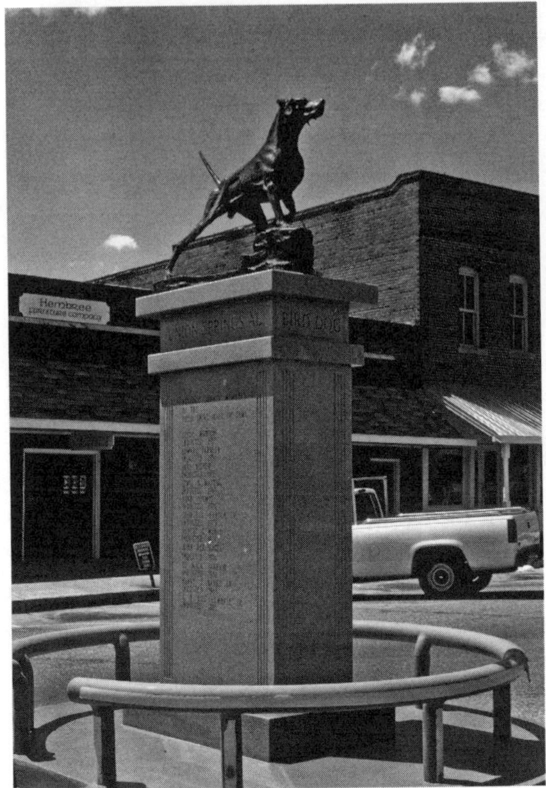

FIG. 1. Bird dog monument by Robert G. Wehle, c. 1985, Union Springs, Alabama. (Photo by the author)

Most of all, when compared with the monuments of the past, today's monuments are afflicted with logorrhea: they are covered with words by their builders, who seem to lack confidence in the ability of visual images to convey their messages. Both the rush to memorialize and the verbosity often arise from an urge to fix the meaning of events quickly and, equally important, to forestall other possible interpretations of the events in question.

To understand these qualities of contemporary commemoration, we need to ask three questions. First, what is the nature of civic monuments? How can we distinguish them from private memorials, on the one hand, and "public art" on the other? Monuments in the strictest sense belong to a repertoire of urban commemorative strategies, which also includes the naming of places, institutions, and public buildings; religious and civic rituals; and the dedication of works of non-memorial art.[3] Furthermore, monuments have not always been the preferred choice, but they have come to the forefront since the 1980s. So we are led next to question the nature and timing of the current monumental impulse. Why so many monuments? Why now? Finally, we must ask about the ways contemporary monuments are realized and the role the monument-building process plays in our society as vehicle for discussing (or evading) sensitive issues. Neither the process nor the role is simple and neither can be papered over by reductive, totalizing concepts such as "collective memory."

Monuments as Commemorative and Didactic Works

Monuments stand at the intersection of several axes along which we Americans organize our place-making and -marking. First, they stand toward the public end of a public-private axis. In graveyards and private spaces, we commemorate people who were significant mostly to their immediate families and friends and we do so in ways that emphasize personal qualities and private roles, even though we often borrow the visual language and epigraphic style of civic monuments to do so. Occasionally, private remembrances spill into the public realm. The roadside crosses and mementoes that are increasingly common along our highways, the memorial murals created by urban gangs, and even a Montgomery, Alabama, flagpole dedicated to "Deceased Past Presidents of Alabama Association of Realtors" are examples. When such commemorations extend beyond the circle of close acquaintances, we enter the realm of the public monument, although sometimes such monuments appropriate the visual forms and textual conventions of private funerary memorials, particularly when they are not publicly sponsored projects (fig. 2).

A second axis leads from specificity to abstraction. The task of monuments is complicated by their traditional reliance on metaphor rather than on expository texts to convey their meanings. They demand a certain cultural knowledge and they are by nature ambiguous: that is the source of their power but their constellation of references may escape the viewer or add meanings unintended by the sculptor. In 1842 Congress debated the fate of Horatio Greenough's statue of George Washington dressed in a toga and seated on a throne.[4] The work had been sent from the sculptor's Italian studio to the Washington Naval Yard, where it sat awaiting a decision about its placement. The debate was occasioned by a proposal that Congress fund a pedestal for the statue, which would then be dis-

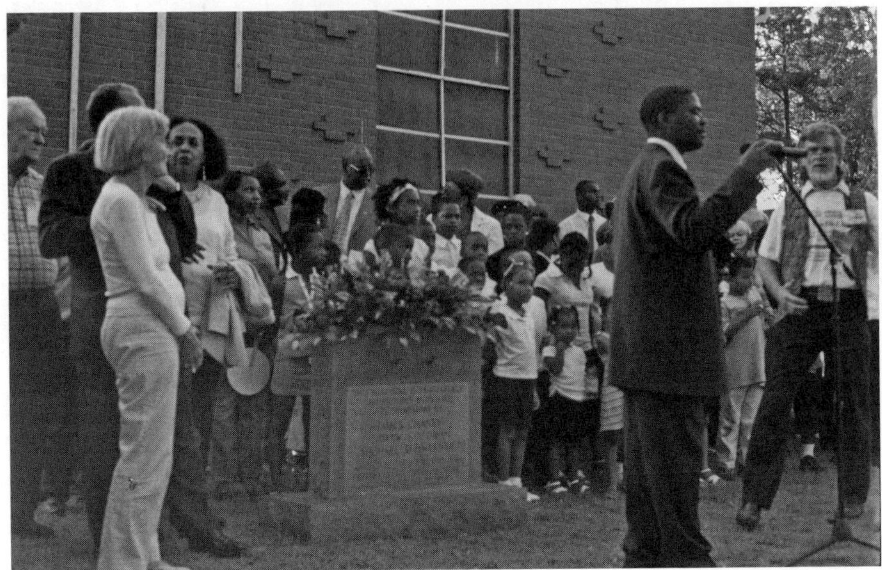

FIG. 2. Chaney, Schwerner, and Goodman monument, c. 1989, Mt. Zion United Methodist Church, Neshoba County, Mississippi. The wreath on top commemorating the fortieth anniversary of the murders of these three young men, placed here on June 20, 2004, follows a common Southern practice of decorating graves on Memorial Day. (Photo by the author)

played in the Capitol. Virginia congressman Henry Wise used the occasion to question the entire metaphorical premise of Greenough's work, from the choice of a semi-clothed Roman god to represent Washington ("a man whose skin had probably never been looked upon by any living" [person]), to the pose, to the Latin inscription. Wise acknowledged that

> he knew all this was dangerous ground to take; he was no artist — on the contrary, in works of art he was a perfect ignoramus. (A voice: "never a truer word.") He spoke from the untutored taste of nature and of an American citizen, who had been taught from his cradle to venerate every thing, little or great, which pertained to the greatest man that ever lived. He preferred seeing Washington as H[o]udon had represented him in the capitol at Richmond, in a lapelled coat and military boots, with epaulets, and a sword by his side.[5]

The ambiguities of visual metaphor in monuments have been explored by such artists as Dan Flavin and Anne Truitt. Flavin, whose works combined commercially available fluorescent-light tubes in various arrangements, created a series of "monuments" to historical figures such as the Russian sculptor-architect Vladimir Tatlin and to personal friends. The mundane materials and the lack of any evident relationship between the works' forms and anything known about the honorees made the nature of the tributes ambiguous. In fact Flavin disavowed any message in his monuments: "It is what it is, and it ain't nothin' else."[6]

"Vernacular" monuments, such as the commercial gravestones used to honor James Chaney, Michael Schwerner, and Andrew Goodman, three civil rights workers assassinated in Neshoba County, Mississippi, in 1964, often evoke a similar ambivalence in their lack of the traditional attributes of monumental commemoration (fig. 3). We expect something more "elevated," more "symbolic," or more "public" to mark such a catastrophic and politically charged event, but the stone "is what it is, and it ain't nothin' else."[7] Conversely, for those with the requisite cultural knowledge, a work such as Anne Truitt's *Southern Elegy* (1961–62), a combination of vertical, black-painted planks that resembles a gravestone without an inscription, seems by its shape and color to elicit mourning without indicating who or what has been lost.[8]

But ambiguity in the visual language of monuments means that they can be read in many ways. In his critique of Greenough's *Washington,* Wise claimed that

> a countryman, entering the rotundo by the library door, and seeing the back of the statue, would very naturally ask who is this? and looking at the inscription would say to himself Simul Acrum. Who is Simul Acrum? (A laugh.) But the next [word — *istud*] would tell him. (Increased merriment.) It was offensive. Mr. W's objection to the statue was that it was not American — it was not Christian; it belonged to another age and country. . . . When standing at right angles to the statue what was the idea it represented? Not that of one seated on a throne — that would not be tolerated here; some had thought it was a garden chair, but Mr. W. should say it was something else that he is sitting on — a throne belonging to an unmentionable temple.[9]

Henry Moore's abstract *Nuclear Energy* (1967), which marks the former site of the Manhattan Project at the University of Chicago, is labeled only with its title,

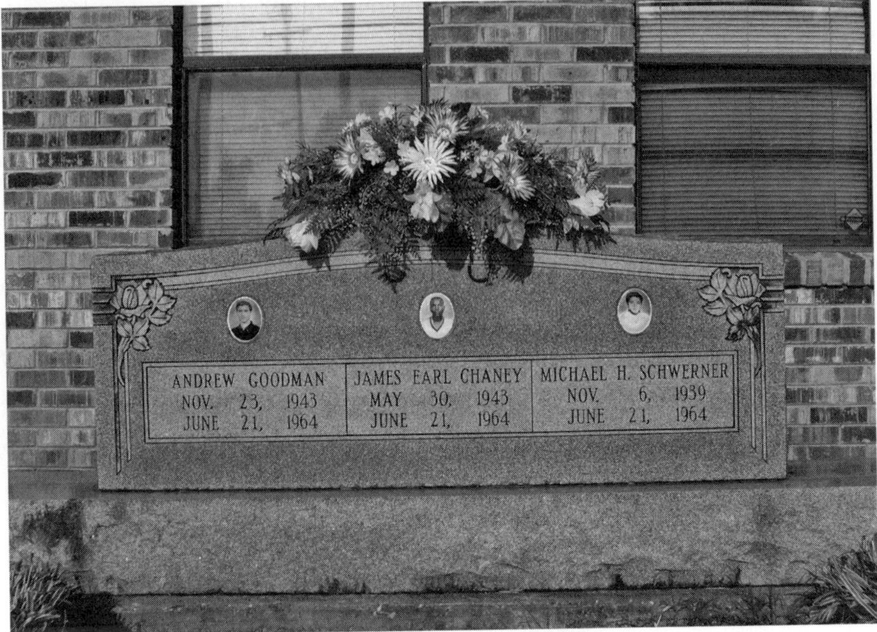

FIG. 3. Chaney, Schwerner, and Goodman monument, 1974, Mt. Nebo Missionary Baptist Church, Philadelphia, Mississippi. (Photo by the author)

date, sculptor's name, and the note, "Man achieved here the first self-sustaining chain reaction and thereby initiated the controlled release of nuclear energy." It may remind one of the abstract beauty of physics or of American ingenuity, but it also resembles a skull, as well as the mushroom clouds over Hiroshima and Nagasaki. Which of these is more apt is left to the viewer. The Washington Monument, seen at night with its stark white color emphasized, its pointed top, and the two red aircraft-warning lights in each face of the upper pyramid resembling eyes, has always reminded me of a Monument to the Unknown Klansman. You cannot control how people will interpret a visual image.

Should that bother us? Increasingly it seems that it does. I think that this is because the nature or task of monuments has been transformed in some subtle way. In defending Friedrich St. Florian's design for Washington's World War II Memorial (1997–2004), the *Washington Post* architectural critic Benjamin Forgey wrote that "a memorial is not a school, it is a shrine. A memorial is not to teach, it is to inspire."[10] But the metaphorical nature of monuments prompts contemporary monument builders to push them along the second axis from the specific-

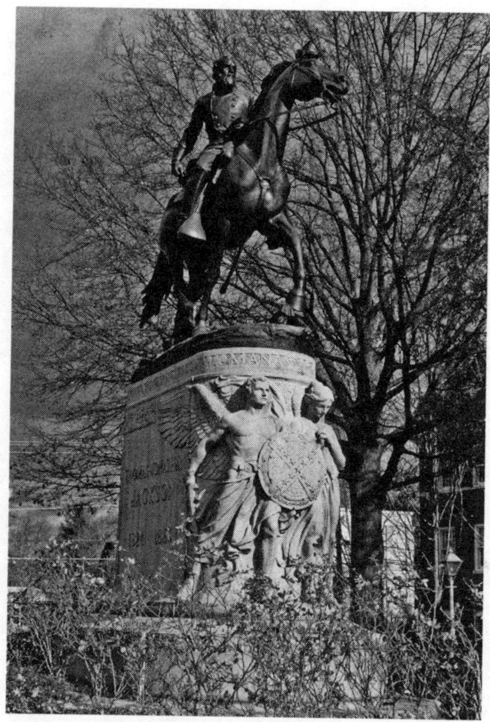

FIG. 4. Stonewall Jackson monument by Charles Keck, 1919/1924, Charlottesville, Virginia. (Photo by the author)

ity of commemoration to the didacticism of contemporary "public art," even as public art in turns slides toward the commemorative purpose of monuments. Los Angeles's *Biddy Mason: Time and Place* ("Biddy Mason's Wall," Sheila Levant de Bretteville and Power of Place, 1989), a public-art work dedicated to an early African American resident of that city, surrounds its many images, including some photographs, with expository texts. The Civil Rights Memorial (Maya Lin, 1989) at the Southern Poverty Law Center in Montgomery, Alabama, a simple inverted cone perched in front of a curved stone wall, is covered with text supplemented by a pamphlet available on-site and by a book that discusses each of the honorees.[11] One might compare these contemporary works to the unannotated allegory of an earlier work such as Charlottesville, Virginia's Stonewall Jackson monument (Charles Keck, 1919/1924), whose classical base, equestrian pose, Confederate battle flag, and proud white youth were assumed to be self-explanatory to the intended audience (figs. 4, 5).

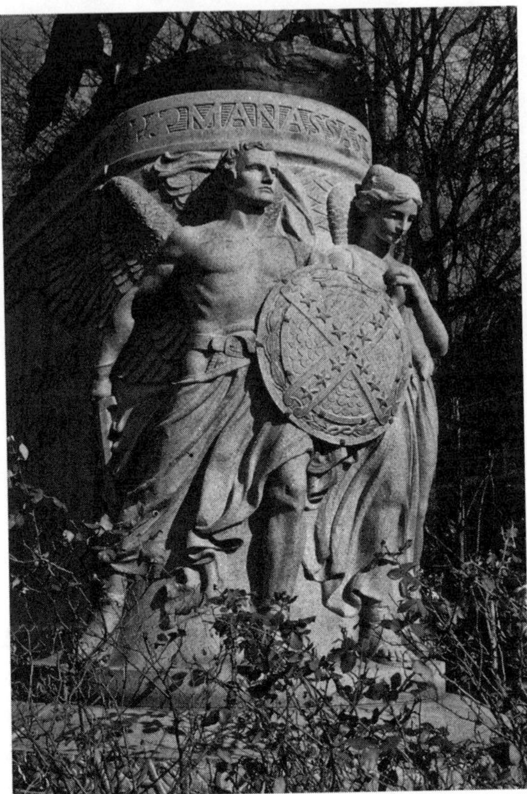

FIG. 5. Detail of Stonewall Jackson monument. (Photo by the author)

Civic monuments and public art now float in a triangle described by literalism, allegory, and formalism. At one corner is the literalism of a monument such as the Marine Corps War Memorial (Washington, D.C., Felix W. de Weldon, 1954), which purports to reproduce a specific historical event, a triumphant moment near the end of World War II when the U.S. flag was raised over the island of Iwo Jima (or, more accurately, when the moment was reenacted for the photographer).[12] Another corner of the triangle is occupied by the allegory of early-twentieth-century civic monuments that celebrated such lofty abstractions as Wisdom, The Triumph of the Law, Justice Receiving Back the Sword Entrusted to War, and Purity.[13] The third point of the triangle marks the flight from both allegory and realism to the pure form that characterized the public art of the mid-twentieth century. These works were often promoted as "free," apolitical, and rational alternatives to the demagogic, realist public art of Fascist and Communist societies.[14] In this Bermuda triangle of metaphor one finds civic monuments such as Cincinnati's *Law and Society* (Barna von Sartory, 1972), which is so abstract as to make its message unclear; didactic public art that is as narrative and representational as any formal civic monument; and the content-free fiberglass menageries of whimsically decorated cows, dolphins, whales, donkeys, elephants, and other creatures that walk (or swim) the streets of early-twenty-first-century American cities, commissioned by civic authorities seeking the least-potentially-offensive public art possible.[15]

The Commemorative Impulse

Why so many monuments? Why now? While Americans have always built monuments, we are currently in the midst of the second of two periods of particularly intense monument-building. Together they have created the majority of the civic monuments that we see around us. The first period encompassed the decades between 1880 and 1930, and especially the years from 1890 to the First World War. This was an era of vast expansion and centralization of economic and political power. The industrial-capitalist economy grew far beyond antebellum bounds and consolidation within and across industries gave certain industrialists, financiers, and corporations significant control over broad segments of the American economy and over those who depended on it. The American nation-state grew proportionately and engaged in some of its first forays into international conflict and imperial rule in Hawaii, the Philippines, and the Caribbean. It was also a time when the United States' grip on much of the North American continent tightened, as European American colonization moved inward in pincer fashion from the East and West Coasts.

If these were decades of national ascent, they were also years of uncertainty, of economic instability and social disorder. Waves of immigrants from eastern and southern Europe and East Asia transformed the ethnic composition of American society, while the oppression of newly freed Southern blacks stimulated migration to the urban North. Politicians and businessmen attempted to discipline the unruly nation by suppressing political dissent and exploiting racial, ethnic, and cultural differences. Like their counterparts in Canada, Australia, South Africa, and other so-called settler nations, they wanted the United States to be a "white man's country."

It was during this period of conflict and transformation that many of our most familiar monuments were constructed, from the Statue of Liberty to Civil War memorials to the legions of bronze politicians, generals, explorers, founders, and businessmen who stalk the streets, parks, and courthouse squares of the United States. Although these monuments appear to be the confident gestures of a newly powerful nation, they are better understood as reassertions of values that monument builders believed needed reinforcement amid turmoil.

This leads us to the first of three rules of thumb about monument-building: *All monuments have a message.* The mere exhortation to remember is a message, of course, but monuments communicate more specific claims as well. They direct us not simply to remember, but *to remember in a certain light.* They *interpret* the subjects they honor. It follows from this that they have an intended audience: people who are thought to need the message.

The subjects of these first-period monuments varied widely, but collectively they narrated a civic mythology, a particular view of American history and society that challenged the new realities of late-nineteenth-century America. They relied on the allegorizing and universalizing qualities inherent in monuments to portray an America in which conflicts and fissures were submerged in a civic unity characterized as progress. The monuments' America was a unique, successful project to bring enterprise, Christianity, and order to a vast, rich, barely occupied world that had been discovered, developed, populated, and further enriched by the individual efforts of Europeans and their descendants.

Here a second rule of thumb is relevant: *Monuments always say more about the people, times, and places of their creation than they do about the people, times, and places they honor.* At the opening of Washington's Lincoln Memorial (Henry Bacon and Daniel Chester French, 1911–22), the critic Lewis Mumford asked, "Who lives in that shrine, I wonder — Lincoln, or the men who conceived it: the leader who beheld the mournful victory of the Civil War, or the generation that took pleasure in the mean triumph of the Spanish-American exploit, and placed the imperial standard in the Philippines and the Caribbean?"[16] The first-period monuments, of which the Lincoln Memorial was a late example, celebrated a time before the waves of new immigrants arrived. They told a tale of "civilization" and "settlement" even as the last of the indigenous peoples of North America were being destroyed or subjugated. They celebrated individual achievement at a time when corporate and institutional power were ascendant. So their stories of Christopher Columbus, Captain John Smith, and Junipero Serra tell us how we should understand the late nineteenth century: as a time when equally bold (white) men could civilize the urbanizing, industrializing wilderness of modern America as their predecessors had done for the "virgin" continent.

It is difficult to miss the similarities between this earlier period and the present era of monument-building. Like the late nineteenth century, the recent decades have been times of political, economic, and demographic upheaval. We have experienced great economic growth and equally drastic economic reorganization and instability: the World Trade Organization, the North American Free Trade Agreement, the downsizing of industrial and governmental workforces, the outsourcing of jobs to foreign countries, the mortgage fiasco, and the destruction of the social safety net bespeak a time when power is once again becoming centralized, but in corporations and international organizations more than in governments. Indeed, globalization has made the nation-state nearly irrelevant, as neoliberal regimes since the time of Ronald Reagan and Margaret Thatcher have sought to dismantle their own power to govern international economic practices.[17] This reshuffling, along with the collapse or reorganization of old empires and the creation of new ones, stimulated a new wave of immigration and demographic transformation, with Latinos, Africans, Middle Easterners, and South and East Asians now forming a significant portion of the American population. At the same time, the civil rights movement, feminism, the gay rights struggle, resurgent religious and political conservatism, and the rehabilitation of militarism in reaction to the defeat in Vietnam have all helped to dissolve or realign long-standing social structures and political coalitions.

So once again monuments are being reared left and right to reassert threatened values. Where the late-nineteenth-century monuments proclaimed the dominance of (Western) Euro-Americans and the importance of individualism in a nation where both were losing importance, contemporary monuments glorify the nation-state (in the many war memorials that have been erected across the United States) at a time when its significance is lessening and they assert the importance of individuals at a time when one often hears the complaint that impersonality and institutional indifference permeate every aspect of daily life. And these new monuments are slathered with texts that approach the length of treatises when compared with the relatively cryptic inscriptions on earlier monuments.

The current monument-building era began with the 1982 dedication of the Vietnam Veterans' Memorial in Washington, D.C. All subsequent monuments—

especially but not only war memorials — stand in its shadow. They take their cues from the visual vocabulary that the designer, Maya Lin, employed or, as in the cases of the additions to the original memorial and to such newer works as the Korean War memorials in Washington (Frank C. Gaylord III and Cooper-Lecky Architects, 1995) and Nashville, Tennessee (Russ Faxon, 1993), or Washington's newly opened World War II Memorial, they explicitly reject it.

Like earlier public monuments, Lin's polished black marble wall with its sober type face employed formal elements borrowed from private funerary monuments to create a mournful mood. But both the defenders and the opponents of the wall read in it a message that transcended sorrow, assuming that the monument was a comment on contemporary American politics. Opponents in particular were convinced that Lin's wall constituted a negative judgment on the Vietnam War and by extension on American military power. They demanded additions to the memorial to transform the negative tone into a positive one. Frederick Hart's life-size *Three Soldiers,* added in 1984, depicted its battle-weary combatants as active figures rather than as the victims that critics found on the wall. A U.S. flag identified the dead as servants of the American state. The addition of Glenna Goodacre's figural Vietnam Women's Memorial (1993) drew wartime deaths in the service of politics into a higher, sacralized realm of sacrifice and loss by evoking the traditional Christian *pietà,* an image of the Virgin Mary cradling the dead Christ.[18] In making these additions to the black wall, Congress and the conservative opposition took a step toward the didactic — toward trying to control viewers' interpretation of the monument and the war — that foreshadowed the later fondness for texts in American monuments of all political persuasions. But they also acknowledged a perennial problem of representativeness and representation that has grown more acute in our time.

By representativeness I refer to the question of how adequately a particular monument embraces everyone it honors. The particularity of the people or events honored in a monument are often hidden behind a façade of abstraction meant to evoke higher purposes and meanings. The deaths of individual soldiers are folded into grand categories such as duty or freedom; the actions of individual leaders come to stand for national greatness; the achievements of individual artists testify to the greatness of a culture. Representation refers to the choice of visual images: how adequately does a monument's form convey the intended message?

American canons of representativeness and representation originated in the aftermath of the Civil War. According to the art historian Kirk Savage, the first

Civil War monuments used images of leaders or allegorical symbols such as eagles to stand for the war and all of its combatants. At the end of the nineteenth century, monument builders began to favor "common-soldier" memorials—idealized representations of single, ordinary fighting men. This choice shifted the monuments' focus from the specific, historic conflict over slavery and mid-nineteenth-century national politics to the abstract, timeless realm of individual duty, thus evading the central issues that provoked the war.[19]

Here we must take note of a third monumental axis, one that connects the collective and the particular. One figure stood for everyone in the common-soldier Civil War monuments but the Vietnam Veterans' Memorial lists every dead American individually rather than trying to categorize or collectivize them. The sheer length of Lin's dramatic black wall gave the comprehensive list (included by order of the competition program) new prominence in American monument-building, even though lists of the dead have been common on local war memorials in the United States at least since the Civil War. But the Vietnam Veterans' Memorial made names obligatory on all sorts of monuments, quasi-monuments, public art, and public works to the point that many of the finalists in the recent World Trade Center memorial competition reflexively proposed to list the names of the dead even though the draft guidelines stipulated that "individual recognition" did not necessarily require individual names.[20]

In keeping with the commercial bent of our times, the naming of honorees elides easily into the "naming opportunity," often with ambiguous results. The inclusion, placement, and form of immigrants' names on the long, gleaming *American Immigrant Wall of Honor* at New York's Ellis Island is determined by donation, while on Los Angeles's *Go for Broke Monument* (Roger Yanagita, 1999), which honors Japanese American soldiers who fought in the American military during World War II, the names of soldiers and the names of donors compete for attention.

If the lack of categorization—as victors, as heroes—on the Vietnam Veterans' Memorial kindled the long-running controversy over the monument's representation of its message, Frederick Hart's *Three Soldiers* reopened the question of representativeness seemingly settled by the list of names. Hart's work is a now-traditional common-soldier monument that serves the same abstracting purpose as the Civil War monuments, blunting the perceived political judgment of the black wall by drawing one's attention to the struggles and determination of living soldiers. But common-soldier Civil War monuments used the image of a generic white man to represent all who participated in the war. Hart's monument divided the common soldier into three different ethnic representatives — a white man, a black man, and a Latino man — but it does not include an Asian American, a Native American, or any of the many other ethnic minorities who fought in the U.S. military. Goodacre's "addition to the addition to the addition" (as Maya Lin called it) fragmented the representation even further by gendering the combatants, although it is testimony to the strength of the common-soldier tradition that the first design for the women's monument proposed a standing "lone Army nurse in combat fatigues." Lin argued in response that everyone was already adequately represented on her wall. "You can have one figurative group that stands for all," she said. "But two figurative groups stand for two."[21] Even to many conservatives, though, the single white male soldier was no longer acceptable as a universal representation. We may have reached the limits of the common soldier's usefulness.[22]

The fragmentation of representation and representativeness is not restricted to the Vietnam Veterans' Memorial. It betrays a broad crisis of confidence in the visual metaphor's power in an increasingly diverse society.[23] In 2002 the plans for a memorial to the firefighters who died at the World Trade Center on September 11, 2001, were revealed. The proposed figural group was a sentimentalized version of a well-known, already sentimentalized photograph of firemen raising a flag over the site (itself an echo of the canonical Iwo Jima photograph and memorial). A petition signed by one thousand rank-and-file firefighters criticized the design for depicting the three men as white, black, and Latino, when the firefighters in the original photograph were all white. The petitioners thought the designers had "sacrificed historical verisimilitude for political correctness."[24] To the dissenters, "the photograph was a symbol of American patriotism," and to alter it for the statue was to alter historical truth. To an official of a black firefighters' union, historical accuracy lay in a statue that would "reflect everyone who sacrificed" on that day rather than confining itself to the accidental details of a photographed moment.[25] Both sides lost sight of metaphor and framed monumental allegory and realism in representation and representativeness as mutually exclusive versions of "truth." The tension between symbolic and literal truth surfaced again when the official monument to the World Trade Center attacks was being designed. The *New York Times* reported that the committee members appointed to select a design for the September 11 memorial were aware of "the publicly expressed hunger for a memorial design specific both to the site and the event." When it became apparent that for technical reasons the memorial design would not reproduce the towers' footprints exactly, one survivor's father told a reporter, "It's very important to me that the dimensions of the tower be properly delineated. . . . To do any less, I think, would not be telling the story. People who come years from now will have no idea what the original dimensions were."[26]

Is contemporary prolixity, then, the product of a coarsening or "dumbing down" of cultural symbols owing to a loss of cultural literacy? Is it a product of growing social fragmentation? Or is there some other way we might account for it? To help us answer these questions we can look to our third rule of thumb (a pendant to number one, which stated that monuments have messages): *Monuments are almost always promoted by interested parties who claim to offer "the nation's gratitude."*[27] By setting a monument in a public space, the builders claim to speak for everyone. This is a fundamental, necessary fiction of monuments, but it *is* a fiction. The public who had a voice in a place such as Charlottesville, Virginia, in 1920, who had the privilege of erecting monuments, and who shared the values and the cultural baggage to understand and identify with the Stonewall Jackson monument was very small and relatively homogeneous (see figs. 4, 5). In fact, that monument was financed by a wealthy businessman, Paul Goodloe McIntire, who chose the sculptor, paid for the monument (and three others), and had the courthouse square redesigned to accommodate it.[28] So at the behest of one man Stonewall Jackson rides across the courthouse square, dwarfing the common-soldier monument erected a decade earlier by the United Daughters of the Confederacy and suggesting that Jackson is the object of gratitude and admiration among all Charlottesvillians, rich and poor, native-born and immigrant, white and black. But the African American–owned *Richmond Planet,* commenting on that city's similar Robert E. Lee monument, cast the claim of consensus in a very different light. "The Negro [worker] . . . put up the Lee Monument," the paper noted, "and should the time come, will be there to take it down."[29]

The narrow definition of the public assumed by the builders of the Stonewall Jackson monument is no longer tenable. A Paul Goodloe McIntire, a United Daughters of the Confederacy, or another powerful, interested party can no longer simply pony up the funds and plop down a monument in a public space regardless of the sentiments of the citizens at large (or at least they cannot do it as easily as they once could). More people and more kinds of people have the political and economic resources to be heard by erecting their own monuments and by opposing those promoted by others. Nearly every monument project since the Vietnam Veterans' Memorial, however innocuous, has come under intense public scrutiny and many have generated bitter quarrels over representation and representativeness.[30] This vehement debate arises not because our society is more diverse or more divided than before or because it has forgotten how to read its common symbols, but because more voices are audible and effective, even though they might not always express their views in palatable or conciliatory ways. Contemporary public battles over monuments are not the result of a breakdown of (an imaginary) former consensus but the products of greater democracy, at least in the symbolic realm.

We are now ready to understand the verbosity of contemporary monuments. Its origin lies in a paradox: contemporary monument builders can no longer rely on the fiction of consensus but they still want to create it. One function of long texts is to make certain that viewers get the right message. Modern monuments want us not simply to remember, but to remember in a particular way.

The Contemporary Monumental Process

Contemporary monument-building perpetuates many of the practices of the first age of monument-building. Memorial projects are organized and carried out by a relatively limited group of interested parties claiming to be the public. The finished works have messages, telling their stories from a particular point of view, with a particular moral. Contemporary monuments say as much about contemporary issues — about the time when they are constructed — as they do about the people and moments they commemorate. The difference is that the audience is more diverse, with more people freer (at least formally) to air their disagreements with the builders, so that once-hidden points of view are more openly aired, although not all are necessarily heard with equal respect.

The ongoing efforts to commemorate September 11, 2001, in New York follows the script precisely. The process has already passed through several stages at this writing. The first was marked by the impromptu memorials that appeared almost immediately on street corners, fences, lampposts, and firehouse walls. Most drew on vernacular practices for mourning violent or accidental private deaths: votive pictures and candles, sacralized everyday objects, and informally presented inscriptions accumulated at sites that were connected, however loosely, with the event. A curious example could be found in midtown Manhattan in the weeks immediately following September 11. In response to the attacks, a bronze

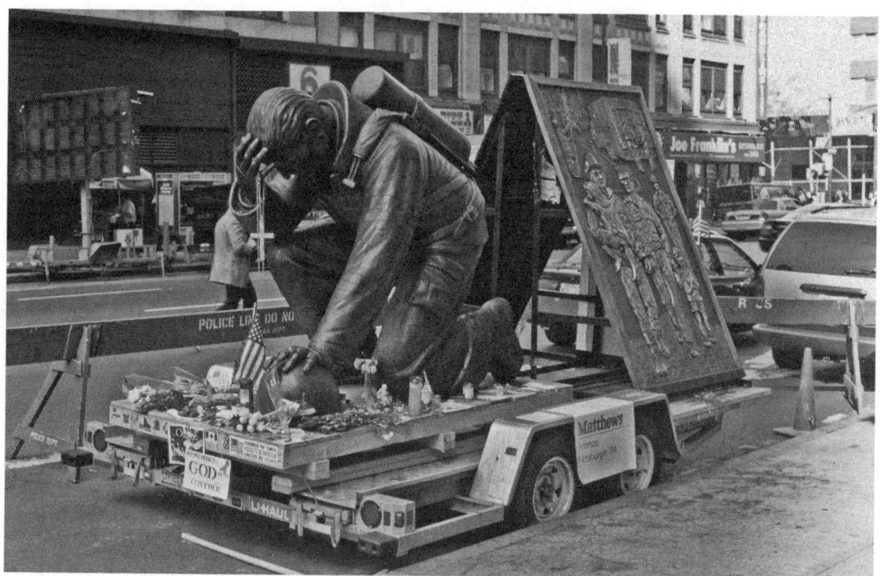

FIG. 6. Rescue workers monument, 2001, as displayed on a New York City street, October 13, 2001. (Photo by the author)

statue and plaque that had been commissioned to honor the emergency-service workers of a Missouri town were donated to the citizens of New York by the town and the foundry. For lack of a site, the oversized work was left on a trailer parked at curbside near the Forty-Second Street entertainment district, far from the World Trade Center site, but it quickly attracted visitors who draped it with rosaries, notes, and other mementoes of the day (fig. 6).

These were improvised gestures by private citizens seeking to come to grips with the trauma at a time when they were still barred from seeing the site itself. They were part of a great flowering of debate and inquiry in the month after September 11 that, as Joan Didion noted, had been smothered by mid-October, as media commentators and the government quickly moved to establish a consensus interpretation.[31] A political-cultural conflict with specific origins and content and a particular context became a clash of cosmic abstractions: "freedom" versus "intolerance," "West" versus "East," "modernity" versus "medievalism." To discuss the event in any other than the sentimentalized terms adopted by everyone from the President of the United States to the *New York Times* to the highly organized survivors' groups was increasingly off-limits.

At this point ground rules for the official memorial competition were published. They adhered to the long-established rituals of monument-building. The memorial was to "recognize each person killed in the attacks in New York, at the Pentagon, and in Pennsylvania [on September 11, 2001] . . . as well as those killed in the bombing at the trade center in 1993," but without establishing "hierarchies of victims" by status or occupation. There was to be an area set aside for families, and the footprint of the destroyed twin towers was to be part of the design. The memorial should contain a tomb for unidentified remains and "may include some surviving elements of the trade center buildings." The finished work should "'inspire and engage people to learn more about the events'" of September 11, but above all it should "reaffirm respect for life, strengthen our resolve to preserve freedom and inspire an end to hatred, ignorance and intolerance."[32]

As in most other civic monuments new and old, the process was driven by interested parties — the contemporary jargon is "stakeholders." At the World Trade Center, the stakeholders were of two sorts. The most visible were the victims' families, who perform the role that such groups as Vietnam veterans or the United Daughters of the Confederacy played in shaping earlier monuments. They met little opposition in claiming the "moral authority" to shape the monument to reflect the ways that they wanted the event and their loved ones to be remembered.[33] These and other stakeholders played the role of the "public": when they said that they would hold "public forums," the organizers of the competition acknowledged, they meant "meetings of specific constituent groups."[34]

Inevitably, there was vehement debate about both representativeness and representation, even among the stakeholders. Some disputed the representativeness of the proposed monument in challenging the guidelines' demand that the dead not be separated by status. The Uniformed Firefighters' Association was particularly adamant that "uniformed rescue workers" be identified as such on the memorial, separating "those who died willingly, risking their lives to save others, as opposed to those who were tragically caught up in the consequences of the attack," while the families of civilian victims felt that all deaths "should be treated with honor and extraordinary respect." Another, echoing Maya Lin's criticism of the Vietnam Women's Memorial, argued, "One memorial could have four separate pieces, but not four pieces for four different groups."[35]

After the consultations with the "constituent groups," a "Panel, Not [the] Public" chose a winner.[36] The panel included a second, unacknowledged group of stakeholders: public officials. They were responsible for accommodating the "many agendas" of a variety of stakeholders — office seekers, subgroups of survivors, developers, art critics, journalists — but needed to do so in ways that would advance their own agendas.[37] There were major political points to be scored as well as equally large political pitfalls to be avoided. So the effective, if not "moral," control of the project eventually passed to a board of directors composed of the kinds of "powerful New Yorkers" who direct most other aspects of the city's cultural and symbolic life.[38]

The balance between the two sets of stakeholders then took yet another turn. One particularly vocal group, led by a victim's sister, claimed "moral authority" over the whole site. Not only should the memorial and its attached museum reflect the survivors' point of view (or that of some survivors), but the entire site should be considered sacred and operated in accordance with their own interpretation of the attack as a simple story of "human decency triumphing over human depravity." The World Trade Center site should "contain no facilities 'that house controversial debate, dialogue, artistic impressions, or exhibitions referring to extraneous historical events.'"[39] They were particularly worried that the Drawing Center and the grandiosely named International Freedom Center might present exhibits that the group considered to be categorically "anti-American." Then they began to question the activities that might occupy sites peripheral to the memorial and even the kinds of books that might be sold in a bookstore adjacent to the site.[40]

Their vehemence obviously took the political stakeholders by surprise. In a bizarre spectacle at the site of the memorial and the "Freedom Tower," New York governor George Pataki warned the International Freedom Center and the Drawing Center that no program would be allowed that offended any survivor or that "denigrates America, denigrates New York or freedom." The *New York Times* cited works shown at the Drawing Center's current site that ridiculed George W. Bush's rhetoric and that illustrated the tortures at Abu Ghraib as examples of the kinds of "anti-American" work that the survivors and the governor wanted to prohibit.[41]

Even those whose interest was limited to the memorial itself doubted the power of the images chosen to convey either the distinctive qualities of September 11 or its gravity and sanctity. The Lower Manhattan Development Corporation (the body supervising the memorial competition as well as the process of reconstructing the World Trade Center site) showed its lack of faith in visual representation early in the process by changing the text of the monument from "killed," as the original guidelines stated, to "murdered by terrorists."[42] When the eight finalists were revealed, letter writers and op-ed columnists denounced them as "cold," "bland," "saccharine and feel-good," therapeutic "psychobabble" fit for "tranquility-inducing public spaces around buildings that are too tall."[43]

The solution, according to several prominent design critics, was to dispense with "democracy" and to allow some artistic genius to create a universally satisfying memorial that could rise above "symbols and politics."[44] The critics' argument was founded in yet another variant of the endless search for consensus, but they missed the point of monuments entirely. Beautiful monuments in the critics' sense are accidents. For a monument's patrons there are far more serious issues at stake than aesthetics.[45] This is why designers and critics are never the majority of competition juries.

Several aspects of the monument-building process, and particularly of its contemporary variant, made such conflicts at the World Trade Center inevitable. The practice of naming individuals and of drawing on mortuary imagery, given such popular force by the Vietnam Veterans' Memorial, renders the World Trade Center's place on the public-private axis ambiguous. Is this a memorial to individual deaths or to some larger concept significant to society at large? The survivors argue that the meaning is larger than individuals—"To me, they're treating 9/11 just like a 3,000-person car crash," said Debra Burlingame, the leader of the anti–Freedom Center coalition—but they and their supporters treat the memorial as a monument to purely private grief, hence the survivors' "moral authority" in deciding how to tell a story that affected the entire nation.[46]

This confusion between monuments' public and private aspects becomes more acute given the characteristic contemporary rush to memorialize the event and to fix its story. In Pataki's words, the memorial would "ensure that . . . the memory of what happened on September 11 will never fade from our hearts." But the program's call for a design that would "reaffirm respect for life, strengthen our resolve to preserve freedom [of what sort?] and inspire an end to hatred, ignorance and intolerance" [in whom?] contained an interpretive subtext.[47] A terrorist act, carried out by a small group of men espousing specific ideas and pursuing particular goals, was recast more generically as a senselessly "horrific attack," decontextualized and given a cosmic meaning that all could accept. Yet even this abstraction concealed an interpretation. By connecting the World Trade Center attacks to the Pennsylvania plane crash and the Pentagon attack and to the 1993 bombing at the World Trade Center but not, for example, to the 1995 terrorist attack on the Alfred P. Murrah Federal Building in Oklahoma City, the locus of "ignorance and intolerance" was made clear.

One correspondent to the *New York Times* demanded, "Leave it raw. Let another generation decide what to put there. We are too hurt to know."[48] Given our rule of thumb about monuments' rootedness in the preoccupations of their own times, there is no reason to believe that a later generation's view of the events would be any truer than this one's. However the immediacy of present anger and grief muzzles active public debate over the events' meanings and their memorialization and precludes difficult or nuanced interpretations of the type that one finds in recent European monuments to the Holocaust, for example.[49]

Do we need consensual monuments? Should we want them if we could create them? Are they appropriate to a democratic society? The political theorist Chantal Mouffe defines true democracy as an "agonistic" polity that airs conflicts fully and openly. In a democracy, one must challenge values, claims, and procedures tirelessly and unceasingly. An illusion of consensus can be sustained only by suppressing evidence, values, and voices, as the unresolved contest over the World Trade Center memorial shows.[50] Monument builders similarly seek to evade conflict and fashion consensus by suppressing specificity in favor of abstraction and indirection. The often-overlooked dedicatory inscription on the Vietnam Veterans' Memorial invokes duty and notes that the names are listed "in the order they were taken from us," as though they were kidnapped or died of a disease, not in wartime in a distant land, as though no one made the decisions that led to their being "taken," as though there were no specific issues being contested by the United States and the Vietnamese.

It is sometimes said that this evasion or indirection is a positive attribute of monuments, that by deemphasizing specific differences and stressing higher, more diffuse values or goals monuments lay grievances to rest and reconcile antagonists. We elevate the Civil War, the civil rights movement, the Vietnam War, or the World Trade Center attacks from the realm of political, social, and military conflict in a specific setting at a specific time with specific rationales to the timeless, sacred, abstract (and therefore content-free) domain of "duty," "sacrifice," or "freedom," but when we make tasteful, vandal-proof artworks in "immaculately maintained" settings that deny conflict, we are derelict in our democratic duty.[51]

Notes

1. "Molinari Backs Monument to Summer of Love," *San Francisco Chronicle,* Mar. 13, 1986, 5; "Rio Vista Dedicates Monument to Humphrey," *San Francisco Chronicle,* Feb. 1, 1986, 3; "Bridge Collapse Commemorated," *New York Times,* May 27, 2003, A20. The Summer of Love monument was never built.

2. "Bridge Collapse Commemorated."

3. For a brief definition of the relationship between monuments per se and the larger commemorative context, see Young, *The Texture of Memory,* 3–4.

4. The work is now on view at the National Museum of American History in Washington, D.C.

5. "House of Representatives," *Niles' National Register* 62 (May 21, 1842): n.p., Xerox, Metropolitan Museum of Art, New York. The parenthetical comments in this and a subsequent quotation from the same source are part of the original text: they record audience interjections during Wise's speech.

6. Dan Flavin, quoted in Cooke and Govan, *Dia: Beacon,* 139.

7. Some such sense of absence seems to have led the State of Mississippi to erect a historical marker at the same site, adding a narrative dimension that might otherwise have been redundant had a more "monumental" monument been present.

8. Meyer, *Minimalism,* 68–70, 74.

9. "House of Representatives."

10. Quoted by St. Florian in "The Making of the World War 2 Memorial," a lecture delivered at the University of Virginia, Feb. 18, 2005.

11. The book is *Free At Last.* For a longer discussion of the message of the Civil Rights Memorial, see Upton, "Commemorating the Civil Rights Movement," 22–33.

12. Goode, *The Outdoor Sculpture of Washington, D.C.,* 189–90.

13. Bogart, *Public Sculpture and the Civic Ideal,* 94–95, 198, 233, and passim.

14. Doss, *Spirit Poles and Flying Pigs,* 44–46; Guibault, *How New York Stole the Idea of Modern Art,* 2–4, 11.

15. Stephen Kinzer, "Art on the Streets Till the Cows Come Home," *New York Times,* Aug. 20, 2001, A1, A13. See Doss, *Spirit Poles and Flying Pigs,* 44, on urban officials' long-standing desire to create "problem-free public spaces."

16. Mumford, *Sticks and Stones,* 141–42.

17. King, *Global Cities,* 93–94; Sassen, *Losing Control?*

18. The choice of sculptor and iconography of this monument also obey a long-standing gender rule of American monument-building that is rarely violated: women can create memorials and be depicted in them serving women or men, but only women can memorialize or be depicted serving women.

19. Savage, *Standing Soldiers, Kneeling Slaves,* 162–208.

20. David W. Dunlap, "Making the Dead Count, Literally," *New York Times,* Nov. 30, 2003, Arts, 40.

21. Phil McCombs, "Senate Backs Women's Memorial; 96–1 Vote Endorses New Statue Saluting Vietnam War Veterans," *Washington Post,* June 15, 1988, B1, B9.

22. See the sculptor Raymond Kaskey's comments on the demand for representation of all branches of the service and "by-the-numbers" depiction of a variety of actors, and his own effort to "cover all the bases" in response, at the World War II Memorial, in Gurney, "Sculpting the World War II Memorial," 105.

23. For a discussion of the struggles over representation and representativeness and the subsequent fragmentation of representation in the Franklin Delano Roosevelt Monument (Lawrence Halprin et al., 1997–2001) in Washington, D.C., see Stein, "The President's Two Bodies," 46–55.

24. Kevin Flynn, "Firefighters Block a Plan for Statue in Their Honor," *New York Times,* Jan. 18, 2002, A21.

25. Dean E. Murphy, "Firefighters Statue to Be Erected Despite Criticism," *New York Times,* Jan. 13, 2002, online edition.

26. David W. Dunlap and Glenn Collins, "How Winning 9/11 Memorial Acquired Its Second Designer," *New York Times,* Jan. 8, 2004, A26; David W. Dunlap, "At 9/11 Memorial, Actual Sizes May Vary," *New York Times,* Feb. 12, 2004, A31. Similarly James E. Young has noted Holocaust survivors' demand for historical literalness and representational imagery in Holocaust memorials as the only adequate representation of their experience, in Young *Texture of Memory,* 9–11.

27. The phrase is taken from a news story detailing the successful campaign for approval of the Vietnam Women's Memorial initiated by a female veterans' organization (McCombs, "Senate Backs Women's Memorial," B1). Similarly, Friedrich St. Florian believes that World War II veterans appreciate his memorial because "a grateful nation had finally paid tribute to them," in St. Florian, "The Making of the World War 2 Memorial."

28. Wunsch, "From Private Privilege to Public Place," 82–83.

29. Savage, *Standing Soldiers, Kneeling Slaves,* 153.

30. See Erika Doss's account of the extended public controversy over Cincinnati's whimsical *Cincinnati Gateway* (Andrew Leicester, 1987–88), in Doss, *Spirit Poles and Flying Pigs,* 197–236.

31. Joan Didion, "Fixed Opinions, or the Hinge of History," *New York Review of Books,* 50 no. 1 (Jan. 16, 2003), online edition, http://www.nybooks.com.

32. Edward Wyatt, "Draft Guidelines Released for Trade Center Memorial," *New York Times,* Jan. 9, 2003, A24.

33. Edward Wyatt, "Some Victims' Families Feel Influence on 9/11 Memorial Slipping Away," *New York Times,* Nov. 16, 2002, A14. In the words of one victim's family member,

the families "symbolically own that land. Legally and technically we don't, but we do" (John King, "Tower Vision," *San Francisco Chronicle,* Jan. 27, 2002, A21).

34. Edward Wyatt, "Panel, Not Public, Will Pick Final 9/11 Memorial Design," *New York Times,* Apr. 9, 2003, A16. The competition was organized and managed by the Lower Manhattan Development Corporation, which has oversight over many aspects of the reconstruction of the World Trade Center site.

35. Edward Wyatt, "Jury for Sept. 11 Memorial Is Facing Spirited Lobbying: Families and Officials Push Their Wish Lists," *New York Times,* May 30, 2003, A26; Glenn Collins, "8 Designs Confront Many Agendas at Ground Zero," *New York Times,* Nov. 20, 2003, A1, A29; Edward Wyatt, "Sept. 11 Memorial Will Pay Tribute to All the Victims, as a Single Group," *New York Times,* Mar. 14, 2003, A25 (quotations). Washington's Korean War Memorial offers an example of the kind of hierarchy that the planners of the World Trade Center Memorial sought to avoid. Front-line soldiers on patrol are represented as three-dimensional male figures while male and female support personnel are confined to a (highly individualized) photo mural of faces. The memorial also lists the individual nations who participated on the United Nations side in the war, but they are merely names, while American soldiers are humanized.

36. Wyatt, "Panel, Not Public," A16.

37. Collins, "8 Designs Confront Many Agendas at Ground Zero," A1, A29; Wyatt, "Jury for Sept. 11 Memorial Is Facing Spirited Lobbying," A26.

38. David W. Dunlap, "Trade Center Memorial Getting More Muscle: Board Meets for First Time Today," *New York Times,* Jan. 5, 2005, A24. A list of the committee members can be found in David W. Dunlap, "31 Named to Raise Funds for Memorial to Sept. 11: Business and Cultural Leaders Lead Drive," *New York Times,* Dec. 2, 2004, C12.

39. Robin Finn, "Fighting for the Underlying Meaning of Ground Zero," *New York Times,* Aug. 12, 2005, online edition, http://www.nytimes.com/2005/08/12/nyregion/12lives.html; website http://www.takebackthememorial.org, quoted in "A Sense of Proportion at Ground Zero," *New York Times,* July 29, 2005, A20.

40. Finn, "Fighting for the Underlying Meaning of Ground Zero"; David W. Dunlap, "Freedom Center's Place at Ground Zero in Question," *New York Times,* Aug. 12, 2005, online edition, http://www.nytimes.com/2005/08/12/nyregion/12rebuild.html; David W. Dunlap, "Arguing the Purposes of the World Trade Center Site," *New York Times,* Sept. 8, 2005, A27.

41. George Pataki, quoted in Patrick D. Healy, "Pataki Warns Ground Zero Cultural Groups Not to Give Offense," *New York Times,* June 25, 2005, A11.

42. Wyatt, "Sept. 11 Memorial Will Pay Tribute to All the Victims, as a Single Group," A25.

43. Scott A. Dergance, Lynn Jericho, and Lisa Chamberlain, Letters to the Editor, *New York Times,* Nov. 21, 2003, A30; Maureen Dowd, "Unbearable Lightness of Mem-

ory," *New York Times,* Nov. 30, 2003, WK9; James Mechalakos, Dorothy Augustine, and Brad Marshall, Letters to the Editor, *New York Times,* Dec. 2, 2003, A30.

44. Herbert Muschamp, "Critic's Notebook: Vision vs. Symbols and Politics at Ground Zero," *New York Times,* Nov. 29, 2003, A15, A20; Michael Kimmelman, "The Ground Zero Memorial's Only Hope: Elitism," *New York Times,* Dec. 7, 2003, AR1, AR47; Michael Kimmelman, "Ground Zero Finally Grows Up," *New York Times,* Feb. 1, 2004, AR1, AR35.

45. When opponents attempt to stop monument projects on aesthetic grounds they inevitably lose, as the opponents of Washington's new World War II Memorial learned (Kevin Keim, "Symbols of Momentous Times: The Architecture of Memory," *Chronicle of Higher Education,* Feb. 27, 1998, B8-B9; Judy S. Feldman, "Memorials and American National Identity," posted on SAH-L, May 30, 2000; Irvin Molotsky, "Design for World War II Memorial Awaits Review, with Detractors Vocal," *New York Times,* July 17, 2000, B6; Arianna Huffington, "A Monument to Distorted Priorities," June 12, 2001, circulated by e-mail).

46. Finn, "Fighting for the Underlying Meaning of Ground Zero."

47. George Pataki, "2003 State of the State Address," *Gotham Gazette,* Jan. 8, 2003, http://www.gothamgazette.com/index.php/city/archives/1557–2003-state-of-the-state-address; Wyatt, "Draft Guidelines."

48. John Armstrong, Letter to the Editor, *New York Times,* Jan. 31, 2004, A30.

49. Young, *Texture of Memory,* 27–48.

50. Mouffe, *The Democratic Paradox,* 69–74, 80–107.

51. Eric Lipton, "Behind Beauty of 9/11 Designs, Devil May Be in Nuts and Bolts," *New York Times,* Nov. 30, 2003, 1, 28.

CATHERINE W. BISHIR

Memorial Observances

When I was growing up in Lexington, Kentucky, one of the most powerful objects in that small, genteel, racially segregated Southern city was the great equestrian figure of John Hunt Morgan at the courthouse square (fig. 1). I did not know much about the famed Confederate cavalry officer, but from his statue I knew he was important and figured he was probably good.

In time, I saw more and more of the results of Southern mythmaking that shaped the environment where I was born and grew up. Well into the 1960s, when I was in college, these included the codified Southern history of antebellum glories, noble sacrifices made during the Civil War, the evils of Reconstruction, and a racially stratified hierarchy that seemed always to have been in place. The landscape of the Old South story was writ large in the Bluegrass area. In those days, the apogee of the University of Kentucky social season was the Kappa Alpha fraternity's Old South Ball, which was a full-bore moonlight and magnolia drama, preceded by a march of college boys in Confederate uniforms down the main street, and culminating in a grand party enhanced by lots of fine bourbon whiskey.

Only much later did I begin to understand the mythmaking that had gone into creating this saga and, just as important, what had been left out of the story, how, and by whom. In time, my curiosity about the South I was born into led me to look more broadly at the process of creating monuments and memories.[1]

Looking at Monuments

Like others who study the formation of public memory, and especially those of us who find monuments an eye-opening entrée to a place's history, I find myself

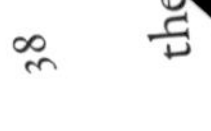

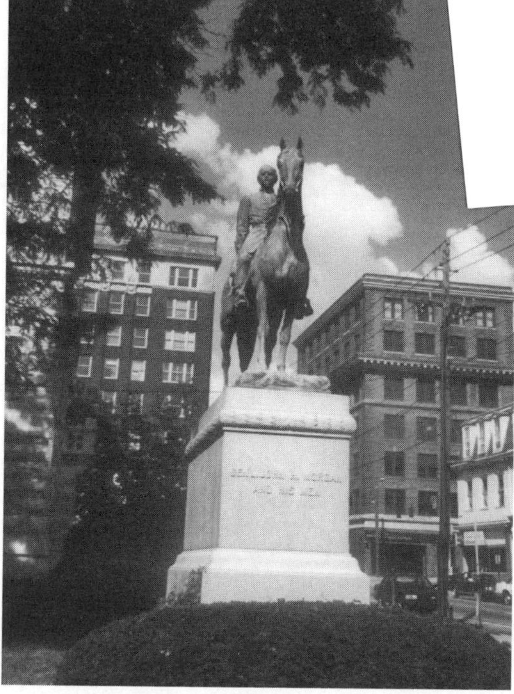

FIG. 1. John Hunt Morgan monument by Pompeo Coppini, Lexington, Kentucky, 1911. (Photo by the author)

looking at monuments and memorials wherever I go. As other essays in this volume show, once we start paying attention to monuments, we become increasingly aware of their defining power in civic places and national identity. At one level, simply by noticing what events and people a community or nation has commemorated, we learn about those aspects of the past. Beyond that, as we examine the monument as a product of its own time, we can ponder questions about who did the commemorating, and when and why. And we can seek to discern what the monument meant in its own time and perhaps what it means in ours.

Monuments of every type capture my attention — plaques marking Lewis and Clark's journey, a lifelike bronze figure of Winston Churchill striding along a street in Paris, and, from the history I actually remember, every commemoration of the civil rights movement and the Vietnam War. All raise questions about who conceived and erected them along with simply telling about the subjects y depict. For me, as a person who grew up in the twentieth-century American South, the most compelling monuments are those that illuminate how Americans addressed the memory and legacy of the Civil War and thereby defined the new nation that emerged.

There are many different ways to encounter monuments, sometimes by chance and sometimes by plan, sometimes fleetingly and sometimes in depth. Often the most striking experience of a monument can occur unexpectedly, when we chance upon a monument "cold" and try to learn its meaning and story simply from the evidence it presents — as it was designed to do. In Chestertown, Maryland, I crossed the street to take a look at a modest marker in a small civic space — and found it one of the most powerful I have ever seen, with the unexpectedness part of its impact (fig. 2). There in that Civil War border state, the marker of 1917 has two sides, each filled with names. The names of the Confederate dead are listed on one side, those of Union losses on the other. Those long columns of names, in the context of both the Civil War and 1917, and the simple text —"Under the sod, the Blue and the Gray / Waiting Alike the Judgment Day"— made it hard to look at anything else.[2]

Even when we visit a monument by intention, there are surprises. We often find that its impact exceeds our expectations. For years I had wanted to visit Gettysburg, Pennsylvania, that battlefield where the direction of the nation's history changed, and the focus of more than a century of memorialization. Yet no amount of reading prepared me for its effect — an effect created by the presence of memorials on the vast landscape. Through the presence of dozens, even hundreds of monuments marking the battlefield, it seemed in a way that the battle was just about to begin. Although I am not a Civil War buff, I had read of the deadly fighting, and especially of Pickett's Charge. I knew that the Union forces had the ridge, and the Confederates commanded by Robert E. Lee were down in the woods across the broad open hillside, preparing to attack. But seeing those lines of tall Union monuments along Cemetery Ridge and looking down across that wide-open slope toward the Confederate lines of Southern memorials conveyed the event in a far more powerful way than books alone can do.

We went down to the edge of the woods to visit the sequence of Confederate monuments. There we found Virginia's heroic and ordered memorial, with General Lee seated calmly on his horse, Traveller, gazing confidently across the field. I was especially looking for the North Carolina monument. Of them all — and we looked at most of them — only that one, a figure group rendered by famed

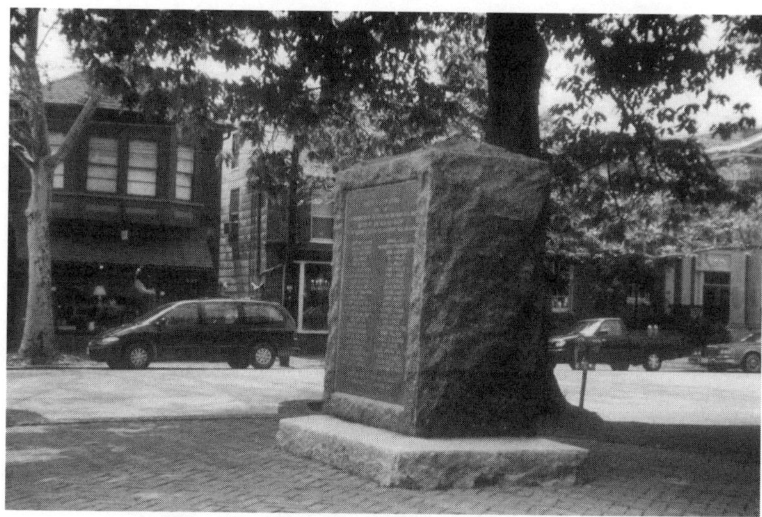

FIG. 2. Memorial to Civil War dead, Chestertown, Maryland, 1917. (Photo by the author)

sculptor Gutzon Borglum and unveiled on July 3, 1929, captured a sense of dread and deep fatigue as well as dogged determination and courage, giving some inkling of the feelings of those about to charge up that hill (fig. 3). Few if any of the memorials in that immense landscape of killing suggest what one scholar has called "about-to-die" moments. But this one does, in the eyes and bodies of the men — no generals, just men — Borglum memorialized. There, as in some photographic images, the men are caught in a moment of contingency. The sculptor "position[ed] the action at . . . the moment at which an individual or group is going to die, but not after they are already dead." In the North Carolina group, it is also the moment at which the men do not know which of them will live, and which will die; they only know they are going to charge.[3]

In some cases, the monument itself raises questions that immediately push for exploration — and broaden our understanding of the past. At Yorktown, Virginia, I was captured by the towering column memorializing the American Revolutionary victory there (fig. 4). While I was gaping at it, I began to read the words — and there are lots of words on this one — about the articles of peace, the United States of America, and the sins of George III. The inscription on the monument lists the names of the colonies north and south and places a strong emphasis on their being "free, sovereign, and independent states." Yet a frieze of

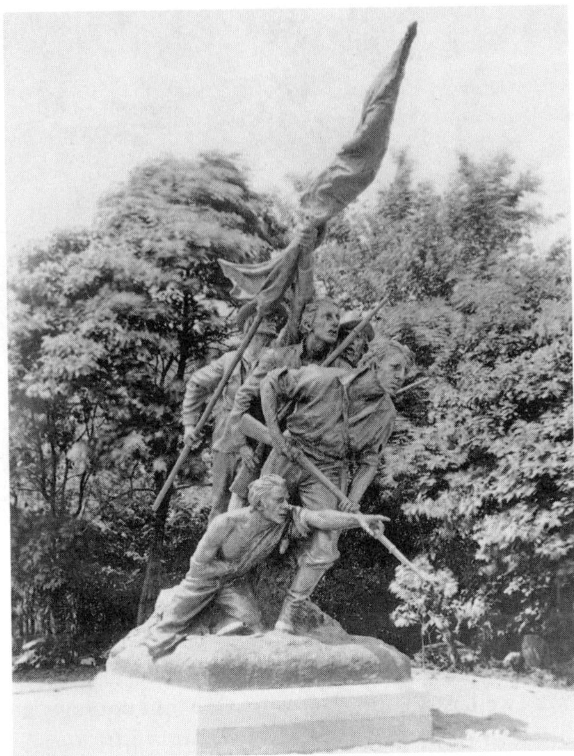

FIG. 3. North Carolina monument by Gutzon Borglum, Gettysburg, Pennsylvania, 1929. (North Carolina State Archives)

classical maidens representing the states, shoulder to shoulder and hand in hand, each topped by a star, is unified by the motto "One country, one constitution, one destiny" (fig. 5). The inscription explains that the monument, dated 1881, was authorized by Congress in 1781 and again in 1880. It was a major national work—planned by leading architects Richard Morris Hunt (chairman of the committee) and Henry Van Brunt and sculpted by nationally renowned artist John Quincy Adams Ward. And thus the questions: What is going on here? Why this towering and costly monument in Virginia *then*?

Seen in the context of its time, the Yorktown Victory Monument's very presence in Virginia and its elaborate iconography take on additional meaning. Although nominally commemorating a 1781 victory, the monument of 1881 stands as one of the first—and most subtly coded—memorials to national reunifica-

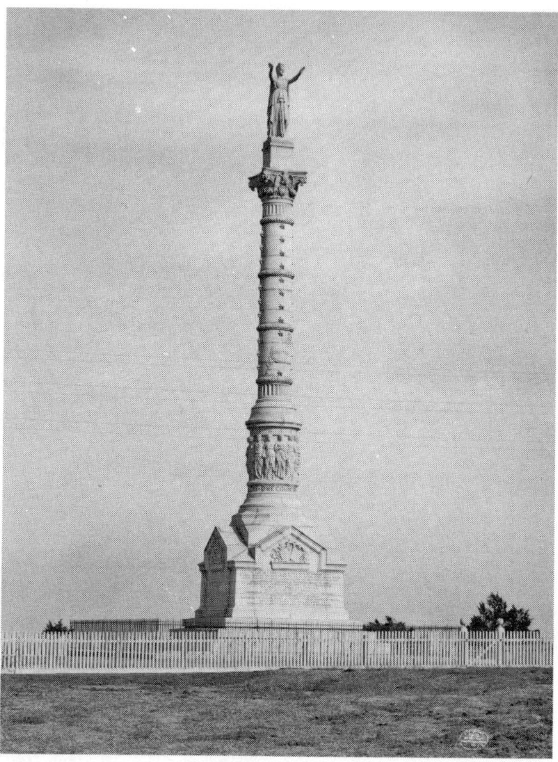

FIG. 4. Yorktown Victory Monument, Yorktown, Virginia, 1884.
Photo by William Henry Jackson, c. 1903. (Library of Congress, Prints and Photographs Division, Detroit Publishing Company Collection, LC-D4-16180)

tion and Southern reentry to the nation. With Reconstruction ended, Virginia was asserting her patriotic prestige in the nation, as a noble sister state and leader in the American Revolution. More important, in 1880 the nation was moving toward sectional reconciliation. Recognition of Southern states as honorable and patriotic parts of the nation in the wake of secession was an important step in that process. And sure enough, a visit to the National Park Service website shows that while the rhetoric surrounding the monument focused on winning American independence in 1781, official reports also stressed the "greatness and prosperity of the nation . . . after a century of various experience," when "thirty-eight free and independent states are shining together in a mighty constellation" —acknowledging obliquely but clearly the Southern Democrats' view of states' rights as part of national reunion. One report of the day characterized the

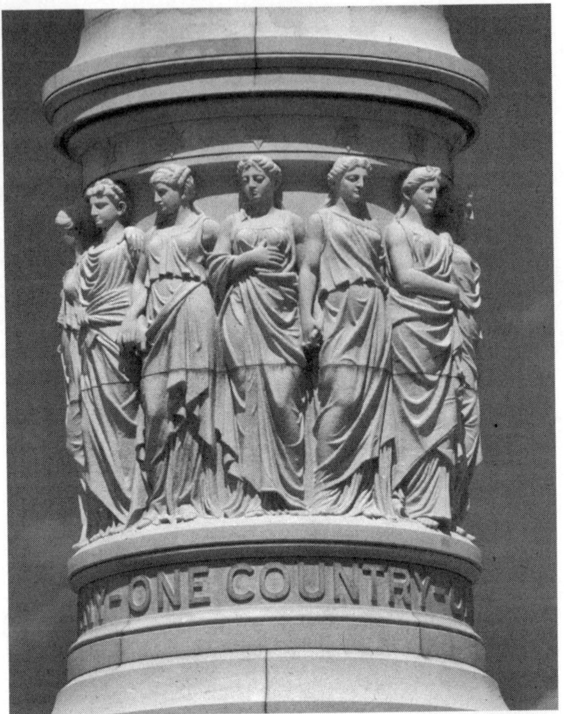

FIG. 5. Detail, Yorktown Victory Monument, showing female figures holding hands. (National Park Service)

Liberty figure atop the column in the words Lincoln used in the Gettysburg Address as "proof of the . . . possibility of a government of the people, by the people, for the people."[4]

The North Carolina Confederate Monument

A close study of another memorial, the North Carolina Confederate Monument in Raleigh, has helped me understand the complexities — the backstories — that lie behind nearly every commemorative monument (fig. 6). For several years, I have explored how memorials define the public sense of history and identity — and more broadly, how the sponsors of the commemorative process edited the history and shaped the society of the South. The story of the Raleigh monument offers a microcosmic but action-packed example.[5]

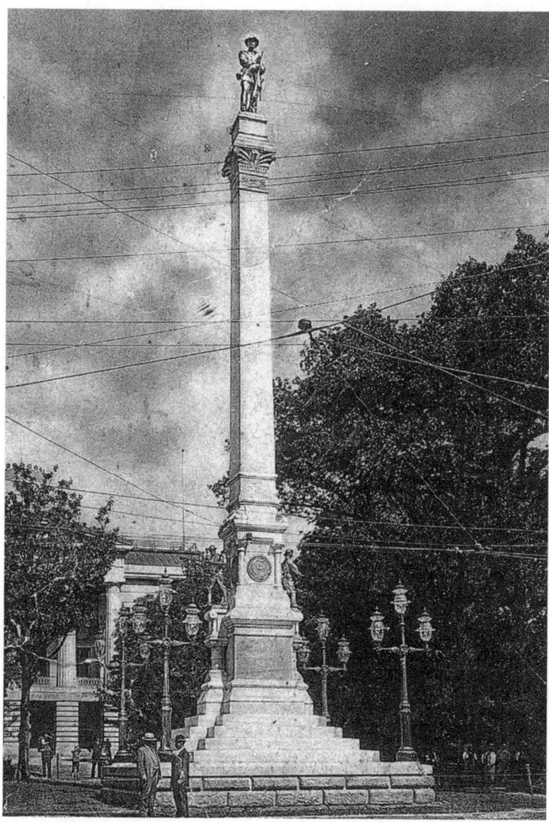

FIG. 6. North Carolina Confederate Monument, Raleigh, 1895. (North Carolina State Archives)

The North Carolina Confederate Monument, a granite obelisk topped by a bronze soldier, stands seventy-five feet tall on the grounds of the State Capitol in Raleigh. Its scale and location suggest that it represents the values of the state and its people. Dedicated in 1895, it conveys the notion that the whole state was unified in the cause of the Confederacy, and that the whole state likewise revered its Confederate heroes enough to place this monument in this prime public place.

In fact, North Carolina had been bitterly divided over the war. The state resisted secession as long as possible, until after President Lincoln called on North Carolina for troops after Fort Sumter. During the Civil War, opposition to the Confederate cause was strong, amounting in some areas to an internal war. Nevertheless, North Carolina became the "Hercules of the Confederacy," and some 35,000 North Carolinians died during military service for the Confederacy — more than from any other state.

The North Carolina Confederate Monument was planned and built during a period of intense political conflict. Opposition to its state funding was strong and vocal, reflecting deep splits in the social and political fabric of the state in the 1890s. Despite political challenges, elite white women — a group important in shaping public monuments and public memory throughout the South and the nation — managed to complete the monument by using every medium — the written word, social rituals, the redefining of a civic space, and above all the monument itself — to define the state's public meaning of the Confederate cause and the direction of the future.

By the early 1890s, when plans for the monument began, Reconstruction was long over and white Democrats, led by the Confederate elite, had regained power. They used the specter of Reconstruction and Republican "Negro domination" to maintain a majority in the legislature, though blacks still voted and there were some black legislators and other officeholders. In 1892, the nation faced growing economic turmoil, and the state's Democrats worried that a "third party" (later the Populists) might divide the white electorate. At this time, Democratic Confederate veterans began a drive for a state war memorial and turned to the Ladies Memorial Association of Raleigh — the LMA — for help.[6]

Formed in 1866 as one of many local LMAs across the South, this organization of elite women and some men had established in Raleigh one of the first new Confederate cemeteries. From 1867 onward, the LMA held annual ceremonies on Confederate Memorial Day (May 10 in North Carolina, Stonewall Jackson's death date). After Reconstruction ended, the LMA made Confederate Memorial Day a major holiday with a great parade and speeches celebrating Confederate valor. In 1892, the LMA responded quickly to the veterans' request, forming the North Carolina Monumental Association (the NCMA, an organization separate from the LMA), with a female "board of management" and a male "advisory board" of prominent Democratic politicians. The NCMA president was Nancy Branch Jones, wife of a leading Democratic politician and daughter of a Confederate general and his widow, who herself was the founding president of the LMA back in 1866.[7]

Like other such groups, the NCMA held Confederate-themed fund-raising events, but money was slow to come. In 1893, the association turned to the largely Democratic legislature for a $10,000 appropriation. The women gathered at the

State Capitol when the bill came up, and "took the House by storm"— crowding the galleries and filling the aisles of the chambers. According to the Democratic *News and Observer* of Raleigh, "In the presence of so many fair patriots, there was no disposition manifested to antagonize the Monument bill." The legislature authorized the funds and further specified that the Confederate monument would be located on Union Square (the Capitol square). The siting underscored the monument as representing the official values and history of the state, and at the same time its sponsors claimed the state's most important public space. With the site chosen, the NCMA commissioned a design from the Muldoon Monument Company of Louisville, Kentucky; signed a contract for $25,000; and continued fund-raising efforts. The group held an elaborate cornerstone-laying event on May 20, 1894, to encourage public support for "the memory of those who laid down their lives for a cause that was just and honorable."[8]

Suddenly the project faced unprecedented challenges — and a radically different public drama. In 1894 Republicans (who included the black voters) and Populists (mainly economically depressed white farmers and other disaffected Democrats) joined forces as "Fusionists." They won a startling victory that made North Carolina the only Southern state where Democrats lost control of the government. The legislature of 1895 was "overwhelmingly Fusionist," with five blacks among the Republicans. This turn of events put the heavily Democratic NCMA in a new position. The monument was proceeding toward completion in April, with full payment of $25,000 due. They had raised $15,000.[9]

When the NCMA turned again to the legislature for help — this time for a loan of an additional $10,000 — the request opened up deep divides that existed in the state. "Do Not Pass It," urged a Populist newspaper, saying public funds should be spent on public schools, not private monuments: "It is not at all certain that any monuments ought to be built on either side to perpetuate the memories of our unnatural civil war. The sooner the rancors and hates of that unhappy struggle are forgotten by both North and South, the better it will be for the whole country." Although the women again filled the legislative chambers when the bill was debated on February 23, 1895, the measure lost in the Senate by a vote of 28 to 8.[10]

Amid the intense racial politics of the day, an unrelated controversy abruptly altered the fate of the monument bill. On February 21, a black House member had offered a resolution honoring Frederick Douglass, the African American leader who had died on February 20, and the House passed it. Democrats and the *News*

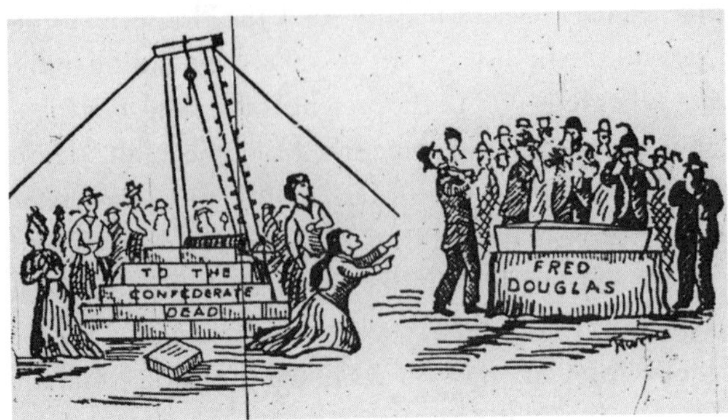

FIG. 7. Political cartoon from the Raleigh *News and Observer,* February 1895.

and Observer pounced on the opportunity. "Miscegenation Legislature Adjourns in Loving Memory of Fred Douglass," the newspaper crowed, "The affair will be a vital blow at the Fusionists" and called on "All patriotic men [to] stand together to preserve the Anglo Saxon civilization." The newspaper then linked the *House's* Douglass resolution of February 21 with the *Senate's* unrelated defeat of the monument bill on February 23. It ran a cartoon on February 24 joining the two. The women, one kneeling, plead, "A land without monuments is a land without memories," while the racially mixed legislators ignore their appeal (fig. 7).[11]

The newspaper's linkage instantly heated up white public outrage and breathed new life into the monument campaign. Legislators dived for cover. Many saw support for the monument as an antidote to the Douglass problem. On February 28 a bill for an appropriation rather than a loan came before the Senate. After long debate and one changed vote, the bill passed 21 to 20. "Glory to God and the Confederate dead," cried a supporter. In the House, still raw from the Douglass furor, debate was bitter. One holdout cited "many letters from his people denouncing the appropriation"—"our duty is to the living and not to the dead." Another said that "the memories of the war should be buried out of sight, he was in favor of digging a hole and burying all monuments." Again the women gathered to play their role in the drama. The bill passed 60 to 38. The *News and Observer* exulted: "And the Women Win."[12]

Almost daily the *News and Observer* reported on the monument and plans for unveiling, scheduled for May 20, 1895, a "patriotic" extravaganza. The near defeat of the monument bill was never mentioned. Yet politics gave both the monument and the unveiling special meaning—celebrating not only the Lost Cause but also the recent triumph over the Fusionist legislators using ploys of race and sex combined in the defense of white Southern womanhood.

Reports building up to the unveiling shared the page with hot racial politics. After a close local election, on May 7 the *News and Observer* proclaimed the triumph of "pure white Democracy"—"The City Still Ours: No Negro Rule in Raleigh." Regularly the NCMA published notices of events for the unveiling, including parties, receptions, and a "Confederate Concert." Ignoring the fact that only their manipulation of the Douglass incident had forced the legislature into funding the monument, the NCMA and the *News and Observer* created an image of universal support for a noble cause. "Everybody and His Wife Coming," ran one headline. Calling on shared memory of the war to draw Populists back to the Democratic fold, sponsors urged "every Confederate soldier" to join the procession in Raleigh "without regard to creed or party."[13]

At the "Great Event," the women took a visible but silent role. Prominent were President Nancy Jones; her mother, Mrs. General Branch; and Mrs. General Stonewall Jackson and her seven-year-old granddaughter Julia Jackson Christian. Only one speaker made even oblique reference to the legislative strife. The completion of the monument depended, he said, on the women's "perseverance which never surrenders. When the voice of woman is heard, saying in her firm and modest way . . . that this monument SHALL be erected, her sweet low voice startles the men from the seashore to the mountains, and behold this polished shaft . . . leaps forth from out [of] the rough quarry at her command." After other long speeches, little Julia Jackson Christian — in a typical unveiling by the youngest generation — pulled the cord and the veil dropped from the monument like "the garments of Elijah."[14]

The "Great Event" attracted some 30,000 people and the attention of the whole state. Even a visiting Northern officer praised the monument and commented that the South would "lose the respect of the world" if it did not thus honor its soldiers. Although many blacks came to observe the event, no mention of them entered official reports. The *News and Observer* proclaimed the day "a perfect success."[15]

The meaning of both the monument and Memorial Day intensified toward the end of the century. In North Carolina, a second Fusionist victory in 1896 put a Republican in the governor's office. In 1898 the Democrats — including key figures from the monument celebration and with the *News and Observer* their "printed voice"—devised a violent "white supremacy crusade." Pulling out all the stops on "Negro domination" and threats to white womanhood, they retook the legislature that year. In 1900 a second "crusade" not only re-won the governor's office but passed a constitutional amendment paralleling those in other Southern states to disfranchise blacks—and effectively removed them from the political arena for more than half a century. When the 1900 Confederate Memorial Day celebration took place, not long before the fateful election, the rhetoric placed special emphasis on shared values in the white populace. "The people of Raleigh of all classes and creeds . . . will join hands and hearts tomorrow in a common cause and decorate with purest flowers the resting places of the fallen soldiers."[16]

Beyond erecting a monument to the Confederate dead, the members of the NCMA had accomplished their goals of advancing the Confederate tradition and reinforcing the social and political hierarchy they believed in. Ostensibly apolitical, they gained state support for *their* version of history as official public memory, which claimed to represent the values of the state as a whole. Standing tall on the public square, the memorial conveys what its sponsors intended. They created a monument and a story that dismissed any hint of conflict or the contingencies of either the war or the creation of the monument itself. More than a century later, hundreds of people pass by the towering monument at the center of the city every day. Few if any know that the story could have turned out otherwise.

Revisiting the John Hunt Morgan Monument

Spurred by my study of other monuments, I have looked anew at the John Hunt Morgan Monument in Lexington. As a child, I took the heroic equestrian figure for granted as a presence in a world dominated by the Bluegrass's Old South identity and the patrician spell of horse breeding and racing. Now I am interested in questions about that monument and its place in public memory and the formation of that identity.[17]

Like other Southern states, Kentucky—at least the Bluegrass region—celebrates the Old South and the Confederate tradition, but with a special twist. In the Bluegrass mystique, standard Old South motifs—columned mansions, belles in hoop skirts, and noble cavaliers in gray—are part of a regionally distinctive blend that incorporates such motifs as the Kentucky Colonel in his white suit; the manufacture of Bourbon whiskey; mint juleps in chilled silver cups on silver trays, served by black hands in white gloves; and magnificent horses nibbling bluegrass in fields surrounded by white fences. The state's Civil War history encompasses tales of the border state in which brother fought against brother; the city's historical markers include commemorations of both Jefferson Davis and Abraham Lincoln. In actuality, the majority of citizens and combatants in Kentucky — which did not secede — were Unionists. Even Lexington and the Bluegrass, more strongly Confederate than many communities, were deeply torn. Yet the popular history of the Bluegrass, and much of Kentucky, ignores the strength of Unionism and focuses on the romantic stories of Confederate partisans and the postwar "genteel tradition." Some have said that Kentucky was the only Southern state that seceded *after* the Civil War. As historian Anne Marshall puts it, the state has always been Southern, but it "became Confederate after the war."[18]

Tying into the Southern imagery is the other vital part of the Bluegrass mystique — the horse industry. Lexington today proclaims itself "The Horse Capital of the World." Rooted in the breeding of saddle horses and racehorses in antebellum days, the Kentucky horse industry has been big money for a century and more. In Kentucky, the idealized Old South culture interacts deeply with the horse industry's aura of tradition, power, beauty, and money that defines the Bluegrass, and indeed the state as a whole, as "horse country." Although transformed radically in the past half century, the romantic image of the rolling horse farms of the Bluegrass — with perfect bluegrass fields, endless black or white painted fences, laboriously built stone walls, and palatial barns — still captures for many an iconic antebellum world. Begun in an agrarian economy based on slavery, the horse business and its landscape changed repeatedly in the late nineteenth century, again with the infusion of moneyed northern horse and society people in the early twentieth century, and more drastically with the corporate development of the industry in the late twentieth century. The corporate and official depiction of Kentucky and the Bluegrass relies on the promotion of the Southern ideal and the Bluegrass landscape. And as shown by scores of books, every tour of the region, and every website about Lexington, the colorful Confederate cavalry leader John Hunt Morgan is a central figure in the living tradition.[19]

A state historical marker summarizes Morgan's story: "John Hunt Morgan (1825–1864). Known as the 'Thunderbolt of the Confederacy,' Morgan was born in Huntsville, Alabama; in 1831 moved to Lexington. After attending Transylvania, he fought in the Mexican War. In Lexington, he prospered as owner of hemp factory and woolen mill. Morgan organized Lexington Rifles Infantry, 1857; later led them to aid Confederacy. Leading cavalry raids behind the enemy lines, General J. H. Morgan disrupted Union supplies and communications. For Southerners, he was the ideal romantic hero. Captured in Indiana-Ohio raid, he escaped and was killed in Greeneville, Tennessee, September 4, 1864. Buried in Lexington Cemetery. Morgan became a courageous symbol of the Lost Cause."[20]

As Morgan's biographer James Ramage shows in *Rebel Raider,* during the war Morgan and his men won legendary stature, with a consciously cultivated reputation for gallantry and daring that boosted Confederate morale.[21] Morgan came from a "good family" with Lexington connections, whose elegant Federal period house is a Lexington landmark. But there was a darker side as well: Morgan's raiders not only struck Union forces throughout Kentucky and into Ohio and Tennessee; they also robbed banks and homes and terrorized civilians. Their guerrilla tactics ignored the rules of "civilized warfare" and brought Morgan into conflict with his Confederate superiors. As historian Anne Marshall observes, even Morgan's brother-in-law and second-in-command, Basil Duke, stated that "an avowal of 'belonging to Morgan' was thought, even in Kentucky, tantamount to a confession of murder and highway robbery."[22]

But after the war, the story changed: "People never forgot that Morgan's men took their horses," explains Ramage, "but upon the passing of the Civil War generation, the robbing of banks and other depredations were seldom mentioned — it was as if they had never happened." As early as 1868, when Morgan's body was brought from Greeneville, Tennessee, to Lexington for reburial, his memorialization served as "a unity fest" for a state eager to reunify. "[I]n a spirit of conciliation and forgiveness, both Union and Confederate veterans marched in the funeral cortege . . . united under the banner of the Lost Cause."[23]

Morgan's magnetism intensified as his men and their heirs gained political power in the state after the war. In contrast to Southern states that had seceded and where Reconstruction policies defined the postwar decade, in Kentucky the Democratic Party held the reins at war's end. Confederate veterans, including many of Morgan's men, won key state positions.[24] Despite repeated challenges to former Confederates' leadership, the process continued as the next generation strengthened Kentucky's racially segregated Jim Crow society around the turn of the twentieth century. Kentuckians like other Southerners polished the Confederate tradition to affirm the legitimacy of the Old South–New South continuum and its racial and social hierarchy. In Kentucky memory, Morgan

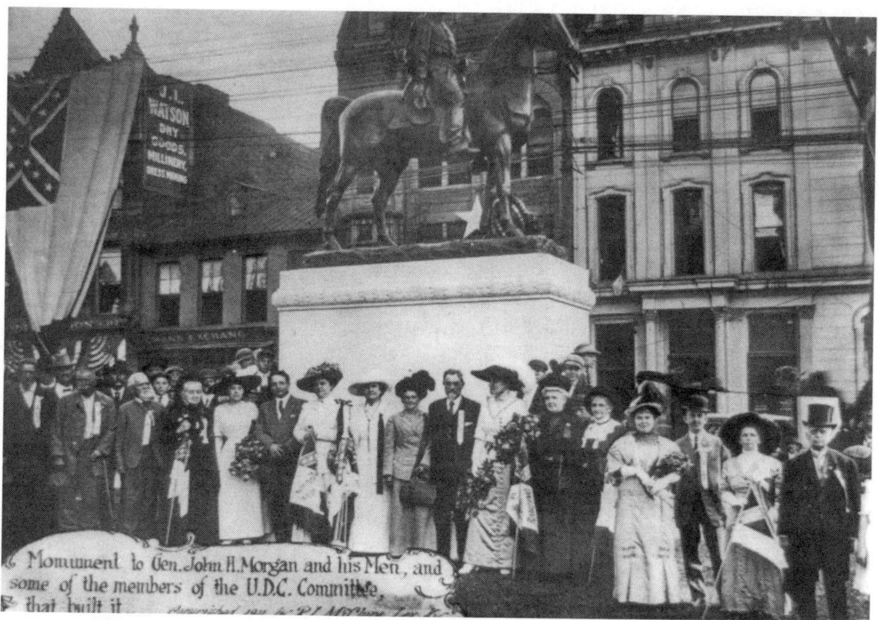

FIG. 8. Monument to John H. Morgan and his men, unveiling ceremony, October 18, 1911. (Library of Congress, Prints and Photographs Division, LC-USZ63-95819)

became "a peerless cavalier, third only to Lee and George Washington."[25] Over the years, the Morgan legacy continued to attract attention as the focus of commemoration, celebrations, history writing, and Civil War tourism.[26]

Creation of the Morgan monument took place during the height of early-twentieth-century Confederate commemoration. The Kentucky United Daughters of the Confederacy (UDC) decided in 1906 to construct an equestrian statue of Morgan in Lexington and selected Italian sculptor Pompeo Coppini from a competition. After considering several models for the general's horse, the sculptor and the sponsors settled on a figure of the general, modeled after his son, and sitting astride a large, idealized stallion. After their fund-raising efforts fell short of the necessary $15,000, the sponsors obtained half the funds from the state legislature in 1910. Thus, like the North Carolina Confederate Monument and many others, a project that began as a private commemoration gained state funding and validation. At the unveiling on October 18, 1911, a crowd estimated at 10,000 filled downtown Lexington, and Morgan's brother-in-law, Basil Duke, presided over the occasion (fig. 8). There was a grand parade including survivors of "Morgan's Men," speeches by the governor and other dignitaries, and festive music including "Dixie" and "The Star Spangled Banner"— a classic demonstration of American patriotism on Southern terms.[27]

Claiming the public square for the Confederate tradition, the larger-than-lifesize figure rises to a height of about twenty feet on its tall stone base. The monument depicts the general in uniform sitting calmly astride a big, muscularly modeled stallion meant to epitomize the ideal cavalry horse of Kentucky. The inscription reads, front and back, "General John H. Morgan and His Men" and "Erected by Kentucky Division United Daughters of the Confederacy."[28]

Like the North Carolina Confederate Monument, the monument itself gives little hint of the "backstory" of its creation. The chief conflict concerned its design, not support for its funding— as highlighted by a popular legend. The story goes that Coppini was supposed to have depicted Morgan riding his favorite horse, a small mare called Black Bess, and that at the unveiling the crowd groaned in stunned surprise to see that it was a stallion instead.[29] Historians have countered this legend by demonstrating that the sculptor and the sponsors had worked out every detail of the design and made it public years before the unveiling. Cheers, not gasps of horror, greeted the unveiling of the monument in 1911.[30]

Still, the legend has a kernel of truth, and it calls attention to a conflict narrative that suggests broader issues at work. There had been disagreement as early as 1908 among the committee members and other influential citizens over whether to show Morgan riding Black Bess or a larger, male horse. Some, including key UDC members, wanted to depict Morgan as he was during the war, and regarded Black Bess essential to historical accuracy. Others, including leaders in the horse industry and other businesses, pressed for a statue that would present the general on a large, impressive horse to convey the appropriate "dignity" and stature. This concept carried the day.

In his accounts of the project, sculptor Coppini focused almost exclusively on the character of the horse. Writing in advance of the 1911 unveiling, he explained simply, "General Morgan's success depended in great measure upon the quality of horses on which his men were mounted. It was the best mounted body of cavalry the world had ever seen"— thus his goal "to produce the kind of horse General Morgan's men used to ride." In his memoir, *From Dawn to Sunset* (1949), Coppini amplified his story. He passed quickly over the committee's disagreement over whether to depict Morgan on "Black Bess" or a "bay horse he was riding in the latter part of the Civil War. The stallion idea prevailed." Coppini emphasized instead his effort to represent "the best there was to be found in a Kentucky saddle horse." He traced his extensive design process in public view: he set up shop in Lexington to model the rider and the horse in clay and produced several versions of the horse before settling on the figures to be cast in bronze. He stressed especially how closely he had worked with "that certain class of men who live only in Kentucky, the good horsemen." He listed among his advisors men who "comprised the 'Who's Who' in Kentucky horsemen celebrities in Lexington." He also cited specific Bluegrass-area horses he studied to create a universal Kentucky ideal. Of horse and rider, Coppini said, "Both are game; both should be great; both should be Kentuckians; that was my aim."[31]

In this depiction, Coppini also created a memorial to suit the times. His Morgan is not the daring cavalryman whirling to foil the enemy nor the gallant knight tipping his hat to the ladies — but a calm and dignified leader in easy control of his stallion, a statesman-like figure of stability more evocative of Richmond's Robert E. Lee equestrian monument than of Kentucky's fiery guerrilla. Like the Lee figure, the relationship of Morgan and his horse also evokes the position of the New South leader in early-twentieth-century society. As Coppini explained, "the man shows a sense of responsibility, but no fear; while the horse is in a pose ready to obey orders."[32]

The rifts in the Morgan monument committee indicate more than personal friction between committee members or even gender differences between the ladies of the UDC and "the horsemen."[33] These conflicts reveal different visions of the meaning and purpose of the monument. For the advocates of the Black Bess version, seeking to honor the Lost Cause and the Confederacy, it was vital to show Morgan in action during the Civil War. But for "the horsemen" and others, it was not the war itself or Morgan's heroism that had the greatest meaning, but rather the Kentucky that had emerged from the war and Reconstruction. For them, the general and his horse stood for the New South order and their place in it, the legitimizing association with Old South mythology and hierarchy, and thus the world they were striving to shape. While nominally it memorializes "General John H. Morgan and His Men," the monument represents white elite business leaders' vision of Kentucky in the early twentieth century, of a city and region in the process of regaining national stature and wealth by becoming the "The Horse Capital of the World."

During the subsequent decades, the Morgan statue attracted a few challenges, but for the most part it remains a marker of gallantry and even patriotism. In recent years, Lexingtonians have expanded memorialization in various directions from the Morgan monument. After complaints about the Confederate tradition's dominance of the public square, a new marker was installed to commemorate the adjoining slave market long ignored in histories of the city.[34] Only a few blocks away, a redeveloped area has been made into "Thoroughbred Park," a simulacrum of the horse farm landscape dotted with idealized bronze horses as carefully rendered as Morgan's giant steed.[35] Today, as for more than a century, the Morgan monument is a central feature in every tour of the Bluegrass, along with horse farm visits, the Keeneland race track, Civil War sites, and antebellum homes. The towering statue, as its makers intended, represents not just a single Confederate raider: it encapsulates the dual character of the Bluegrass mystique and social hierarchy, idealizing at once the Confederate and Old South tradition and the power of the Kentucky horse and horsemen. Amid a fast-changing landscape and economy, this combined mythology still dominates the identity and shapes the values of Lexington and of Kentucky.

WITHIN HALF A CENTURY after the Civil War, Americans had transformed the meaning of the Civil War, and national reunification was taking place on Southern terms. As some say, the North had won the war, but the South won the peace. With Southern Democrats in control of a Jim Crow society as well as writing the history books, in the early twentieth century not only the conflicts over memorials but whole chapters of history — dissent and internecine conflict during the Civil War, post-Reconstruction black political participation, white supremacy campaigns — simply dropped out of official public memory. Recent historians have challenged these accounts, just as citizens have challenged the racial and class structures defined at the turn of the twentieth century. Yet in the popular memory, as defined by the established leaders at the turn of the twentieth century, the story has changed but little. By putting in permanent, public form a single version of the past, the creators of these monuments laid lasting claim to their definition of the past and set the terms by which they meant to shape the future.

The more I look at monuments, the more I find that wherever they may be, and whatever their form and apparent purpose, we can learn the most from them by asking not merely what they commemorate but who was doing the commemorating, and when, and why. In short, what is (and was) this monument really about? We can uncover much more about the person or event memorialized and, beyond that, explore the forces, people, motivations, times, struggles, and choices that produced it. Although I know that I can seldom find out everything I would like to know about most of the monuments I see, I know the possibilities are there. In studying the history of the North Carolina Confederate Monument in Raleigh and in asking questions about the John Hunt Morgan Monument in Lexington, I have expanded my comprehension of how people shaped the history and public memory of their communities to suit their values. By questioning the process as well as the product of that history-making, we can begin to understand the world we have inherited and, with any luck, think anew about the direction of the future.

Notes

My thanks to the Henry F. duPont Winterthur Museum for a 1987 fellowship to study the roles of monuments and architecture in forming public memory in the South.

1. Bishir, "Landmarks of Power," 5–46, republished in Brundage, ed., *Where These Memories Grow.* My thinking about monuments and memorials has benefited greatly from conversations with Fitzhugh Brundage, Jerry Cashion, Jeffrey Crow, Gaines Foster, Kirk Savage, and Dell Upton. My perspective has been informed especially by Foster, *Ghosts of the Confederacy;* and Savage, *Standing Soldiers, Kneeling Slaves.* Also valuable are Jacob, *Testament to Union;* and Mills and Simpson, eds., *Monuments to the Lost Cause.*

2. The Chestertown memorial was given by James A. Pearce, dated June 1917, and dedicated to "the patriotism and valor of a once divided but now united country," indicative of an emphasis on national unity in the face of war in Europe.

3. On "about-to-die" images in journalism, see Zelizer, "The Voice of the Visual in Memory," 168–70. See also Craven, *Sculpture at Gettysburg;* Martin, *Confederate Monuments at Gettysburg;* Weeks, *Gettysburg;* and *Commemorations Attending the Presentations and Unveiling of the North Carolina Memorial on the Battlefield of Gettysburg, Wednesday, July 3rd, 1929* [1929]. In 1986, the state dedicated a second North Carolina marker at Gettysburg, at the spot almost to the Union-held ridge, where North Carolina troops in "the Pettigrew-Pickett Charge" went "farthest at Gettysburg" on July 3, 1863 — "within ten paces of the stone wall to their front" reads the marker. For facts and images about the Gettysburg monuments, see http://www.usa-civil-war.com/Gettysburg; and Frederick Hawthorne, "Gettysburg: Stories of Men and Monuments," reproduced at http://www.gdg.org/Research/Authored%20Items/monmen.html. North Carolinians of the Confederate tradition had long been defensive about the state's contribution to

the Confederacy, believing that Virginians especially had improperly denigrated Tar Heels' sacrifice and valor. They saw the state memorial at Gettysburg as a step in rectifying the record — and taking their proper place in American as well as Southern history. How sculptor and sponsors translated this motive into one of the battlefield's greatest works is another part of the saga.

4. A monument to commemorate the victory at Yorktown was approved by the Continental Congress on October 29, 1781, but never built. After deferring a request from Fredericksburg, Virginia, for the memorial, in 1879 Congress authorized a study for the project, and with the encouragement of citizens from north and south (including the legislature of North Carolina), on June 7, 1880, Congress authorized $100,000 for its construction. The cornerstone was laid in 1881, and the monument was completed in 1884. For segments from the official report from that time, see http://www.nps.gov/colo/Ythanout/VicMonument2.htm. Thanks to Kirk Savage and Dell Upton for insights on this monument's place in history. Reunification on Southern terms included national acceptance of Southern racial and political policies, which culminated in the Supreme Court's ruling on *Plessy v. Ferguson* in 1896, legitimizing the "separate but equal" doctrine. See Ayers, *The Promise of the New South* on this period.

5. This discussion is adapted from Bishir, "'A Strong Force of Ladies,'" 455–91.

6. Raleigh *News and Observer,* March 24, June 15 and 19, 1892, and May 20, 1895.

7. *News and Observer,* July 16, Sept. 10–12, 1892, and Feb. 16–14, 1893; clippings in Branch Family Papers, North Carolina State Archives, Raleigh, North Carolina.

8. North Carolina Monumental Association Minutes, in Branch Family Papers; *News and Observer,* May 24, 1894, and May 20, 1895.

9. Edmonds, *The Negro and Fusion Politics,* 37–38; Trelease, "The Fusionist Legislatures of 1895 and 1897," 280–309.

10. *News and Observer,* Feb. 20–22, 1895; *The Caucasian,* Feb. 21, 1895.

11. The "land without memories" parallels language quoted in the preface to a poem, "A Land Without Ruins," by Father Abraham Joseph Ryan, favorite poet of the Lost Cause. The preface includes the language, unattributed, "A land without ruins is a land without memories — a land without memories is a land without history." This poem, and others by Father Ryan, would have been known to both the members of the North Carolina Monumental Association and the readers of the *News and Observer.*

12. *News and Observer,* Feb. 22–March 8, 1895.

13. *News and Observer,* various dates, March–May 1895.

14. *News and Observer,* May 20, 1895; undated clippings in Branch Family Papers.

15. *News and Observer,* May 20, 1895; undated clippings in Branch Family Papers.

16. *News and Observer,* May 20, 1895; undated clippings in Branch Family Papers.

17. If politics in Kentucky are "the damnedest," the historians are surely the kindest; I am grateful for the gracious welcomes and assistance of those who know the most about

Morgan and his place in Kentucky history, especially James Ramage and Anne Marshall, and for their kind help, Marty Perry, Mark Wetherington, and Bill Marshall.

18. Conversations with David Morgan and Camille Wells, April 2005; Anne E. Marshall to author, April 24, 2005. In her study of historical memory and the Civil War in Kentucky, Marshall shows how "white Kentuckians used the aristocratic bearings of the Lost Cause to embellish their southern identity" to affirm the social and political structure that went with it. See Marshall, "'A Strange Conclusion to a Triumphant War'"; and Marshall, *Creating a Confederate Kentucky.* My thanks to Dr. Marshall for sharing her findings with me; quotation from Marshall to author, April 24, 2005. The mythmaking permeated nearly every aspect of popular and elite culture, including works of poetry and fiction in the "local color" school and the proponents of the "genteel tradition." This trend, which began in the mid-nineteenth century, attained full and lasting flowering in the twentieth century.

19. The idealized Bluegrass landscape is part of a package of created memory that extends unbroken (except by war) from the antebellum golden age to the present. As one descendant of "horse people" puts it, in a place whose economic engine depends on tracing equine bloodlines, the concern for the lineage of humans is hardly a surprise (J. B. Scott to author, May 8, 2005). For a critical analysis of the horse imagery of the Bluegrass, see Schein, "Normative Dimensions of Landscapes," 199–218.

20. Marker no. 1809, http://www.history.ky.gov.

21. Ramage analyzes Morgan's stature as folk hero in *Rebel Raider,* 1–7. The first Civil War novel by a Kentucky writer was *Raids and Romance of Morgan and His Men,* published in 1864, the year of Morgan's death, and of about sixty Kentucky Civil War novels, over half featured Morgan and his men. See Ward, *A Literary History of Kentucky,* 67–68.

22. Ramage, *Rebel Raider,* ix–x; Duke quoted in Marshall, "'A Strange Conclusion to a Triumphant War,'" 252.

23. Ramage, *Rebel Raider,* 258, 256.

24. Ibid., 252–53, 256. On Union commemorations, see Marshall, "'A Strange Conclusion to a Triumphant War,'" 254–56.

25. In Lexington, Lost Cause apologists even succeeded in having a sixth-grade history textbook censored in 1908 "because it described [Morgan's men's] looting of private property on the Great Raid." See Ramage, *Rebel Raider,* 256.

26. Ibid., 257–59. Ramage, ibid., 258, counted in Kentucky more than twice as many historical markers to Morgan and his adventures as to any other person or event (including Daniel Boone) — which now total about eighty. For current organizations and events commemorating Morgan, see http://www.history.ky.gov; http://www.thinkwestkentuocky.com/monuments; and http://www.lexingtonrifles.com.

27. Milward, "The Unveiling of the Morgan Statue," 52–56.

28. Emerson, comp., *Historic Southern Monuments,* 140, cites the measurements of the horse as twenty hands high, the rider seven feet tall, and the base eleven feet high; courtesy of Marty Perry. The Morgan figure is one of only two equestrian statues in Kentucky commemorating a Civil War figure. The other is of General John B. Castleman, best known as a founder of the American Saddlebred Association.

29. This story has received recent retelling in Loewen, *Lies across America,* 164–65. The local prank of painting the horse's testicles in brilliant colors (one of innumerable such pranks among equestrian statues) is characterized as a protest of depicting "Bess" with balls. Loewen states that the monument is inscribed "General John H. Morgan and his Bess" and quotes from a long poem entitled "The Ballad of Black Bess," which he cites as an anonymous Kentucky ballad. In fact, the monument inscriptions make no mention of Bess, only of General Morgan and his men, and the satirical ballad by Kentucky writer Bruce Denbo dates from the 1950s. The legend and the painting pranks continue to the present; as one reporter said, "The old story is just more entertaining than the truth." See clipping, Dec. 4, 1981, courtesy of James Ramage. See also http://www.visitlex.com.

30. For accounts correcting the "picturesque myth" about the unveiling, see Milward, "The Unveiling of the Morgan Statue," 52–56; Burton Milward, "Morgan Statue Unveiled," *Lexington Leader,* Oct. 16, 1961, courtesy of James Ramage and Marty Perry; and Ramage, *Rebel Raider,* 257. It appears likely that the disagreement within the monument committee remained a bitter issue for disconsolate Black Bess advocates, and the story was reconfigured over the years into the more dramatic story of a shocked public at the unveiling event.

31. Coppini, *From Dawn to Sunset,* 163–65.

32. Coppini quoted in Emerson, comp., *Historic Southern Monuments,* 140, and a photograph of the statue (or a model for it) is pictured on 141. "The picture and data were furnished by Mrs. E. D. Potts." On the Robert E. Lee equestrian monument in Richmond, where there was intense debate over how to depict both horse and rider, see Savage, *Standing Soldiers, Kneeling Slaves,* 129–61. My ideas about the depiction of the relationship of man and horse derive from Savage's analysis of the Lee figure: he comments that the establishment of the image of Lee as representative hero of the South and his depiction on his horse constituted a coded definition of mastery "not in the obvious territory of race relations," but "rather in the relationship of the hero to his animal servant, the horse Traveller." See Savage, *Standing Soldiers, Kneeling Slaves,* 133.

33. Coppini's account in *From Dawn to Sunset* does not make clear whether it was he or "the horsemen" who pushed for a more impressive horse than the black mare. Some accounts ascribe it to the sculptor, without explaining the role of the horse businessmen. This is a topic of further research.

34. In "Normative Dimensions of Landscape," Schein points to the racialized landscape of the courthouse square and calls for public acknowledgment of its history of the

adjoining Cheapside Street as a slave auction site. The marker (#2122) was installed in 2002.

35. See Schein, "Normative Dimensions of Landscape," on the Thoroughbred Park. On issues affecting the traditional horse farm landscape of the region, see the organization Bluegrass Tomorrow, http://www.bluegrasstomorrow.org; and The Center for Historic Architecture and Preservation (CHAP) at the University of Kentucky, including documentation and analysis of Bluegrass racing landscapes and farm properties in the Bluegrass, http://www.uky.edu/Centers/Preservation/projects.

MARK A. PETERSON

Stone Witnesses, Dumb Pictures, and Voices from the Grave

Objects, Images, and Collective Memory in Early Boston

THE FOUNDERS OF Boston, Massachusetts, were English Puritans, and Puritanism shaped Boston's cultural practices and habits in profound ways, giving a particular cast to local aspirations and methods for preserving the past, and creating a heritage that would linger well into the early national period.[1] With respect to the question of which aspects of the past were important to preserve, the intense spirituality of the Puritans tended to favor the eternal over the fleeting, deep truths over surface characteristics. With respect to the question of how to remember the past, Puritans were iconoclastic — they understood the power of physical objects or visual images in molding human perceptions, but they feared the potential for idolatry inherent in "graven images," and claimed to prefer to substitute words for objects whenever possible. Yet their use of words was always intensely metaphorical, folding language back on objects, and deriving power from those objects.[2] This essay begins with the Puritan founders of Boston and moves forward in time through the Revolutionary era and beyond, examining a variety of media through which New Englanders strove to preserve the past, in the context of these specific tensions over what to preserve and how to preserve it. An imaginary stroll through the libraries, portrait galleries, and graveyards of the colonial period will help us to understand the shifting forms that the most powerful commemorations of the American Revolution in Boston and the surrounding countryside would take.

THE DAWNING OF historical consciousness begins with the awareness of death; with the passing of particular individuals, and with the general realization of human mortality. The act of thinking historically, of remembering the past, always means thinking about the dead and coming to terms with death. From the very beginning of New England's settlement, and stretching back into its roots in Puritan England, this impulse to dwell on the significance of death was particularly strong, and it profoundly shaped Bostonians' historical sensibility. Since Puritans claimed to favor words over objects as means to convey meaning, biographical forms of writing were tremendously important to them as a way to preserve the memory of the dead, but biographies of a peculiar sort. The central background text for understanding Puritan biography was the work of the sixteenth-century English Protestant John Foxe, whose *Book of Martyrs,* as it was known, an immense compendium of the sufferings of Protestants in the early years of the Reformation, stands as the great code, the essential template, for all subsequent efforts in this line. The formal title of Foxe's work was *The Acts and Monuments of the Christian Church,* a striking image, in which the written words contained in the biographies became the equivalent of both the evanescent "acts" and the durable "monuments" of the church, embodied in its martyred members. But the point of Foxe's biographies was not to glorify the specific qualities or actions of individual martyrs, but to show how each life spoke the larger truths of Protestant Christianity. Foxe all but effaced the personal and particular in favor of the general and universal.[3]

With Foxe's text as a starting point, the desire to find universal truths in the lives of exemplary individuals became an essential part of Puritan spirituality. Even so distinctive a feature as a person's name was thought to contain a deeper and not entirely personal meaning. A favorite Puritan strategy for commemorating the dead was to see what hidden anagrams the departed's name contained. To cite one example, when the early Massachusetts governor Thomas Dudley died, the letters of his name were rearranged to spell out the phrase, "Ah, Old, Must Dye," an appropriate recognition of the power that death holds over all mankind. As a mnemonic device, this technique is remarkably effective — once one encounters this anagram, it is difficult to see Thomas Dudley's name without thinking, "Ah, Old, Must Dye."[4] Remembering Thomas Dudley means remembering death as well.

The earliest biography written in Boston fell squarely within this tradition, an account of the life of the town's first minister, John Cotton, written in 1658 by his successor in the Boston pulpit, John Norton. The title of this work, *Abel Being Dead, Yet Speaketh,* was drawn from a biblical verse which declared that although Abel was killed by Cain, through his faith in God, Abel's voice could still be heard from the grave.[5] As Norton put it, "By Faith, Abel being dead many thousand years since, yet speaketh, and will speak whil'st time shall be no more. That the living speak is no wonder: but that the dead speak, is more than miraculous.... To preserve the memory of the blessed with the Spices and sweet Odors of their *Excellencies* and *Weldoing,* recorded to posterity, is a super-Egyptian embalming." This was the purpose of Puritan biography, to embalm the spirits of the dead and make them speak, to allow future generations to hear their voices from the grave, but with an emphasis on their enduring spiritual qualities, on "any *excellency* in the Sons of mortality, that may outlive Death." To this end, Norton claimed to prefer words over visual images: "Dumb pictures of deserving men answer not ingenuous minds capable to retain the memorial of vertue, the real effigies of their Spirits."[6] To focus on "dumb pictures," or on the mortal features of the subject that would not outlast the grave, only distracted from the larger exemplary purpose that these memorials were meant to serve. For this reason, Norton's biography of John Cotton can tell us a great deal about the nature of Puritan spirituality, but very little about the fleeting events of the life of his subject.

Although Norton's life of John Cotton set the mold for Puritan Boston, the great practitioner of this genre was John Cotton's grandson, Cotton Mather, whose *Magnalia Christi Americana* (1702) aspired to be an American version of Foxe's *Acts and Monuments,* an immense compendium of biographies of New England's leading magistrates and ministers, all cast in the same exemplary mode. In the scope of his achievement, Mather's work set the standard for New England historical writing and influenced the process of memory-keeping for decades to come.[7] And yet, despite his insistent moralizing, his constant search for the spiritual significance behind mundane events, the obsessive energy with which Mather pursued the details of his subjects' lives and carefully recorded their actions and words began to undercut the larger purpose of the exemplary biography. Today, historians can profitably read Mather for purposes other than those intended, as his volumes are filled with the mundane, ephemeral details that works like Norton's life of Cotton omitted. In the title of Mather's biography of his father, he referred to the great Increase Mather as "ever-memorable," and in the son's vivid rendering, those memorable qualities had more to do with the father's distinctive personality and dramatic life than with his exemplary Christian spirit.[8]

As the seventeenth century gave way to the eighteenth, literary memorials remained the dominant form of memory-keeping in Boston. But despite Puritan preferences for word over image, visual means of preserving the past were not entirely absent from colonial Boston. One art form in particular, the portrait, was made to perform a function in visual terms strikingly similar to that of the exemplary biography. The portrait in figure 1 depicts a man named Robert Jannys, who served as mayor of the English town of Norwich in the early sixteenth century, a century before the Puritan migration to New England began. Norwich was a major city in East Anglia, the region from which many of New England's founders came, and a source of their cultural inheritance — a city where portraits like this one were hung in the streets as part of celebrations such as the annual guild day. Jannys's portrait is a striking example of the *memento mori* tradition in European portraiture. The skull in the hands of Robert Jannys, but even more so, the decaying skeletal figure looking over his shoulder, reminds the viewer that the earthly power of this man is no match for the power of death — the fact that the skeleton and not the mayor holds the scepter clinches the argument. So even though this "dumb picture" of a "deserving man" does capture the personal features of Jannys that will not outlive Death, the vivid presence of Death in the picture is there to make this otherwise "dumb" portrait speak, to turn the viewer's thoughts to the inner virtues of the subject: *memento mori,* remember death, and attend to the spiritual qualities that will outlast the grave.[9]

As Puritans from East Anglia migrated across the Atlantic and founded New England, this tradition moved with them, exemplified in figure 2, a self-portrait painted in the 1680s by the merchant-artist Captain Thomas Smith of Boston.[10] The pose and the omnipresent skull repeat the pattern of Robert Jannys and other earlier mayors of Norwich, although Captain Smith manages to squeeze in more of the details of his own life, with the naval battle in the upper left perhaps meant to illustrate a major event in his mercantile career. Here, it would seem that the desire to remember the particular, the personal, is competing with the universal fact of death's dominion. Yet the self-composed poem that Smith places below the skull gives added emphasis to the *memento mori* message:

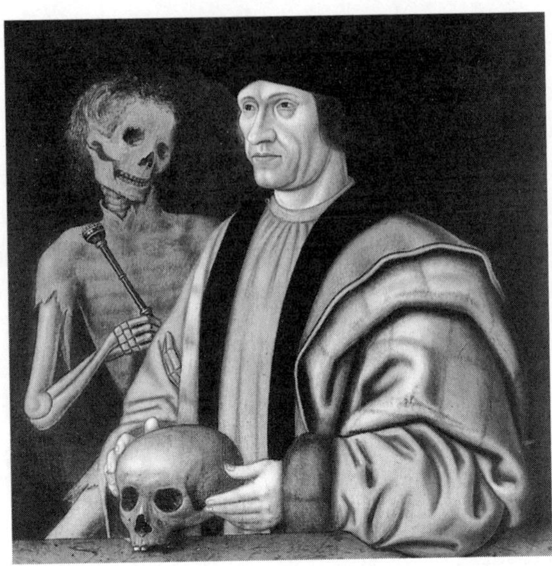

FIG. 1. Portrait of Robert Jannys, Mayor of Norwich, 1517 and 1524, artist unknown. Oil on panel, 77.5 × 61 cm. (Norfolk Museums and Archaeology Service [Norwich Castle Museum and Art Gallery])

Why why should I the world be minding
Therein a World of Evils finding;
Then farewell World: Farewell thy Jarres
Thy Joies thy Toiles thy Wiles thy Warres.
Truth sounds Retreat: I am not Sorye.
The Eternal Drawes to him my heart
By Faith (which can thy Force subvert)
To crowne me (after Grace) with Glory.

The written text, together with the skull that rests upon it, bids farewell to the "toils and wars" of life that the painting depicts, and death, although victorious, brings the promise of eternal life to come. Thomas Smith's self-portrait is not a dumb picture, but one that projects a voice from the foreshadowed grave.[11]

By the eighteenth century, as new cultural forces in Boston begin to compete with Puritanism, the typical Boston portrait gradually departs from the *memento mori* and the exemplary biography traditions — skulls and references to death's dominion recede, and the specific features of the individual's life are given greater

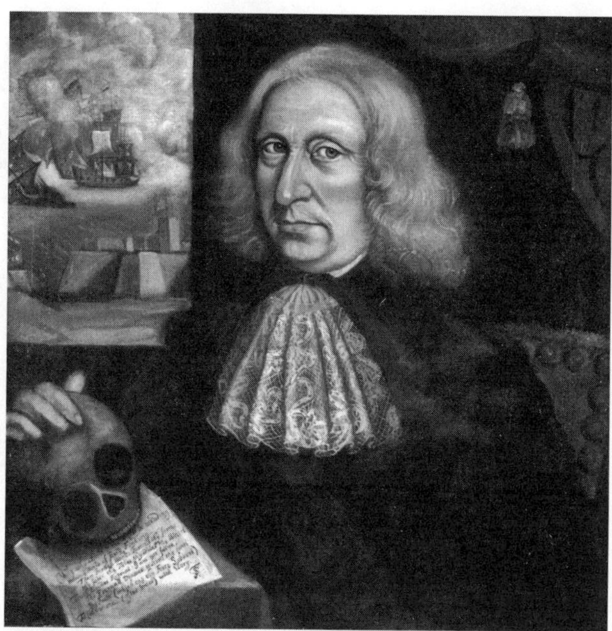

FIG. 2. Captain Thomas Smith, self-portrait, c. 1680. Oil on canvas, 62.9 × 60.4 cm. (Worcester Art Museum, Worcester, Massachusetts, Museum purchase)

prominence. Portraits even of Puritan ministers, like Cotton Mather or Thomas Prince, another leading historian among Boston clergymen, lose the grim *memento mori,* even if the sermons they preached continued to preserve the tradition. But in figure 3, perhaps the most famous portrait by New England's finest artist, the John Singleton Copley portrait of Paul Revere, painted only a few years before his midnight ride, we see the striking shift. The pose is traditional, but the skull has now been replaced by one of Revere's silver teapots as an appropriate spheroid of contemplation. The symbol of death's dominion over man gives way to an emblem of man's dominion over the plastic world. It is Revere himself and the glory of his achievements, not an abstract reminder of human mortality, that this painting is meant to portray, and the virtues it celebrates are more worldly than spiritual.

It would seem that as a means for preserving the past, the portrait has come a long way, and that the Puritan preference for the eternal over the ephemeral, the general over the particular, has been reversed by the time of Copley's Revere.[12] Yet

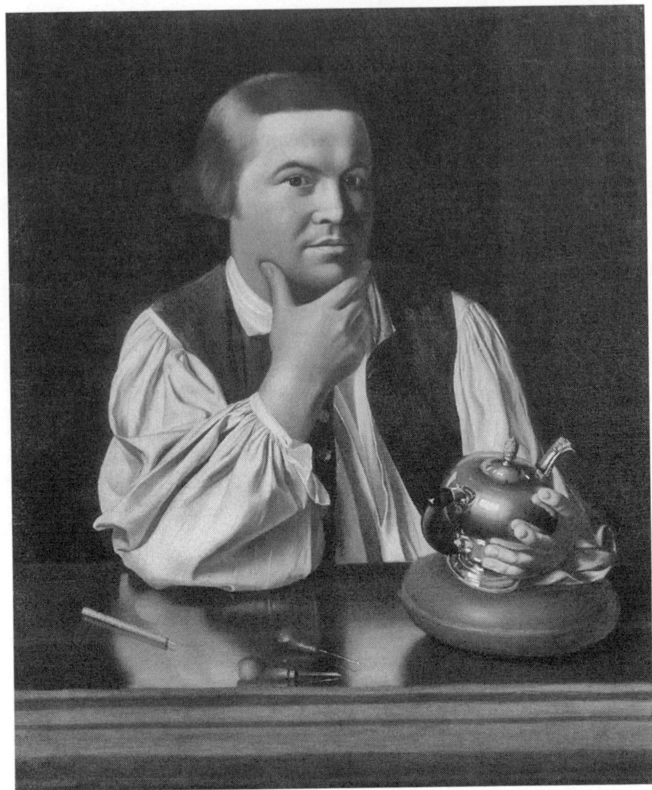

FIG. 3. *Paul Revere,* 1768, by John Singleton Copley, American, 1738–1815. Oil on canvas, 89.22 × 72.39 cm. (Museum of Fine Arts, Boston, Gift of Joseph W. Revere, William B. Revere, and Edward H. R. Revere, 30.781; photograph © 2013, Museum of Fine Arts, Boston)

even Revere's teapot partakes of a spectrum of sacred and secular meanings that silver signified in early New England. By the time of Copley's portrait, Boston craftsmen had for more than a century been making silver vessels that served as bearers of spiritual meaning within New England's religious traditions — the substitution of teapot for skull is an innovation within, not an abandonment of, this tradition of pictorial memory.[13] Nor does the *memento mori* disappear from Boston; it even resurfaces in the age of mechanical image-making with a c. 1848 daguerreotype of Dr. John Collins Warren, chief surgeon of the Massachusetts General Hospital and nephew of Joseph Warren, the martyred hero of the Battle of Bunker Hill (fig. 4). But we should consider the possibility that when placed

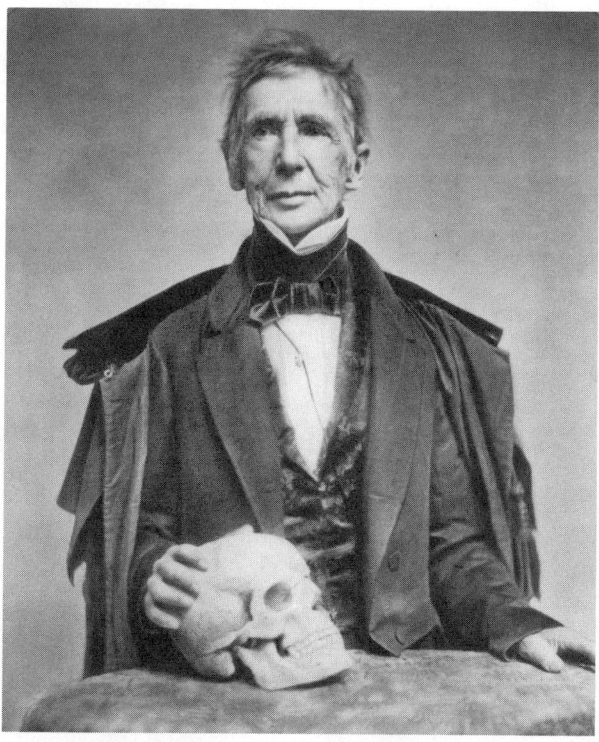

FIG. 4. Daguerreotype of Dr. John Collins Warren, c. 1848. (Harvard Medical Library in the Francis A. Countway Library of Medicine)

under the hands of Boston's foremost physician in the hopeful era of romantic reform, the skull may now signify mankind's growing dominion over death as much as death's eternal power over humanity.[14]

Another form of memory preservation, seemingly more durable if less expressive than the portrait, was the gravestone. From the beginnings of Puritan settlement, gravestones of necessity performed a version of the *memento mori* tradition. The simple representation in stone of the fact of a person's death, marking the spot where their physical remains were interred, served as a reminder to all who viewed it that death was omnipresent. The *memento mori* tradition dominated the Puritan century in gravestone art. The preponderance of skulls, crossed bones, and figures of death or of time snuffing out life's candle overwhelmed the occasional touches of individual identity — the brief acknowledgments that the

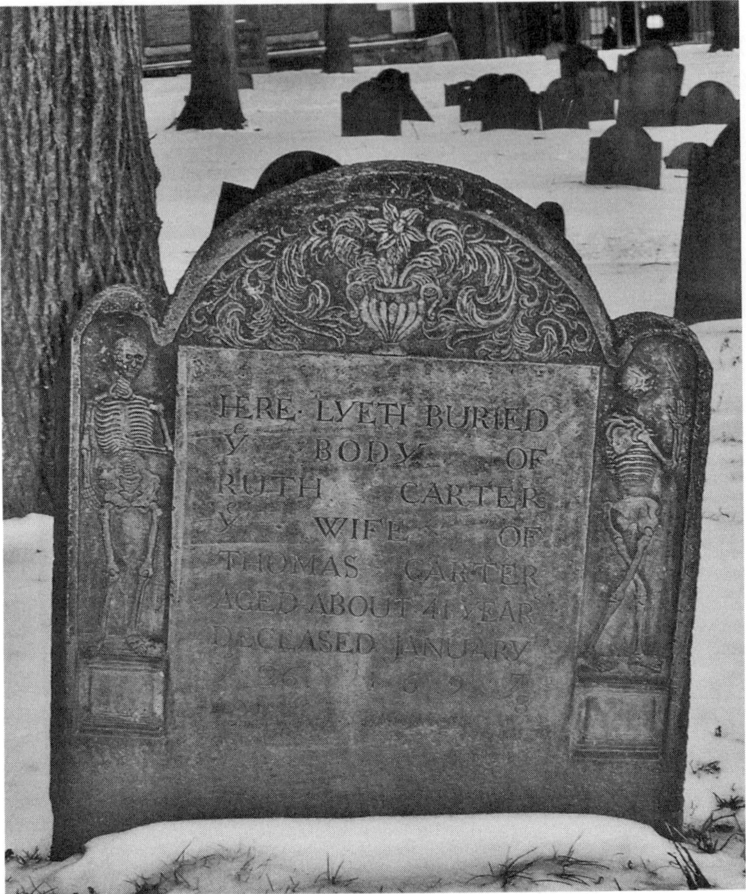

FIG. 5. Gravestone of Ruth Carter, c. 1697, artist unknown, Old Granary Burying Ground, Boston, Massachusetts. (Photo by the author)

departed had served as a deacon, or had performed some distinctive version of the role of exemplary wife and mother — that managed to work their way onto Puritan gravestones (fig. 5). For the few who did inscribe verse epitaphs on their tombstones, the message was generic and universal, warning the passing reader to prepare for a similar fate. The oldest stone in Boston's Granary Burying Ground that bears an epitaph in verse, the grave of Hannah Allen, reads: "Stay! thou this tombe that passeth by / And think how soon that thou mayst die." A stroll through a seventeenth-century Puritan burying ground will tell you more about Puritan spirituality than it will about the lives of the individuals buried there.[15]

Yet gravestones, like portraits, began to evolve as the seventeenth century gave way to the eighteenth. Graven imagery more frequently depicted the promise of glory in the afterlife than the fact of death itself— the skulls became angels, and wings and cherubs gained in prominence. Furthermore, the individuality of the person emerges in greater detail in the occasional epitaphs written for the departed. One remarkable gravestone in an old cemetery in Hardwick, Massachusetts, tells the story of Ebenezer Cox, an officer in the Massachusetts provincial forces in the colonial wars with France, who died in 1768 at the age of forty-two:

> Beneath this stone a noble Captain's laid
> Which for his King and Country was Display'd
> His Courage that no Terrors could Disarm
> Nor when he faced ye Foe his fear Alarm
> But now he's Conquer'd & ye silent Grave
> Can boast that power ye French could never have
> In six campaigns Intrepid trod ye Field
> Nor to ye Gallic Foe would ever Yield
> At last he's gone we hope where wars do cease
> To spend a whole eternity in Peace.

The closing sentiment is reminiscent of the poem depicted in Captain Thomas Smith's self-portrait, but the weight of detail is now given over to the life of the individual (fig. 6).

This transformation in gravestone art was captured in a comical sketch written by Nathaniel Hawthorne in the 1830s, entitled "Chippings with a Chisel," cast in the form of a running dialogue between the narrator, who speaks for modern ways, and an old stone carver named Wigglesworth, a name borrowed from the famous seventeenth-century Puritan author of the apocalyptic poem *Day of Doom.*[16] No matter what the personal characteristics or life history of the customer who enters his shop, Wigglesworth always wants to use the same old traditional "lugubrious emblems of mortality" for their prospective tombstones, while the narrator prefers the personal, the expressive, the hopeful. When the conversation during a customer's visit to choose a tomb for a departed relative yields "at least a dozen simple and natural expressions" suitable for engraving, old Wigglesworth rejects the notion: "No, no, there is a good deal of comfort to be gathered from these little old scraps of poetry, and so I always recommend them in preference to any new-fangled ones."[17] But by the 1830s, society's preference

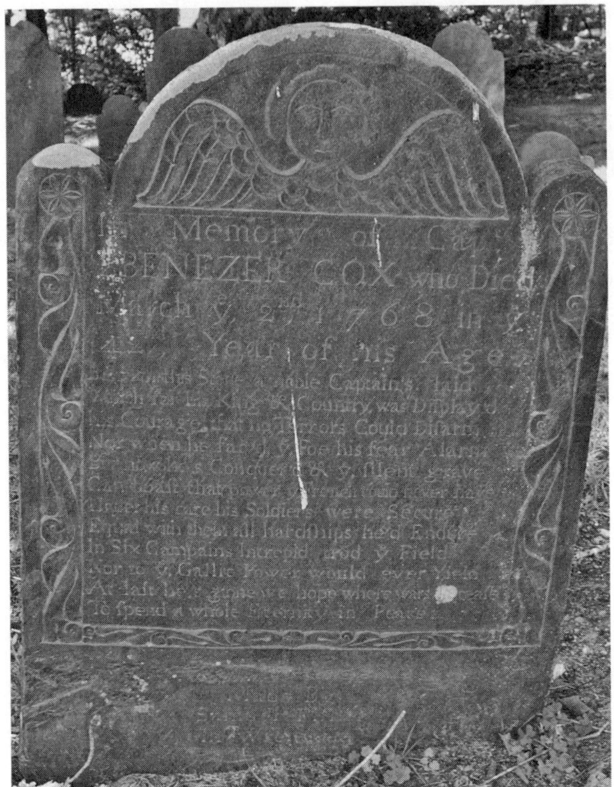

FIG. 6. Gravestone of Ebenezer Cox, c. 1768, artist unknown, Hardwick, Massachusetts. (Photo by the author)

for the new-fangled had finally won out and was embodied in the newly opened Mount Auburn Cemetery in Cambridge, founded in part to solve Boston's problem of inadequate space for burying its dead. One stone in particular at Mount Auburn captures this fully. The grave of Dr. Charles Thomas Jackson, a pioneer in the use of ether for painless surgery, lists his many personal accomplishments, and then appends a new-fangled sort of poem:

Thy godlike crime was to be kind
To render with thy precepts less
The sum of human wretchedness
And strengthen man with his own mind.

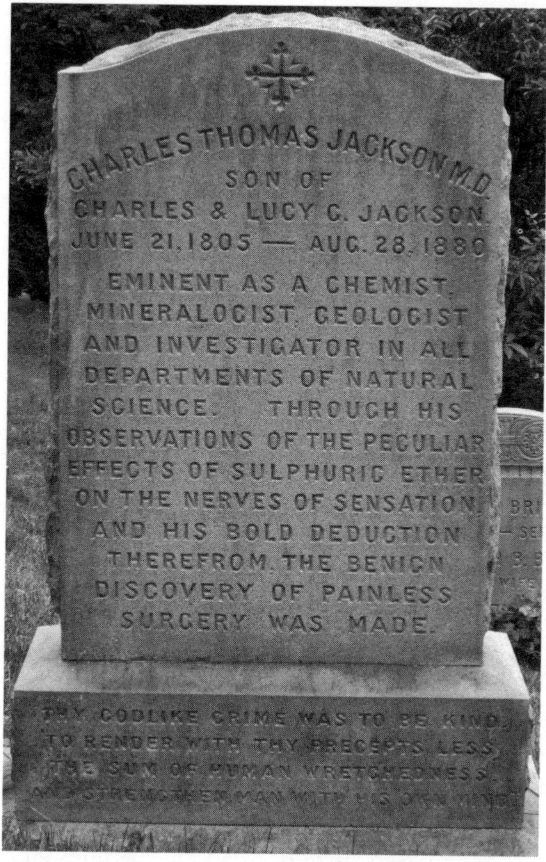

FIG. 7. Gravestone of Dr. Charles Thomas Jackson, c. 1880, Mount Auburn Cemetery, Cambridge, Massachusetts. (Photo by the author)

By calling up this promethean imagery, Jackson's gravestone, ironically enough, goes quite far toward denying death's dominion over humanity—we have here the stone equivalent of the daguerreotype of Dr. Jackson's colleague Dr. John Collins Warren (fig. 7).[18]

Through the use of words, images, and objects, the Puritan legacy bequeathed a variety of means for preserving the past, especially for the lives of individuals and the exemplary qualities they embodied. But what was missing from colonial Boston was any tradition that combined these forms for the preservation of specific events in the region's history. In fact, Cotton Mather drew special attention to the absence of historical monuments in Boston, and at the same time indirectly explained the reason for it, when he published the earliest recorded history of the town of Boston. As he was engaged in assembling his massive collection of biographies for the *Magnalia,* Mather also saw the need to preserve some testimony of the ways in which the town of Boston had received divine assistance during its early history. In April 1698, Mather preached a sermon which he later published under the peculiar title, *The Bostonian Ebenezer.*[19] The word "ebenezer" was borrowed from an Old Testament verse, in which the prophet Samuel set up a stone monument, giving thanks to God for delivering the children of Israel from imminent destruction by the army of the Philistines: "Then Samuel took a Stone, and set it up, — and called the Name of it, Ebenezer, saying Hitherto the Lord hath Helped us," as the Hebrew word "ebenezer" means literally, a stone of help.

In his sermon, Mather took this biblical example of commemoration and attempted to apply it to Boston's history, but with characteristic Puritan precautions. He reviewed other instances where biblical patriarchs like Jacob and Joshua "have used sometimes to Erect Monuments of Stone, as durable Tokens of their thankfulness to God," but he also pointed out that "they so did it, as to keep clear of the Transgression forbidden in Lev. 26.1, *ye shall not set up any Image of Stone in your Land, for to Bow down unto it.*"[20] Mather recognized the danger that the memorial itself, rather than the divine meaning behind the event it commemorated, might become the object of veneration. To avoid this potential for idolatry, he felt it necessary to translate the medium for commemoration from stone into an intangible form: "Boston, a place where the Remarkable Help received from Heaven by the People, does loudly call for an Ebenezer, . . . but my Sermon shall be this Day, your Ebenezer, if you will with a Favourable and a Profitable Attention Entertain it."[21] Mather's peculiar "ebenezer," his literary memorial stone, exemplifies the tensions and preferences that Puritans brought to the task of commemoration. But in the actual text of his history of Boston, Mather struggled to find specific events that deserved an ebenezer, literary or concrete. The Lord's divine assistance to seventeenth-century Boston consisted mainly of disasters averted — hurricanes that spared the town or French fleets that never got around to attacking.

The American Revolution would change all this, and through the cataclysmic events that altered the course of Boston's history, the way its memory would be preserved changed as well. By this time the Puritan legacy was starting to fade, and the New Englanders who began to approach the problem of commemorating the Revolution displayed a certain degree of confusion about what to remember, and how to remember it — were they remembering the dead, preserving the distinctive features of the lives and the heroic deeds of the individuals killed in the bloody conflict, or were they constructing ebenezers to preserve the deeper meaning, the motivating spirit that lay behind historic actions and events? Should their memorials be durable objects, stone witnesses, or would words and rituals be the better way to resurrect these voices from the grave?

During the resistance movement of the 1760s and 1770s, the commemoration of major events like the Boston Massacre were conducted through public ceremonies that combined various features of traditional colonial rituals — the parades, pageantry, and brawling of Pope's Day, "please to remember the 5th of November, gunpowder, treason and plot," with the feasting, toasts, speeches, and sermons characteristic of Harvard College Commencements.[22] But the shocking outbreak of open warfare on April 19, 1775, at Lexington and Concord, as well as the vicious battle two months later on June 17 in Charlestown, called for more profound efforts to preserve the memory of these dramatic events.

While the Revolutionary War was still being fought, the 19th of April was annually observed in the solemn manner of the Puritan fast day, or day of humiliation. In Lexington, the militia would assemble and accompany the entire town to a worship service in the meetinghouse on the green, "to drop a tear upon the graves, and mourn over the ashes of their slaughtered friends."[23] The ritual was more closely related to a funeral service, an acknowledgment of the power of death and an attempt to remember the fallen individuals, than a general commemoration of the patriotic cause or a tribute to the "spirit" behind the glorious event. It was not until 1799, as the eighteenth century came to a close, that the citizens of Lexington took the lead in moving from language and ritual to durable object by setting up a stone equivalent of the ebenezer that Cotton Mather had constructed in literary terms for Boston a century earlier.[24] In that year, the stone obelisk shown in figure 8 was erected and inscribed with the names of the individual martyrs — Robert Munroe, Jonas Parker, Samuel Hadley, Jonathan Harrington, Issac Muzzy, Caleb Harrington, John Brown, and Ashael Porter — as if it were a tombstone. But after the fashion of Cotton Mather's biographies and those of John Foxe before him, the rest of the inscription linked the meaning of their deaths to a higher cause: "The blood of these Martyrs was the Cement of the Union of these States, then Colonies; and gave the Spring to the Spirit,

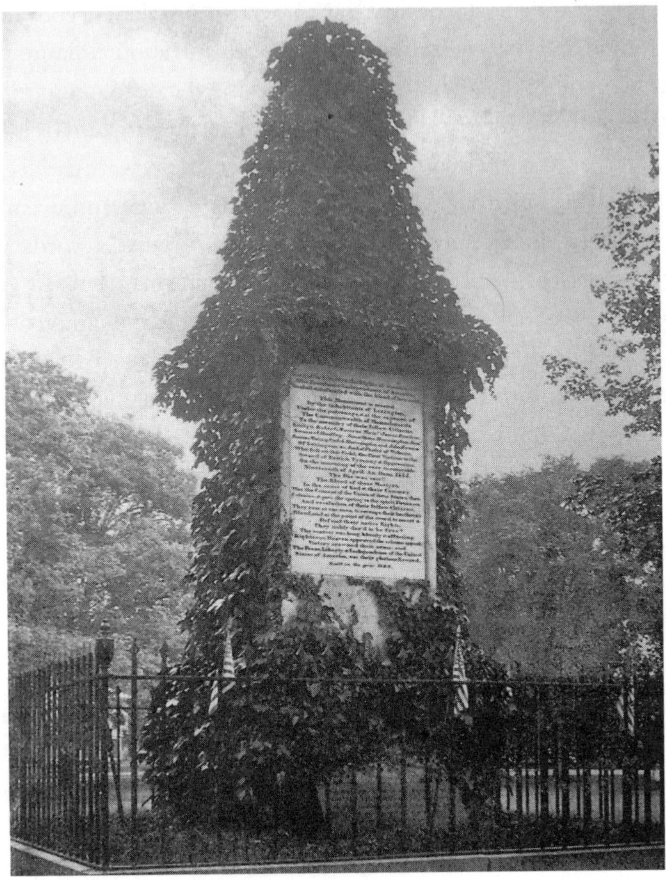

FIG. 8. Memorial Obelisk on Lexington Green, 1799, Lexington, Massachusetts. (Courtesy, American Antiquarian Society)

Firmness, and Resolution of their Fellow-citizens. They rose as one Man to revenge their Brethren's Blood, and at the Point of the Sword to assert and defend their native Rights." Yet in Lexington, the confusion over whether they had erected an elaborate gravestone for individual heroes, or an ebenezer commemorating the spirit of revolution, was still evident in 1835, on the sixtieth anniversary of the battle. The remains of the minutemen killed that day were disinterred from their resting places in the nearby cemetery, carried in an elaborate procession with a military escort to the meetinghouse, where a funerary oration was delivered by Edward Everett, and then, finally, entombed in a mahogany "Sarcophagus" placed in a stone vault behind the monument on the green (fig. 9).[25]

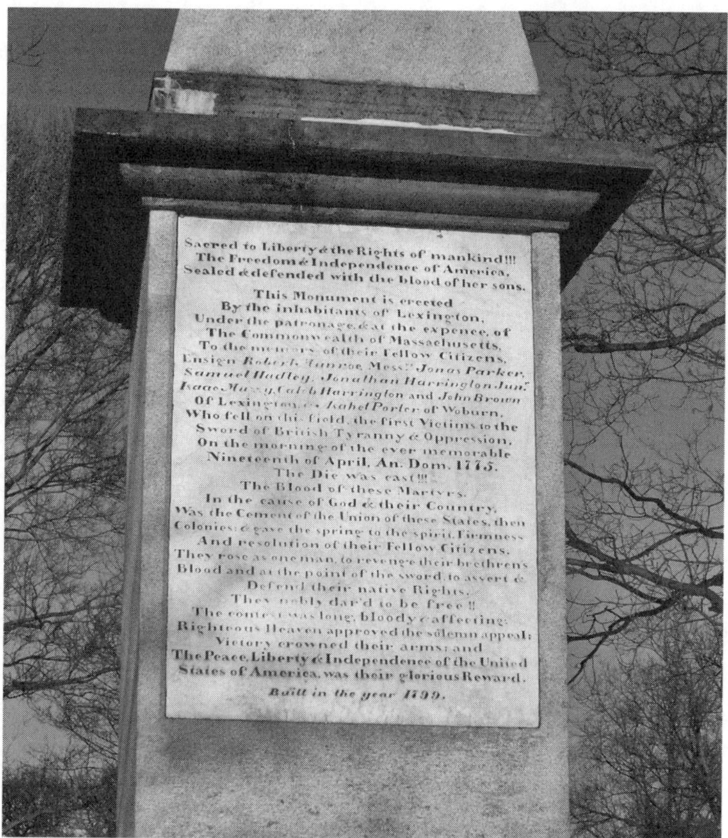

FIG. 9. Detail, Memorial Obelisk on Lexington Green.
(Photo by the author)

Meanwhile, in Charlestown, at the site of the Battle of Bunker Hill, the problem of defining a suitable form of memorial evolved somewhat differently. The town was largely destroyed during the battle, and only slowly rebuilt in its aftermath, so that the first recorded celebration commemorating the battle took place eleven years later, on June 17, 1786, the day on which the Charles River Bridge was dedicated. Patriotism and commerce were linked that day by a grand procession, led by war heroes and corporate investors in the bridge, beginning at the Old State House in Boston, winding its way into the North End and across the new bridge to Charlestown, accompanied by thirteen-gun salutes fired from cannons on Copp's Hill and Bunker Hill, and concluding with general feasting and elaborate toasts at the site of the battle itself.[26]

But after these celebratory and self-congratulatory beginnings, eight years later Charlestown would adopt the funerary approach in the construction of its first monument on the battleground. In 1794, the Charlestown Masonic Lodge erected a "Tuscan pillar," some eighteen feet high and surmounted by a gilt urn, bearing the initials and age of Joseph Warren, the martyred major-general who was killed in the battle. Although the physical remains of Warren had been reinterred in Boston in 1776, the Charlestown monument served as a substitute tombstone for Warren — its inscription read, "In memory of Major General Joseph Warren and his Associates [unnamed], who were slain on this memorable spot, June 17, 1775." And then, in a verse inscription echoing the seventeenth-century voice from the grave, but with a patriotic rather than a religious message, the tombstone cried out to passersby: "None but they who set a just value upon the blessings of Liberty are worthy to enjoy her. In vain we toiled; in vain we fought; we bled in vain, if you, our offspring, want valor to repel the assaults of her invaders!" Only the death of the individual hero was marked specifically by the monument, but the message of the epitaph offered a secularized version of the old Puritan gravestone's injunction to prepare for death.[27] That this pillar was made of wood, as was the similar commemorative column designed by Charles Bulfinch and erected on Boston's Beacon Hill at about this time, suggests a certain confusion over just how long these memorable messages were meant to last.[28]

The next stage in Charlestown's commemorative evolution, the movement to build the monument that still stands today on Bunker Hill, arose out of a controversy begun in 1818, when General Henry Dearborn, who fought in the battle, published an account of the battle in which he impugned the character and conduct of General Israel Putnam. The fact that Putnam was no longer alive to defend himself pointed to the emerging problem that now, more than forty years after the outbreak of the war, the Revolutionary generation was dying off, and before long there would be *no* living witnesses to these momentous events, making it all the more important to create stone witnesses in their stead. The controversy brought renewed attention to the battle, and soon the Bunker Hill Monument Association, led by Daniel Webster, Edward Everett, and John Collins Warren, whom we met earlier, developed their incredibly ambitious plans for a massive obelisk on the site, replacing the old Masonic pillar to Joseph Warren.[29] The foundation stone was laid in 1825 by the visiting French hero Lafayette, but the monument remained unfinished until 1843, due largely to the costs and difficulty of erecting such an enormous ebenezer. It might even be said that more divine assistance was needed to complete the monument than was given to the patriots in the battle it was meant to commemorate. Size was clearly important to its builders — in the words of the historian of the association, George Washington Warren, "There is no danger whatever that the obelisk now erected on Bunker Hill will ever be battered down by a hostile power, or that its massive material will be disjointed and used for works of military defence.... It will always be its own great defender.... It will stand ever, fast-rooted in our Earth, impregnable ... nor can it ever be deemed offensive, or even inappropriate in form, as commemorating the success of the great Cause itself, for which men gave their lives, and not simply as expressing the merited praise of their heroic death."[30] The gargantuan size of the memorial dwarfed the significance of any individual human action or any words that might be written on the side — this would be no gravestone remembering an individual, but a super-Egyptian ebenezer, a gigantic stone witness to the glory of a righteous cause (fig. 10).

Yet despite the confident words of George Washington Warren, there were critics of the Bunker Hill monument who did think it offensive and inappropriate. The Charlestown Masonic Lodge insisted that a model of its old monument to Joseph Warren be placed within the new one, while another critic, William Ladd, decried the idea of a giant obelisk as unnecessarily belligerent, an aggressive trophy to the nation's glory rather than a suitable "token of gratitude and honor to the mighty dead."[31] Ladd's objections went unheeded, but he pointed to the deeper problem. The desire for ever-larger stone structures that would speak for themselves and endure forever was coming dangerously near to idolatry, a celebration of the community's power and will to build such massive monuments, rather than a reminder of the meaning of the events they stood for. But in the 1830s, New England's leading literary figures began to catch up with the monument builders, and in their own subtle way, created memorials to the Revolution as powerful and enduring as any cast in stone.

In 1835, the year the Lexington minutemen were reinterred beside the obelisk on the green, Nathaniel Hawthorne wrote one of his many historical sketches that invoked Puritan traditions from the colonial period, but brought them forward into the Revolutionary era and beyond. In "The Gray Champion," Hawthorne retold the story of Boston's "other" rebellion begun on April 18 — the overthrow in 1689 of the tyrannical royal governor Edmund Andros. To give that ill-remembered event a dramatic center, Hawthorne resurrected a legendary character, the spirit of one of the English Puritan regicide judges who con-

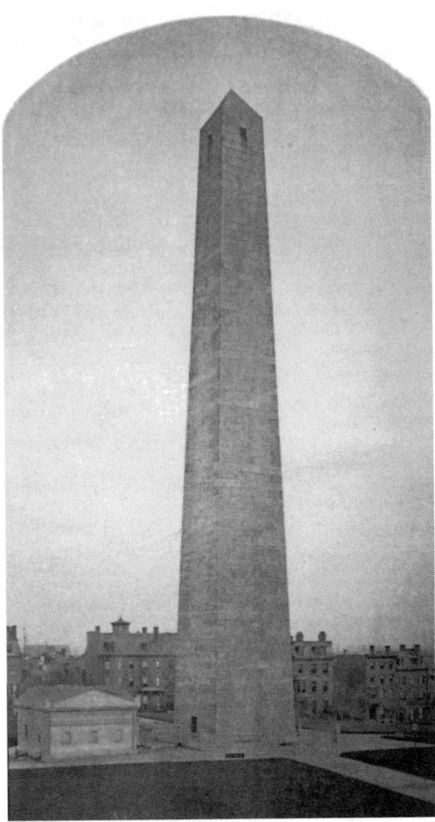

FIG. 10. Bunker Hill monument, 1842, Charlestown, Massachusetts. (Courtesy, American Antiquarian Society)

demned Charles I to his death and had fled to New England after the Restoration of Charles II. Hawthorne's story placed this ghostly figure at the head of the rebellion against Andros. After heroically stopping the governor's military procession and giving the townspeople courage to rebel, the mysterious spirit melts "slowly into the hues of twilight, till, where he stood, there was an empty space. The men of that generation watched for his reappearance, in sunshine and in twilight, but never saw him more, nor knew when his funeral passed, nor where his grave-stone was." And yet, in his conclusion, Hawthorne asserts that this ghostly Puritan, who "had staid the march of a King himself, ere now," will appear again whenever the descendants of the Puritans are to show the spirits of their sires. . . . When eighty years had passed, he walked once more in King Street. Five years later, in the twilight of an April morning, he stood on the green, beside the meeting-house at Lexington, where now the obelisk of granite, with a slab inlaid, commemorates the first fallen of the Revolution. . . . He is the type of New England's hereditary spirit; and his shadowy march, on the eve of danger, must ever be the pledge that New England's sons will vindicate their ancestry.[32]

In this subtle sketch, Hawthorne resolves the tensions in Puritan traditions for remembering the dead and commemorating the deeper meaning behind their deeds. By drawing on a real historical figure like the regicide judge, yet treating him so abstractly as to remove any specific human traits and make him into nothing more than a "spirit" of patriotic virtue, Hawthorne's story follows in the tradition that Foxe began in his *Book of Martyrs.*[33] And yet by placing this figure on Lexington Green, on the very spot where the stone monument now marks the grave and lists the names of the town's fallen heroes, Hawthorne associates the abstract with the particular, and the evanescent with the concrete, building a bridge between various forms of commemoration, a bridge which links the distant past of the Puritan era with the Revolutionary generation and projects its spirit into the present.[34]

A year later, Ralph Waldo Emerson would follow Hawthorne's lead in the poem he was commissioned to write for the dedication of Concord's Revolutionary memorial. Not to be outdone by their Middlesex neighbors in Lexington and Charlestown, the citizens of Concord also undertook commemorative efforts as the Revolutionary generation began to fade from the scene in the 1830s. Here too, the process was not without controversy. Purists favored the site along the Concord River by the North Bridge where the fighting between minutemen and regulars actually began, while commercial interests favored the center of town, where tourists might liven their business, especially given the fact that the North Bridge itself had long since vanished. Eventually, monuments were built in both locations, but the purists won the initial round and built a modest obelisk in 1836 on the east bank of the river, near the spot where the war began. For the official dedication ceremony, the town called on its favorite son to provide a commemoration in verse to complement the stone witness (figs. 11 and 12).[35]

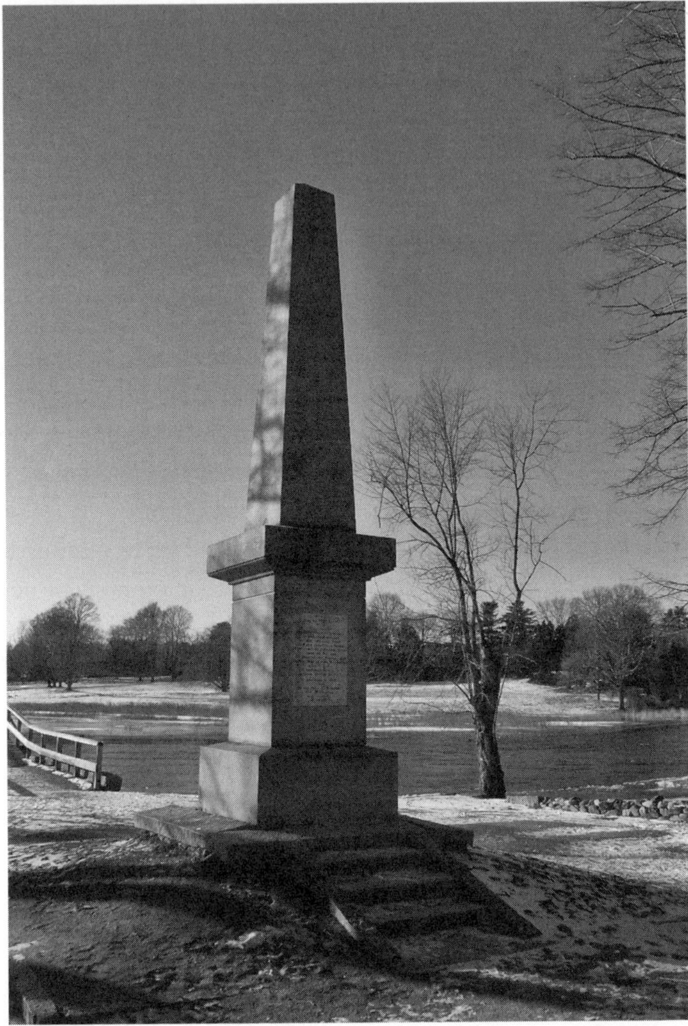

FIG. 11. Concord Battle monument, 1837, Concord, Massachusetts. (Photo by the author)

It is necessary to read Emerson's "Concord Hymn" in its entirety to get past the too familiar "shot heard round the world." This phrase has become such a cliché that it obscures the profound way in which Emerson, like Hawthorne, weaves together the particular and the general, the evanescent and the permanent, reviving and then resolving the tensions inherited from the Puritan tradition.

By the rude bridge that arched the flood,
Their flag to April's breeze unfurled,
Here once the embattled farmers stood
And fired the shot heard round the world.

The foe long since in silence slept;
Alike the conqueror silent sleeps;
And Time the ruined bridge has swept
Down the dark stream which seaward creeps.

On this green bank, by this soft stream,
We set today a votive stone;
That memory may their deed redeem,
When, like our sires, our sons are gone.

Spirit, that made those heroes dare
To die, and leave their children free,
Bid Time and Nature gently spare
The shaft we raise to them and thee.[36]

The poem's two imperfect rhymes convey the larger story that Emerson is telling: flood stood, stone gone. In four brief stanzas, Emerson remembers those "embattled farmers," as well as the "foe" who died along side them, and yet effaces their particular qualities, dwelling not on the heroic actions but on the deeper "spirit" that "made those heroes dare to die," to stay the flood of historical inevitability for a brief moment. And although he recognizes the value of the "votive stone," the durable object, as a device for preserving the memory that might "redeem" past deeds for present and future generations, he also acknowledges, in his reference to the absent bridge, that physical memorials, no matter how sturdy, are themselves subject to time's ravages. Emerson therefore appeals in traditional Puritan fashion to the spiritual, to the evanescent meanings conveyed in his own words, to preserve the meaning of the stone "when, like our sires, our sons are gone."

Another generation later, on the "eve of danger" that Hawthorne's "Gray Champion" had forecast, Henry Wadsworth Longfellow would return to these complex problems of patriotic commemoration embedded deeply in New England tradition. In 1861, in the wake of the secession of the Southern states and with the threat of war looming, Longfellow would revisit the midnight ride of

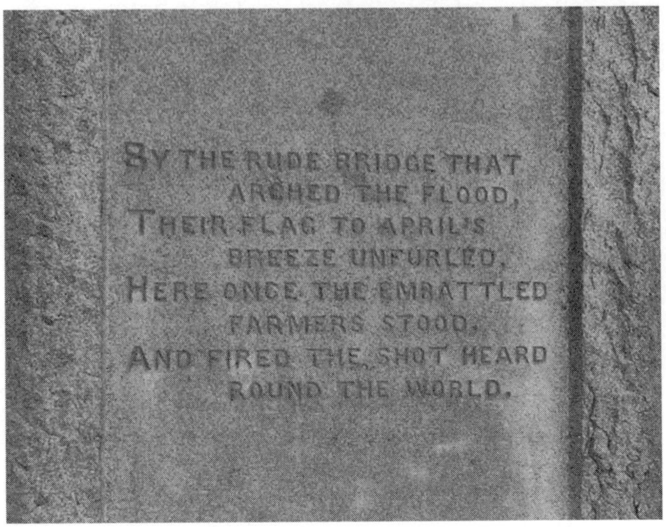

FIG. 12. Detail of Minuteman statue by Daniel Chester French, 1875, Concord, Massachusetts. (Photo by the author)

Paul Revere and attempt to apply the meaning of that event to the national crisis.[37] It has become something of a commonplace to criticize Longfellow for his historical inaccuracies, his histrionic myth-making, and "Paul Revere's Ride" has received a thrashing from the critics, both historical and literary, in the years since it was written.[38] But Longfellow's poem is worthy of defense within the context of commemoration, and even praise for its profound awareness of the depths of New England's traditional forms for creating and preserving memory. As with Emerson's "Concord Hymn," we have to slip past that familiar first stanza, with its insistent rhythms and rhymes, "Listen my children, and you shall hear / Of the midnight ride of Paul Revere, On the eighteenth of April, in Seventy-five; / Hardly a man is now alive / Who remembers that famous day and year." Clichéd, yes, but it recognizes that the need for memorials is greatest at the moment when living memory is disappearing, as it most certainly was in 1861, when even children alive in '75 would have been very old.

Despite the criticism the poem receives for making Revere a greater hero than he really was, the striking thing about the remainder of the poem is how little of Revere there is in it. After the opening stanza in which he gives a few brief instructions to a "friend," the character of Revere speaks not another word — we never actually see or hear him giving anyone the alarm. No details of his personality are revealed; his individuality, that bold and fleshy immediacy so apparent in Copley's portrait, is completely effaced in Longfellow's rendering. And the poem's overall mood is dominated not by any sense of heroic achievement, but by somber meditations on death and the dead. The long third stanza dwells at length on Revere's unnamed friend (though surely Longfellow knew the name of Robert Newman) who climbs the tower of the Old North Church, "Where he paused to listen and look down / A moment on the roofs of the town / Beneath in the churchyard lay the dead, / In their night encampment on the hill, / Wrapped in silence so deep and still / that he could hear, like a sentinel's tread, the watchful night wind, as it went creeping along from tent to tent, and seeming to whisper, 'All is well.'"

This wind that stirs among the graves there on Copp's Hill, beneath the Old North Church, where Cotton Mather lay buried, this breeze that reassures the dead Puritans in their "night encampment" that "all is well," will soon return, as we watch the silent, faceless Revere ride through the ghostly villages of Middlesex County. Again, eerily, almost nothing happens in this poem. As "he" rides through Medford and Lexington, no minutemen or redcoats appear, no battles are fought. All Longfellow offers are fearful images: "the damp of the river fog, that rises as the sun goes down," and the "spectral glare" in the meetinghouse windows, "aghast at the bloody work they would look upon." In Concord, the night wind we encountered on Copp's Hill reappears as "the breath of the morning breeze blowing over the meadows brown," but that breeze whispers death to "one who was safe and asleep in his bed, who at the bridge would be first to fall, who that day would be lying dead, pierced by a British musket-ball." Like Emerson's "Concord Hymn," Longfellow acknowledges the "embattled farmer" without naming him, and then transfers him instantly from sleep to death, by way of the breeze, the breath, the spirit of revolutionary resistance, without depicting any heroic action whatsoever. In fact, at this point in the poem, where an account of the heroism of the minutemen would seem like a natural resolution, the culmination of Revere's ride, Longfellow renounces the need to recount the history of the battle at all. Instead he writes, "You know the rest. In the books you have read, How the British regulars fired and fled." What "Paul Revere's Ride" preserves for future generations is not the historical particulars, but the spirit, the breeze, the "midnight message," "a voice in the darkness, a knock at the door, and a word that shall echo forevermore, . . . borne on the night-wind of the Past, through all our history to the last." In this, we can hear deliberate echoes of

Cotton Mather's cry in his *Magnalia,* uttered in trepidation as the last of Boston's founding colonists were dying out, and the living memory of the colony's origins was dying with them, that "whether New England may Live anywhere else or no, it must Live in our History!"[39] With these works of Revolutionary commemoration, Hawthorne, Emerson, and Longfellow found new means to resolve the tensions over public commemoration inherent in Boston's history from the time of its Puritan origins, by folding together the literary and the spiritual with the monumental and the particular in the contest over how the past should be remembered and redeemed.

Notes

1. Although historians have accurately traced the changes in New England's Puritan religious culture in close detail, my claim for this measure of cultural continuity is informed by the work of David D. Hall, who argues for the ways in which various forms of culturally produced "debris" can linger long after their creation or their immediate utility; see Hall, *Worlds of Wonder, Days of Judgment;* and Hall, ed., *Lived Religion in America.* For excellent general studies of memory and the American Revolution, see Purcell, *Sealed with Blood;* and Kammen, *A Season of Youth.* My own approach to understanding continuity and change in cultural forms such as memory practices has been shaped by reading the work of Pierre Bourdieu on cultural production and the idea of the "habitus"; see Bourdieu, *The Field of Cultural Production.*

2. On Puritan iconoclasm, see Phillips, *The Reformation of Images;* Aston, *England's Iconoclasts;* and Duffy, *The Stripping of the Altars,* 565–93. On the use of objects in Puritan spiritual development, see Peterson, "Puritanism and Refinement in Early New England," 307–46.

3. Foxe's work has been published in dozens of American editions over the centuries, many of which are held by the American Antiquarian Society in Worcester, Massachusetts. See, for instance, *Foxe's Book of Martyrs,* which includes updates on Protestant martyrology added by American clergymen.

4. On anagrams in early New England funeral elegies, see Brown, "'Boston Sob Not,'" 306–39.

5. Hebrews 13:4.

6. Norton, *Abel Being Dead, Yet Speaketh,* 3–4, emphasis in original. The copy of Norton's work owned by the American Antiquarian Society once belonged to Increase Mather, John Cotton's son-in-law and Norton's colleague among the Boston clergy, and contains Mather's marginal annotations.

7. Mather, *Magnalia Christi Americana.* On the influence of the *Magnalia* on New England and American historiography, see Bercovitch, *The Puritan Origins of the Amer-*

ican Self; Woolsey, "Staging a Puritan Saint"; and Felker, *Reinventing Cotton Mather in the American Renaissance.*

8. Mather, *Parentator.*

9. Miller, "The Puritan Portrait," 153–84; Dresser, "The Background of Colonial American Portraiture," 19–58.

10. On the importance of Norwich, the county of Norfolk, and the region of East Anglia to the New England Puritan migration, see Anderson, *The Great Migration Begins;* Anderson, *New England's Generation;* and Thompson, *Mobility and Migration.*

11. See Miller, "The Puritan Portrait," 179–82; and Allard, "The Painted Sermon," 347.

12. Rebora et al., *John Singleton Copley in America,* 246–49; Prown, *John Singleton Copley,* 1:74–75; Dubuque, "The Painter and the Patriot," 1–5; Fischer, *Paul Revere's Ride,* 2–4.

13. Peterson, "Puritanism and Refinement in Early New England," 307–46.

14. Linden-Ward, *Silent City on a Hill,* 148.

15. On Puritan gravestones, see Ludwig, *Graven Images;* and Benes, *The Masks of Orthodoxy.*

16. Wigglesworth, *Day of Doom.*

17. Hawthorne, "Chippings with a Chisel," 622.

18. Linden-Ward, *Silent City on a Hill,* 325–27.

19. Although originally published as a separate pamphlet, *The Bostonian Ebenezer* was later included in the *Magnalia;* see the Hartford 1853 edition, 1:90–104.

20. Mather, *Magnalia,* 1:90, emphasis in original.

21. Ibid., 1:91.

22. On Pope's Day (Guy Fawkes Day) parades and spectacles, as well as Harvard College Commencements, see Morison, *Harrison Gray Otis, 1765–1848,* 7–11; and Benes, "Night Processings."

23. Zabdiel Adams, *The Evil Designs of Men,* 36.

24. Indeed, the text used by a clergyman to commemorate Lexington's hundredth anniversary as an incorporated town was the same one Cotton Mather chose for *The Bostonian Ebenezer*—1 Samuel 7:12; see Williams, *A Discourse,* 3. Williams uses the same ebenezer imagery as Mather does to describe the process of commemorating Lexington's past.

25. Everett, *An Address,* 52–62.

26. Warren, *The History of the Bunker Hill Monument Association,* 6–9.

27. Ibid., 9–10.

28. Whitehill, *Boston,* 82–84; Kirker and Kirker, *Bulfinch's Boston,* 79–81.

29. Warren, *The History of the Bunker Hill Monument Association,* 31ff.

30. Ibid., 178.

31. Ibid., 175–77.

32. Hawthorne, "The Gray Champion," 242–43.

33. The abstract, generic Puritan represented by the mysterious regicide was also useful for Hawthorne in terms of negotiating the nuances of the historical memory of Puritanism in New England. The most prominent flesh and blood Puritan to stand up to Andros on April 18, 1689, was Cotton Mather, but by the 1830s, Mather's popular reputation was so bound up with the Salem witchcraft debacle that he was essentially unusable as a representative of the Puritan tradition of resistance to tyranny. In the popular mind, Mather was a tyrant who had worked up the witchcraft craze, and therefore was not the symbolic figure to oppose another tyrant.

34. Wilson, "Web of Secrecy," 515–48.

35. On Concord's conflicts regarding the commemoration of the Revolution, see Gross, "The Most Estimable Place in All the World," 1–15; and Gross, "Commemorating Concord."

36. Emerson, "Concord Hymn," 125.

37. For the full text of Longfellow's poem, which was first published in *The Atlantic Monthly* in January 1861, see Longfellow, "The Landlord's Tale," 25–29.

38. For an overview of the development of mythology surrounding Paul Revere and his ride, see Fischer, *Paul Revere's Ride,* 327–44. Yet Fischer is among those who underestimate the depth of Longfellow's understanding of New England's commemorative traditions; see Fischer, *Paul Revere's Ride,* 331–33.

39. Mather, *Magnalia,* 1:27.

THE TRIUMPHAL MARKER

JHENNIFER A. AMUNDSON

Staging a Triumph, Raising a Temple

Philadelphia's "Welcoming Parade" for Lafayette, 1824

A LACK OF internal strife and external aggression made the years following the War of 1812 prime for the development of nationalist sentiments in the United States. Presiding over this "Era of Good Feelings," President James Monroe promoted the strength of his country through his eponymous doctrine, which warned the countries of Europe from interfering with other independent nations, while recognizing that America neither developed without nor existed in isolation from them. A profound expression of America's character of self-sufficiency and gratitude was initiated by the invitation that Monroe extended to his Revolutionary War compatriot the Marquis de Lafayette in 1823. Lafayette's volunteerism on behalf of the American cause was legendary: the high-ranking official in the French army had foregone pay while serving brilliantly at Yorktown alongside his longtime friend George Washington, who was now deceased and nearly deified. In 1824 Lafayette returned to the nation that he had helped to found a half century earlier. Because the French general's popularity and profile necessitated a lengthy journey, Lafayette would eventually conduct a thirteen-month tour through all twenty-four states, during which he was honored as "the Nation's Guest."

The growing influence of America's press spread the idea that the lengthy tour was a single communal celebration in which each city and state along the circuit was one scene within a broader play. None commanded the spotlight as did Philadelphia, where the rituals of celebration were performed with greater energy, enthusiasm, and expense than in any other American city. For eight days, dinners, balls, receptions, fireworks displays, and other festivities honored the

Frenchman for his role in the country's independence, as well as the state's and city's role in the Revolution. These celebrations united a variety of precedents to develop a specifically American language of commemoration, one that communicated the belief that the country had achieved the greatness of Rome while remaining distinct from Europe, and that gained fluency with elite classical learning while remaining inclusive of all citizens. Among the lengthy slate of activities and their associated artifacts, three elements of Lafayette's very first day in Philadelphia established a cohesive language designed to impress certain ideals upon the public memory. The initial procession expressed republican virtue and industry in a format which blended ancient precedent with modern activities; neighborhoods manifested civic pride by participating in the construction of temporary monuments that adapted classical forms to suit their American context; the city's buildings were transformed, both for the short and long term, by both construction and social activities that exemplified the values represented by Lafayette himself. In fact, the most enduring aspect of Lafayette's visit was such a transformation: the renovation of public understanding of an extant building, once a nearly obsolete state house, now a significant monument of American independence. These events cast America as the reincarnation of grand ancient civilizations and Philadelphia as its capital of culture and liberty.

Procession: The Republican Triumph

Alternately identified as the "Welcoming Parade" or "Grand Civic Procession," the most spectacular event of the week evidenced the common Federal period practice of blending Greek and Roman sources, a tradition as long standing as any in the new country.[1] The Roman-coined *capital* of America's Greek-inspired *democracy* had once been stationed in Philadelphia; likewise, the parade's path was defined in some districts by architecture inspired by both Greek and Roman precedents. Through this blending of ancient sources with more modern ones, the parade and its material accoutrements were designed to suggest historical heritage as well as American modernity. As an activity, the parade manifested a symbolic language that had been assembled from sources that were either classical or modern, and presumably "American." Citizens represented contemporary achievements in commerce, education, the trades, and professions. The country they celebrated was young and innovative; their own achievements were perceived as being the culmination of historical progression dating back to the ancients.

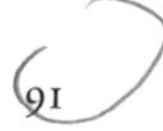

The very form of the parade drew from recent and ancient precedents. It seemed natural that the "Athens of America," as Philadelphia had become known, should host its own Panathenaic procession. This ancient festival honoring Athena processed from Athens's Dipylon Gate and proceeded through the *kerameikos,* or potter's quarters, through residential and market districts toward the temples on the Acropolis. In Philadelphia the parade likewise stretched through every type of urban quarter — residential, commercial, religious, and cultural — to its "sacred" end. While inspired by this Greek example, Philadelphians followed a Roman precedent more closely. Contemporary writings consistently refer to the Welcoming Parade as a "triumph," alluding to the highly regulated Roman military procession that began at the outskirts of the imperial capital and processed along a lengthy route, passing through various neighborhoods and near certain monuments, toward its conclusion at the Capitoline.[2] The Athenian parade was primarily focused on its conclusion, when a new *peplos* would be presented to Athena. In Rome, the activity of the parade itself was sacred, from the army's cleansing passage into the city to the culminating activity of sacrifice at a temple.

Because the Arrangements Committee was so well aware of this ancient example, it is instructive to consider the means by which its members understood the Roman rite and translated its celebratory language into a modern American tongue.[3] The requisites for a proper Roman *triumphus* were largely ignored after the fall of the empire; in the sixth century Justinian and his court celebrated what would more properly be termed the *adventus,* which is like the *triumphus* in being a kind of entry parade for an emperor after a campaign or long journey, but differs from it as not necessarily being tied to military activity and thus lacking spoils of war.[4] Since the precise Roman ceremonies had become obscured even by the sixth century, and continued to be so through the development of such celebrations into the modern period, it is not surprising that nineteenth-century Philadelphians presented a version of the *triumphus* that would have bewildered the Roman Senate.

In lieu of a triumphator proper, Philadelphia's procession focused on Lafayette as a personification of America's victory, cleansing the Roman precedent of its avaricious and violent overtones. One contemporary author compared the "American triumph" as superior and more virtuous than its ancient precedent; it was an example "of the *moral sublime.*" Although a tyrant could command "pomp and glitter [and] all that *art* can do," he could not demand "the heartfelt offerings of a free people" which were accorded to Lafayette.[5] Similarly emphasizing America's preeminence by comparisons with Rome, the "Ode to Lafayette," distributed by the city's printers, includes the following lines directed toward a general who fought for independence rather than imperialism:

> Thy course through the land shall a triumph be,
> Such as conqueror ne'er attended;
> For the glories that shall be shower'd on thee,
> With no tear of grief shall be blended.[6]

Transforming the triumph's meaning by suppressing its original martial overtones was of the greatest importance in southeastern Pennsylvania, settled and still largely populated by Quakers.[7]

The rewriting of the Roman military triumph as an American civic spectacle appealed to greater numbers than this particular group of pacifists alone, as revealed in newspapers that suggested it was "not merely the soldier," but rather Lafayette as "[the great] friend of universal liberty" who was honored by the procession.[8] The imperial plunder, including slaves and stolen art, that customarily accompanied the Roman victorious was replaced in the American triumph by the "free people" of Philadelphia and the industry they enjoyed as a result of their liberty. In addition to the printers operating their presses, other groups illustrated such rewards while the parade was under way, including trade societies displaying banners with inscriptions extolling the "wisdom and courage" of Lafayette and Washington, to whom they owed "the free exercise of industry."[9] In this aspect the parade was more Greek than Roman, bearing closer resemblance to the Panathenaic procession in which all free Athenians honored the goddess while celebrating the peaceful relations among the Greek city-states.

In addition to their awareness and use of the ancient past, by 1824 Americans could review their own history to enhance Lafayette's fête. In general, Philadelphians revealed a growing respect for the colonial setting of their earliest history and a specific interest in events like the Grand Federal Procession that was held on July 4, 1788. Celebrating the ratification of the Constitution, it set the standard for later American pageants in both its character and organization. Much of its path was traced by later parades, including Lafayette's, which concluded at the same point on Chestnut Street. The act of reiterating those earlier steps made the later parade a historic reminder, a reflection of the interdependence between

Revolution and Constitution, while enriching the display by conjoining American with ancient history.[10]

This blending of traditions was brought to bear for about five hours on September 28, 1824, when the static grid of Philadelphia was transformed by the creation of a new street, the dynamic parade route threading its way through neighborhoods selected by the Arrangements Committee. Certain standing buildings, witnesses of past events or prophets of future accomplishments, as well as areas of population concentration, swayed the decisions of those who planned the route. Cutting an irregular course through the eastern part of the city's regular grid, the thoroughfare emphasized the difference between William Penn's drawing-board plan and the reality of settlement in the city (fig. 1). Laid out in 1683, centuries before Philadelphia's population would fill the plan that spans the distance between the Delaware and Schuylkill Rivers, its checkerboard was lopsidedly settled by growing crescents ebbing from its eastern edge at the Delaware. Intended as the city's primary east–west thoroughfare, High Street (presently Market Street) was deprived of its ceremonial potential by the pragmatically located market sheds stretching down its center from Second to Eighth Streets. Of Penn's five planned parks, the square designated "Centre" was actually quite remote from the center of population and activity; parade planners would look elsewhere for their principal celebratory locus. Rather than heed Penn's ideal scheme, they sought the symbolic center of the city by considering the history of the urban fabric in the Revolutionary story, which had fixed the importance of certain buildings and their associated institutions. Primary among them was the half-empty, partially obsolete Old Pennsylvania State House that marked the parade's conclusion at Chestnut Street between Fifth and Sixth Streets.

The Welcoming Parade began three miles north of the city with a review of some 6,000 military volunteers. Led by infantry and cavalry, Lafayette was conducted in an open barouche drawn by six horses. Representing virtually all walks of life in Philadelphia, thousands of marchers processed amidst crowds of more than 100,000 spectators: a staggering number for a city whose population reached only about 80,000 at the time.[11] The three-mile parade comprised diverse trade societies and numerous other groups, including umbrella makers, coopers, farmers, priests, professors, and public officers. While most participants wore special garments for the day, some groups chose to ornament the route with their professional energies. The printers were especially active, producing

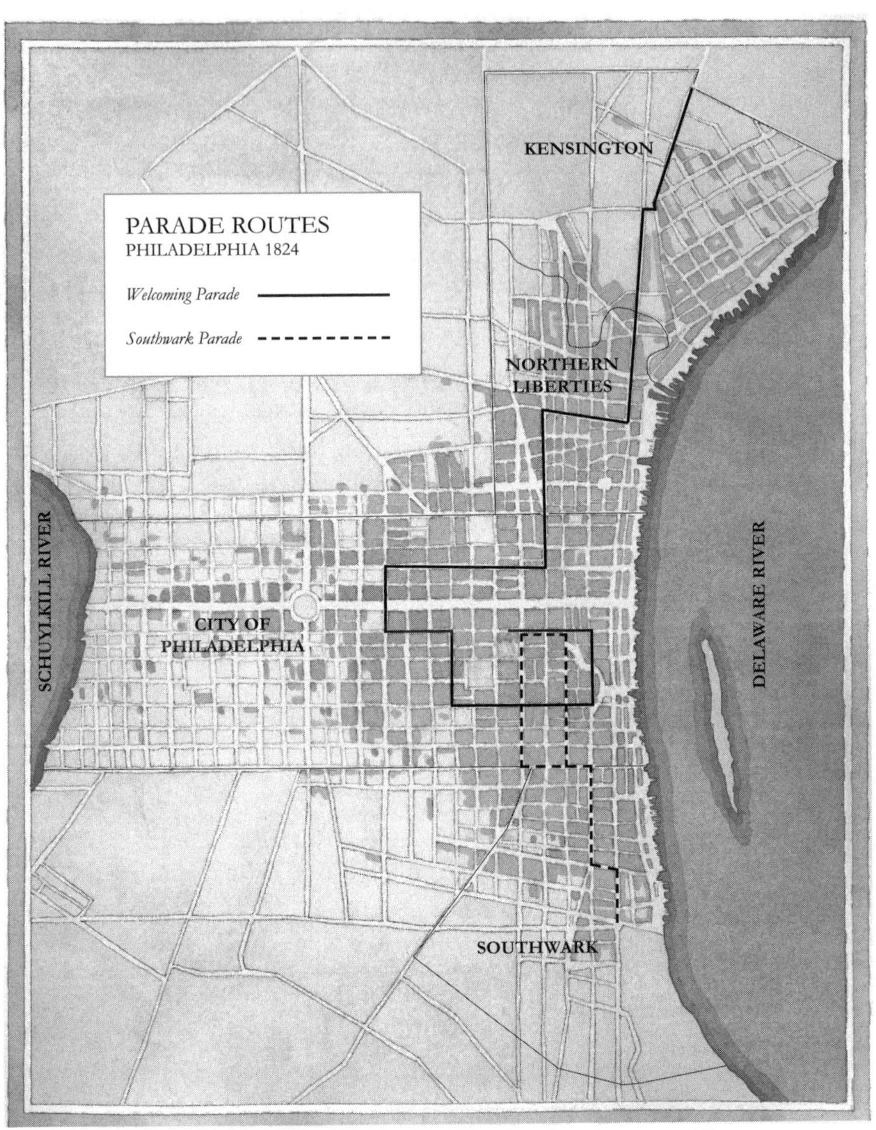

FIG. 1. Plan of Kensington, Northern Liberties, the City of Philadelphia, and Southwark, ca. 1824, showing the paths of the Welcoming Parade and Southwark Procession. (Drawing by Andrew C. Gander)

and distributing an inspirational broadside from an operable press mounted on a float.[12]

The first leg of the thirty-block-long parade (fig. 2) was framed by plain but handsome buildings, several of which represented Philadelphia's lengthy and varied religious history. Along Fourth and Arch Streets the procession passed a series of churches and meetinghouses built by Reformed Calvinists, Presbyterians, Roman Catholics, Methodists, German Lutherans, and Quakers. A contemporary guidebook suggests that the buildings were not particularly extravagant architectural specimens, but instead "large and neat" structures. They welcomed Lafayette with representations of the city's colonial and religious heritage, the former of which was being reassessed for cultural significance while the latter remained a thriving influence on daily life.[13]

Lafayette's path was planned to showcase both time-honored and recent architecture that housed and symbolized Philadelphia's considerable religious, financial, social, and cultural resources. Toward the center of the city, a growing number of new buildings designed by such notable architects as William Strickland, Benjamin Henry Latrobe, and John Haviland presented the classically inspired architectural face of the city. Managers of institutions who expected visits from Lafayette heightened the city's festive appearance through the display of banners, bunting, and other decorations on their structures. Buildings that were scheduled to accommodate special activities were accorded even more elaborate embellishment. In perhaps the most extreme example, Strickland directed a sweeping reconstruction of the interior of the Chestnut Street Theatre (near the center of the city and the parade route's conclusion) to accommodate 1,600 revelers in what would become the city's largest ballroom.[14]

The Welcoming Parade's westward route on Arch Street, the most efficient choice for the parade's longest arm, highlighted some of the city's monuments which represented urban expansion and development.[15] Turning south along Eleventh Street, Lafayette processed through one of the most quickly expanding and tastefully appointed parts of the city, home to several institutions which represented urban development and social improvement. These included the Pennsylvania Institute of the Deaf and Dumb, housed in a "large and convenient" building, and the domed quarters of the Academy of Fine Arts.[16] Advancing again toward the river, east along Chestnut Street, the parade passed other significant institutions: just north on Ninth Street stood the grand neoclassical manse erected by the city in an unsuccessful attempt to entice the president of the

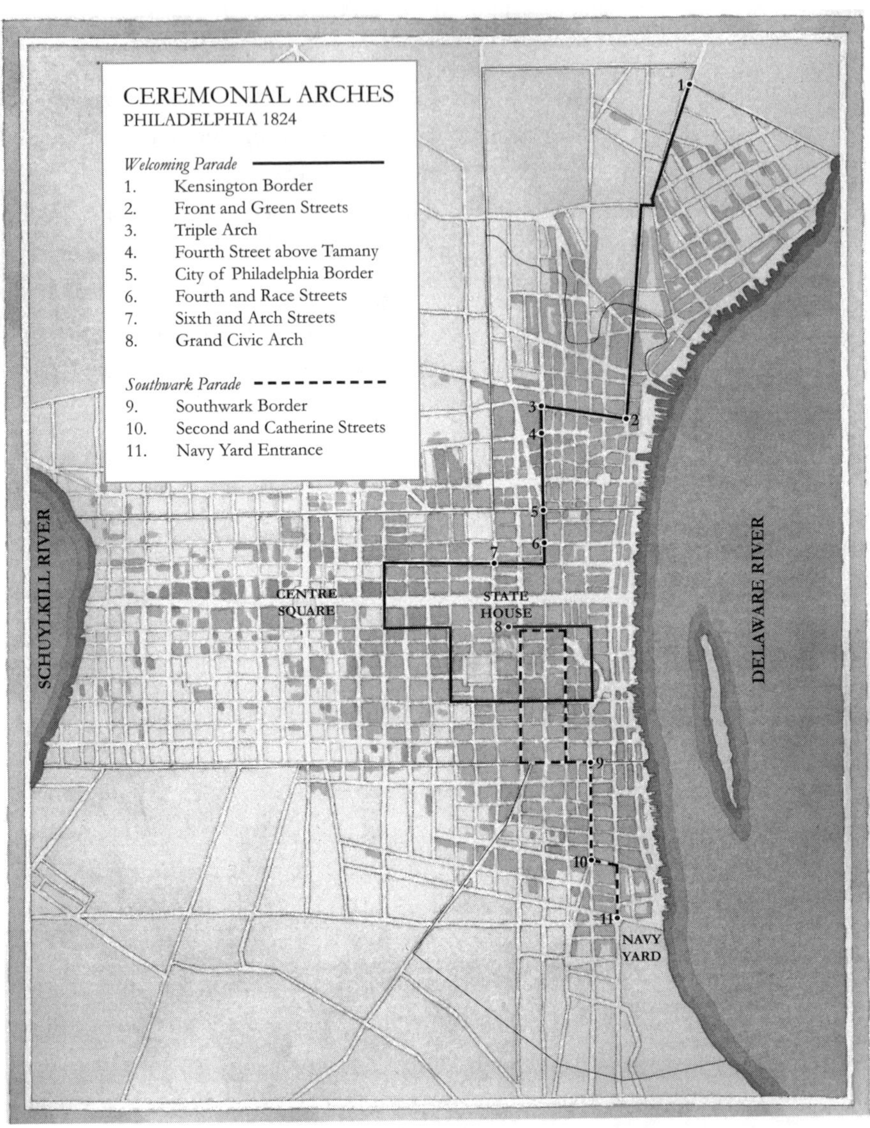

FIG. 2. Plan of the City of Philadelphia with locations of ceremonial arches noted, ca. 1824. (Drawing by Andrew C. Gander)

United States; after the government's departure for Washington it was used as a classroom building for the University of Pennsylvania. Nearby on Eighth Street construction was under way for a new building designed by Strickland for the benevolent Musical Fund Society.[17] The full city block to the southwest of Eighth and Spruce Streets was occupied by the Pennsylvania Hospital, its first building constructed in 1755; subsequent additions made it one of the largest institutional buildings in the country. During Lafayette's visit, its floors were strewn with wreaths and sand into which compliments to the general were traced.[18] Among a number of recent buildings representing stylish architectural modes, Haviland's 1823 Greek Revival St. Andrew's Episcopal Church stood nearby on Eighth Street. It and other ecclesiastical edifices in the vicinity were testament to the continued religious life in the city evidenced in the first leg of the procession, as well as proof of the city's architectural innovation.

Eighteenth-century row houses lined Spruce Street, on which the procession traveled eastward. Here, and in other such neighborhoods, both homes and businesses were altered for the occasion of the parade by having window sashes and fanlights removed and balconies constructed to make viewing from inside of buildings more commodious. Home owners, especially the wealthy and those along the parade route, decorated their windows with ornaments of marble and alabaster, fruit, candles, and colored lamps. Spruce Street was also dotted with ecclesiastical landmarks and benevolent institutions like St. Joseph's Orphan Asylum, built in 1789. Nearby stood the Walnut Street Prison, a substantial stone building that represented strides in penitentiary reform that originated in Philadelphia and had been influential on both sides of the Atlantic.[19] The final segments of the parade also passed through residential neighborhoods like Society Hill, home to some of the wealthiest residents of the city.[20] North along Second Street and west on Chestnut Street, the procession returned to one of the more established parts of the city, many of its buildings rebuilt or under reconstruction. The financial center was defined by a series of orderly buildings, including five insurance offices established in the first decade of the century. Among them stood the celebrated white marble Bank of Pennsylvania by Latrobe and the U.S. Custom House, another marble building designed by Latrobe's pupil Strickland. Chestnut Street included four more banks in a variety of modern architectural styles.[21] This neighborhood was set aglow with nighttime illuminations; one particularly impressive display at the older U.S. Bank had the effect of presenting "the whole building [with] the enchanting appearance of transparent marble."[22]

Both colonial and early Gothic Revival buildings nearby had been recently rough-cast in imitation of stone; this treatment had become increasingly popular throughout Philadelphia, reflecting the change of taste that accompanied the Greek Revival's recent advent in the city. Near the route's conclusion, the banking quarter gave way to an intellectual center featuring the headquarters of the American Philosophical Society, the Library Company, Loganian Library, and Charles Willson Peale's art and natural history museum. A Friends' school on Fourth below Chestnut Street taught ancient languages, mathematics, and natural philosophy, while the Apprentices' Library, housed in Carpenters' Hall, instructed the laboring classes in "reading and valuable information."[23]

Lafayette, who was more familiar with colonial red-brick Philadelphia than the Federal period's classically inspired marble and rough-cast "Athens of America," was impressed by the city's architectural developments, but even more so by patriotic scenes set for him in and around them. Particularly moving was the brand new marble building on Chestnut Street modeled on the Parthenon. Strickland's Second Bank of the United States was made even more impressive for this occasion; decorated not only with festoons and bunting, the bank served as a pedestal for surviving veterans of 1776.[24] This tableau framed living reminders of the Revolution — Philadelphia's earliest patriots — with the Greek architecture of one of the city's most modern buildings. As the bank (an enterprise of the federal government) was hailed for its architectural associations with the foundations of Greek democracy, likewise the veterans were understood to be foundational to American democracy. Together the city's establishments — from meetinghouses to penitentiaries, from libraries to hospitals — revealed its citizens' aspirations to foster intellectual progress, moral development, health, and social improvement within impressive settings that blended America's colonial past with classical antiquity. They provided an instructive architectural frame for Lafayette's winding circuit, a three-dimensional architectural history chronicling the city's growth from foundation to revolution and independence.

Participation: The Civic Arch

Philadelphians celebrated the liberty that had been won from an oppressive monarchy by making the Welcoming Parade a widely inclusive opportunity for participation on a variety of scales. Citizens were aware that the "magnificent pageant" relied on contributions from "everybody . . . direct or indirect."[25] Individuals took part not only in the passive observation of the proceedings but also by their purchase of tokens that ornamented their regular dress; the scores of such products as handkerchiefs, cravats, fans, slippers, and buttons featuring Lafayette's name and portrait confirmed the popularity of this most intimate form of adornment available to most Philadelphians. Gathering in groups defined by vocation, citizens marched in the parade and represented trades and professions. Entrepreneurs erected grandstands and risers at key locations along the parade route and charged a fee for those perches which offered improved vantage points.[26] In many ways Philadelphians changed the face of their city for the great festival, in both individual and communal efforts, as well as to both symbolic and entrepreneurial ends.

The most striking example of this broad civic participation were the dozen or so temporary triumphal arches erected specifically for the Welcoming Parade, which remained standing for the duration of Lafayette's stay in Philadelphia. The selection of this monument type, raised along the parade route in keeping with the imperial Roman tradition, clearly conveyed the vision and aspiration of the young country.[27] Departing from the ancient custom whereby such monuments were financed by a central authority, and more in keeping with modern European practice for such ephemeral markers, all but one of Lafayette's arches were proposed by and paid for by smaller bands of citizens and wealthy individuals who lived in the neighborhoods through which the parade passed. Although Lafayette's secretary, Auguste Levasseur, recorded their total number as thirteen, no other primary evidence confirms this figure.[28] Certainly the reporters who chronicled each Lafayette event to the last detail, from the enumeration of menu delicacies to the specially made levee room upholstery designs, would not have neglected such a significant item. The absence of direct numerical symbolism is important, for a citywide control would have been required to erect exactly thirteen arches. The grassroots efforts that are to credit for the arches' construction offer evidence for a certain enthusiastic expression of republicanism among many of Philadelphia's citizens.

Just as the nature of the triumphal procession had been altered to reflect the "moral sublime" evidenced in the American character, the arches too were tailored to suit their republican context. While some symbolic figures were adopted with only a change in their meaning rather than their form (most conspicuously, the messenger-eagle of Jupiter, god of the sky and patron of Rome, had been chosen as recently as 1782 as America's national symbol), in many instances imperial and "pagan" ornaments were modified to express the patriotic values of the democratic nation. Images of divinities, sacrifices, and apotheosis were replaced by the founding fathers, state seals, and national symbols. A local paper praised their decidedly American character, noting that their decorations "evinced ingenuity as well as high moral feeling and ardent patriotism."[29] Even the designation of the "triumphal" arches was changed, and with great specificity, as unpublished documents reveal. The concerted effort to focus the procession on peace and community involvement, rather than war and military personnel, prompted an Arrangements Committee secretary to amend meeting minutes by crossing out the original signifier "triumphal" and replacing it with the term "civic."[30]

A variety of sources reveals the position of eleven arches along Lafayette's parade path (see fig. 2).[31] The length and detail of their descriptions in the press are relative to the prominence of their location and size within the city and its associated townships to the north and south. Twenty-first-century Philadelphia has its roots in several separate settlements along the Delaware River that would maintain political autonomy until the mid-nineteenth century: the Cartesian grid at the center which marked the official bounds of the city proper, flanked to the south by Southwark and to the north by the Northern Liberties and Kensington. Most of the identifiable arches were concentrated toward the margins of the settlements, and most of these — with rare and important exceptions — maintain a common form and ornamental approach defined by their geographic arrangement.

At Kensington's northern border, an "elegant" triple arch with "marbled" columns supported a dark green attic level with slogans welcoming Lafayette and featured portraits of Franklin and Washington (*arch 1* in fig. 2).[32] Roman arches often constructed such lineages of power by linking family names across monuments.[33] Similarly, the Kensington arch united the figures that had made significant contributions to America's history, with Philadelphia as their stage. To ensure that the point was made, the arms of the United States and those of Pennsylvania were exhibited on the side arches as well, emphasizing the relationship of national and local figures and government. In the place of a quadriga, which would have appeared at the top of a Roman arch, a large sculpted American eagle spread its wings over a patriotic and appreciative inscription.

Three more arches greeted Lafayette in the northern suburbs. The arch at the intersection of Front and Green Streets (*arch 2* in fig. 2) bore another welcoming

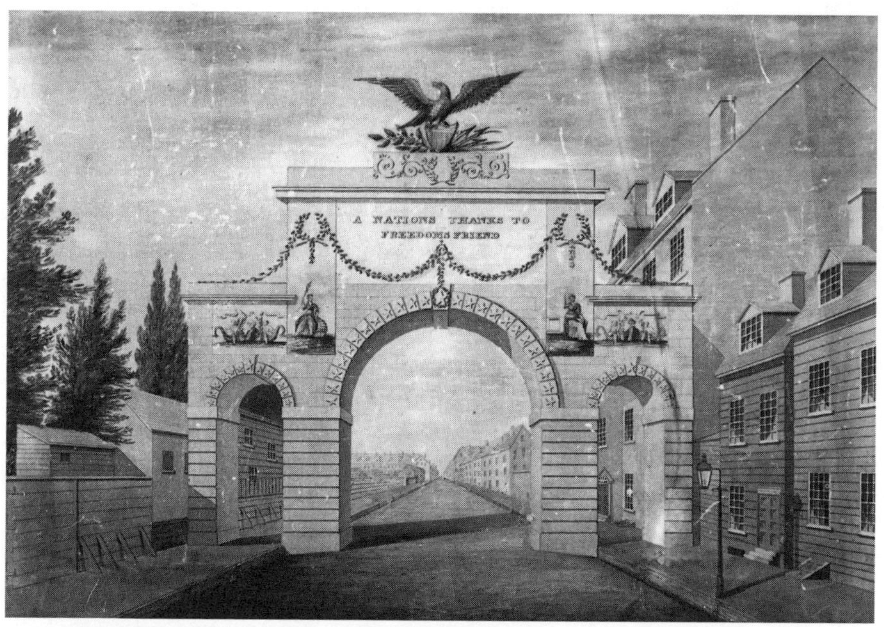

FIG. 3. Triple Arch, intersection of Front and Arch Streets. The original caption read, "Triumphal arch erected in honor of Lafayette in Philadelphia, 1824 by Samuel Honeyman Kneass." (Independence National Historical Park)

inscription that evoked the American flag.[34] Several blocks to the west, a triple arch spanned the street and its flanking sidewalks (*arch 3* in fig. 2 and fig. 3). Over its side arches thirteen stars represented the original states; the attic inscription read, "A Nation's Thanks to Freedom's Friend."[35] The final arch outside city limits, spanning Fourth Street above Tamany (*arch 4* in fig. 2), must have been rather unassuming as it escaped the notice of observers who focused their attention on grander urban adornments.[36]

This opening leg of the parade passed through neighborhoods traditionally populated by artisans, carpenters, grocers, tailors, mariners, captains, blacksmiths, and furniture makers,[37] a variety of citizens who can be generally described as the patrons of the arches. While their relative wealth and cultural aspirations were expressed in these large arches (at least two of them with triple openings), residents of the city proper, with greater numbers of merchants and skilled workers, were not to be outdone by their neighbors to the north. Crossing the city limits on Fourth Street near Vine, Lafayette was met with the spectacular sight of another grand arch set amidst a veritable Arcadian ensemble. Representing each of the states, twenty-four young women, clad in white and adorned with garlands of flowers, scattered blossoms before the barouche and sang a commemorative ode to the general.[38] The arch here (*arch 5* in fig. 2) was painted to appear as if it were hewn from thirteen massive rough-stone blocks, each of which bore the name of an original state. Pennsylvania's geographic and political centrality was highlighted by its enduring nickname, with the state name and arms appearing on the keystone, fundamental to the stability of any arch. Female figures that might have represented Valor and Victory in Roman arches were replaced by allegories designated Prosperity and the Genius of Liberty for the American triumph. Lengthy inscriptions, decisive dates of the Revolutionary War, and names of patriots and military heroes (Lafayette's figured prominently) completed the composition.[39] Just one block farther south, an arch on Race Street (*arch 6* in fig. 2) was made remarkable by the appearance of a live eagle above the attic level,[40] while another, its description lost, appeared at Arch and Sixth Streets (*arch 7* in fig. 2).[41]

From this point, the parade circled counter-clockwise through the city to its end point, passing no other temporary monuments except the final one, which was the culminating expression of the Americanized classicism introduced by these preceding seven (*arch 8* in fig. 2 and fig. 4). The most elaborate of the temporary monuments was the only one financially supported by the city (fig. 5). The judiciously named Grand Civic Arch measured 45 feet wide by 35 feet high and was constructed on a wooden frame with stretched canvas painted in imitation of stone.[42] Utilizing painting, sculpture, and architecture in a cohesive act of commemoration — as architect Iktinos and sculptor Phidias had collaborated on the Parthenon — sculptor William Rush, painter Thomas Sully, and architect William Strickland worked together in the creation of new American iconography. Like the Victory figure which holds a laurel wreath over the emperor in an interior relief from the Arch of Titus, the nineteenth-century design included two frames supporting a wreath over the keystone, reiterating Pennsylvania's designation as the Keystone State. With the lavish painting of the city's seal by Sully above, the symbol underscored the fact that it was not a single ruler, but political and geographic entities that were triumphant in the American victory. In lieu of the quadriga, which would have suggested political strength as a function of military might to imperial Romans, its top was adorned with two allegorical figures carved by Rush, *Wisdom* and *Justice*. Each promised peaceful resolutions to conflict rather than the force signified by the horse and chariot. Such ornament

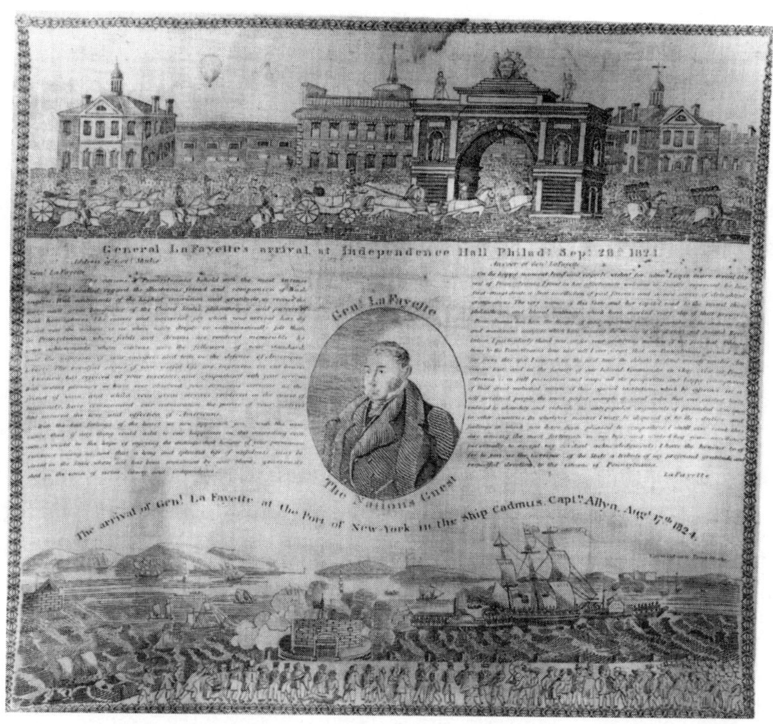

FIG. 4. Welcoming Parade, with image of procession including Lafayette's barouche near the Grand Civic Arch. The original caption read, "Lafayette's Arrival at Independence Hall." Linen handkerchief, 1824. (Courtesy, Winterthur Museum)

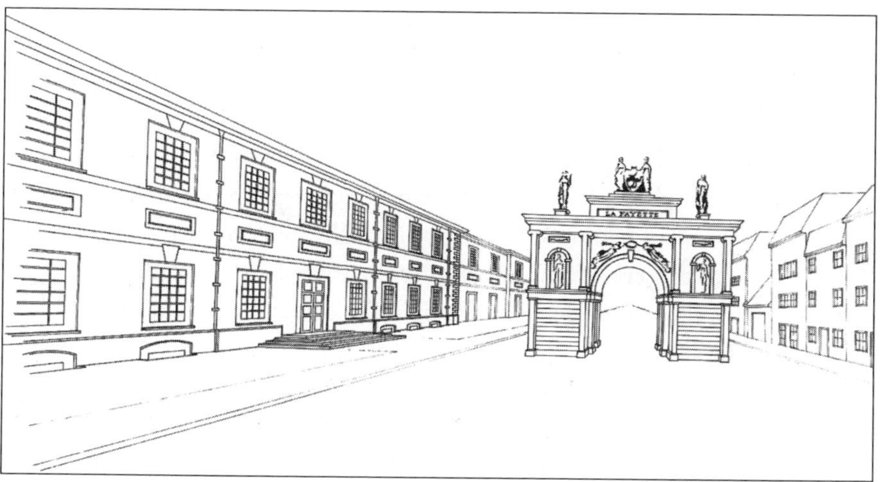

FIG. 5. Grand Civic Arch on Chestnut Street near the Old Pennsylvania State House. (Drawing by Jonathan Flager)

encouraged the civilized manner of modern government, and stressed the role of many minds in the creation and preservation of one nation.

The formal language of the Welcoming Parade's civic arches suggested that the citizen-patrons who raised them shared a cohesive set of ideals with the Arrangements Committee's aesthetic values and vision for representing the city, state, and country. Stars and stripes, eagles (live or sculpted), classical architectural motifs, and other similar expressions of patriotism appear repeatedly among the arches. Archived and published commentaries demonstrate the manner in which the arches were seen as symbols of regional pride; the Kensington arch was "most tastefully decorated, doing credit to the judgment and patriotism of our brethren *in that section*" of the city.[43] Such an emphasis reveals the common understanding of the residents' character to the north of town and on the waterfront, where merchants and artisans raised the arches in expressions of native and national pride, and in a cohesive formal language that linked Philadelphia's neighborhoods, as did the procession whose route they marked.[44]

Yet the general harmony expressed in the Welcoming Parade arches was disturbed by discord to the south. By the nineteenth century the district that shared Philadelphia's southern border had gained a certain gritty reputation when compared with either the city or its northern suburbs. Lodged more often in houses built of timber rather than brick, Southwark's residents were expected to be more boisterous and less prosperous than their neighbors to the north. Their most common institutional affiliation was the region's greatest employer, the Naval Yard, rather than the more culturally esteemed institutions to the north, or the networks of artisan trades in the Northern Liberties.[45] Although a delegation from Southwark was included among the marchers in the parade, the procession itself did not enter the district, and passed its northern boundary by just two city blocks. While simple logistics dictated that the general's procession from New Jersey and into Philadelphia would pass through the Northern Liberties and Kensington, the citizens of Southwark perceived the choice to route the procession away from them as evidence of prejudiced views and political strategy.[46] In response, the Southwark residents proposed their own celebration for Lafayette (see fig. 2).

A later procession would conduct the general from his temporary residence on Third Street through Southwark to the Navy Yard. As had been done for the Welcoming Parade, the Southwark route would be distinguished with a series of civic arches, three of which are known to have been raised. Like those to the north, the Southwark arches possessed a legible arch form and similarly employed patriotic slogans, classically derived symbols, and references to the Revolutionary War. However, whether a matter of economy or a self-conscious expression of individuality, they reveal a somewhat different approach and attitude. At Southwark's border (*arch 9* in fig. 2), a laurel-festooned arch was erected with columns entwined with evergreens. Its keystone was inscribed with Lafayette's name, and the arch itself bore inscriptions on each side.[47] A remarkable construction some four blocks to the south, on Second near Catherine Street (*arch 10* in fig. 2), utilized four large trees joined in pairs by their boughs and brought together and secured by "strong tackles," with a large triangle hung in the center.[48] The nature of this arch spoke more of the ingenuity and the trades which populated this district than an inherited classical heritage. The final arch, at the entrance to the Navy Yard (*arch 11* in fig. 2), was further evidence of the local sentiment. Recalling Lafayette's procurement of a ship for aid in the war, its inscription read, "I will purchase and equip a vessel myself."[49] With its brash slogan suggesting, perhaps, the residents' self-sufficient, individualist character, this arch highlighted the role that their craft played in Lafayette's endeavor as much as it suggested the role that the general played in the nation's history. The pageant and arches in Southwark also reveal that the classical tradition was flexible enough to accommodate the patriotic expressions of wealthy merchants of the north as well as shipbuilders of the south, even when those expressions varied in tone.

Transformation: Temple of Liberty

Although the Southwark procession was an important segment of the festivities that marked Lafayette's stay in the city, the Welcoming Parade captured the attention and imagination of citizens who experienced it in Philadelphia and those who read about it across the country. Central to its significance was the landmark chosen as the procession's culmination, and the transformation of its meaning in Philadelphia, and to the country, as a result of the pageant. The Welcoming Parade concluded in front of a suite of buildings constructed across a span of sixty years but stylistically unified through their use of such colonial idioms as red brick, white trim, belt courses, dentil moldings, and cupolas. The Old Pennsylvania State House (1732–53) is flanked to the south by the Old Supreme Court (1790–91) and to the north by Congress Hall (1787–89). The Grand Civic Arch stood before and at the center of the ensemble, marking the point where

Lafayette's carriage halted. Its classically inspired design was meant to enhance the setting already graced by the extant buildings, ensuring their commemorative function, and adding a layer of significance to this site which already had been, and continues to be, an important gathering place for displays of patriotism in Philadelphia. The monument was evocatively designed with the proportions of an arch buried by accumulated debris, communicating the impression that it had survived time and trauma, like those ruins illustrated in archaeological folios popular in the early part of the nineteenth century. It also suggested that the nearby buildings, and the institutions they housed, would be likewise durable and resilient. Symbolizing enduring values of the Republic, the figural sculptures *Wisdom* and *Justice,* resting on the arch's attic level, called attention to the flanking buildings: Justice, with scales and sword, signified the Supreme Court; and Wisdom, known by her books, snake, and mirror, represented Congress Hall.

From one perspective, the State House was a curious choice, as all traces of governmental activity which it once housed had departed from its halls.[50] Alterations in its use, as well as the physical addition of commercial offices along its north front, had disfigured the building from its original appearance. Yet in spite of these changes, the place where Lafayette disembarked and poised himself to meet the people sustained an important position in American memory. Although mostly abandoned and much neglected, it remained the stage and backdrop for key scenes in the story of 1776. Heightened by the presence of Lafayette, who had taken part in the making of these memories, the building was charged with a strengthened significance that would forever alter its position, not only in Philadelphia's urban structure but also in the landscape of American history.

The Old State House was Philadelphia's answer to the Capitoline and Parthenon, the terminations of the Roman triumph and the Athenian Panathenaea, respectively. Like them, it was a site of civic and sacred relevance, for no finer a temple of republicanism could be imagined than the location of the first Continental Congress, the building in which both the Declaration of Independence and the Constitution were signed. Echoing activities in the Capitoline, where Roman generals sacrificed to Jupiter before taking up the sword, it was in the State House that Lafayette first vowed his support of the American Revolution. Like the Panathenaea, this procession ended with a presentation and tribute paid within a building. At the conclusion of those ancient parades, a solitary general, or small number of worthies, would scale monumental flights leading to the inner sanctum. In Philadelphia, Lafayette climbed only a few steps to enter the American temple, and then invited all the citizenry to join him. Once inside, they presented gifts to him, as did the ancients to their icons. Although the building's original functional utility had waned, its symbolic function increased. Now, with its purpose in Lafayette's parade, the Old State House was elevated to the standing that it still enjoys in America today.

On a daily basis Lafayette conducted receptions in the building that helped codify its revived meaning. These levees were staged in the East Room beneath a full-length wooden sculpture of Washington, which was positioned where the Speaker once oversaw the business of the Continental Congress.[51] This image was doubly significant, for Washington both received Lafayette's offer of support for the cause in this building and led the army which achieved independence from Britain. Reflecting the ancestor sculptures of ancient Rome by recalling the founding fathers, the sculpture supervised the proceedings in effigy form. It also replicated Greek cult images, reinforcing suggestions in contemporary newspapers that the spirits of the early patriots dwelt within the building's brick confines.

Each afternoon, for a few hours, the Old State House was a stage on which representatives of all walks — clergy, university professors, the chamber of commerce, and the children of public schools — acted out the fruits of liberty and democracy. Lafayette's secretary wondered at the "picture of the most perfect equality" presented by scenes in which "mechanics with their hardened hands and uprolled sleeves, . . . the magistrate and plain-clad farmer stood together."[52] These daily events cemented the ideals suggested in the greeting that met Lafayette as he alighted before the building; the mayoral address declared that the immortal fame, virtue, and service of Lafayette's compatriots were manifest in the building itself, and that "this hallowed Hall . . . may emphatically be called the Birthplace of Independence."[53] Later in the century a historian of the city would record that Lafayette's visit was to credit with "having stimulated patriotic feelings which had long lain dormant and directed the popular mind toward the history of the American Revolution, and to the contemplation of the claims which the services of the fathers of the republic had upon posterity."[54] Ultimately, it was not gallons of rough-cast, embroidered cravats, toasts invoking the ancients, marble porticoes, or even canvas arches which could best manifest the ideals of the Revolution. It was rather the activity within the nearly century-old State House that was the primary catalyst for evoking a lasting change in the public memory. Like the city itself, the East Room was transformed — to some, "consecrated"—during Lafayette's visit, and became known as the Hall of Independence, a designation that would eventually expand to include the whole building.[55] In 1824, the building that Americans had previously referred to as the Old Pennsylvania State House — when they happened to refer to it at all — was rejuvenated as Independence Hall.[56]

AS EMPEROR AUGUSTUS had boasted that he found Rome a city of brick and left it one of marble, Lafayette's parade left a corridor of canvas classicism and rough-cast antiquity in its wake. The most enduring remnant of the lavish week-long affair in the autumn of 1824 is not so tangible as the arches and buildings which marked the parade route, but is rather a shift of perception: the renaming and repositioning of the State House in the mind of Philadelphians and Americans as Independence Hall, a vessel in which the spirit of Washington and Jefferson has been joined by others through the centuries, as is revealed by the more recent additions of bronze plaques commemorating such notable icons as Lincoln and Kennedy. The building was the focus of Lafayette's Welcoming Parade and the stage for the most important of events of his stay in Philadelphia. The individual and group activities there reflected the extensive participation that was to credit for the nature of the various celebrations, primarily the Welcoming Parade. Its aesthetic resulted from a joint effort of city councilors who planned the route to pass through certain districts and near specific buildings, neighbors who worked together to design and erect temporary arches along the parade route, institutions and home owners who changed the physical nature of their houses through temporary construction, and individuals who became living ornament for the spectacle by adorning themselves with specially made buttons, ribbons, and cravats. Human activity had transformed virtually the entire city into a capital of liberty, which had at its ceremonial center an old-fashioned brick building, now consecrated as a temple of independence.

Notes

1. Newspapers accentuated ancient analogies through the week. For example, Lafayette was greeted by the parade's chief marshal "in the toga of peace." Inscriptions added to building lobbies invoked the names of Pompey, Cato, Caesar, and Brutus. At a ball held at Washington Hall, a toast was raised to "Greece regenerated, wishing her a Washington for a leader, and a Lafayette for a friend." See the *US Gazette* (Oct. 8,

1824), quoted in Brandon, *Lafayette, Guest of the Nation,* 75, and Levasseur, *Lafayette in America in 1824 and 1825,* 1:142–43.

2. Lafayette's secretary, Auguste Levasseur, also made the comparison, referring to himself as "narrator of this journey, or rather triumph." See Levasseur, *Lafayette in America in 1824 and 1825,* 1:158. For analysis of the Roman triumph, see Favro, "The Street Triumphant," 152–58.

3. The Arrangements Committee, a twenty-one-member group of representatives of different city councils, appointed marshals to represent Philadelphia as well as the city's major suburbs to the north and south, which remained distinct administrative units until 1854. See Brandon, *Lafayette, Guest of the Nation,* 67.

4. Further characteristics that distinguish the *triumphus* from the *adventus* (as well as a third rite, the *ovatio,* which was open to generals) and their practice in the Byzantine empire are included in Mango, "The Triumphal Way of Constantinople and the Golden Gate," 173–74. See also McCormick, *Eternal Victory,* 16, 90.

5. *Pictorial Life of General Lafayette,* 189, emphasis in original.

6. "Ode to Lafayette," written by James N. Barker on request of the Printers of Philadelphia. Printed in Idzerda, Loveland, and Miller, *Lafayette, Hero of Two Worlds,* 130.

7. At least one member of the Society of Friends was motivated to write to the Arrangements Committee to explain that the "military character" of certain events would prohibit Quaker participation. In lieu of the planned military salute, he urged the committee to consider greeting Lafayette with children bearing baskets of flowers: "It is desirable for the honor of the city that the reception of La Fayette and the marks of respect shewn to him should be as much of a *civic* nature as possible; at least that the affair should not be wholly military." Letter from John Hallowell to Joseph S. Lewis, Sept. 27, 1824, emphasis in original, in Lafayette Arrangements Committee Papers (hereafter Committee Papers), Historical Society of Pennsylvania (HSP).

8. *Poulson's American Daily Advertiser* (Sept. 30, 1824).

9. Meeting Minutes for Aug. 21, 1824, in Committee Papers, HSP. See also Levasseur, *Lafayette in America in 1824 and 1825,* 1:15, 141–43.

10. Even so, the different character of parade ephemera in each reveals a significant alteration between the generations that staged them. The 1788 parade concluded with a presentation of a modestly scaled ship, a model of one of the vessels that played key role in the Revolutionary War effort. In 1824 the city raised a larger, grander monument whose Roman prototype clearly communicated the aspirations of the young country, as well as its shifting historical consciousness.

11. Brandon, *Lafayette, Guest of the Nation,* 69.

12. *Pictorial Life of General Lafayette,* 197.

13. For example, the Arch Street Meeting House (1804) had been enlarged in 1811, just a decade before Lafayette's visit. Other churches in the area had also been recently either refurbished or enlarged. See *Philadelphia in 1824* (Philadelphia: Carey & Lea, 1824), n.p.

14. The *US Gazette* (Oct. 8, 1824), quoted in Brandon, *Lafayette, Guest of the Nation,* 91.

15. Arch Street lay near the bulging center of Philadelphia's western population expansion away from the Delaware River. The westward pull of the parade route along Arch Street helped to decentralize the tens of thousands of visitors to the city who lined the streets and who could not be accommodated by High Street, which was made unsuitable for such parades by the stalls that cluttered several of its blocks.

16. The Institute of the Deaf and Dumb was established in 1820; in 1824 its new quarters designed by John Haviland were under construction to the southwest at the corner of Broad and Pine Streets. The Academy of Fine Arts was founded in 1805 as one of the first such establishments in the country and dedicated to providing "elegant and rational recreation for the public" and a "school for young artists." The academy boasted extensive and expansive galleries, yearly exhibitions, a library, a collection of antiquities, and ancient and modern sculptures and paintings by Rubens, Titian, Canova, and others. See *Philadelphia in 1824,* n.p.

17. Founded 1820, the Musical Fund Society existed to provide relief for needy musicians and their families and also to serve the cultivation of taste and proficiency in musical art among the population. See *Philadelphia in 1824,* n.p.

18. The floors of the Pennsylvania Hospital, founded in 1750 and added onto in 1755, 1796, and 1804, were embellished with inscriptions that communicated such sentiments as "Welcome, La Fayette, to this Asylum of the afflicted — May thy days be ended without experiencing any of their sufferings" and "In thy presence, La Fayette, we forget our sufferings." See the *US Gazette* (Oct. 8, 1824), quoted in Brandon, *Lafayette, Guest of the Nation,* 91.

19. Its earliest construction dating to 1774, the Walnut Street Prison was a monument to the international fame of Pennsylvania's prison system. The prominence of this building is reflected in the fact that a contemporary guidebook printed in 1824 devoted thirteen pages to detailing it, and only ten to describing all of the city's colleges and universities together. See *Philadelphia in 1824,* n.p.

20. These included the Powell, Shippen, Hamilton, Rush, and Bingham families. See Schweitzer, "The Spatial Organization of Federalist Philadelphia, 1790," 45–46.

21. Latrobe's Bank of Pennsylvania was reportedly the "most pure model of Grecian architecture in the country." Ornamented with some of the country's first architectural sculpture, the Custom House included, in an attic niche, the allegorical figure *Commerce* carved by the city's first sculptor, William Rush. The bank row included the North American Bank, which was the oldest bank in the country, and Latrobe's Philadelphia Bank, a "neat and correct specimen of the Gothic style," "recently roughcast and colored in imitation of marble." See *Philadelphia in 1824,* n.p.

22. *Poulson's American Daily Advertiser* (Sept. 30, 1824).

23. The main object of the Philosophical Society was the cultivation of the "exact

sciences," history, "moral science," and general literature. From the building's niche, the image of Franklin had peered since its construction in 1785. The professional and social mission of the Apprentices' Library was to "elevate people whose situation in life often leads them into danger of evil habits." See *Philadelphia in 1824,* n.p.

24. The scene was recorded to possess "from its venerable character, and its associations . . . one of the most striking incidents of the occasion." See Bowen, *A History of Philadelphia,* 90. See also *Poulson's American Daily Advertiser* (Sept. 30, 1824).

25. *Pictorial Life of General Lafayette,* 198.

26. Newspapers advertised the relative prices of stands erected for the festivities. While places throughout town were available for a few coins, seats on one "well-built balcony on Chestnut near fifth," at the parade's end point, demanded from one to three dollars. See *Poulson's American Daily Advertiser* (Sept. 27, 1824).

27. For the triumphal processions, the Romans erected temporary arches that were later replaced by permanent ones. No records indicate that Philadelphians planned to build permanent monuments to replace the ephemeral markers raised across their city. Philadelphia was not unique in raising arches of this nature, which appeared in Lafayette parades in several other cities across the nation.

28. Accessible evidence confirms only eleven arches in Philadelphia; no newspaper account or other available description records thirteen, or any total count for that matter. However, Levasseur's count has been repeated in much of the scholarship that treats Lafayette's American tour. See Levasseur, *Lafayette in America in 1824 and 1825.*

29. *Poulson's American Daily Advertiser* (Sept. 30, 1824).

30. Meeting Minutes, Aug. 19, 1824, in Committee Papers, HSP.

31. The most significant among the sources include the published account of Auguste Levasseur's committee meeting minutes, newspaper clippings, and oral history records held at the Historical Society of Pennsylvania. See Committee Papers, HSP.

32. The *Evening Post* (Sept. 25, 1824), quoted in Brandon, *Lafayette, Guest of the Nation,* 67.

33. In the first century, Augustus erected arches for his family flanking the Temple of Divius Julius, literally constructing an imperial family line in the Forum Romanum.

34. "May the Star Spangled Banner of Columbia Ever Shield La Fayette and Welcome Him to Our Shores." See the *Evening Post* (Sept. 25, 1824), quoted in Brandon, *Lafayette, Guest of the Nation,* 67.

35. The *Evening Post* (Oct. 2, 1824), quoted in Brandon, *Lafayette, Guest of the Nation,* 70.

36. Committee Papers, HSP.

37. Schweitzer, "The Spatial Organization of Federalist Philadelphia," 46.

38. Adapted by Benjamin Mayo, the song's lyrics were reprinted in the *US Gazette* (Oct. 1, 1824), and included such lines as, "What are nations / What their stations / When compared with freedom's host; / What are mighty monarchs now / While at Freedom's

shrine we bow / Pride of princes, strength of kings / To the dust fair freedom brings." See Bowen, *A History of Philadelphia,* 87–88.

39. The motto read: "The Sons of Freemen welcome the Hero who 'burned to shed his best blood in the cause of liberty.'" On the left of the base a painted female figure appeared with the inscription, "Prosperity, the result of Industry"; opposite and on the right, a painted figure, the *Genius of Liberty,* was paired with the motto, "Liberty the result of bravery." On the reverse of the arch were the dates 1781 and 1776, with the names of such patriots as Hancock, Adams, Franklin, and Hamilton. See Bowen, *A History of Philadelphia,* 87–88.

40. Newspapers made much of the bird being perched "in all its natural majesty" on this "very splendid arch." See the *Evening Post* (Oct. 2, 1824), quoted in Brandon, *Lafayette, Guest of the Nation,* 71.

41. Oral history of Margaret Flannery, Dec. 1, 1895, in Committee Papers, HSP.

42. The timber-framed, canvas-wrapped Grand Civic Arch, designed by Strickland and painted by Chestnut Street Theatre scene painters, is discussed in Meeting Minutes, Aug. 20–21, 1824, in Committee Papers, HSP. See also the *Evening Post* (Oct. 2, 1824), quoted in Brandon, *Lafayette, Guest of the Nation,* 72.

43. The *Evening Post* (Sept. 25, 1824), quoted in Brandon, *Lafayette, Guest of the Nation,* 67, emphasis added.

44. Schweitzer, "The Spatial Organization of Federalist Philadelphia," 43.

45. Ibid., 48, 50–51.

46. See meeting minutes of Sept. 1, 8, 10, 17, 18, and 24, 1824, in Committee Papers, HSP.

47. The north front read, "the man whom we delight to honor" and the south, "The Friend of Liberty." See the *US Gazette* (Oct. 4, 1824), quoted in Brandon, *Lafayette, Guest of the Nation,* 88.

48. The *US Gazette* (Oct. 4, 1824), quoted in Brandon, *Lafayette, Guest of the Nation,* 88.

49. Ibid.

50. Since its completion in 1753 it had served a variety of purposes: originally the capitol of the Province of Pennsylvania, later it was home to both the Continental Congress and (briefly) the federal government. Having fallen into a state of disrepair after the Commonwealth's legislature moved inland to Lancaster in 1799, in 1824 its only tenant was Charles Willson Peale's museum on the second floor. (At least one Philadelphian was uneasy about the undignified tenant of the building; archived meeting minutes reveal a request to remove the museum sign from the former State House: "The New Yorkers and others will say that you put Lafayette in the 'Philada Museum.'" Letter from anonymous citizen, Sept. 7, 1824, in Committee Papers, HSP.) From time to time the idea of demolishing the decidedly outdated building had been proposed.

51. Rush sculpted this image of Washington in 1815. It was moved to the East Room in 1824 with portraits of such patriots as Penn, Franklin, Morris, Hopkinson, Jefferson, Hancock, Adams, Madison, and Monroe to enrich the room for Lafayette's levees. See *Poulson's American Daily Advertiser* (Sept. 30, 1824).

52. Levasseur, *Lafayette in America in 1824 and 1825*, 1:141–44.

53. The *Evening Post* (Oct. 2, 1824), quoted in Brandon, *Lafayette, Guest of the Nation*, 74.

54. Scharf and Westcott, *History of Philadelphia*, 609.

55. By the end of the decade its surrounding area, now known as Independence Square, would become the "symbolic heart and most sacred site" of the city. See Davis, *Parades and Power*, 31. For a broader study of the building's changing meaning across time, see Mires, *Independence Hall in American Memory*, esp. 67–73, for the impact of Lafayette's visit on the building's history.

56. Not even the Arrangements Committee foresaw the change; throughout their meeting minutes the building is referred to as the "state house," in Committee Papers, HSP.

ELLEN M. LITWICKI

"Liberty Regulated by Law"

Civic Instruction on the George Washington Inaugural Centennial in Chicago

> And the beginning, as you know, is always the most important part. . . . That is the time when the character is being moulded and easily takes any impress one may wish to stamp on it. . . . It seems, then, our first business will be to supervise the making of fables and legends, rejecting all which are unsatisfactory; and we shall induce nurses and mothers to tell their children only those which we have approved.
> — Plato, *Republic*

IN FEBRUARY 1887 the Union League Club (ULC) of Chicago, which numbered among its members the leading business and professional men of the city, inaugurated annual public exercises for Washington's Birthday, for the express purpose of providing civic and patriotic education to Chicagoans. Seven months later civic elites in Philadelphia staged a three-day commemoration of the centennial of the Constitution. In the wake of this celebration, an editorial in *Century* magazine proposed to make Constitution Day, like Washington's Birthday, an annual festival of civic education that would exert a "direct patriotic influence" on Americans. "Merely to group about a national idea," the editor asserted, "is an incalculable influence in making our people homogeneous and sympathetic."[1]

The calls for a revival of Washington's Birthday and the institution of Constitution Day sounded the opening salvo of a campaign by civic elites to seize control of American public celebrations. The late nineteenth century witnessed an explosion of civic celebrations in the United States. Several developments converged to produce this crusade. Rapid industrialization after the Civil War had produced impressive wealth for American capitalists, as well as a bitter struggle between them and their employees for control of the workplace and the fruits of capitalism. In addition, the immigration that industrialists encouraged to provide a plentiful, inexpensive, and docile workforce brought together an unprecedented variety of ethnic and racial groups. American industrialists, along with veterans organizations, hereditary societies, and educators, viewed these developments with varying degrees of apprehension, and each determined that patriotic and civic education would go far in the direction of solving the problems of the late nineteenth century. Civic celebrations constituted one element of their program, and also represented the attempt of business and professional men to legitimize their position as the civic leaders of Gilded Age society.

THE LATE NINETEENTH CENTURY was a fertile period for the invention of holidays. In the 1860s Civil War veterans created Memorial Day and Confederate Memorial Day, while African Americans and Radical Republicans invented a variety of emancipation holidays. Labor unions created Labor Day in the 1880s, and immigrants introduced a variety of ethnic holidays. As these holidays suggest, public celebrations in this period showcased both the diversity and the tensions of American cities. In Chicago, one of the most ethnically diverse and conflict-ridden of those cities, immigrants, African Americans, labor unions, socialists, and Civil War veterans each commemorated their own holidays by the 1880s. Even the Fourth of July, rather than uniting Chicagoans, had fragmented into dozens of picnics, races and games, dances, parades, speeches, and fireworks displays. Chicago had not even sponsored a common celebration for the nation's centennial in 1876, leaving this to the city's Irish and German immigrants.[2] Moreover, commercial excursions, amusements, and sporting events increasingly offered attractive alternatives to public celebrations of the Fourth and other holidays.

Civic-minded business and professional men viewed the fragmented and commercialized celebrations of the late nineteenth century as symptomatic of the anarchy they believed threatened Chicago. They determined to address this problem by transforming patriotic holidays into vehicles for the creation of urban order and unity. They found the antidote to the chaos they perceived around them in law and order patriotism, and they concluded that public celebrations of patriotic holidays might furnish the perfect occasions for the civic and patriotic education necessary to transform immigrants and recalcitrant workers into good citizens and loyal Americans. As the sponsors of such exercises, these self-proclaimed civic elites could script them in order to construct a patriotism based on law and order and civic duty, which would transcend the ethnic, racial, class, and sectional loyalties that they viewed as threatening the nation's health.[3]

Between 1889 and 1909 a cohort of civic-minded financiers, merchants, and manufacturers in Chicago organized huge public events to commemorate the centennial of George Washington's inauguration, the quadricentennial of Christopher Columbus's arrival in America, and the centennial of Abraham Lincoln's birth. It was no accident that these efforts began in earnest in 1887. On May 4, 1886, a rally of strikers in Chicago's Haymarket Square had been disrupted by a bomb that sparked a police assault on the crowd and ended in the deaths of several officers and civilians. For civic elites this "murder" of police officers at Haymarket provided proof of the lawlessness and anarchy of the labor movement, as well as the potential threat posed by unassimilated immigrants. To elites Haymarket symbolized the anarchy that ensued from unrestrained liberty. They began their holiday campaign shortly thereafter.

Taking the leading role in the Chicago effort to spread the message of law and order through holiday celebrations was the Union League Club. One of the city's most exclusive clubs, it had been founded in 1879, spurred by political corruption and the railroad strike of 1877, in order "to encourage and promote by moral, social and political influence, unconditioned loyalty to the Federal Government, and . . . to inculcate a higher appreciation of the value and sacred obligations of American citizenship." Its members constituted a cross-section of the city's most prominent men. They were financiers and attorneys, presidents of banks, heads of merchandising and manufacturing concerns, investors in real estate, and traders in commodities. Contemporaries hailed them as self-made men and representative citizens. They took as active an interest in the development of their city as they did in their businesses. Member Charles L. Hutchinson, for instance, president of the Corn Exchange Bank and the Chicago Board of Trade, had many and varied civic and philanthropic concerns. He sat on the board of directors of the University of Chicago and served as a trustee of the Chicago Orphans' Asylum, and he was president of the Art Institute and superintendent of St. Paul's Universalist Sunday School. A biographer of banker Elbridge Keith, who served as president of the ULC, noted that he was "always prominent in benevolent work, and actively interested in anything tending to the benefit of Chicago and good citizenship generally."[4]

Self-conscious civic leaders such as Hutchinson considered themselves not only well-qualified but duty-bound to educate other Chicagoans, particularly the largely immigrant working class, in patriotic Americanism and good citizenship. Without a doubt their motives were self-serving. If working-class Chicagoans could be won over to the Union League Club's vision of patriotic citizenship, they would form a more compliant workforce. This does not mean, however, that the men of the ULC were not sincere in their conviction that their version of patriotism and citizenship was the correct one. On the contrary, they believed sincerely that disorder threatened the health of the city and the republic and that they could offer a solution.[5]

The Union League Club ushered in its campaign of civic and patriotic education with its 1887 Washington's Birthday celebration. George Washington, the American exemplar of civic virtue, provided a fitting vehicle for both patriotic education and national unity. The first president, according to a ULC orator, "had been selected by the world as a supreme civic representative of virtue" and was thus "an ideal public man." Speaking at the club's Washington banquet that year, writer James Russell Lowell urged members to vote for the "political statesman" rather than the politician and to break the "absolute slavery to party" that corrupted American politics and made politicians the slaves of their ignorant constituents. "The duty of the more intelligent," Lowell warned, "is to govern the less intelligent." This duty was construed in racial and ethnic terms as well; Lowell asserted that the United States would "last just so long as the traditions of the men of English descent who founded it are dominant there."[6]

The challenge to the men of the Union League Club was how to create an electorate that would put the political statesman in office. They found their answer in holiday civics lessons. Two years later Jacob Cox addressed the public at the club's Washington exercises. Claiming that the recent "anarchist outbreak" in Chicago "was simply an outburst of European methods among men who lacked the qualities which make an American citizen," Cox warned that immigrants must assimilate to Anglo-American civic values. "The perpetuity of our freedom," he argued, "depend[s] upon assimilating to the native American type the new elements which immigration adds to our population."[7]

Members of the Union League Club believed that their financial success and concern with the public good, as demonstrated by their cultural and civic philanthropy, qualified them to dictate the terms of that assimilation and justified their claim to the mantle of Washington and political statesmanship. Their

Washington celebrations featured public lectures on citizenship by men like themselves, prominent in business, finance, government, and letters. By 1889 the club was congratulating itself on the fruit borne by these exercises, which were, proclaimed president George Bissell, "more and more becoming the instrumentalities out from which the best thoughts of our public men flow into our political and social currents, and thus become creators of public opinion, and encouragements to higher citizenship."[8]

That same year the Union League Club embarked on a much more ambitious undertaking, that of organizing a massive citywide celebration for the centennial of Washington's inauguration. If annual commemorations of Washington's Birthday were a good way to educate the public, the centennial provided the opportunity for a veritable feast of civic education. At a February meeting the club members resolved to celebrate the centennial on April 30 "by organizing as many gatherings as can be arranged for satisfactorily, of Americans, whether native or foreign born, who are devoted to the Constitution of the United States and to Republican institutions — to liberty regulated by law." The club heralded the inauguration of the new government under the Constitution as "the real birth of the United States, as a nation." Although the Declaration of Independence had been a great milestone in national history, the ULC claimed that "it was surpassed by the affirmative act which made us a constitutional government and united people."[9]

It was not surprising that the businessmen of the Union League Club, fearful of revolt from their employees, focused on the establishment of the government of laws under the Constitution and the first president, rather than on the act of revolution embodied in the Declaration of Independence. The secretary of the executive committee even proposed that the inaugural celebration would provide a badly needed corrective to the excessive liberties of the Fourth of July. The Fourth, he explained, "is a day calculated to arouse enthusiasm for independence . . . a day for the removing of barriers, a day that is understood too much by the children . . . as a day for license, freedom from law and restriction." In contrast, celebrating the anniversary of Washington's inauguration would "give emphasis to our Constitution, to creation rather than destruction, . . . to rejoice not that we have thrown off the yoke of England, but that we are a nation with national ideas and a history."[10]

To arrange the celebration, club members created a planning committee of seventeen men who constituted a cross-section of the city's elite, including

Hutchinson and another bank president, Mayor John A. Roche, three attorneys, two judges, and four heads of manufacturing or merchandising concerns. The planning committee enlisted the support of a broad spectrum of middle- and upper-class Chicagoans by inviting them to serve on a larger general executive committee and fourteen additional committees, ranging from the committee on the school celebration to the committee on pyrotechnics. Small businessmen, newspapermen, attorneys, clergymen, bankers, and school officials (including the only three female committee members) dominated the membership of these committees, along with a sprinkling of clerks and salesmen. Working-class Chicagoans were conspicuous by their absence.[11]

As testament to the celebration's assimilative goal, a number of ethnic businessmen and journalists sat on the planning committees. The committee of seventeen had deliberately enlarged the executive committee in order to enlist "the cooperation of representative citizens of foreign birth or extraction." These representatives included journalists such as Alex Mastrovalerio, editor of *L'Italia,* and Herman Raster, editor of *Illinois Staats Zeitung,* as well as businessmen such as Peter Kiolbassa. At a meeting on February 11, Samuel Allerton, chairman of the executive committee, suggested the ULC's agenda when he told these men that the committee hoped "that there may be awakened in you, . . . that patriotic sentiment which will move you to go to your own people and say to them: 'It is time for us to become Americans,' which will inspire you to teach your children the American patriot's love for the Stars and Stripes, the emblem of liberty."[12]

Involving the entrepreneurs and intelligentsia of both the native- and foreign-born population in the centennial planning was only one step in ensuring the celebration's popularity. To reach the city's religious believers, the organizers enlisted clergymen to lead religious services and to serve as orators at the schools and meeting halls. The organizers established a committee to arouse interest in the celebration across the entire region, hoping to spur commemorations in other towns. Rather than rely on the largesse of wealthy men, the executive committee decided to raise the $25,000 necessary for the celebration in small subscriptions from the populace, "thereby cementing their interest in the celebration" by making every subscriber a "shareholder" in the enterprise. Despite this rhetoric, most of the money probably came from the middle and upper classes, and from businesses. The finance committee had subcommittees for virtually every type of business in the city, from laundries, candy makers, and meat markets to the Board of Trade, bankers, and "capitalists."[13]

The Union League Club had resolved early in the planning stages to secure the "participation of all, young and old, native and foreign-born, in commemorations and exercises which would tend to develop interest in national life and quicken patriotic impulses." Organizers appealed to working-class Chicagoans by encouraging their employers to give them a holiday; there was even a "committee on suspension of business." The planning committee took particular pains to involve the city's schoolchildren in the centennial, following Plato in reasoning that "in the warmth and enthusiasm of youth are found the best soil for planting the seeds of patriotism." The school celebration committee recruited teachers to teach their students patriotic songs and recitations, assign patriotic essays, and give "daily lessons in the constitutional and political history of our country," so that the children might participate actively in the celebration. To appeal to the diverse population of the city's schools, the speakers committee invited local ethnic and African American leaders to speak at the school exercises. The day's main orators included Chicago rabbi E. G. Hirsch and Congressman John Mercer Langston, Virginia's first elected black congressional representative. The program committees involved the populace in the mass meetings by offering them resolutions to approve, by recruiting volunteers rather than professionals for the choruses, and by picking popular patriotic tunes that the crowd could sing. The committee on decorations encouraged people to decorate their homes and businesses appropriately and patriotically for the occasion. Finally, organizers appealed to the popular love of spectacle by providing evening fireworks displays. There was only one constituency whose cooperation the ULC did not actively solicit, and that was organized labor. Not surprisingly, given the anti-union views of club members, no labor representatives sat on the celebration committees, and the program did not include a trades procession.[14]

The program that the executive committee developed, under the ULC's guidance, was a masterwork of civic education. The club directed that "speakers should not only unfold the Constitution before their hearers, but that *patriotism* itself be *defined,* as a comprehensive term embracing most of the duties incident to our relation to society as well as to government." Religious services, mass meetings of citizens, school exercises, and fireworks displays were the means the organizers chose to inculcate in Chicagoans the proper spirit of patriotism. The instruction began in the churches. Some thirty local churches held special services on April 30, replete with patriotic songs and sermons on the importance of religion in America's development. Pictures of Washington and U.S. flags served as visual inspiration to the congregations. Following the church services came exercises in the city's public and private schools. After flag-raising ceremonies at each school, students and their parents gathered for programs of student recitations, original essays, and patriotic songs. The older children listened to addresses by business and professional men on Washington's life and patriotism. Before heading home, each student received a souvenir medal of the occasion, the better "to fix in their memories the lessons contained in the school exercises."[15]

Children and churchgoers were not the only targets for civic instruction. That afternoon an estimated one hundred thousand adults attended nine mass meetings organized by the planners. To provide the proper patriotic atmosphere, the meeting places had been decorated profusely with flags and bunting, flowers, wreaths, and portraits of Washington. Although Chicago's population was too large to permit one celebration, the ULC did its best to ensure that all participants had the same experience. The program at each meeting was the same, the simultaneity of the exercises replicating the goal of national unity. At three o'clock each chairman called his meeting to order with a brief address and then turned the floor over to the chaplain, who led the audience in a prayer of thanksgiving. A band then played national airs and a volunteer chorus led the audience in song. The chairman next read regrets from "prominent men" who could not attend Chicago's celebration, to impress upon the audience the importance of the occasion. After this he read a series of resolutions for the day, which the crowd approved by acclamation. Finally, two orators at each meeting delivered speeches on the history of American liberty, Washington's patriotism, and the wisdom of the Constitution. To close the exercises, the chorus and audience sang "America," including a special "centennial stanza."[16]

That evening the Union League Club hosted a banquet for the orators and distinguished guests, while the populace attended three fireworks displays, which gave final imprint, in visually spectacular form, to the patriotic lessons of the day. Some four hundred thousand Chicagoans exclaimed at set pieces that included the Capitol, "its dome a scintillating ball of white flames"; the word "America," in every shade of the rainbow; Washington's head, "as large as the sphinx"; and the first president taking the oath of office. The elites, sated with good food and wine, and the people, sated with gunpowder and pyrotechnics, finally called a halt to the centennial festivities near midnight.[17]

In the aftermath of the celebration, members of the Union League Club congratulated themselves on the success of their brainchild. Member Joseph

Medill's *Chicago Tribune,* for example, proclaimed that the event demonstrated "the deep patriotic sentiment of the people, . . . [and] their devotion to the National Union." And well they should congratulate themselves. In the space of three short months, the men of the ULC had developed a celebration for the inaugural centennial that spread their version of law and order patriotism to a large portion of Chicago's population. They had announced that they intended that the centennial should "awaken the people to a realizing sense of the blessings they enjoy under free institutions . . . [and] serve to kindle anew the fires of patriotism." The organizers, led by the ULC, had carefully designed the day's exercises and instructed speakers to define this patriotism as liberty regulated by law.[18]

According to the men of the Union League Club, the most important duty of citizenship was obedience to the law, and the importance of the Constitution lay in its check on liberty. In their view, unregulated liberty led to license and anarchy; in contrast, regulated liberty brought progress and prosperity. In keeping with the theme of liberty under law, most of the orators at the day's mass meetings were representatives of authority, either governmental or religious. The eighteen speakers included former mayor Carter H. Harrison, two judges, six clergymen, two congressmen, the county superintendent of schools, a professor, and an attorney. Rev. S. J. McPherson, a Presbyterian, echoed this sentiment at one of the mass meetings, proclaiming that "the two ruling ideas of American history are liberty and order." Rabbi E. G. Hirsch, speaking at another meeting, found the difference between French and American notions of liberty to be instructive. Whereas the French Constitution did nothing to control public passions, he explained, "liberty according to the American idea is always wedded to law and to responsibility." Even the members of the Union League Club were not released from this instruction. Although they hardly needed reminding, Supreme Court justice John Harlan told them at their banquet not to "forget that the liberty for which our fathers fought is liberty secured and regulated by law, not the liberty of mere license."[19]

Orators provided their listeners with vivid examples of the liberty of license. Hon. Peter Hendrickson informed the audience at one mass meeting that "the five years from 1783 to 1788 are the saddest and darkest in our history" and rejoiced that the ordered liberty of the Constitution had put an end to the anarchy of the Articles of Confederation. Other speakers referred to the Confederacy as another example of the lawlessness unleashed when the Constitution was ignored and states' rights placed above the federal union. But labor strife, which weighed most heavily on the businessmen and financiers who organized the celebration, served as the chief illustration of the anarchy brought on by unregulated liberty. American workers had no cause for discontent, J. M. Thurston told Chicagoans at another mass meeting, for the United States was "the only country where labor is fairly paid; where the industrious working man, out of the accumulated savings of his daily toil, can pay for the pleasant home in which he lives and send his children to the public schools." Thurston warned that anarchists and other dissenters were not welcome in America. "The government of the people," he thundered, "must never be endangered by the dissemination of those monstrous theories which would overturn all government for anarchy and subvert all society to the dominion of unbridled passion and brute force." One could never learn this lesson too young. Thomas Cratty instructed the students of Scammon Elementary School in their duty to root out such dissent. "Revere our flag, love it," he exhorted them. "If any little one should see anyone disrespectful to our flag, place your little fist under his nose and say 'stop.' . . . [I]f you see the flag of anarchy, socialism, or communism, stamp on it, tear it down and trample it in the dust."[20]

The centennial organizers thought it particularly important to teach these lessons to immigrants, who had not been reared in the "ordered liberty" of the United States. Immigrants received the message that those willing to Americanize were welcome; those who were not could return to Europe. Thurston asserted that "no man must be permitted to profane the sanctuary of liberty with his unholy presence who does not subscribe with his whole heart and soul to the tenets of our Constitution." L. D. Thoman cautioned that citizenship should not be granted indiscriminately: "The American republic should no longer confer citizenship without some evidence that the honor is being worthily bestowed." This evidence, Thoman believed, should include an understanding of the Declaration of Independence and the Constitution. Rev. David Utter was more blunt, informing students at Harrigan School that it was time to close the doors: "We do not need any more people now from foreign lands." For the most part, however, the civic elite remained optimistic about immigrants' capacity to assimilate, given the will and the proper civic instruction. "Our nation is an empire of immigrants," Judge Richard Prendergast proclaimed at one mass meeting. "The republic was founded . . . for every man who was born upon this continent or who would come to these shores willing to assume and to discharge the duties of citizenship."[21]

As befitted a celebration organized by the city's business leaders, orators also made sure that Chicagoans understood the prominent role of commerce and industry in the progress of the nation in its first century of liberty under law. Peter Hendrickson argued that if the Constitution was the central pillar of the nation, the invention of the steam engine was the second: "The Federal Constitution and the steam engine are the great twin products of Anglo-Saxon intelligence and enterprise." The morning addresses at the schools were made "by men who had won distinction in professional and commercial life," whom the Union League Club considered to be particularly appropriate to demonstrate to the city's youth "the beauties of a government of the people, for the people, and by the people."[22]

Despite the large audiences who heard the Union League Club's version of patriotism and liberty under law on the Washington inaugural centennial, it is difficult to assess whether Chicagoans took to heart the intended lessons. Although the attendance at the mass meetings was higher than for most Chicago celebrations, it nevertheless comprised only about 15 percent of the city's adult population, which meant that the majority of Chicagoans either had to work or had found other things to do on their holiday. The existing records unfortunately leave few clues as to the composition of the crowds at the mass meetings, making it almost impossible to ascertain how many workers and immigrants actually took part.[23]

Certainly the day's patriotic lessons did not end labor strife or socialism in Chicago. A German-language socialist paper reported that "[m]any American workers undisturbed tended their business," rather than attend the meetings, perhaps because their employers refused to give them a holiday. The article claimed disdainfully that the only people celebrating were "the native rowdies, who were lacking enthusiasm because the wealthy failed to fill them up with brandy," and "the newly immigrated, who wandered around . . . and vainly looked for something which would appear to them more beautiful and grand than similar things in their respective home-country." The paper was particularly scathing in its criticism of the school exercises for "stuffing the brains of our dear youth with patent-patriotism."[24]

Nor did the exercises convince many immigrants that assimilation should proceed on elite terms. The Union League Club reported that the ethnic members of the executive committee had decisively vetoed a proposal to have separate meetings for immigrants, but German military and fraternal organizations, apparently dismayed by the lack of a procession, staged their own through the downtown streets. And the city's Czech community sponsored exercises that followed the official program but gave all the leading roles to Czechs, undermining the ULC's Americanization message by suggesting that they could be good Americans while remaining loyal Czechs. Moreover, some school exercises were apparently conducted in foreign languages. At the Polk Street School, for instance, Italian children listened to speeches in their native tongue, while a private German-English school featured exercises in both languages. At the latter school the German and American colors intertwined and Henry Frick, a proprietor, countered the ULC's implication that immigrants had little to offer America by telling students that "the virtue of patriotism [was] inherent in the German character." Frick pointed to Revolutionary War heroes General John Peter Muhlenberg, Baron Friedrich Wilhelm von Steuben, and General Baron Johan DeKalb as evidence that Germans had played a key role in establishing the American nation and government.[25]

The role of African Americans in establishing and preserving the American union also got short shrift at the celebration, and black Chicagoans doubtlessly listened with skepticism to the paeans to law and order patriotism and the Constitution that had permitted slavery. One of the Union League Club's invited speakers used his platform to dissent from the organizers' lily-white version of American history. Congressman John Mercer Langston had worked as an abolitionist, aided fugitive slaves in Ohio, helped to assemble the Fifty-Fourth Massachusetts Volunteer Infantry Regiment during the Civil War, led postbellum campaigns for black suffrage, established Howard University's law school, and served as consul-general in Haiti and as president of a black college in Virginia before winning his seat in Virginia's delegation to the U.S. Congress, where he continued to fight for black rights in the face of emerging segregation and disfranchisement laws. Langston was thus keenly aware of the struggle waged by African Americans for their liberty and political rights in America. Although he acknowledged the importance of the Constitution in his centennial oration, he challenged the Union League Club's disdain for the Declaration of Independence. Indeed, he cast his vote for the latter as the preeminent document in American history. "The animating principle of our government, its inspiring and controlling spirit," Langston insisted adamantly to his Chicago audience, "is defined in the immortal words of the Declaration: 'We hold these truths to be self-evident; that all men are created equal.'"[26]

Although limited, this evidence of dissenting and alternative views suggests that while the Union League Club carefully designed the Washington inaugural centennial exercises to speak to as many of Chicago's diverse inhabitants as possible, the results were mixed. The centennial organizers found perhaps the most fertile ground for civic instruction in the schools, echoing Plato in explaining that "the youthful mind is the proper place to inculcate lessons of virtue and wisdom" because "it is in a state of receptivity." Unlike adults, who could choose whether or not to attend a mass meeting or church service, schoolchildren provided the ULC with a captive audience. Organizers resolved to continue the education begun on the centennial by establishing "a course of education in our public schools, to fill the minds of our children with a knowledge of our history and with a veneration for our great men." This civic education, they argued, would make the student into a patriotic adult who would "respect the laws" and "love his country." Such patriotism, organizers claimed, would ultimately serve an assimilative function, "obliterat[ing] the line of nationality."[27]

The Union League Club made good on its resolution to develop civic education in the schools. In 1890 the club added a children's program to its annual Washington's Birthday exercises. Some nine thousand schoolchildren attended exercises in the Auditorium and Central Music Hall, where they sang patriotic songs, including a special "Ode to Washington" penned by the superintendent of schools, and listened to speeches defining the first president's virtues. Rev. Dr. H. W. Bolton, for instance, recounted a string of anecdotes that illuminated the young George's studious habits and obedience to his mother. Rev. Martin L. Williston presented a stereopticon lecture with scenes of Washington's career and the Revolution. Williston himself exemplified the ULC's message of liberty under law. He served as secretary of the fledgling Society of Patriotic Knowledge, which "taught a boy to say: 'I will be obedient to the laws of the school and the laws of the state.'" In 1895 the Union League Club moved its school celebration of Washington's Birthday to the city's schools, in a bid to reach a larger percentage of the student population. The club retained sponsorship and control of the school celebrations, distributing song sheets and supplying orators to the schools. As a further stimulus to this program of civic education, club member Joseph Medill's *Chicago Tribune* in 1900 offered cash prizes and published the ten best student essays on George Washington.[28]

The seed of patriotism planted in the Washington inaugural centennial, then, arguably bore its best fruit in Chicago's schools, with their captive and malleable audience. The Union League Club, joined by school officials and such patriotic organizations as the Sons and Daughters of the Revolution, the Grand Army of the Republic, the Society of Patriotic Knowledge, and the American Flag Day Association, had established civics instruction as a fixture in the nation's public schools by the turn of the twentieth century, inculcating in schoolchildren their vision of law and order patriotism on Washington's Birthday as well as other holidays.[29]

The hearts and minds of their parents proved more difficult to win, however. Immigrants and African Americans were often eager to pledge their loyalty, but they did so on their own terms, asserting their rights to full citizenship without necessarily subscribing to the Union League Club's restrictive definition of patriotic Americanism. Organized labor similarly proclaimed its patriotism while it fought for the rights of workers against employers, including ULC members. Socialists condemned the ULC's brand of patriotism as a capitalist sham to keep workers enslaved. The bulk of Chicagoans demonstrated their indifference by simply staying away from the centennial exercises and subsequent celebrations. It is noteworthy that by far the largest attendance on the centennial came at the fireworks displays. While these may have been intended as visual reinforcement of the day's civic lessons, most of the spectators probably came for the sheer spectacle and entertainment value. The George Washington inaugural centennial and its aftermath, in sum, reveal both the efforts of the new civic elite to legitimize its power in the city and the limits of that power. Although members of the Union League Club, along with other self-professed civic leaders in Chicago, organized similarly massive and inclusive civic celebrations for the Columbian quadricentennial in 1892 and the centennial of Abraham Lincoln's birth in 1909, the city's diverse constituencies continued to participate in such events in their own way and on their own terms.[30]

Notes

Portions of this essay are adapted from my book *America's Public Holidays*, 148–64.

1. *Chicago Tribune*, Feb. 23, 1887; Douglas, *The American Book of Days*, 460; "Constitution Day," *Century*, December 1887, 327.

2. Litwicki, *America's Public Holidays*, 151; Litwicki, "'Our Hearts Burn with Ardent

Love for Two Countries,'" 3–4. On the fragmentation and development of holidays in this period, see Litwicki, *America's Public Holidays.*

3. On the formation of the late-nineteenth-century elite, see Baltzell, *The Protestant Establishment,* 1–21, 110–39. On the reshaping of public behavior in this period, see Boyer, *Urban Masses and Moral Order,* 121–87; Levine, *Highbrow Lowbrow,* 184–200; Bennett, *The Birth of the Museum,* 27–28, 51–53; Gilbert, *Perfect Cities,* 28–40.

4. *The Chicago Clubs Illustrated* (Chicago: Lanward Publishing Co., 1888), 55. Biographical information found in John J. Flinn, ed., *The Hand-Book of Chicago Biography* (Chicago: Standard Guide Co., 1893), s.v. "Hutchinson, Charles"; "Chicago Biographies and Miscellaneous Articles from the *Chicago Tribune* 1900–01," bound typescript, Newberry Library, Chicago; *The Biographical Dictionary and Portrait Gallery of Representative Men of Chicago, Wisconsin, and the World's Columbian Exposition* (Chicago: American Biographical Publishing Co., 1895), s.v. "Keith, Elbridge." The cost of belonging to the Union League Club provides one indication of the wealth and status of its members. The initiation fee was two hundred dollars and annual dues were eighty dollars. Only the exclusive Chicago Club, a social organization, was more expensive.

5. Smith, *Urban Disorder and the Shape of Belief,* 15. On the "civic-uplift" zeal that swept American cities in the 1890s, see Boyer, *Urban Masses and Moral Order,* 162–66.

6. *Chicago Tribune,* Feb. 23, 1887.

7. *Union League Club. Exercises in Commemoration of the Birthday of Washington, February 22, 1889* (Chicago: P. F. Pettibone & Co., 1889), 25–26.

8. Ibid., 49.

9. *The Nation's Birthday: Chicago's Centennial Celebration of Washington's Inauguration. April 30, 1889* (Chicago: Slason Thompson & Co., 1890), 4–5, 11.

10. Ibid., 21.

11. All the committees and their members were listed in ibid., 317–25. Occupational data was located for 386 of the 476 committee members in *The Lakeside Directory of Chicago, 1889* (Chicago: Chicago Directory Co., 1889).

12. *The Nation's Birthday,* 6–7.

13. Ibid., 9–10. The book does not provide an accounting of individual subscribers, making it impossible to tell how many small subscriptions came from working-class or ethnic Chicagoans.

14. Ibid., 8, 101, 104–7; *Chicago Tribune,* May 1, 1889.

15. *The Nation's Birthday,* 14, emphasis in original, 37, 16–17. For descriptions of the exercises held in various schools, see ibid., 107–53; and *Chicago Tribune,* May 1, 1889.

16. *The Nation's Birthday,* 159–68.

17. Ibid., 285–86; *Chicago Tribune,* May 1, 1889.

18. *Chicago Tribune,* May 1, 1889; *The Nation's Birthday,* 14–15.

19. *The Nation's Birthday,* 176, 211, 248–49, 258. Occupational data on speakers was determined from their titles and from *The Lakeside Directory, 1889.*

20. *The Nation's Birthday,* 131, 143, 183–84, 243.

21. Ibid., 137, 183, 199, 214.

22. Ibid., 245, 106.

23. Chicago's total population in 1890 was 1,099,850. Adult population (21 and over) was estimated at about 60 percent of the total, based on figures from *School Census of the City of Chicago, 1884* and *Report of the School Census Taken May, 1908.*

24. *Chicagoer Arbeiter-Zeitung,* May 1, 1889, in the Chicago Public Library Omnibus Project, comp. and trans., *The Chicago Foreign Language Press Survey* (Chicago, 1942), section III, B.3, "Holidays."

25. *The Nation's Birthday,* 146, 153; *Chicago Tribune,* May 1 and 2, 1889.

26. *The Nation's Birthday,* 237. Biographical information on Langston, an Oberlin College graduate, found at Oberlin College Archives, "John Mercer Langston (1829–1897)," http://www.oberlin.edu/external/EOG/OYTT-images/JMLangston.html. On other Langston speeches, also see Litwicki, *America's Public Holidays,* 58, 60–61.

27. *The Nation's Birthday,* 21, 101–2, 104, 167.

28. *Chicago Tribune,* Feb. 23, 1890, Feb. 23, 1895, and Feb. 22 and 23, 1900; *Union League Club. Exercises in Commemoration of the Birthday of Washington, Februrary 22, 1890* (Chicago: S. A. Maxwell, 1890).

29. On civic education, see O'Leary, *To Die For,* 172–93; Litwicki, *America's Public Holidays,* 174–90; Hemenway, "An Analysis of Civic Education."

30. On these celebrations, see Litwicki, *America's Public Holidays,* 164–74.

RICHARD M. SOMMER AND GLENN FORLEY

The Democratic Monument

The Reframing of History as Heritage

THE NOTION that monuments are the most explicit physical manifestation of cultural heritage has become commonplace in the United States. Yet, the emergence of the term "heritage" to describe the selective preservation, reconstruction, or fabrication of artifacts from the past is itself historical. As David Lowenthal has pointed out, modern conceptions of heritage are no longer circumscribed by familial acts of inheritance and tradition but rather are a part of popular culture.[1] Paradoxically, in the United States this more popular notion of heritage is based in the material culture of what had been the domain of "traditional heritage"— in house museums of notable individuals, in period rooms highlighting original furnishings, and in restoration villages offering a "living history." History, in turn, has become more hermeneutic and self-conscious about questioning received ideas, ranging from Eric Hobsbawm's writings on the invention of tradition to the museum installations of Fred Wilson. In societies aspiring toward democracy, especially those like the United States whose populations are ethnically diverse and are characterized by high rates of immigration, the oscillation between contention and consensus around which aspects of the past are shared can be reformulated as the distinction between history and heritage. History-making begins by opening the past to scrutiny. Heritage, as Lowenthal notes, makes the past familiar and consumable. The monument is the medium, and monument-making is the process through which not only to measure the vagaries that exist between history and heritage but also to understand the consequences of substituting one for the other.

In what follows, we will examine a period in American history, specifically the emergence of the Cold War, when monuments and monument-making are acutely put in the service of reframing the past as heritage. By monument, we refer to a very broad spectrum of objects and landscapes, from permanent, figurative constructions such as built landmarks and geological formations to trails or sustained events that cover large territories. By expanding the definition of monument to include landscapes, trails, and events alongside more figurative objects, we are acknowledging the tension that exists in American culture between the redemptive possibilities and exceptional nature of the open landscape and the civilizing pedagogy of the civic monument, and how this has changed the very identity of the monument in recent history. More specifically, we will be exploring relationships between two midcentury "monuments": the 1949 proposal for Independence Mall, a three-block-long greensward framing Independence Hall, and the 1947 tour of the Freedom Train, a traveling exhibit of original and facsimile documents central to American history.

As monument-making schemes, Independence Mall and the Freedom Train depended on Cold War notions of American exceptionalism. This version of exceptionalism promoted concepts such as liberty and freedom as the rights and obligations of the individual citizen rather than as a collective entitlement as they had been during the New Deal. During the Cold War, the notion of an American heritage supplanted history by supporting an exceptionalist view of the United States, one that emphasized the nation's revolutionary origins as the birthright of each citizen. Although highly individualist conceptions of freedom were already an aspect of the laissez-faire industrial economies of the nineteenth century, the Cold War period saw a new equation of freedom with liberal capitalism, merged into an all-purpose notion of "free enterprise." At this time, the free (pursuit of) enterprise promoted the American way of life and galvanized opposition to totalitarian and communist regimes.

Independence Mall

During World War II, a group of civic leaders in Philadelphia promoted the scheme for the Independence National Historical Park and its centerpiece, Independence Mall. The professed purpose of the park was to highlight buildings and sites associated with Philadelphia's role as the "Cradle of Liberty" during the Revolutionary period. The plan proposed to raze three city blocks in the Olde City to create the mall, the focal point of which was Independence Hall, formerly the Pennsylvania State House.

The circumstances surrounding the creation of Independence Mall illustrate the symbiotic relationship between an emerging historical preservation movement and ever-escalating modes of modernization. The rise of historic preservation movements in the United States (as elsewhere) assuaged feelings of loss and nostalgia that came in the wake of convulsive cultural changes brought by modern industrialization. During the antebellum period, particularly in growing mercantile cities such as Philadelphia, there was little consciousness of a shared national history. Following the Civil War, political faction, rapid industrialization, and mass immigration qualified efforts to stabilize the country through invoking national unity. One attempt to find common origins around which to unify the country was the effort to raise and promote public interest in the American Revolution and the country's shared colonial past.

In Philadelphia, public interest in the colonial past centered on the State House complex, known since the early nineteenth century as Independence Hall. As the site of the first Continental Congress, the signing of the Declaration of Independence, the framing of the United States Constitution, and prior to its move to Washington, D.C., the Capitol of the United States, the importance of the State House complex to the history of the nation's first, formative years only started to be understood early in the nineteenth century. Yet, the State House was not established as a historic site at this time. It remained an active public building until the end of the nineteenth century. Following the transfer of the state capital to Harrisburg, Pennsylvania, the State House complex functioned as Philadelphia's City Hall and the state's federal courts. From 1802 to 1828, the State House lodged the first public Museum of Natural History in the United States, established by the painter Charles Willson Peale.[2] Moreover, areas near Independence Hall were active sites of intellectual debate and sometimes-violent political and social clashes. For example, in 1838 a group of abolitionists raised funds to build Pennsylvania Hall. It was built approximately three blocks from Independence Hall along Sixth Street (now part of the mall) specifically to facilitate the exercise of free speech on issues related to slavery. Pennsylvania Hall's proximity to Independence Hall exposed the hypocrisy in the state and federal governments' refusals to either take up the question of slavery or to allow such debates to occur in Independence Hall. In an expression of growing hostility toward the group of abolitionists behind the erection of Pennsylvania Hall, a group in which both women and African Americans took, for that time, unusually public roles, a mob torched the building three days after it was opened. While saving nearby buildings, Philadelphia's fire brigade allowed Pennsylvania Hall to burn down. The construction of Pennsylvania Hall, its short life of sponsoring protest, and its torching are as much a part of the history of the mall site as are better-known Revolutionary events.[3]

Although Charles Willson Peale had already stated in the early 1800s that Independence Hall would be "a building more interesting in the history of the world, than any of the celebrated fabrics of Greece and Rome!" the building did not begin to emerge as a true shrine until after the much-heralded visit of the Marquis de Lafayette to Philadelphia in 1824.[4] The marquis's tour of the city included a reception in the State House's Assembly Room redecorated as a "Hall of Independence." Thereafter the entire State House building began to be regarded as "Independence Hall." This shift in perception precipitated a series of projects to "restore" the hall and its outbuildings and square to their condition at the time of the American Revolution. These projects gathered momentum leading up to the 1876 centennial celebration of American independence.[5]

MEASURING THE MOTIVATION for, and effect of Independence Mall, brings into play the difference between history and heritage — that is, the difference between a shifting and a fixed view of the past. The history of Independence Hall is bound up with the material and social history of Philadelphia, which from its inception was influenced by both the utopian and pragmatic aspects of William Penn's plan for the city. When the Pennsylvania State House was built in the early 1730s, it occupied a very different city from the one William Penn envisioned just a half century prior. In Penn's vision, Philadelphia was to have been a "wholesome . . . green country town": a "holy experiment" in religious tolerance combining the pastoral order of a seventeenth-century English gentleman's country farm with the market and communal functions of a city.[6] Penn's originating 1683 checkerboard plan, with its east–west orientation spanning two rivers, was consistent with his desire to balance utopian ideals with the exigencies of real estate and land governance (fig. 1). Nevertheless, the Pennsylvania State House and its yard were built at the western fringe of a typical colonial port town of crowded blocks with stately Georgian faces and haphazard, sometimes treacherous, alleys and mews. The practical orientation of the State House, with a south-facing yard and north-facing street elevation looking toward the city's later massive expansion to the north, stands in contrast to the east–west orientation of Penn's plan.

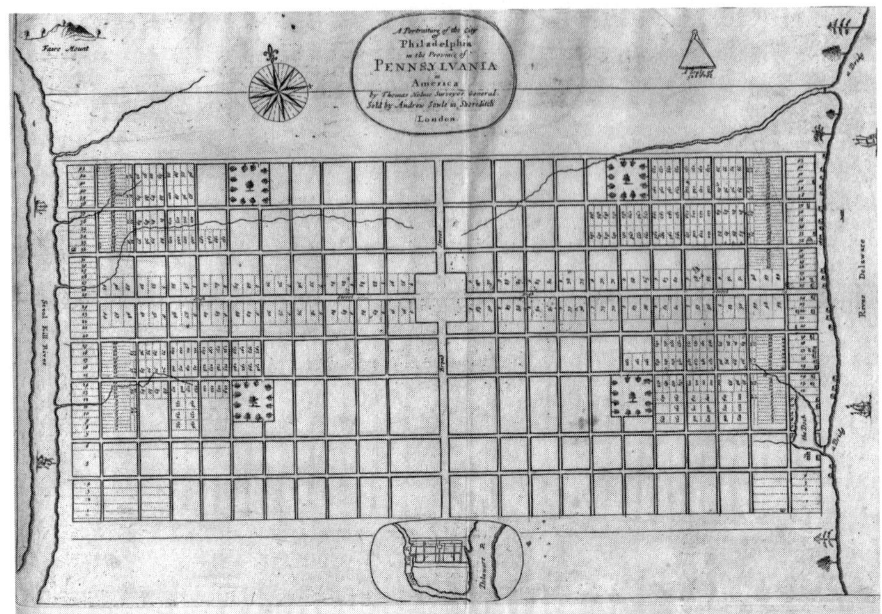

FIG. 1. *A Portraiture of the City of Philadelphia in the Province of Pennsylvania in America.* 48 × 33 cm. Sold by Andrew Sowle, Shoreditch London, (1683). (Haverford College Quaker and Special Collections, Haverford, PA)

Ironically, the nineteenth century brought both the realization and the eclipse of Penn's colonial plan. By the middle of the century, unbridled growth had allowed the city to reach its western riverfront. The city's five public squares, once relegated to dumping grounds and occasionally even omitted from city maps, reemerged as regulated civic open spaces, providing relief from a scale and density of development never anticipated by Penn. The preponderance and extension of the grid as a nineteenth-century planning device coincided with the consolidation, in 1854, of the various townships in Philadelphia County under one municipality. Spurred by the explosive growth of the Industrial Revolution, Philadelphia's population multiplied by thirty times over the course of the nineteenth century. Center City Philadelphia, though still understood as the core, was by the turn of the twentieth century just one-tenth of an expanding metropolis.

By 1900 Philadelphia had transformed radically from a walking city to a sprawling metropolis. The original colonial city at the eastern edge of Center City, which contained Independence Hall and the Liberty Bell, had become, in the eyes of many, ramshackle. Factories and other imposing structures from the nineteenth century overshadowed the remnants of the colonial period. Commercial and business interests that had once flourished there were moving westward. Like Penn's ideal plan, the colonial city and its State House appear to have been twice eclipsed: first, by the completion of Penn's colonial plan and the relocation of City Hall and commercial interests westward to Central (now Penn) Square, and second, but almost simultaneously, by the recasting of the entire city's geographic limits.

In the early 1900s, anticipating the city's role in the 1926 sesquicentennial of the American Revolution, Philadelphia undertook a series of ambitious urban planning projects. Two projects, the Fairmount (now Benjamin Franklin) Parkway and the Delaware (now Benjamin Franklin) Bridge drew on Beaux-Arts-derived planning principles of the City Beautiful movement. Although essentially transportation driven, these projects had the effect of creating two new monumental entryways into the city. The Fairmount Parkway prefigured Independence Mall by introducing the potential for large-scale development to renew a "blighted" sector of the city. The Fairmount Park Art Association as well as other civic and professional organizations conceived and supported both projects.[7]

After more than one hundred years of failed attempts to build a bridge that would span the Delaware River from Camden, New Jersey, to the eastern shore of Philadelphia, the growing use of the automobile precipitated the construction of the Delaware Bridge, which was completed in 1928. If the Fairmount Parkway established a planning precedent for the mall, the Delaware Bridge brought more direct traffic pressures to the Olde City, especially to the areas around Independence Hall. The massive landing of the bridge fell between Race and Vine Streets and ended in a plaza fronting one of Penn's original squares, now Franklin Square. Drawing twice as many cars as anticipated, the suspension bridge created a sweeping, panoramic aerial view of the colonial city, allowing visitors and Philadelphians to rise up from the labyrinth of the city's oldest precincts and view these areas as a whole, from the vantage of their early, maritime formation. The relentless car traffic and the visual scrutiny of the new automobile tourist created pressure to transform the area, particularly the precinct around Independence Hall.

Alongside Philadelphia's efforts to introduce infrastructural improvements, including the bridge and parkway constructions, was an emerging narrative of the city's central role within the nation's heritage. A surge in patriotism after World War I had increased the status and veneration of the Independence Hall complex and the Liberty Bell enshrined therein. Temporary viewing stands, constructed adjacent to Independence Hall on Chestnut Street, served the frequent patriotic parades, pageants, and rallies held there. A consequence of the increased use of the hall site was that the workaday uses, decaying condition, and eclectic architecture of the surrounding area came to the attention of the city fathers. They found the older buildings on Chestnut Street facing Independence Hall especially distasteful, and hoped to replace them with a plaza that would more permanently serve patriotic events. Between 1915 and the adaptation of an official park plan in the mid–1940s, approximately twelve plaza proposals emerged, with the architect Paul Cret's proposal being perhaps the most sophisticated.[8]

The idea to build a vast public green along the three blocks facing Independence Hall did not come from planners or architects such as Paul Cret but grew out of two other, more curious, influences. In 1928 Dr. Seneca Egbert, professor of hygiene at the University of Pennsylvania, conceived the scheme that most directly influenced the making of the mall. His proposal was apparently a response to a 1925 Philadelphia City Council proposal to abate traffic congestion at the Benjamin Franklin Bridge Plaza by diverting traffic from the plaza to Market Street through the creation of a grand boulevard, mid-block between Fifth and Sixth Streets. Egbert proposed "the development of a Concourse or Esplanade between Independence Hall and the plaza at the west end of the Delaware Bridge that should serve as a permanent and impressive Sesquicentennial memorial of the historic events incident to the founding of the nation."[9]

No drawing is known to exist of this scheme, but Egbert did draft an elaborate report outlining his proposals. Several aspects of the scheme he outlined were present in the plan finally implemented in the late 1940s. Egbert justified his boldest proposition to demolish three city blocks stretching from Independence Hall on Chestnut Street to the Bridge Plaza on Race Street — more than twenty acres — by citing a widely held fear that at any time a fire could consume one of the area's abandoned or dilapidated buildings and spread to Independence Hall or another cherished colonial edifice. His other influential proposals included the widening of Fifth and Sixth Streets to accommodate increased traffic from the bridge, the creation of a central pedestrian esplanade "possibly as broad as Broad Street," the creation of a plaza for events fronting Independence Hall, the accommodation of underground parking, and the building of a new subway stop.[10]

Perhaps even more influential than the physical proposals was Egbert's supposition that the new mall would raise tax revenues by increasing the assessed value of the three cleared blocks, resulting in an increase in the perceived value of adjacent properties and the district as a whole. Egbert also implied that the historic value of the Olde City could be mined to commercial advantage. To achieve a project of this magnitude, Egbert foresaw the need for a structure through which various state and city agencies could cooperate, a concept that anticipated the urban renewal scheme that allowed the mall to be built several decades later.

Before Philadelphia even considered building the mall envisioned by Egbert, replicas of Independence Hall had been set on vast greens in other parts of the United States. In the late 1920s, Henry Ford tried to purchase Independence Hall to make it the frontispiece for the Edison (later Ford) Museum he was building adjacent to Greenfield Village in Dearborn, Michigan. Competing with the Rockefellers' project of re-creating colonial Williamsburg, Ford was vying to assemble the most "real" replica of America's colonial and industrial past. When Philadelphia would not sell Independence Hall, Ford reproduced it and attached it to a shed with its back (yard-facing) tower elevation set against a public green (fig. 2). An exact-scale replica of Independence Hall was reproduced for the Pennsylvania Building at the New York World's Fair in 1939. At the fair, the replica of Independence Hall fronted the end of a grand axis of state buildings along a National Mall–like reflecting pool within the fair's "Government Zone." In these and numerous other civic buildings that more or less copy Independence Hall during this period, it is worth noting that the yard, rather than the street elevation of the original, is positioned as the symbolic front. This indicates how prior to the creation of the mall, the Chestnut Street elevation that now faces Independence Mall was considered by many to be secondary to the building's identity.

The outbreak of World War II and the bombing of Pearl Harbor brought a renewed interest in Independence Hall and the Liberty Bell as symbols of patriotism. Starting in 1941, Edwin O. Lewis, a charismatic, highly persuasive, well-connected judge and president of the Pennsylvania Society of the Sons of the Revolution, mounted a campaign to build the three-block-long mall that Egbert had envisioned. Lewis engaged Roy Larson, an architect and senior member

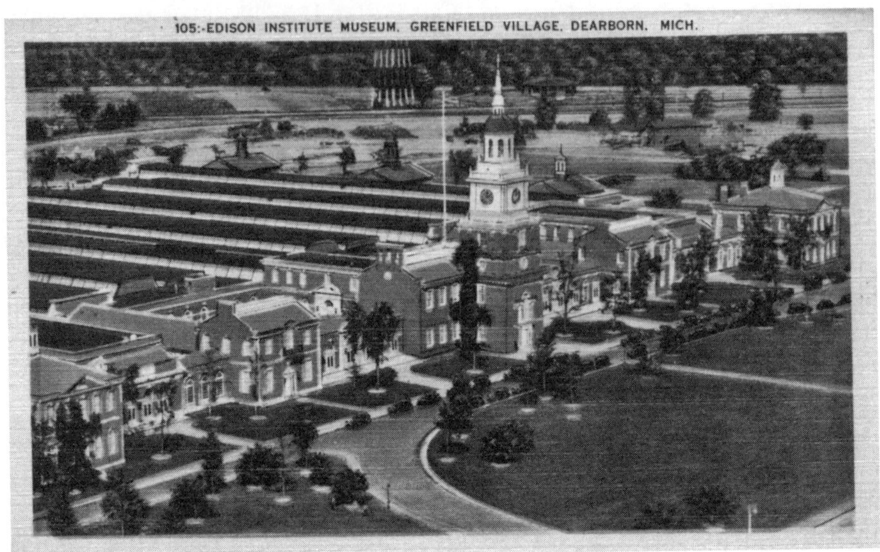

FIG. 2. Henry Ford Museum, Greenfield Village, Dearborn, Michigan, undated postcard. (Author's collection)

of Paul Cret's staff, to make the new plan. Mindful of the potential for federal support for the construction and management of the mall, Lewis conceived the project as a national park that eventually would include the entire complex of buildings associated with Independence Hall. Before Judge Lewis's commission, Larson had made a proposal in 1937 that cleared the three blocks north of Independence Hall and drew liberally from Egbert's scheme. Larson later revised his plan to have the park scheme include important historic structures on two partial blocks to the east of Independence Hall. This is the plan that was eventually implemented after the U.S. Congress approved the construction of the national park in 1949.[11]

In hindsight, it appears the mall was a critical element in a Faustian bargain made by Philadelphia's civic leaders to leverage the hallowed Independence Hall and the bell it houses — the shrines most central to the city's legend — to a wholesale reform of the colonial city. In the process, hundreds of buildings and businesses had to be taken by eminent domain and demolished, including the polychrome Guarantee Trust Company and the Provident Life & Trust Company Bank and Office Building designed by Frank Furness.[12] Before the formation of Independence Mall, this area's discrete set of colonial buildings and artifacts could be valued for the way their modest form and casual arrangement connoted the humble beginnings of American democracy (figs. 3 and 4). Among the many ironies that attend the mall's creation is that by drawing on crudely conceived, eighteenth-century European classicism, planners of the mall erased historical artifacts that might have been great assets to the site. By contrast, on the blocks running east of Independence Square, the National Park Service originally employed the strategy of selectively pruning those buildings lacking a vintage appropriate to a national park dedicated to colonial history. Nevertheless, the combination of the Park Service's pruning strategy and the monumental axis of Independence Mall set the stage for re-gentrification of nearby areas, especially Society Hill.

The creation of the mall and its environs suggests a now-common process by which a city's historic form and stock of historic buildings can be leveraged to stimulate both public and private investment in decaying areas. Linking a patriotic-themed memorial to an infrastructure-driven urban redevelopment project was not unique in the early decades of the twentieth century; the Jefferson National Expansion Memorial in St. Louis, Missouri, which was conceived in the early 1930s and evolved, like the idea and execution of the mall in Philadelphia, over the following three decades, was a prime example of the type. The mall project is unique in that it brought together planning movements with highly diverging agendas for the built environment. Abating traffic from the Benjamin Franklin Bridge provided the initial stimulus for the project. Then it became a project of framing and historically "preserving" a hallowed shrine. The mall was ultimately achieved through a nascent form of urban renewal. Reverence for Independence Hall received its greatest boost from the Colonial Revival during the 1920s — a movement that was critical to the maturing of a historic preservation consciousness in the United States. The grandiose scale of the mall — an obvious mismatch with the diminutively scaled Independence Hall — was a result of lingering City Beautiful ambitions that coalesced in the early years of the twentieth century.[13] The grandiosely scaled mall was mostly intended to do for Independence Hall (Philadelphia's old City Hall) what the Fairmount Parkway had been seen to do for the new City Hall: create a grand civic corridor to a monumental building and in the process manage traffic. Nevertheless, Independence Hall is a fraction of the size of Philadelphia's newer City Hall and is a monument by virtue of its history, not its size.

By aligning with a network of national parks and related tourist sites rather

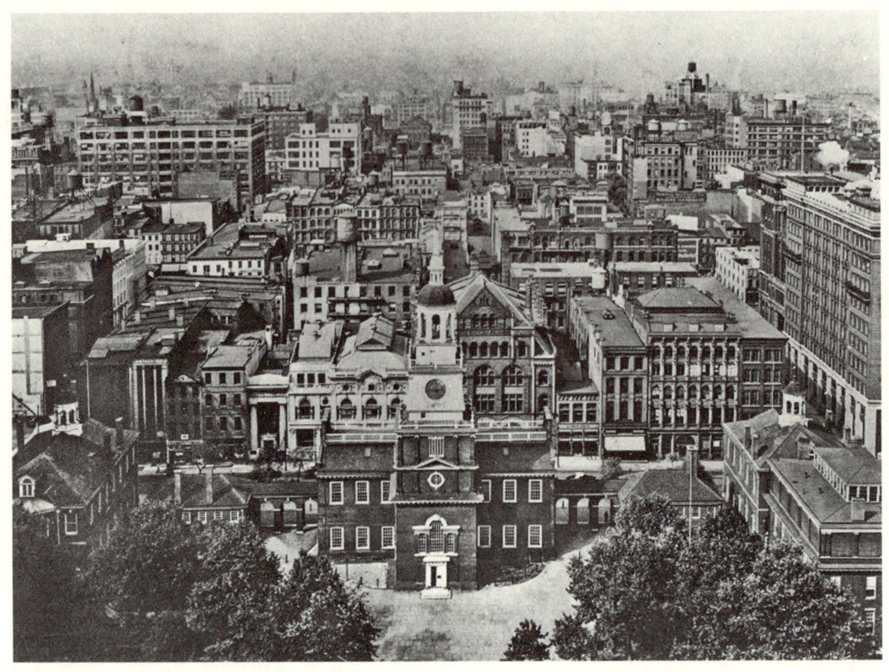

FIG. 3. Independence Mall area, n.d. (Photo courtesy of *Philly*History.org, a project of the Philadelphia Department of Records)

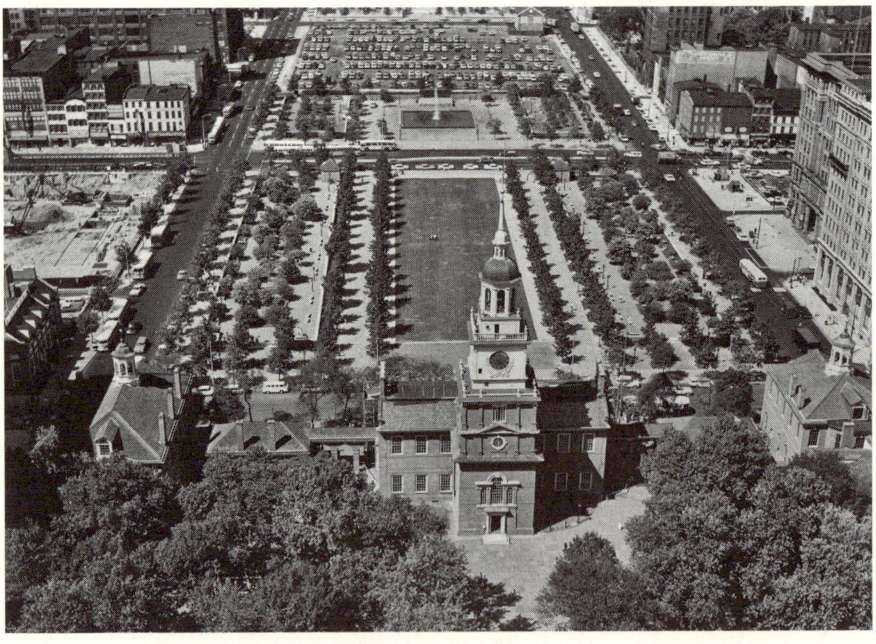

FIG. 4. Independence Mall area, after 1964. (Photo courtesy of *Philly*History.org, a project of the Philadelphia Department of Records)

than with the material history of Philadelphia, Independence Mall indicates how, at a time when metropolitan areas such as Philadelphia were dissipating into the suburbs, the aesthetic chosen for the symbolic areas at the center was one that put a premium on cleanliness, easy automobile access, and open, verdant vistas. Penn's Greene Country Towne was finally going to be realized, but at a scale that could be appreciated only from a moving automobile.

Independence Mall presaged the larger redevelopment of Philadelphia's downtown in the postwar period. With the 1949 appointment of Edmund Bacon as the powerful executive director of the Planning Commission, the mall project became a linchpin for his renewal schemes. The mall took more than a decade to complete. During this period Bacon proposed, and partially achieved, a plan that wrapped the original borders of Penn's colonial plan with expressways (fig. 5). Bacon's scheme, and a similar, more artistically rendered proposal by Louis Kahn, in essence isolated the "original" city from the rest of Philadelphia in a manner similar to the way in which the Independence Hall complex had been isolated from the city that had grown up around it. This reification of the city to the essence of its old and new formations is captured in a famous sketch by Kahn in 1952, in which Independence Hall appears to be the only building left standing in a city protected at its original borders by citadel-like parking structures (fig. 6).[14]

The late nineteenth century established a precedent for using politically symbolic events and sites to herald American greatness. These events included Philadelphia's own International Exposition held in 1876 for the centennial of the American Revolution, and the World's Columbian Exposition held in Chicago in 1893—both of which stimulated new plans and visions for their respective cities. A major theme of these events was the shared colonial "heritage" of the United States and how this heritage helped reinforce the cohesion of the expanding "Union" after the Civil War. The patriotic motivation for Independence Mall extends from this period. Although aesthetically a City Beautiful project, the mall was only achieved after being recast as an urban renewal project that linked the postwar ethos of free enterprise to the remaking of decaying cities.

Independence Mall framed the buildings associated with national independence as central figures in a heritage narrative of national origins. In erasing a portion of the mercantile fabric fronting Independence Hall, the open and axial space of the mall not only provided a retroactive civic presence for the hall but also contributed to investing the Chestnut Street façade of Independence Hall with monumentality it did not previously have. This abstract and large-scale

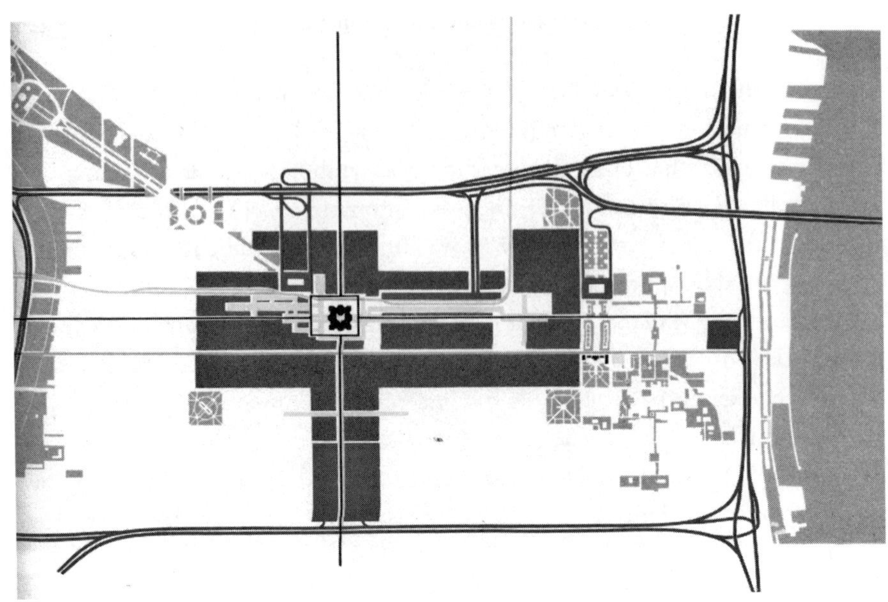

FIG. 5. Plan of Center City Philadelphia, 1962. (From *Design of Cities* by Edmund Bacon, copyright © 1967, 1974 by Edmund N. Bacon; Used by permission of Penguin, a division of Penguin Group [USA]

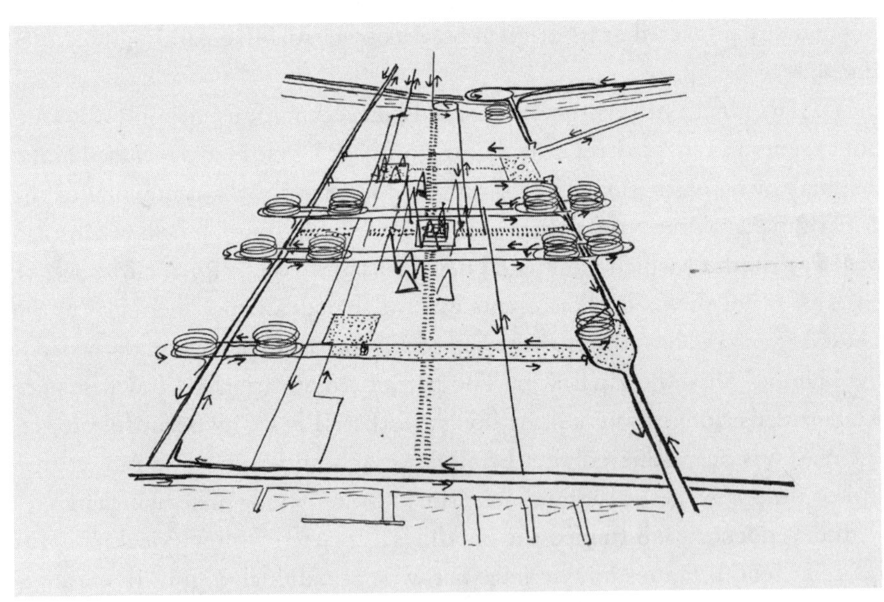

FIG. 6. Louis Kahn, Sketch for Philadelphia, 1952. (Louis I. Kahn Collection, the University of Pennsylvania and the Pennsylvania Historical and Museum Commission)

monumentality shifted Independence Hall out of history and into heritage. In consecrating the singularity of the historical event that occurred within it — the signing of the Declaration of Independence — the newly monumental Independence Hall suggested a more stable civic authority highlighted by a narrative of the political origins of the United States that belied its mercantile beginnings. That is, heritage emphasized the episodic act of political independence (the signing of a document occurring in a particular building) over a more extended history of mercantile independence (the development of the colonial American city).

The Freedom Train: 1947–1949

In displaying foundational and pivotal documents in American history as evidence of an inexorable American project of preserving, as well as expanding, freedoms, the Freedom Train repeated Independence Mall's formulation of heritage over history. A yearlong traveling exhibition at the onset of the Cold War, the Freedom Train was a veritable rolling reliquary that, in presenting salient documents from America's past, transformed the contingencies of history into a written heritage. Heritage is in this context an effort to form an ostensibly more durable set of social codes, behaviors, and political beliefs. As the uncritical reception of history, heritage as conveyed aboard the Freedom Train promoted the notion of the "good citizen," a morally upright figure adopting conventional gender roles whose central concerns were family, nation, and God. For the good citizen individualism, tempered by civic duty and national allegiance, could best be funneled into the pursuit of free enterprise. Moreover, as the president of the National Association of Manufacturers noted earlier in the decade, free enterprise was "simply human nature — human desire — expressing itself in a free land."[15] The Freedom Train's promotion of heritage, embodied in the good citizen and expressed in the calculated resonance of original historical documents, sustained the Cold War locution of free enterprise by subsuming the history of the struggle for protecting individual and institutional rights and freedoms within the contemporary endeavor of unrestricted individual (and corporate) material productivity.

American industry, through the efforts of the Advertising Council, played a central role in promoting free enterprise. As a public relations group organized within the advertising industry and conceived at the outset of World War II, the Advertising Council promoted the social benefits of advertising and, consequently, business through noncommercial, tax-deductible public service advertising campaigns. The notion of public service advertising was introduced by James W. Young of the J. Walter Thompson Company at a November 1941 meeting between the Association of National Advertisers and the American Association of Advertising Agencies. Young was addressing the Depression's impact on advertising revenue, the nation's impending involvement in the war, and a nervous sense that the advertising industry's credibility was gradually eroding. His proposition of noncommercial advertising as a form of public relations was based on his claim, "We [advertising agencies] have within our hands the greatest aggregate means of mass education and persuasion the world has ever seen — namely, the channels of advertising communication."[16] Known as the War Advertising Council throughout World War II, the group organized ad campaigns to sell war bonds, to encourage the development of victory gardens, and to promote conservation of resources for the war effort. In the transition from war to peacetime, the group, renamed the Advertising Council, justified its continued role as a "liaison" between business and government by claiming that should business "scrap its information leadership . . . there would then exist no coordinated method for informing and inspiring the people, or securing public action."[17]

For one of the group's first postwar projects, Thomas D'Arcy Brophy, then director of the Advertising Council and president of the ad agency Kenyon and Eckhardt, Inc., proposed an exhibit of "American Heritage" as a means to address "a loss of faith in our traditions."[18] The idea meshed with what was seemingly a simultaneous proposal by William Coblenz, assistant director of the Public Information Division at the Department of Justice, for a "Liberty Train," a display of documents from the history of the United States juxtaposed with documents from Germany's Third Reich (the war crime trials at Nuremberg were taking place during this period).[19] A meeting of government officials and business leaders organized by the office of Attorney General Tom Clark merged the proposals of the Advertising Council and Justice Department. The result was the Advertising Council's 1947 campaign entitled "Our American Heritage," featuring the Freedom Train (fig. 7).[20] Rather than place an exhibit on liberty in the context of a recently vanquished enemy, officials of the Truman White House placed it within the context of America's new, Cold War opponent, the Soviet Union. According to Attorney General Clark, a survey of historical documents emphasizing American freedom, in contrast to Soviet tyranny, would, "reawaken in the American people the loyalty it is known they have for the American way of life."[21]

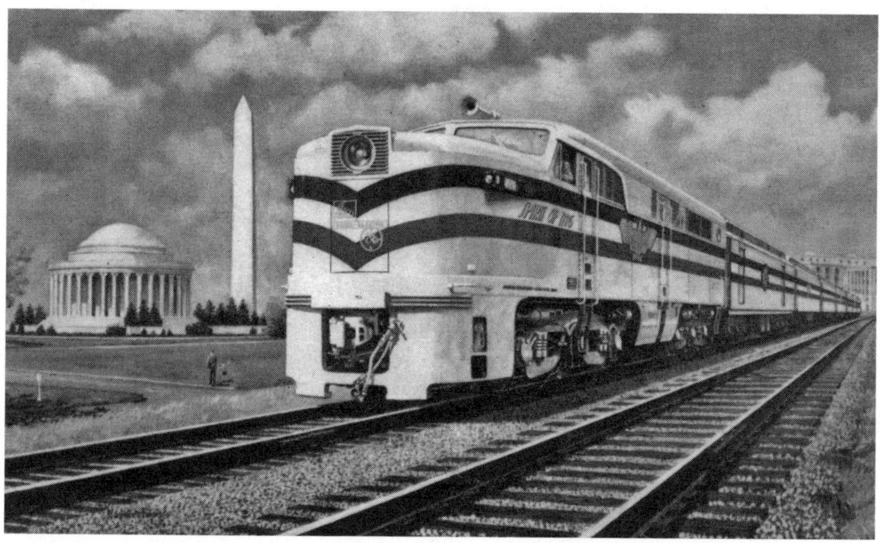

FIG. 7. Official Freedom Train postcard, American Heritage Foundation, 1948; artwork, Howard Fogg. (Author's collection)

The Eastman Kodak Company coordinated the campaign and recruited ten advertising agencies to volunteer in the development of newspaper and magazine advertisements, billboards, train cards, radio promotions, and informational guides. The Advertising Council noted how this media strategy offered "an increased awareness of [Americans'] individual rights and liberties as guaranteed by the Federal Constitution and expressed in other historical documents . . . [as well as] a more extensive participation by citizens in the affairs of nation, state, and community, and in fulfilling the duties of American citizenship."[22] The Diorama Corporation of America designed the exhibit cars, and the exhibit's director for the adjutant general of the army was responsible for the construction of the train.[23] The exhibit was to be instructive and informative.

Within the emerging field of public relations there was, however relative, a distinction to be made between propaganda and education. One of the originators of public relations, Edward L. Bernays, made the argument in his 1923 book *Crystallizing Public Opinion* that public relations had an educational value — that it is "commendable, enlightening, instructive," while propaganda is "insidious, dishonest, misleading."[24] For Bernays, education was for shaping a uniformity of opinion, of developing a "public conscience." In this respect, the Advertising

Council was one additional "force," along with parents, schools, churches, and media, in shaping public opinion and in guarding against the infiltration of foreign ideology.

On February 14, 1947, the Advertising Council established the American Heritage Foundation to officially sponsor the Our American Heritage campaign. Winthrop W. Aldrich, then chairman of Chase National Bank, served as chairman of the foundation's board, and Thomas D'Arcy Brophy served as its president. A White House conference on American heritage held on May 22, 1947, announced that the Freedom Train was to be "constructed as a National Shrine," with its main theme being "the message of democracy, its significance, and the responsibilities of the individual to it."[25] The inaugural departure of the Freedom Train tour from Philadelphia's Broad Street Station on September 17, 1947, coincided with the 160th anniversary of the signing of the U.S. Constitution.[26] At Independence Hall, Attorney General Clark read a message from President Truman that drew its theme from the Truman Doctrine, which had been outlined just six months earlier.[27] Referring to the train's documents as "our common heritage of freedom," Truman said, "It is a heritage which we Americans must share with the world, for in this noble heritage of freedom for the individual citizen, without distinction because of race, creed, or color, lies the world's great hope of lasting peace."[28] Nevertheless, on March 21, 1947, President Truman issued an executive order authorizing current and prospective executive branch employees to be subject to loyalty investigations, an indication that a shared commitment to American heritage was apparently insufficient to ensure national fealty.[29]

The Freedom Train oscillated uncomfortably between its propagandistic role of forwarding narrow, ahistorical notions of American freedom and its ostensibly public service role of defining citizenship. Consisting of an engine named the "Spirit of 1776," three exhibit cars, and four service cars, the Freedom Train displayed 132 documents and artifacts, originals as well as copies (fig. 8). The earliest document was a 1493 description by Christopher Columbus of his voyage across the Atlantic and his exploration of "the islands of India." The most current document was a September 2, 1945, entry from the log of the USS *Missouri* recording Japan's surrender to the Allied powers. In between were original documents, such as Roger Williams's 1644 work "The Bloody Tenent of Persecution," a statement on religious freedom; Thomas Jefferson's 1776 rough draft of the Declaration of Independence; Abraham Lincoln's 1863 Gettysburg Address; and Francis Scott Key's 1814 manuscript of the "The Star Spangled Banner."[30] The primary donors

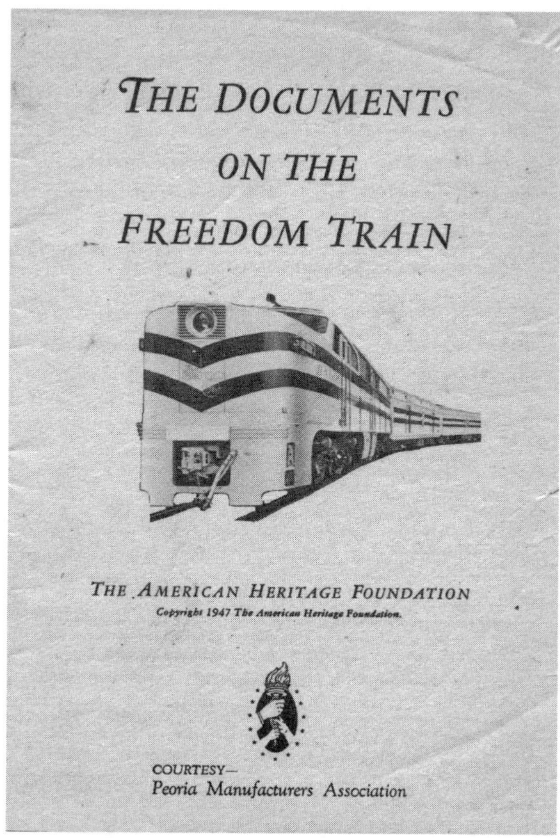

FIG. 8. *The Documents on the Freedom Train,* American Heritage Foundation pamphlet, 1947. (Author's collection)

of the exhibition materials were the National Archives, Library of Congress, American Philosophical Society, Colonial Williamsburg, university libraries, federal agencies, and private collectors.[31] The statements and documents from American history not chosen for display were as telling of the political intentions of the project as those that were included. Missing were any documents related to the progressive New Deal policies of Franklin Roosevelt. Conspicuously absent was Roosevelt's 1941 State of the Union address, espousing a globalism of "four essential human freedoms": Freedom of Speech, Freedom of Worship, Freedom from Want, and Freedom from Fear.[32] To heighten a sense of their authenticity, the exhibitors displayed the documents in the manner of hallowed religious relics.[33] Rather than interpret their meaning and invite an active engagement with the ideas the documents represented, the displays promoted a passive acceptance of the documents' inherent value. At the end of the exhibit each visitor was asked to sign the Freedom Scroll and to take the Freedom Pledge:

> I am an American. A free American.
> Free to speak — without fear
> Free to worship God in my own way
> Free to stand for what I think right
> Free to oppose what I believe wrong
> Free to choose those who govern my country.
> This heritage of Freedom I pledge to uphold
> For myself and all mankind.[34]

The week preceding the arrival of the Freedom Train in each city was called "Rededication Week," during which civic groups, schools, and places of worship, assisted by material prepared by the American Heritage Foundation, held rallies, parades, educational events, and religious ceremonies expanding on the general theme of citizenship. Freedom of Religion Days, Veterans Days, Women's Days, Organizations Days, American Family Days, Youth Days, Freedom of Expression Days, and Good Citizenship Days represented an effort to posit the individual citizen as a participating member within tradition-bound and community-oriented social groups.[35]

The campaign's main publication, *Good Citizen,* as well as a nationally released eleven-minute film *Our American Heritage* narrated by Joseph Cotton supplemented local community group activities.[36] Similar to Rededication Week, *Good Citizen* outlined nine points for "good citizenship." Among them were voting, jury duty, paying taxes, supporting public schooling, and above all, respect for the family as a repository of virtue (fig. 9). The final section on the family, given the recent history of displacing Japanese Americans in the United States to internment camps during World War II, evokes a particular irony in promising, "To the degree that all other duties of citizenship have been fulfilled, your home will be your castle, secure from the threat of confiscation, and those in it safe from detention camps and firing squads."[37]

Anticipating national and international interest in whether the "freedom" that was being celebrated was available to all citizens equally, the organizers in-

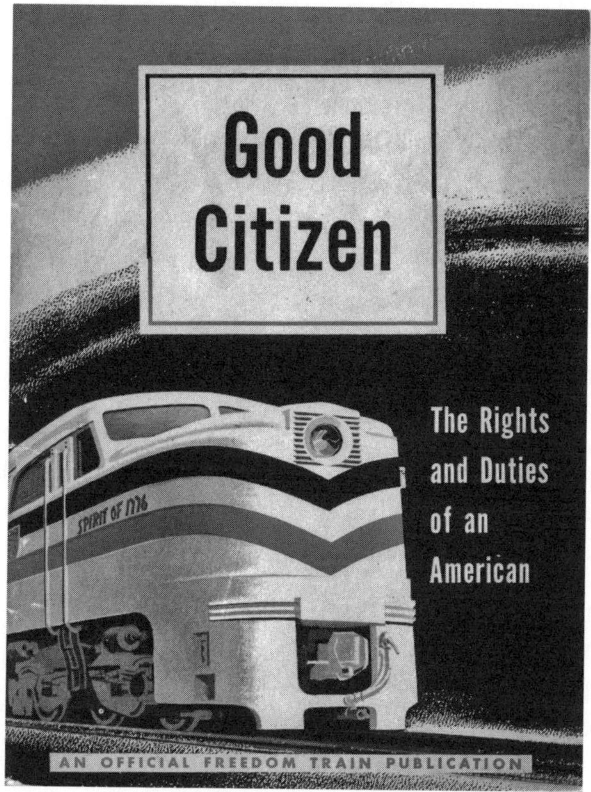

FIG. 9. *Good Citizen: The Rights and Duties of an American,* American Heritage Foundation pamphlet, 1948. (Author's collection)

sisted that access and tours through the train be, in all cases, racially integrated. Birmingham, Alabama, and Memphis, Tennessee, refused to comply and were dropped from the tour.[38] Georgia altered one of the service cars in order to exhibit the Confederate Constitution and other Southern documents on the Freedom Train's tour. That the sponsors of the Freedom Train refrained from linking the project to the direct promotion of any commercial or corporate interests speaks to the degree to which they believed "free enterprise" would be served best through the promotion of Americanism above all else.

Yet, as Henry Steele Commager noted in an article published coincident with the beginning of the Freedom Train tour, the promotion of Americanism was a thin disguise for intolerance toward dissent and criticism. Commager asked:

> What is the new loyalty? It is above all, conformity. It is the uncritical and unquestioning acceptance of America as it is — the political institutions, the social relationships, and the economic practices. It rejects inquiry into the race question or socialized medicine, or public housing, or into the wisdom or validity of our foreign policy. It regards as particularly heinous any challenge to what is called "the system of private enterprise," identifying that system with Americanism. It abandons evolution, repudiates the once popular concept of progress, and regards America as a finished product, perfect and complete.[39]

Unlike the zeitgeist to which Commager alluded, the Advertising Council not only shaped but also quantified Americanism. In its 1947–48 annual report, the Advertising Council noted:

> A test study to determine whether or not the Freedom Train campaign was successful in clarifying understanding of the meaning of freedom and in creating a more specific awareness of the duties of good citizenship was conducted in a relatively small industrial town in March. This study revealed that the people's concept of freedom was broadened considerably by the campaign. Seventy-five percent defined freedom in objective, rather than personalized terms following the campaign, whereas only 61 percent had done so beforehand. Also, "before" and "after" questions showed that the awareness of the qualifications of citizenship was increased by about 35 percent.[40]

Running concurrent with the Freedom Train was an Advertising Council campaign on free enterprise. ESSO Standard Oil coordinated the "American Economic System" campaign under the organizing theme of "The Better We Produce, The Better We Live." Emphasizing the relation between mass production and rising living standards, yet also recognizing labor's right to collective bargaining, the Advertising Council stated that the objective of the campaign was "to promote a better understanding of how the American economic system works so that Americans will not only have a greater appreciation of its benefits but [would] be better able to refute the arguments of those who would destroy it."[41] The publication for the campaign, *Miracle of America*, joined with the publication *Good Citizen* in tying the moral underpinning of the individual to providential guidance and the exceptionalist foundations of the nation.

During a single week in October 1947, as the Freedom Train entered its second month on tour, events revealed the deep fissures within American society that belied the Freedom Train's call to rally around a homogeneous notion of American heritage. On October 24 the National Association for the Advancement of Colored People (NAACP), with W. E. B. Du Bois as its principal author, submitted to the United Nations "An Appeal for Redress" to protest ongoing racial discrimination, segregation, and disfranchisement of African Americans.[42] The same day, the House Un-American Activities Committee questioned eleven "unfriendly" witnesses regarding Communist infiltration of the motion picture industry, leading to the blacklisting of the Hollywood Ten the following month. On October 29, the President's Committee on Civil Rights issued its report "To Secure These Rights," outlining the gap between a foreign policy based on the promotion of freedom and ongoing racial discrimination in the United States. Later that year *Pravda,* the state newspaper of the Soviet Union, denounced the Freedom Train as "hypocrisy on wheels," noting, "Hired radio liars, provincial Senators and 'selfless' businessmen, atomic diplomats and pro-Fascist philosophers advertise freedom so hard they foam at the mouth." The Freedom Train escaped comparison with its less sober predecessor — the agitprop trains of the early period of the Soviet revolution.[43]

After traveling some 37,000 miles, the Freedom Train tour ended in Philadelphia on January 22, 1949.[44] During a period of sixteen months, the train stopped in 322 cities. More than 3.5 million visitors viewed the exhibit. The popularity of the Freedom Train was, in part, attributable to the marketing strategies of the Advertising Council. Bringing the central documents of American history directly to the people had a popular, democratic appeal. Moreover, the choice of a train offered to revive consciousness, however briefly, of the central role the railroad played in the expansion and modernization of the United States. Nevertheless, the cultural and economic value of the train in the United States had begun to wane in the postwar period. In 1934 the railroad industry had seen it necessary to form its own public relations arm — the Association of American Railroads — in order "to bring about a better public understanding and appreciation of railroad progress, achievements and problems" and to elicit "a more friendly sentiment toward the railroads."[45] The railroad industry was also facing an inexorable challenge by the Good Roads movement that had its own rhetoric of linking freedom and individual enterprise ("Freedom of the highways is a basic human right") with the notion of a network of interstate highways.[46]

For some, however, the Freedom Train was less a historic relic of unvarnished American enterprise than a glaring example of institutional racism and segregation. Coinciding with the inauguration of the train, the *New Republic* published a poem by Langston Hughes expressing his skepticism about the symbolic value of the Freedom Train, particularly in the segregated South. Hughes wrote, in part:

> Who's the engineer on the Freedom Train?
> Can a coal black man drive the Freedom Train?
> Or am I still a porter on the Freedom Train?
> Is there ballot boxes on the Freedom Train?
> Do colored folks vote on the Freedom Train?
> When it stops in Mississippi will it be made plain
> Everybody's got a right to board the Freedom Train?[47]

Before and during the Freedom Train tour, successive Supreme Court rulings and congressional legislation addressed the segregation of railroad dining cars, railroad station waiting rooms, and interstate travel. Ironically, the military force aboard the Freedom Train guarding the exhibition of documents espousing freedom was still officially segregated for the first half of the tour.[48]

Perhaps nostalgia for an American frontier forged by the railroads made a train the fitting vessel for an exhibit program that correlated democratic freedoms with free enterprise. Free enterprise was, as such, a notion conceived to open a new frontier based on the marketing of the American way of life. Nevertheless, the railroads contributed to forming an industrial, urban geography, and the material circumstances revealed by train travel and train stations inevitably exposed fissures in the more ideological, less land-based promises of free enterprise. These inconsistencies were not lost on social critics in the period following the tour. In 1952 William H. Whyte observed in his book *Is Anybody Listening?*: "Look at many ads—particularly the Free Enterprise ones . . . the terms are those of Main Street: shady lawns, barbecue dinners in the back yard, mansarded roofs, the town firehouse, church suppers, and so on. . . . But do most Americans live on Main Street? The greatest single proportion live in the dirty, smelly city. But this is something we do not like to face, for the problems that urban life has wrought are among the most disagreeable we have to meet."[49] Whyte's comment suggests

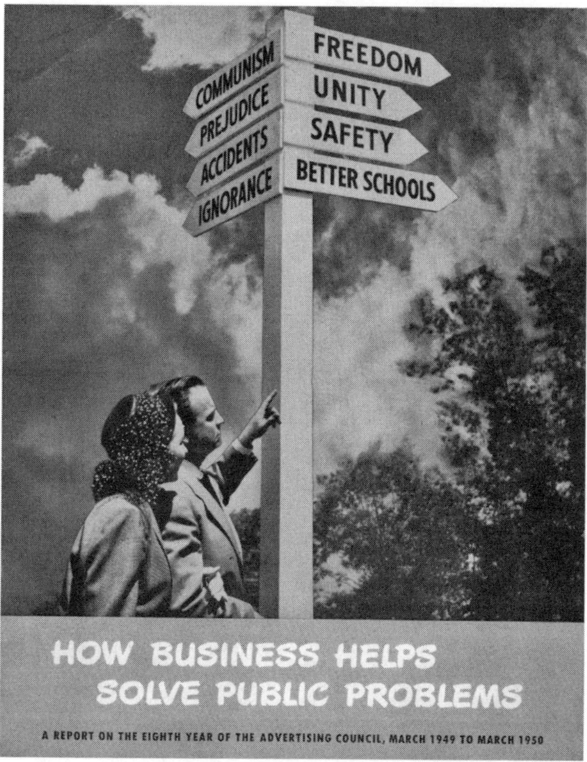

FIG. 10. Cover of Advertising Council Eighth Annual Report, 1949–50. (Courtesy, Ad Council Archives, University of Illinois Archives, RS 13/2/02)

that the alliance of business and government behind the Freedom Train had as its aim to construct a Potemkin village that could shape a complaisant citizenry more amenable to a harmonious heritage than to a dissonant history and contemporary reality (fig. 10). Nevertheless, the geographic nexus of the Freedom Train remained the city — a testing ground for the contingencies rather than the verities of democracy and freedom (fig. 11).

Conclusion: From History to Heritage

Paradoxically, in the effort to ground the concept of free enterprise in the ostensibly more durable and permanent construct of American heritage, the Independence Mall and Freedom Train projects reinscribed their subjects — historic

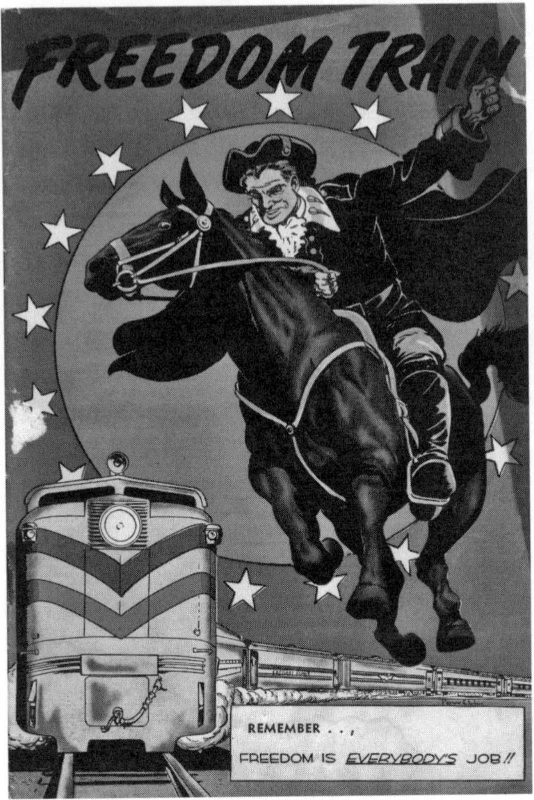

FIG. 11. *Freedom Train* comic book by Algred M. Klein, with cover art by Bob Powell, 1948. (Author's collection)

buildings and documents — within a modern context. The midcentury urban renewal strategy of replacing the aging, incremental city with a "modern" one, and saving only certain historical artifacts, had the effect of heightening a sense of the new through its juxtaposition with what was clearly old. This redevelopment strategy merged well with the mall project's effort to emphasize America's colonial heritage above all else by isolating Independence Hall and setting it on a modern stage of national proportions.

Alternatively, the sponsors of the Freedom Train provided unprecedented public access to a historic array of documents heralding the evolution of political freedoms in the United States. Despite this stated purpose, it was the railroad taken as an allegory of a free and mobile America and the use of the most sophisticated, modern advertising techniques and promotional media then available that account most for the tour's popularity and historical impact. By employing the emerging techniques of urban renewal and public relations, respectively, the Independence Mall and Freedom Train projects succeed as emblems of national identity that severed American heritage from other American traditions of political iconoclasm and dissent. Moreover, within a Cold War context, heritage not only sustained a liberal individualism but also, more broadly, could counter a Marxist end of history that entailed the supplanting of the capitalist system. In its promotion of a complaisant body politic, this form of American heritage had to pose an effective alternative to a teleological history of revolution. It accomplished this by shifting the focus from revolution to a less politically volatile material culture of authenticity, achievable through the consumption of artifacts — original or reproduced. Living history, as history in suspension, replaces history in development.

The assumption of a national heritage depends, as does an individual's birthright, on the transmission of traditions, unquestioned, from one generation to the next. Yet, the very idea of an American heritage runs against the grain of American history, where successive waves of immigration and access to wealth and property have fundamentally challenged the notion that values and culture are inherited rather than made. Competing accounts of the histories Americans share, as opposed to the heritage they inherit, are constantly being amended and are part of the critical process by which democracy is renewed. Knowing that George Washington lived, however briefly, and housed slaves on the exact parcel of the mall that now enshrines the Liberty Bell, or that abolitionists fought to extend the definition of human rights on a nearby site only a half century later, does not diminish the first president of the United States or sully the Liberty Bell as a symbol. Quite the opposite: these histories illuminate the nation's unfinished and hard-fought movement toward a more expansive definition of human rights and social emancipation. Moreover, the concept of heritage, in its effort to make the past "congenial," cannot account for the location of Washington's slave quarters on the site of the mall.[50]

Independence Mall and the Freedom Train's positioning of the notions of independence and freedom as long-established fixtures of American heritage contrast with the radical promise of democracy as an ongoing historical project. Independence Mall's formal strategy of establishing a new ground to highlight a historic figure evaded the complex history of the site in favor of recovering a (false) sense of origin. In the case of the Freedom Train, despite efforts to circumscribe the public reception of significant documents of American history, there remains a democratic spirit and an unpredictable potential in making historic texts, and especially the ideas they represent, available in the everyday space of the city. In a democracy, the function of commemorative forms such as a monument or a trail is not primarily retrospective and regenerative, but prospective and contingent, causing us to be mindful of the myriad ways in which history can actually be made. Both the mall and the train demonstrate that in a society seeking more democratic forms of expression, it is history rather than heritage that enables the monument to be identified with — and perform — in the service of democracy.

Notes

1. Lowenthal, *Possessed by the Past,* 63.

2. At this, the country's first public, popular museum, Peale combined his portraits of luminaries from the American Revolution with paleontological finds, including the mastodon from Newburgh, New York, which Peale advertised as "the great *incognitum.*" Constructing a prehistoric lineage for America, Peale's museum rejected late-eighteenth-century efforts to legitimize the American project in the light of natural history.

3. Pennsylvania Hall Association, *History of Pennsylvania Hall.*

4. As quoted in Greene, *The Intellectual Construction of America,* 197.

5. Mires, *Independence Hall in Public Memory,* 133–39.

6. For an account of the first plans for Philadelphia, see Reps, *The Making of Urban America,* 152–53.

7. Farnham, "Staging the Tragedy of Time," 258–79; and Brownlee, *Building the City Beautiful.*

8. Gibson, *Cultural Landscape Report, Independence Mall,* 27–28.

9. Ibid., 28.

10. Ibid., 29–32.

11. Ibid., 63.

12. For an account of opposition to the wholesale clearance of the mall site mounted by the Park Service's architect, Charles E. Peterson, see Greiff, *Independence,* 49–58. See also Lewis Mumford's later criticism in "The Skyline."

13. The actual character of the mall, as completed, was, on the two southernmost blocks, a banal mix of an emerging modernism and an academic style derivative of Cret's work, and on the northernmost block, a more abstract composition by the landscape architect Dan Kiley (who also designed the Jefferson National Expansion Memorial Grounds).

14. For a further account of Independence Mall in the context of Edmund Bacon's Planning, see Sommer, "The Urban Design of Philadelphia."

15. Frederick C. Crawford, "Competitive Free Enterprise and the Common Man," address before the Economic Club of Detroit at the Book-Cadillac Hotel, Detroit, Michigan, February 15, 1943, New York Public Library pamphlet, 12.

16. As quoted in Griffith, "The Selling of America," 390.

17. War Advertising Council, *From War to Peace,* 5.

18. As quoted in Griffith, "The Selling of America," 398.

19. Bradsher, "Taking America's Heritage to the People," 229.

20. Griffith, "The Selling of America," 398.

21. "Meeting Is Called on 'Freedom Train,'" *New York Times,* May 16, 1947, 11.

22. Advertising Council, Sixth Year Annual Report, 1947–48, New York Public Library.

23. Monaghan, *Heritage of Freedom,* 146.

24. Bernays, *Crystallizing Public Opinion,* 212.

25. American Heritage Foundation, "Conference at the White House."

26. H. Walton Cloke, "Martin Denounces Communism Aides," *New York Times,* September 18, 1947, 23.

27. Truman, "Special Message to the Congress on Greece and Turkey: The Truman Doctrine," 176–80.

28. H. Walton Cloke, "Truman Asks U.S. to 'Share Liberty,'" *New York Times,* September 17, 1947, 23.

29. "President Orders Investigations to Remove All Disloyal Employees," *New York Times,* March 23, 1947, 1. Loyalty took on a broader public role during the Freedom Train tour. In opposition to the celebration of May Day by the political left, the Veterans of Foreign Wars organized a Loyalty Day parade in New York City in 1948. The parade became an annual event, although with increasingly smaller turnouts. See Alexander Feinberg, "750,000 Witness Loyalty Turnout," *New York Times,* May 2, 1948, 3.

30. Of the 132 items exhibited, only 20 could be said to address issues of freedom and liberty directly. Some 50 documents were political, that is treaties, governmental, proclamations. Some 32 were military, with more than half of these dealing with World War II. For a list of items exhibited, see Monaghan, *Heritage of Freedom.*

31. Ibid., 145–47.

32. "Eighth Annual Message," 2855–61.

33. The *New York Times* reported on the security measures taken. Inside the windowless exhibition cars, "Each document and book will be enclosed between sheets of Lucite plastic, one-half-inch thick. The plastic sheets, in turn, will be anchored by star-headed bronze bolts inside steel cases, and the cases will be covered with shatterproof double-glass sheets and imbedded into steel walls with uniquely designed security screws." See "Precautions Taken For Freedom Train," *New York Times,* August 28, 1947, 25.

34. American Heritage Foundation, *Good Citizen,* 74.

35. Bradsher, "Taking America's Heritage to the People," 241.

36. "Democracy Dramatized," *New York Times,* September 22, 1947, 6.

37. Not insignificantly perhaps, Tom Clark's position in the Roosevelt Justice Department, prior to becoming Truman's attorney general, was to coordinate the displacement of Japanese Americans out of their homes and into internment camps.

38. "Freedom Train to Skirt 2 Cities: Many in South Lift 'Jim Crowism,'" *New York Times,* December 25, 1947, 1.

39. Henry Steele Commager, "Who Is Loyal to America?" *Harper's,* September 1947, 195.

40. Advertising Council, Sixth Year Annual Report, 1947–48, New York Public Library.

41. Advertising Council, Seventh Year Annual Report, March 1948–March 1949, New York Public Library.

42. George Streator, "Negroes to Bring Cause Before U.N.," *New York Times,* October 12, 1947, 52; and George Streator, "U.N. Gets Charges of Wide Bias in U.S.," *New York Times,* October 24, 1947, 9.

43. "*Pravda* Assails Freedom Train," *New York Times,* December 5, 1947, 9.

44. "U.S. Tour Is Ended by Freedom Train," *New York Times,* January 9, 1949, 50. Soon after, Congress extended the tour of the Freedom Train for another two years. See "Freedom Train Backed," *New York Times,* February 15, 1949, 27.

45. Association of American Railroads, *An Outline,* 66.

46. National Highway Users Conference, *Highway Transportation.*

47. Hughes, "Freedom Train," 27.

48. Although President Truman issued Executive Order 9981 desegregating the military on July 26, 1948, racism and discrimination continued to be an issue beyond the tour of the Freedom Train. See Dudziak, *Cold War Civil Rights,* 86–90. C. Vann Woodward notes that Congress and the military, fearing negative public reaction, kept silent about the executive order, resulting in delaying the implications of the order until 1953. See Woodward, *The Strange Career of Jim Crow,* 136–37.

49. Whyte, *Is Anybody Listening?* 30, 32.

50. David Lowenthal writes, "History and heritage both refashion the past in present garb. But the former does so to make the past comprehensible, the latter to make it congenial." See Lowenthal, *Possessed by the Past,* 148.

THOMAS J. CAMPANELLA

"As a Witness upon the Field of History"

The American Elm as Commemorative Vessel in Nineteenth-Century New England

By the turn of the nineteenth century, Americans had planted along their streets and avenues one of the greatest urban forests in history, comprised largely of a single species of tree, the American elm. "Elm Street" became one of the iconic landscapes in America, a delightful fusion of nature and artifice as well as an idyllic environment in which generations of Americans came of age. But even before the species was planted in large numbers as a street tree — a trend begun by village improvement societies in New England in the 1850s — the American elm was well known throughout the region as a "witness tree"— a living commemorative vessel associated over the years with significant historical events and acts of patriotism and resistance. By the end of the nineteenth century, nearly every village, town, and city in New England had a "great elm" in its midst that was linked to persons or stories from the hallowed past.

There were a number of reasons why this came to be — why, of the dozens of tree species native to the woodlands of early New England, it was the elm that came into such exalted service. The New England colonists took an early liking to the elm, for it grew like a weed and quickly attained a remarkably beautiful form — like a great green fountain of limbs and branches. But the tree had also gained a prominent place in the colonial landscape as a result of the forest management practices of Native Americans and the timber economy of the colonists. Local tribes fired the fields and woods periodically to clear ground for crops and freshen browse for game. Doing so burned some areas readily, while other places — riverbanks, boggy lowlands, and floodplains — were largely spared the flames. As a result, certain tree species were favored and others kept at bay. Oak, hickory, and pine on drier upland sites were killed off or stunted, while trees in the moist bottomlands were able to live long and grow to great size. And of the native bottomland species, *Ulmus Americana* attained the greatest height and largest crown mass. The elms encountered by the colonists would have been ancient, truly magnificent specimens. It is hardly surprising the tree made such a lasting impression on the Yankee imagination.

But the elm was also not a terribly useful tree to the colonists, a fact that—ironically—perpetuated the good fortune of the species. Elm wood was considered poor in quality compared to oak, maple, beech, pine, hickory, and other species. It is tough and fibrous, difficult to plane, and prone to warping. And because it had low commercial value, timber cutters often left big elms behind while they picked off the choicer trees all around; they were not worth the tremendous effort of felling. These great elms were almost always solitary specimens (*Ulmus Americana* rarely grows in pure stands, one of the reasons why Elm Street was such an artificial—and fragile—creation), and they gained further prominence in the landscape as their compatriots fell. Great elms thus emerged from smoke and axe blades standing nobly in the fields and meadows that were gradually cleared from the bottomland woods. In time, these trees became a fixture in the colonial landscape, gradually accumulating about their trunks a range of associations that endeared them to the hearts and minds of the local population. In a sense, the tree's greatest asset was its beauty; it was useful for little else.

In a land lacking the picturesque ruins that gave the European landscape such historical depth, Americans looked instead to nature for appropriate vessels for their own accumulating history. Here was (in the European view, of course) a bright, fresh land unburdened by the detritus of history. As William Tudor wrote of the American scene in 1819, "Our picturesque objects of an artificial kind are vastly fewer than those in older countries," though the landscape was "better without them." Like many Americans, Tudor believed that "the sight of these grisly, hideous remains conjure up the ideas of baronial oppression, feudal slavery, and monkish delusion . . . and awaken painful recollections in the midst of the most smiling scenery." America was, instead, a "happy region of freedom"; wherever one looked he beheld "the unpolluted soil of liberty."[1] And in that soil grew immense old trees that, to American eyes, made better monuments than all the marble in Rome.

The old elms of Yankee field and wayside, left behind by the pioneers or planted in garden and dooryard by the first settlers, acquired a range of symbolic meanings that transformed the trees into far more than keepsakes of the forest primeval. For a people yearning for a tangible history of their own, old elms endowed the landscape with temporal depth. Like rubble on the Appian Way, an aged elm served as a yardstick of cultural time; as Berkshire minister Orville Dewey wrote of the Great Elm of Sheffield, Massachusetts, such a tree was "a witness upon the field of history."[2] Nehemiah Adams, writing in 1838, was even more specific: an aged elm, he argued, "is to antiquity with us what a pyramid is in Egypt."[3] And the eminent landscape theorist Andrew Jackson Downing could only agree: "If we have neither old castles nor old associations," he wrote in *Rural Essays,* "we have at least, here and there, old trees that can teach us lessons of antiquity, not less instructive and poetical than the ruins of a past age."[4]

Trees were ideal for such service because they were alive. Trees undergo a cycle of birth, growth, maturation, decay, and death not unlike a human being. Subtle life processes are continually at work in a tree, transforming and renewing it with the seasons and the years. Unlike architectural monuments, an aged tree is both part of the past and a living presence. The American elm, moreover, grows so fast that it can attain an appearance of great age in a relatively short period of time. A sapling elm present at some historical event — the passing of General Washington, for example, or the founding of a town — would "look the part" within a few short decades. Tall and spreading, elms imparted an air of antiquity to a village scene, and endowed upstart Yankee villages with an atmosphere of historical legitimacy. Oliver Wendell Holmes understood this function well: "A life of between two and three centuries seems a long one in a new country like ours," he wrote in 1890, "and 'the old elm' is often the most ancient monument of a New England village."[5] Many grand and storied Yankee elms were presumed much older than they actually turned out to be, keepsakes from "the unknown ages," wrote Adams, "which preceded the arrival of the Pilgrims."[6]

This role of the elm as a witness to history was remarked upon by many literate observers. Charles Joseph Latrobe, English author of *The Rambler in North America* (1835), concluded that the "air of comparative antiquity" of the Connecticut River valley was due to its abundant elms — hallmark of "long and steady cultivation." Old elms (or old-looking elms) helped "throw a degree of interest over the country," he wrote, "which contrasts agreeably with that air of rawness and newness which is imprinted upon the works of man."[7] And as the pace of life quickened with the coming of the Industrial Revolution, such keepsakes were cherished even more. At the Amoskeag Manufacturing Company in

New Hampshire, workers circulated a petitioned in 1853 to spare an elm which was to be felled for a new mill building. They argued that the "beautiful and goodly" tree should be saved simply because it recalled a lost age "when the yell of the red man and the scream of the eagle were alone heard on the banks of the Merrimack, instead of two giant edifices filled with the buzz of busy and well-remunerated industry." The Amoskeag elm was, the workers claimed, "a connecting link between the past and present."[8]

Totemic witness elms were commonplace throughout New England during the nineteenth century. The Great Elm at Springfield, Massachusetts, among the oldest and largest trees in New England, dominated the center of the city for decades. So did the great Pittsfield Elm, which stood like a immense maypole anchored in the town square. In Winthrop, Massachusetts, the Gibbons Elm was said to have "witnessed . . . much of the history of the town." In 1912, an extraordinary farewell ceremony, attended by some 3,000 people, was held in honor of the ailing tree. A poem was commissioned for the occasion—"The Old Elm"—and read as the three-hundred-year-old plant was ceremoniously felled. In his monograph *The Historic Trees of Massachusetts* (1919), James R. Simmons described the event as "one of the most remarkable gatherings ever held in honor of a tree."[9] Scores of other towns possessed a great elm that served as iconic centerpiece in the daily life and collective history of the community.

None was more famous, however, than the Great Elm of Boston Common, the subject of dozens of paintings, poems, children's stories, even patriotic ballads. The tree was honored chiefly for its presumed antiquity, and was long thought to be a relic from aboriginal times. Indeed, "No citizen now living can remember," wrote John W. Hamilton in 1875, when the Old Elm "was not venerable for its years and its history."[10] An anonymous poet provided imaginative elaboration:

When first from Mother Earth you sprung,
Ere Chaucer, Spenser, Shakespeare sung,
Or Puritans had come among
The savages to loose each tongue
In psalms and prayers.
These forty acres, more or less,
Now gayly clothed in Nature's dress,
Where Yankees walk, and brag and guess,
Were but a howling wilderness
Of wolves and bears.[11]

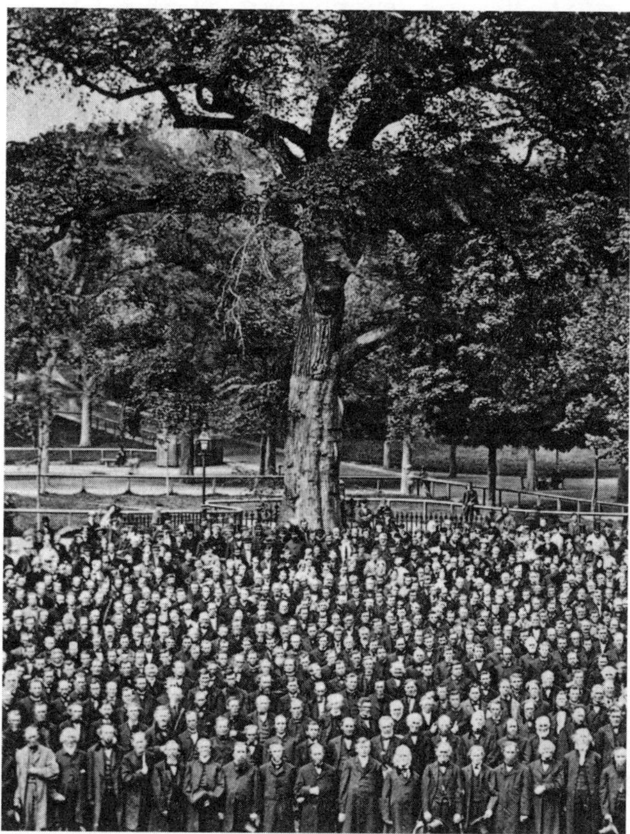

FIG. 1. Gathering of Methodist ministers under the Great Elm of Boston Common, 1866. (From Hamilton, *Memorial of Jessie Lee and the Old Elm*, 1875)

But science was swayed as well. "This tree," wrote J. C. Warren, then president of the Boston Society of Natural History, "we must venerate as a visible relic of the Indian Shawmut; for all its other native trees and groves have been long since prostrated; the frail and transient memorials of the Aborigines have vanished; even the hills of Trimountain cannot be distinguished." Only "this native noble elm" remained to connect past and present (fig. 1).[12]

By the 1850s the Great Elm was already gnarled and picturesque, and certainly looked every bit the autochthonous relic it was thought to be. Its increasing decrepitude and the predations of storms and gravity only seemed to magnify the tree's mystique. Finally, on a windy winter night in 1876 (at precisely 7:17 p.m.), the tree came crashing to earth. The *Boston Herald* reported that, within hours, the Common was swarmed with relic hunters who "crowded upon the trunk, and, with knife in hand, were not long in gratifying their found desire by getting such souvenirs as they most prized." In this way, "A good deal of the tree, in fact about all of the smaller limbs and branches, were taken away before the police could prevent it."[13] Oliver Wendell Holmes, Boston's jocular poet laureate, was quick to pen verse in eulogy:

The darkened skies, alas! have seen
Our monarch tree laid low,
And spread in ruins o'er the green,
But Nature struck the blow;
No scheming thrift its downfall planned,
It felt no edge of steel,
No soulless hireling raised his hand
The deadly stroke to deal.[14]

If many Yankee elms were honored primarily for their great antiquity, others held more fixed and specific historical associations. In the Yankee imagination the majesty and noble bearing of an elm made it an ideal candidate for the commemoration of hale deeds and great souls. Elms bore memory well, at least in an age before Dutch elm disease. Naturalist Donald Culross Peattie put it best: "If you want to be recalled for something that you do," he wrote in *A Natural History of Trees,* "you will be well advised to do it under an Elm."[15]

Name-bearing monument elms were landmarks in many nineteenth-century New England villages and towns—and cities, too. They were among the first symbols of collective remembrance to occasion the American scene—what Michael Kammen has called "repositories of memory."[16] Most of New England's monument elms were linked, in some large or small way, with the founding generation and the Revolutionary War. These trees served to remind citizens to whom they owed their freedom. As one writer put it years later, "We need such monitors in our public places . . . to arrest our headlong race, and bid us calmly count the cost of the empire we possess."[17] Monument elms typically gained their historical value serendipitously—and the link between tree and deed could be rather tenuous indeed. Many monument elms said to have sheltered a passing Washington or Lafayette were, upon death and a tally of growth rings, shown to have been no more than knee-high seedlings on the momentous occasion.

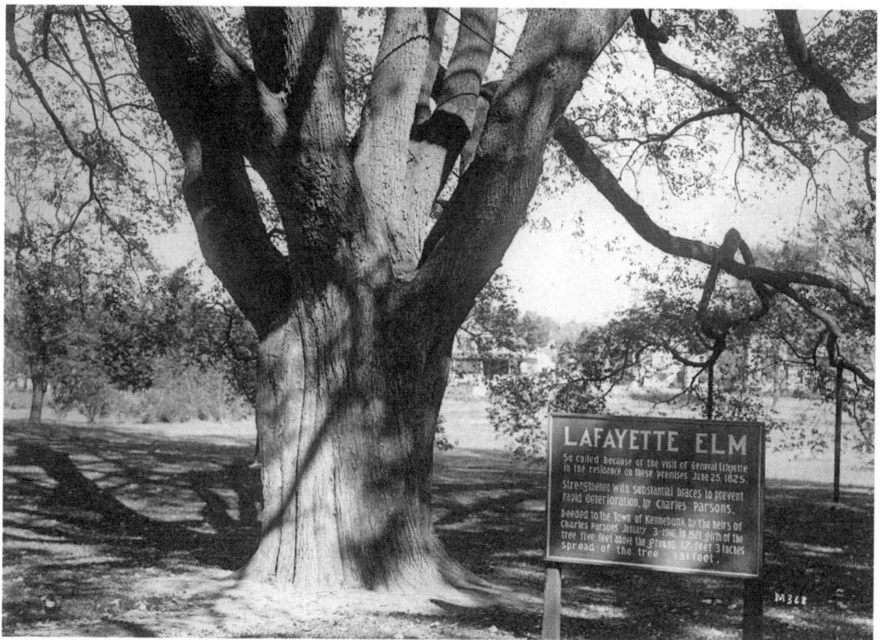

FIG. 2. The Lafayette Elm, Kennebunk, Maine; photo by E. H. Wilson, 1926. (Courtesy of Photographic Archives of the Arnold Arboretum, Harvard University)

Moreover, elms had an uncanny ability to draw significant events into their orbit. Naturalist Lorin L. Dame observed this of Boston's Great Elm: "whatever took place anywhere on the Common," he wrote, "gravitated into the history of the big elm."[18] Mere proximity to a historical event was often enough to endow an elm with lasting fame. The Marlboro Elm in Marlboro, Massachusetts, for example, began its career as an anonymous tree growing near the house of a Tory sympathizer who had been shot during the Revolution.[19] But over the years the house was sold and fell into disrepair, and the event once associated with it eventually relocated to the elm. When the great French general Lafayette visited a home in Kennebunk, Maine, in 1824, it was an elm nearby that became chief vessel of the event's memory (fig. 2). Lorin Dame observed that in Deerfield, Massachusetts, there was "hardly a spot . . . marked by a monument which is not also marked, at no great distance, by an old tree." And in time the relationship between the two inverted: the magnificent Deerfield elms—"witnesses of the events commemorated by tablets"—became more famous than the stone markers they once supplemented.[20]

By the middle of the nineteenth century such sylvan markers of local history or distinguished sons numbered in the hundreds. The Boxford Elm of Essex County, Massachusetts, celebrated a historic encounter between colonists and local tribesmen. Near the site of the tree in 1701 a meeting was held in which the purchase of town land was arranged. In the transaction, the colonists acquired title to considerable acreage in exchange for two shillings in silver and "Rum and vittles enouf." The tree that eventually bore the memory of the event was not planted for another fifty years. Yet, as it aged and took on an appropriately aged look, it was bestowed the town's creation myth.[21] The Cushing Elm of Hingham, Massachusetts, set out in 1729, bore the name of its planter but gained fame when it sheltered a company of Cohasset militiamen on their way to defend Boston. The tree, described as a "marvel of strength and symmetry," was ever after linked to these patriots and "the illustrious dead."[22]

Often the work of assigning historical associations to a particular elm fell to the antiquarian. Henry Howe of New Haven took it upon himself to christen some of the city's "most noble trees" in 1883, suggesting "names for each by which they shall hereafter be known."[23] Before this, New Haven had only one name-bearing elm — a tree planted on the day of Benjamin Franklin's death in 1790 and known as the Franklin Elm (fig. 3). Howe snipped freely at the broadcloth of history in the course of his project. One elm at the African Congregational Church — known locally as the "African Church Elm"— Howe renamed unapologetically in honor of Wesley, founder of Methodism, whose first flock in New Haven had earlier occupied the site.[24] Other memory-bearing elms were named after "representative men" in New Haven society — merchants, bankers, educators, and other luminaries of the local empyrean. Needless to say, Howe's elms were patrician trees. Rare indeed was the elm named for a woman, in New Haven or anywhere else. One of the few had been dedicated to the great soprano Jenny Lind — the "Swedish Nightingale" who took midcentury America by storm. In 1852 Lind toured western Massachusetts and sang in Hatfield beneath an elm — known afterward as the Jenny Lind Elm.[25]

No single historical figures had more namesake elms than George Washington. Under a brace of elms in Holliston, Massachusetts, Washington was said to have rested on his return from Boston in 1789.[26] The Great Elms at both Wethersfield and Springfield allegedly sheltered the great man, and were often referred to by his name. At Palmer, Massachusetts, stood another Washington Elm, which, according to tradition, witnessed two passages of the great man — in

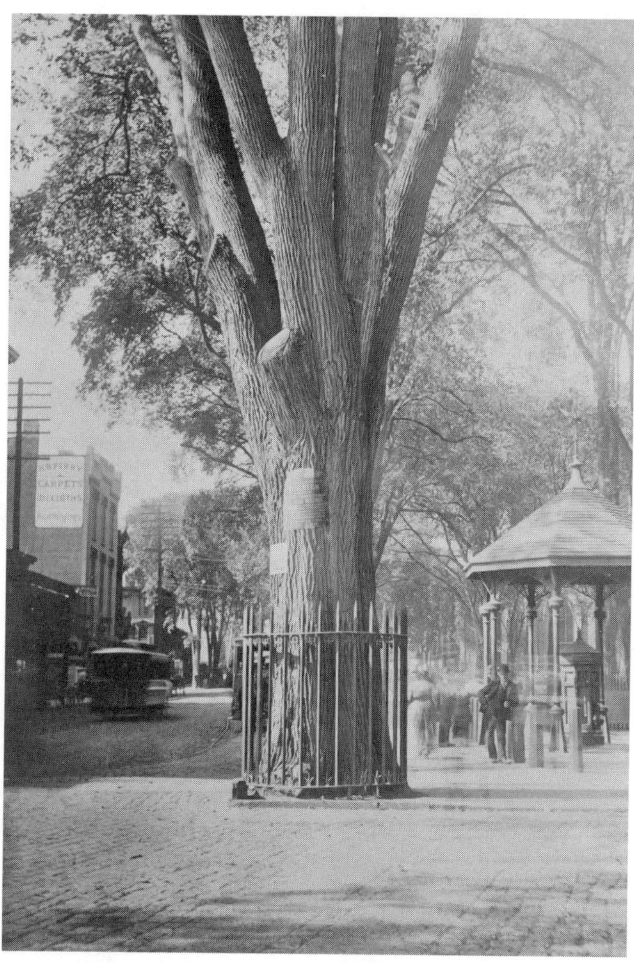

FIG. 3. The Franklin Elm, New Haven, Connecticut, c. 1860. (Library of Congress, Prints and Photographs Division, LC-USZ62-117871)

1775 and in 1789.[27] But none of these trees had the exalted status of the Washington Elm at Cambridge, Massachusetts — the greatest of all Yankee name-bearing elms, and the most famous tree in America until its death in October 1923. The Washington Elm was one of the top tourist attractions in Boston for decades. Visiting dignitaries made obligatory tours of the tree, and its image was imprinted on hotel chinaware, furniture upholstery, postcards, stereographs, even a United States postage stamp (fig. 4). It was the subject of songs, rhymes,

Decoration Day speeches, and reams of patriotic verse. James Russell Lowell's "Under the Old Elm" was only the best known:

> Historic town, thou holdest sacred dust,
> Once known to men as pious, learned, just,
> And one memorial pile that dares to last;
> But Memory greets with reverential kiss
> No spot in all thy circuit sweet as this,
> Touched by that modest glory as it passed,
> O'er which yon elm hath piously displayed
> These hundred years its monumental shade.[28]

The origins of the Washington Elm story can be traced to the first great mustering of American forces during the Revolution. Three months after the initial firefights at Lexington and Concord, Washington was summoned to Massachusetts to assume command of the Army of the United Colonies. He arrived at Cambridge on July 3, 1775, to take up his new post and review the troops on Cambridge Common. Myth and fact have long blurred the true course of the day's events. The traditional version of the story holds that Washington took command with great drama and gravitas, and "beneath the wide-spreading branches of the patriarch tree" that was to bear his name.[29] But the association of this seminal event with the Washington Elm was largely a manufactured one, an "invented tradition" of the mid-nineteenth century. As Eric Hobsbawm has written, invented traditions — usually based partly in truth — seek to "establish continuity with a suitable historic past." They often appear during periods of convulsive change, when a "rapid transformation of society weakens or destroys the social patterns for which 'old' traditions had been designed."[30]

In Cambridge, that moment came in the 1840s. The town's population, which numbered fewer than 3,500 persons until 1820, nearly doubled a mere ten years later — and then doubled again by 1845.[31] Much of this population boom was due to a massive influx of immigrant workers fueled by the industrial development of East Cambridge. The founding of the City of Cambridge in 1846 summarized the metamorphosis of "Old Cambridge"— a predominantly Anglo-Saxon community fiercely proud of its role in the founding of the nation — into a polyglot metropolis. The origins of the Washington Elm tradition also appear to date to this societal transformation. The narrative was invented, as it were, to provide continuity with a past under siege by the forces of industrial modernization.

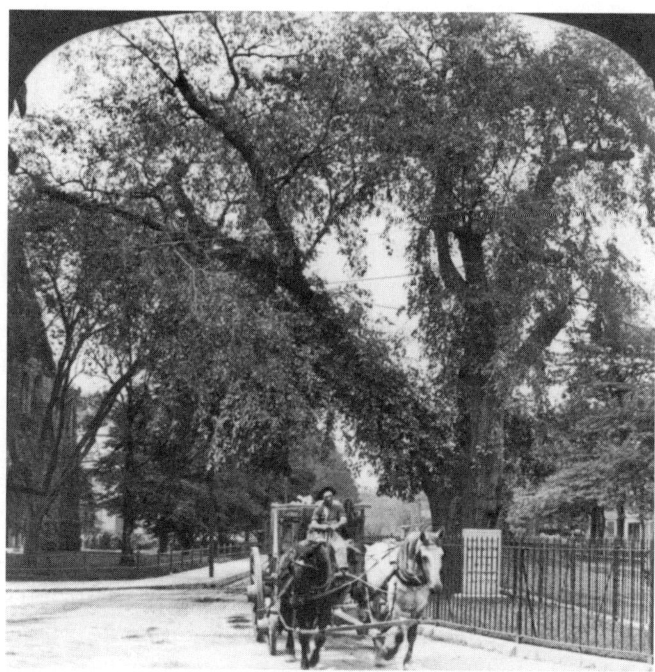

FIG. 4. The Washington Elm, Cambridge, Massachusetts, c. 1890. (From Dame, *Typical Elms and Other Trees of Massachusetts,* 1890)

Prior to the 1840s, the Washington Elm is wholly absent from local histories, Revolutionary-era accounts, or traveler's descriptions. Indeed, for more than half a century, the story seemed nonexistent.[32]

Another contributing factor was a flush of nationalism that accompanied the presidency of Andrew Jackson. The Jacksonian years brought a resurgent interest in America's colonial past, a new sense of piety and gratitude toward the founding generation (which was then fast disappearing) and a fresh interest in "relics of our national infancy."[33] Ralph Waldo Emerson reflected on the irony of all this filial devotion in a land so fresh with youthful possibility: "Our age is retrospective," he wrote in "Nature"; "It builds sepulchres to the fathers."[34] Or it invented sepulchral elms. Although the precise source of the Washington Elm tradition is not known, it appears to have involved an imaginative antiquarian named John Langdon Sibley. In an 1837 issue of *The American Magazine of Useful Knowledge,* Sibley related that under a "Glorious old tree" Washington "drew his sword as commander-in-chief of the American army, for the first time." The witness Elm was thus worthy of reverence as a "sacred memorial of the past and the present." "Amidst the changes which have taken place in the world, and particularly in America and New England," Sibley reasoned, this tree "stood out like a watchman" guarding the grave of memory."[35]

Sibley had some help, however, from none other than the great fabulist Washington Irving, who invoked the elm and its glorious associations in his 1855 *Life of George Washington*.[36] And during the centennial in 1876, the Washington Elm gained further fame when the diary of a colonial woman named Dorothy Dudley was published. The document, whose author claimed to have witnessed Washington on the Common, contained a breathless firsthand account of the day's events and placed Washington and the elm at center stage. The Dudley diary found its way into many a schoolbook before it was shown to be a fraud — the work of an anonymous soul punch-drunk on patriotic sentiment.[37] Other writers contributed similarly fabulous embellishments. In one particularly imaginative account from 1874, Washington had evidently built a *platform* in his Elm, in which he was "accustomed to sit and survey with his glass the country round."[38]

However specious its provenance, the Washington Elm story became part of the nation's mythological canon. In 1864, during a surge in patriotism brought on by the Civil War, a granite tablet was placed at the base of the tree with an inscription from the pen of Henry Wadsworth Longfellow. "UNDER THIS TREE," it claimed, "Washington first took command of the American Army, July 3rd, 1775."[39] By 1875, the centennial of Washington's arrival at Cambridge, the Elm tradition was firmly ensconced as patriotic truth. A spectacular celebration in July of that year focused on the tree. The Elm's lower limbs were adorned with bunting, and one intrepid soul affixed an American flag to a limb at the very top of the tree.[40] The Elm's symbolic power lasted well into the twentieth century. "In the heart of every American who loves the history of his country," wrote J. R. Simmons in 1919, "there dwells a degree of respect and gratitude for this living representative of olden time."[41] As late as 1936, writer Erle Kauffman could claim: "Of course every boy and girl knows that it was an elm tree at Cambridge, Massachusetts, that shaded General George Washington . . . when he took command of the Continental Army." For Kauffman, it was the Washington tree that made *Ulmus Americana* "America's tree of glory."[42]

With scrutiny, however, the Washington Elm tradition began to unravel. In 1923 a short article in the *Cambridge Tribune* demonstrated that the tree was no relic of the aboriginal forest but an elm planted by a long-forgotten farmer — one of six of nearly identical age located at five-hundred-foot intervals along Garden Street, the old edge of the Common. The trees were apparently planted around 1700 as part of "a methodical plan" to provide shade for livestock — and perhaps amenity for the town's inhabitants.[43] Then, in a meticulously crafted essay published in 1925, a local historian named Samuel F. Batchelder accused the "traditionalists" of overlooking a floodtide of evidence that proved the Washington Elm story was just that — an elaborate story. But wrecking a sacred piece of patriotica was not something done lightly: Discrediting the Washington Elm story, Batchelder suggested, "would be as painful a shock to our historic equilibrium as to declare the truth that the Declaration of Independence was not signed on the Fourth of July."[44]

Washington was said to have taken command of the troops on July 3, 1775, in the ceremony described by Sibley and others. But Batchelder could produce no evidence to support either date or event. Washington was indeed in town on July 3, but spent the entire day inspecting fortifications elsewhere in Boston. As the troops themselves were busily constructing trenches from Malden to Roxbury, it is impossible that the entire army could have been summoned to the Common to cheer their new general. The Provincial Congress had in fact specified, on June 26, 1775, that the reception for Washington at Cambridge be "without any expense of powder, and without taking the Troops off from the necessary attention to their duty at this crisis."[45] Hauling in the troops at such a perilous moment would have been reckless indeed. And as for Washington's wheeling about memorably on a stallion — as had been described by Sibley — his own letters reveal a man in "poor health" and "a good deal fatigued."[46]

The role of the hallowed tree was equally suspect. As Batchelder reasoned, it was unlikely that Washington would have sought to shelter himself from the sun in front of a lot of hardscrabble farmers whose respect he needed to earn. This was not the idolized *pater patriae* of later decades: in 1775 Washington was still a little-known Southern gentleman on Yankee turf — a man who had come, moreover, to replace a popular New England commander — Artemus Ward. Languishing under a shade tree would have been no way for a new leader to appear before men he was to send into battle.[47] Indeed, the actual transfer of authority between the generals most likely took place across the Common at Artemus Ward's headquarters.

But in spite of himself Batchelder was troubled by the "persistent association" of the Washington and the Elm, and conceded than the story must contain some grain of truth. If Washington did not take actual command of the colonial troops in a ceremony under the Elm, perhaps he did *something* near or under the tree — even if it was no more than stop by it briefly, perhaps as General Ward rode out to greet him on the morning of July 2, in the pouring rain.[48] In the end it hardly mattered. Irrespective of the precise role — if any — the Elm played, it had long ago been ensconced as the principal vessel bearing memory of the historical event. The legend refused to die, in spite of Batchelder's revisionism and long after the tree itself had passed from the scene.

By the end of the nineteenth century the once-noble Elm had been marooned on a traffic island, surrounded by streetcar tracks and a sea of asphalt. Its great crown had been mercilessly pruned and a series of iron rods and bands supported what was left of its rotting limbs. The storied hulk finally succumbed to gravity on October 27, 1923. A Parks Department crew had been dispatched earlier that week to remove a projecting limb. As they did so, the entire tree — sodden from recent rains — toppled over.[49] Word spread rapidly that the icon had fallen, and soon a crowd gathered, followed by crewmen who had been instructed to cut up and haul off the remains. A reporter from the *Cambridge Tribune,* claiming to represent several historical societies, attacked the Superintendent of Parks as he arrived: "I forbid you to put a saw on it!" he shouted."[50] The crowd swelled and became unruly as relic hunters scrambled for pieces of the tree. The sole patrolman on scene was quickly overwhelmed by "Nearby residents and Radcliffe girls," reported the *Cambridge Chronicle,* who "went to work with the saws and axes of the park employees to remove souvenirs."[51]

The fall of the Washington Elm made national news, with some reports claiming that the tree's demise was the work of Communists.[52] Most related the story with heavy patriotic sentiment. "In the recent death of the Washington Elm," the *Chronicle* moaned, "the city and the nation have suffered an irreparable loss from our historic memorials. No other tree in all the world was so dear to American hearts. Thousands of pilgrims annually wended their way to the Cambridge common to see uplifted its venerable form whose spreading branches served to kindle anew the fires of patriotism in their pent-up souls. Indeed the passing of this precious relic has inspired thousands of Americans with a sense of almost personal human loss such as one might feel with the passing of a great figure in our country's history." With the passing of the Washington Elm, "the last surviving eye-witness" of the Revolution had gone. Its loss eliminated a monument "greater than sculptured marble and more lasting than any tablet of bronze or granite."[53]

A commission was appointed shortly after to determine the fate of the remains — now placed under lock and key in a city warehouse — and to recommend an appropriate memorial to the Washington Elm. Once a vessel bearing the memory of a historical event, the Washington Elm was now itself an object of veneration.[54] The Washington Elm came to overshadow the very event it shaded — and to which it owed its original significance. It even nearly caused the removal of another monument to Washington in Boston. Walter Gilman Page, chairman of the Commonwealth's art commission, seriously proposed moving the great equestrian statue of Washington in Boston's Public Garden to the site of the late Elm.[55] Concerned "that the traditional sentiment . . . not end with the death of the original," James Michael Curley — Boston's mythic mayor — offered his municipal neighbors a young scion of the Washington Elm, raised from a cutting taken years before.[56]

But efforts to properly commemorate the Washington Elm remained unresolved for decades, and produced little more than a medallion in the pavement marking the former location of the tree.[57] In 1949, Frank Boland, proprietor of the nearby Commander Hotel (whose stationery and chinaware carried an image of the Elm), initiated a campaign to commemorate the commemorative tree. Doing so reopened debate over the veracity of the Washington Elm tradition. Leonard Craske — a popular classicist better known for his sculpture of the fisherman at Gloucester, Massachusetts — had already been commissioned to design a bas-relief. He depicted precisely the scene of patriotic pomp that made Batchelder wince. After consultation with the U.S. Army's Historical Division, some of the grosser inaccuracies were eliminated.[58] With Harvard historian Samuel Eliot Morison's input, Boland and Craske edited the caption to read, "General George Washington, having taken command of the Continental Army, reviews the troops on Cambridge Common from under the elm that grew near this spot, July 3, 1775."[59] This too failed to pass muster, and by the final casting, the elm had been purged from the text; the tree was now but a mute companion to an equestrian Washington. The unveiling of Craske's piece, on July 3, 1950, was itself a grand occasion, and included a parade, "Dress Retreat," fireworks, and a banquet featuring "elm soup." One of the honored speakers was a young congressman named John F. Kennedy.[60]

As for the tree itself, the Parks Department received hundreds of requests for fragments — from "people of all classes and conditions," from colleges, genealogical associations, historical societies, fraternal lodges, women's clubs, elementary schools, veteran's organizations, the Mount Vernon Ladies' Association of the Union, and even from the Smithsonian Institution. One man, who claimed Washingtonian lineage, wished to craft a box for buttons said to be from the general's coat. A sculptor offered to "carve a likeness" of Washington from the wood of the tree. Another suggested that a pair of chairs be made for the president and vice president of the United States.[61]

In the end, hundreds of small cubes were cut from the limbs of the Washington Elm, each labeled with a brass plaque and sent to prominent individuals around the country. Fragments of the main trunk were sent to the governors of various states and territories, and a polished cross-section was presented to the museum at Mount Vernon. At least one picture frame was made, to hold a likeness of the late tree itself. Gavels were fashioned, too, and a pair presented to the senate and house of representatives of each state.[62] Smaller cuts of the historic wood were sent to the governments of thirty-two countries.[63] Freed from its post of two hundred years, the remains of the Washington Elm — New England's most famous witness tree — sped around the world.

Notes

This essay is adapted from chapter 3, "The Witness Tree," of Campanella, *Republic of Shade,* 45–68.

1. Tudor, *Letters on the Eastern States,* 271–72.
2. Dewey, *An Address Delivered Under the Old Elm Tree in Sheffield,* 5.
3. Adams, *Boston Common,or Rural Walks in Cities,* 16.
4. Downing, *Rural Essays,* quoted in Goode, "Andrew Jackson Downing on Trees," 191.
5. Holmes, "Introduction," in Dame, *Typical Elms and Other Trees of Massachusetts,* 8.
6. Adams, *Boston Common, or Rural Walks in Cities,* 16.
7. Latrobe, *The Rambler in North America,* 43.
8. Quoted in Gutman, *Work, Culture, and Society in Industrializing America,* 29. Also see Kammen, *Meadows of Memory,* 143–45.
9. Simmons, *The Historic Trees of Massachusetts,* 133–34.
10. Hamilton, *Memorial of Jessie Lee and the Old Elm,* 47.
11. Quoted in Ibid., 49.

12. Warren, *The Great Tree on Boston Common,* 17.

13. "The Boston Elm: The Famous Tree Succumbs to the Gale," *Boston Herald,* February 16, 1876.

14. Dame, *Typical Elms and Other Trees of Massachusetts,* 49.

15. Peattie, *A Natural History of Trees,* 239.

16. The phrase is from Kammen, *Meadows of Memory,* 150.

17. Drake, *Historic Mansions and Highways around Boston,* 268.

18. Dame, *Typical Elms and Other Trees of Massachusetts,* 51.

19. Ibid., 79–82.

20. Ibid., 101.

21. Simmons, *The Historic Trees of Massachusetts,* 61–62.

22. Ibid., 27.

23. Howe, "New Haven's Elms and Green," 6.

24. Ibid., 8.

25. Wells and Wells, *A History of Hatfield,* 223.

26. Letter from Thomas A. Dickinson, in the *Framingham Tribune,* quoted in Simmons, *The Historic Trees of Massachusetts,* 54–55.

27. Simmons, The *Historic Trees of Massachusetts,* 85–86.

28. Lowell, "Under the Old Elm," 74–89.

29. "Diary of Dorothy Dudley," quoted in Batchelder, "The Washington Elm Tradition," 50.

30. Hobsbawm, "Inventing Traditions," in Hobsbawm and Ranger, eds., *The Invention of Tradition,* 1–4.

31. Paige, *History of Cambridge,* 452.

32. Batchelder, "The Washington Elm Tradition," 54.

33. Quoted in Miller, *Errand into the Wilderness,* 205.

34. Emerson, "Nature," quoted in Kazin, *A Writer's America,* 50.

35. Sibley, quoted in "The Washington Elm," 143–44.

36. Irving, *Life of George Washington,* 318.

37. Morison, "Proposed Tablet Under Washington Elm."

38. Drake, *Historic Mansions and Highways around Boston,* 268.

39. The tablet is located on Cambridge Common adjacent to the former site of the Elm.

40. Dame, *Typical Elms and Other Trees of Massachusetts,* 27.

41. Simmons, *The Historic Trees of Massachusetts,* 15.

42. Kauffman, "The Elm," 222.

43. J. Gardner Bartlett, in the *Cambridge Tribune,* November 3, 1923, reprinted in "The Washington Elm," 145–46. The Cambridge Cow Common originally extended as far west as Linnaean Street. The Washington Elm, located at the present intersection of Mason and Garden Streets, was the first of the six elms.

44. Batchelder, "The Washington Elm Tradition — Is It True?

45. Lieutenant Colonel E. M. Harris to John B. Atkinson, May 4, 1949, unpublished letter, Cambridge Historical Commission, Cambridge, Massachusetts.

46. Washington, quoted in Batchelder, "The Washington Elm Tradition," 73.

47. Batchelder, "The Washington Elm Tradition," 56–57. Washington was thus the *second* commander of the American Army — a point, Batchelder allowed, which was "not generally appreciated."

48. Ibid., 73–75.

49. "The Washington Elm," 143.

50. "Some Interesting Work about the Famous Washington Elm," [n.d.], unpublished affidavit, Cambridge Historical Commission.

51. "Washington Elm Finally Topples," *Cambridge Chronicle,* October 27, 1923.

52. Charles M. Sullivan to Gary Griffith, September 25, 1996, unpublished letter, Cambridge Historical Commission.

53. "A Tribute to the Washington Elm," *Cambridge Chronicle,* July 4, 1925.

54. Or as George Crabbe put it, "Monuments themselves Memorials need." Quoted in Lowenthal, *The Past Is a Foreign Country,* 323.

55. "Washington Elm Is Cut Up and Stored," *Cambridge Chronicle,* November 3, 1923.

56. "Mayor Curley Makes Offer to Cambridge," *Cambridge Chronicle,* November 10, 1923.

57. A later medallion still marks the spot, though it is indistinguishable from a manhole cover.

58. Lieutenant Colonel E. M. Harris to John B. Atkinson, May 4, 1949, unpublished letter, Cambridge Historical Commission.

59. Frank A. K. Boland to Hon. Michael J. Neville, December 28, 1949, unpublished letter, Cambridge Historical Commission.

60. The bas-relief was later stolen, and had to be recast from a plaster model now located in the lobby of the Sheraton Commander Hotel. See Eliot B. Spaulding, "Stolen Bronze Memorial Recast for April 19," *Cambridge Chronicle,* March 20, 1975.

61. "Many Interested in Historic Elm," *Cambridge Chronicle,* December 1, 1923.

62. "A Tribute to the Washington Elm," *Cambridge Chronicle,* July 4, 1925.

63. Batchelder, "The Washington Elm Tradition," 47.

THE WEIGHT OF HISTORY

ALISON K. HOAGLAND

Unresolved

The Italian Hall Memorial in Calumet, Michigan

In Calumet, Michigan, the memorial to the worst tragedy of the copper-mining district consists of a masonry arch salvaged from the Italian Hall where the incident took place (fig. 1). Standing in the center of a grassy lot with modest landscaping, the arch is neither triumphal nor mournful. The incident that it commemorates is not obvious from the design of the memorial, and it is only after reading text that a visitor can understand what the memorial references. Yet it is this very lack of explicitness and commitment that makes the memorial so effective, because it commemorates a highly contested and unresolved event. The community's complex memory of the tragedy is reflected in a memorial that is understated and incomplete.

Set in the middle of a lot on the edge of Calumet's commercial center, the memorial consists primarily of a stone and brick archway, adorned with brass plaques contributed by donors to the memorial effort. Brick paths, concrete benches, shrubbery, and a flagpole define the space, while several signs relate the story. One side of a large Michigan Historical Site marker describes the event; the other side gives the history of the building. A smaller stone marker displays a photograph of the Italian Hall. And in the rear of the lot, a "Historical Women of Michigan" sign relates the story of one activist present at the Italian Hall tragedy, Anna Clemenc. The reliance on signage indicates that the arch alone does not tell the story. The arch reminds us that the building of which it was once a part was demolished, indicating a lack of community support for its preservation and suggesting the divided feelings about the tragedy. The arch stands disconnected, acting as sculpture as much as building fragment. The story that it memorializes is incomplete.

Tragedy

Five months into a bitter strike in Michigan's Copper Country in 1913, the Western Federation of Miners held a Christmas party for strikers' children. About 500 children and 175 parents crowded into the second floor of Italian Hall. The partygoers played games, sang songs, and, late in the afternoon, lined up to receive presents from Santa Claus. Then disaster struck. Someone apparently yelled "Fire!" and panic-stricken partygoers raced down a wide flight of stairs to reach the main exit. But someone tripped and fell and others on top of them, until dozens of bodies lay at the foot of the stairs, crushed. Seventy-three people died that day; fifty-eight of them were children. Tragically, there was no fire, and thus no need to rush. The official cause of death was suffocation.[1]

This tragedy resonated throughout the Copper Country and the nation at large. Opinions differ on the cause and the effect of the tragedy, the strike, management-worker relations, and the company's role in the community. The Italian Hall tragedy has as much capacity to divide the community as to unite it. The fact that seventy-five years elapsed before the event's commemoration also points to the division in the community. Copper Country residents could not forget the tragedy, but they did not always want to remember it either.

To understand the import of this tragedy, several contexts must be established. One concerns the copper-mining district in Michigan known as the Copper Country. Located on the Keweenaw Peninsula, which juts up into Lake Superior in the northwest corner of the state, the Copper Country was the nation's prime source of copper from the mid–1840s to the mid–1880s. Although Butte, Montana, surpassed its output in the late 1880s, Michigan nonetheless continued to increase copper production until after World War I. One company dominated the industry and produced half the dividends: the mighty Calumet & Hecla Mining Company, headquartered in Boston, Massachusetts. About fifteen other companies worked deposits in the seventy-five-mile-long district.

The labor force had gone through several transformations. The earlier miners tended to be Englishmen — especially Cornishmen — as well as Scots, Irish, and Germans. Cornishmen and Scots tended to rise to management positions. By the late nineteenth century, new workers came from Finland, Eastern Europe, and Italy. These workers tended to receive unskilled jobs and lower pay, and it is among these workers that unionists found their greatest support.

The Western Federation of Miners (WFM), a leftist union associated with

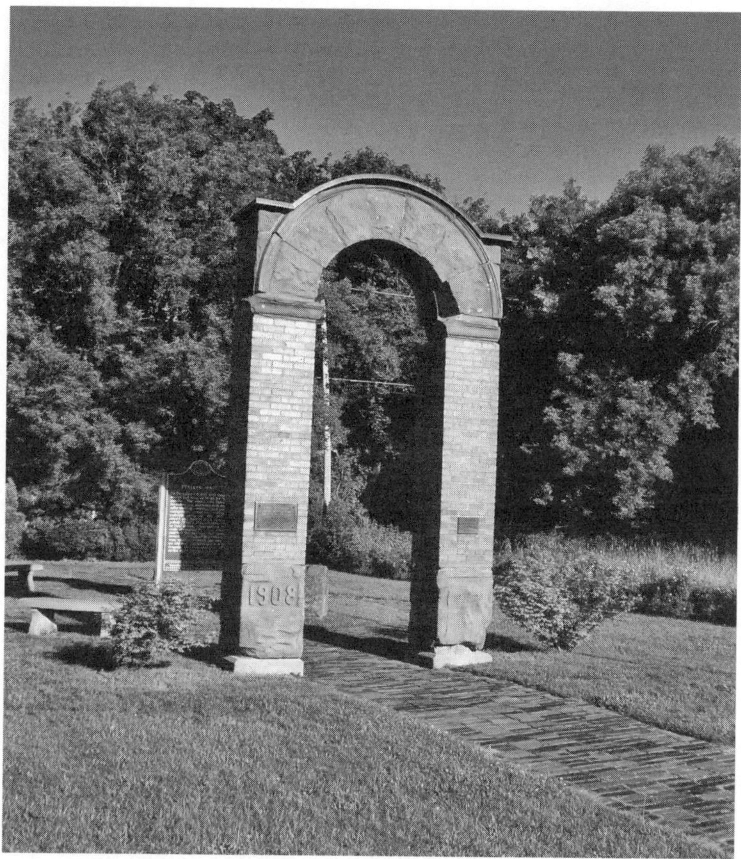

FIG. 1. The Italian Hall Memorial consists primarily of an archway salvaged from the building in which seventy-three people, mostly women and children, died. (Photo by the author)

metal mining in the Rockies, sporadically attempted to organize the Copper Country, beginning in 1904. By 1913, the WFM claimed 9,000 members in the Copper Country and the union locals readied for a confrontation. The national executive board urged caution, fearing that they did not have the financial resources to support a strike. But the locals held a referendum and when the members voted to strike, the executive board reluctantly supported them. In letters to mine managers, the Copper Country's District Union No. 16 enumerated its demands, which included shorter hours, higher pay, two men on each rock-drilling machine, and recognition of the union. The mining companies unilaterally re-

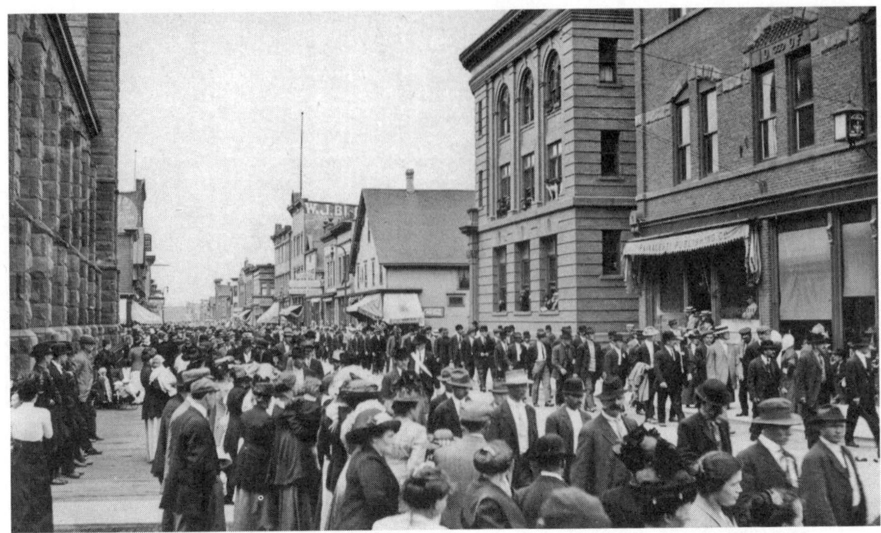

FIG. 2. Unionists parade in downtown Calumet. (Quincy Mining Company Collection, Box 1 F. 9 [Donor: Louis Koepel], Michigan Technological University Archives and Copper Country Historical Collections)

fused to meet with union representatives, and on July 23, 1913, WFM members walked out and shut down all of the mines in the Copper Country, putting 15,000 men out of work.[2]

The strike lasted for eight-and-a-half months, with popular support shifting frequently (fig. 2). For the first few weeks, the strikers seemed to have the upper hand, with the mines shut down and the companies' management refusing to negotiate. To maintain order, the governor sent in the National Guard, which was largely seen as supporting the companies. In mid-August, some of the companies resumed operations on a small scale. As the governor withdrew troops, the companies replaced them with contract detectives and also deputized their own loyal men. Strike-related violence on August 14 resulted in the deaths of two strikers and a wave of sympathy flowed toward the unionists.[3] Clashes on the streets were an almost daily occurrence, as strikers paraded and endeavored to discourage strikebreakers. Union-supporting women, particularly Anna Clemenc, also paraded defiantly, attracting insults.

Company managers drew on many resources. Their well-funded lawyers obtained injunctions against parading. They imported strikebreakers and deputies to keep the mines functioning. They provided space and resources to the National Guard troops. A pro-management group calling itself the Copper Country Commercial Club published propaganda on their behalf. In November a Citizens' Alliance formed, serving as an anti-union organization. After three strikebreakers were killed on December 6, public sentiment seemed to shift toward the side of the companies. It was in this highly charged atmosphere that the Italian Hall disaster occurred.

The violence and social divisions that marked the Copper Country strike of 1913–14 were not unusual, as the late nineteenth and early twentieth centuries witnessed a number of highly violent strikes. Labor violence reflected new conflicts in industry, as management attempted to consolidate control over an increasingly hierarchical workplace and an increasingly immigrant workforce responded by organized confrontations. Some of the most violent conflicts in the early twentieth century occurred in the mining industry. At the same time as the Copper Country strike, Colorado coal miners, organized by the United Mine Workers of America, were on strike in Ludlow. When the Colorado Fuel & Iron Company evicted them from company housing, the strikers set up tent colonies. In April 1914 (just as the Copper Country strike was ending), the National Guard fired machine guns and rifles into the colony during a day-long assault, then set fire to the tents in the evening. The bodies of eleven children and two women were found the next day in a pit beneath one of the tents. These victims were among the estimated ninety people who died in strike-related violence in Colorado alone.[4]

Given the intensity of feeling about labor-management conflicts in general, and the Copper Country's strike in particular, it is no wonder that the Italian Hall tragedy was instantly politicized. Public sentiment immediately shifted back to the strikers. Donations to a relief fund amounted to $25,000 within a day. Charles Moyer, president of the WFM, rejected this charity, however, maintaining that the "union will bury its own dead." Some observers saw this as a missed opportunity. Luke Grant, an investigator for the U.S. Commission on Industrial Relations, suggested that the union could have used public sympathy deriving from this tragedy to force the companies to negotiate.[5] But the opportunity was lost. Two days later, the county sheriff's men confronted Moyer and an assistant in their hotel room, shot Moyer during a struggle, and put them on a train out of town. Public support for the strike began to slip away, as did the support of the national union. Finally, in April, the locals voted to abandon the strike effort.

The Italian Hall tragedy remained the most prominent incident of the long and bitter strike. Its impact was compounded by the fact that, while there was a clear sense of a wrong having been committed, no one was ever charged with a crime. A few days after the tragedy, the coroner held an inquest, summoning seventy witnesses. His verdict, issued on December 31, 1913, was that the cause of death was "by suffocation, the same being caused by being jammed on the stairway leading to the entrance of the Italian Hall . . . and the stampede was caused by some person or persons within the hall, unknown to the jury at this time, raising an alarm of fire within the hall."[6] Two unresolved questions haunt the history of this event, affecting the way that the incident persists in public memory. One is the question of who, if anyone, cried fire? And the second one is how did people die? Why were they trapped in a stairwell?

Witnesses differed widely on who had raised the alarm. At the coroner's inquest, twenty-six witnesses heard a man cry "Fire!" They described the perpetrator variously as dark, fair; moustached, clean-shaven; wearing a hat, wearing a cap. Witnesses differed on where in the hall the perpetrator stood. Some placed him by the door, others in the back of the hall. As the *Miner's Bulletin* reported, "a fiend in the shape of a man sneaked up the stairway leading to the hall, opened the door and waving his arm cried 'fire, fire!' then quickly making his way to the street where he disappeared in the gathering darkness." Seven witnesses said he was wearing a button; three identified it as a Citizens' Alliance button. But fourteen did not see a button on the man at all. The unionists felt strongly that the Citizens' Alliance or other pro-company men precipitated the disaster. Much of the questioning at the inquest was designed to counteract this, pointing out that union representatives checked for union cards before allowing people to enter the party. And although others noted that identification was not checked later in the day, the coroner's finding included the statement "that no person or persons was allowed inside of the hall where the celebration was being held without producing a union card or having some member of the union vouch for them before they be allowed admittance."[7]

Other explanations surfaced. Perhaps someone cried for water, which in Croatian sounds very much like the word for fire. Another account emerged in 1982, when Leslie Chapman of Calumet related a story that he had heard fifty-eight years earlier in Butte. In 1924, an unknown dying man confessed that he and his partner "were both single men and drunk and thought we'd have some fun. As we walked by the hall we decided to holler fire and watch the people come down.

We didn't know it would turn out bad. We both left town afterward."[8] Some witnesses never heard a cry of "Fire!"

The second unresolved question concerns the pile-up in the stairway and its cause (fig. 3). Witnesses described a rush to the stairs, someone tripped and fell, causing others to fall, creating a pile of people that just got bigger. Eyewitness John Antila described it as "just a moving mass down the stair." Others, approaching from the outside, found a mass of bodies four or five feet high, packed so tightly that people could not be removed from the front; rather, rescuers went in the back of the building to the top of the stairs, and pulled people off the top. Eyewitness Charles Meyers described it as "a mass mostly all children mixed up and tangled in one mass in front of the door, that I don't believe any children got out. I tried to pull some of these children but I could not, they were so tight and tangled up I could not do anything." When asked how many people were in the stairway, he estimated two hundred or more, and said, "It was just one scream, they were squeezed so tight they could not give a loud sound. It was just a scream, and death showed in almost all their faces especially the lower ones." The *Miner's Bulletin* described the tragedy: "The way was made for the children first and they filled the stairway so full and crowded from the rear so fast that some of the children were swept off their feet. These little bodies acted as stumbling blocks for those who followed and within a few seconds the stairway was a mass of bleeding, crushed, dead and dying humanity."[9]

In the midst of a bitter strike, a theory arose as to why so many died in the stairway. The union claimed that detectives in the employ of the companies held the doors shut and prevented exit. This account showed up first in a special edition of *Tyomies,* the Finnish-language newspaper, on December 26, 1913; the next day sheriff's deputies raided the newspaper's offices and charged four employees with "publication of matter that might have the effect of inciting a riot." Perhaps because of this intimidation, neither the union local's newspaper, the *Miner's Bulletin,* nor the national union's publication, *The Miners Magazine,* charged that deputies had held the doors shut. At the inquest, only two witnesses reported that deputies blocked the doors, while sixteen testified that they had not.[10] Some witnesses pointed out that some officials at the scene prevented people from entering and compounding the mess.

By the 1950s, though, another explanation had surfaced; some people alleged that the doors opened inward, thus preventing egress. This explanation has gained wide acceptance, even appearing on the Michigan Historical Site marker.

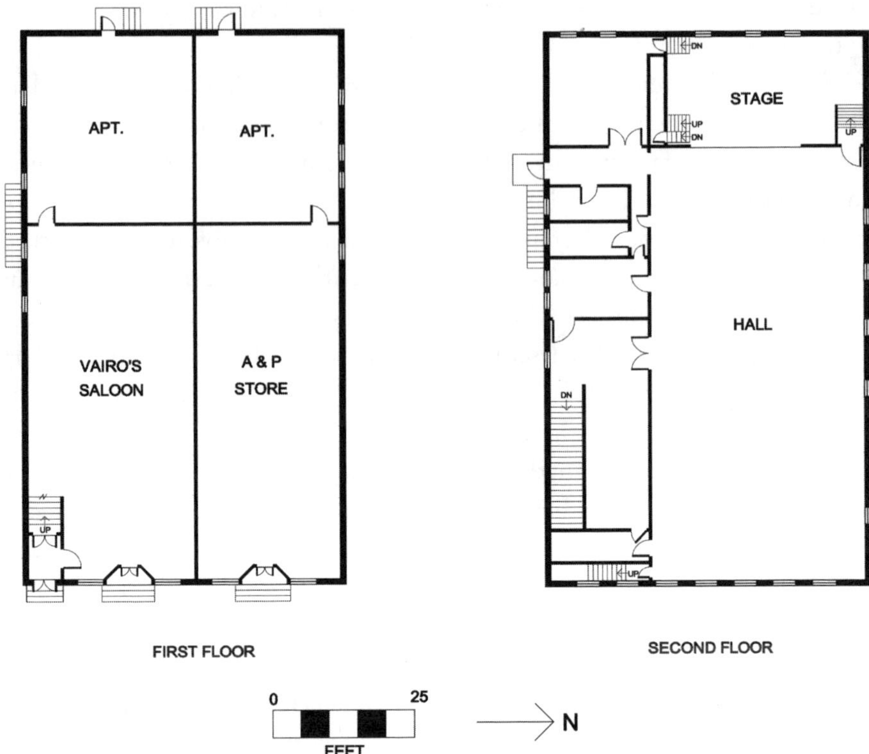

FIG. 3. First- and second-floor plans of the Italian Hall. Conjectural drawing based on contemporary accounts and photographs; the building was not measured before demolition. (Drawing by Chris Merritt and the author)

But this is clearly a latter-day explanation; not one witness at the coroner's inquest mentioned inward-opening doors. The pro-company *Daily Mining Gazette* specifically said that the doors opened outward, and neither union publication, the *Miner's Bulletin* or *The Miners Magazine,* alleged inward-opening doors, an explanation that might, in fact, absolve deputies from holding doors shut.[11]

The Italian Hall had had previous experience with inward-opening doors, as well as with disasters. The Società Mutua Beneficenza Italiana was a benevolent society organized in 1875 along ethnic lines. In 1890, its nearly completed hall collapsed in heavy winds. The organization rebuilt the next year, producing a large wooden building on a stone foundation, divided into two stores on the first floor, with a second-floor hall. In 1904 this building was cited by the marshal for

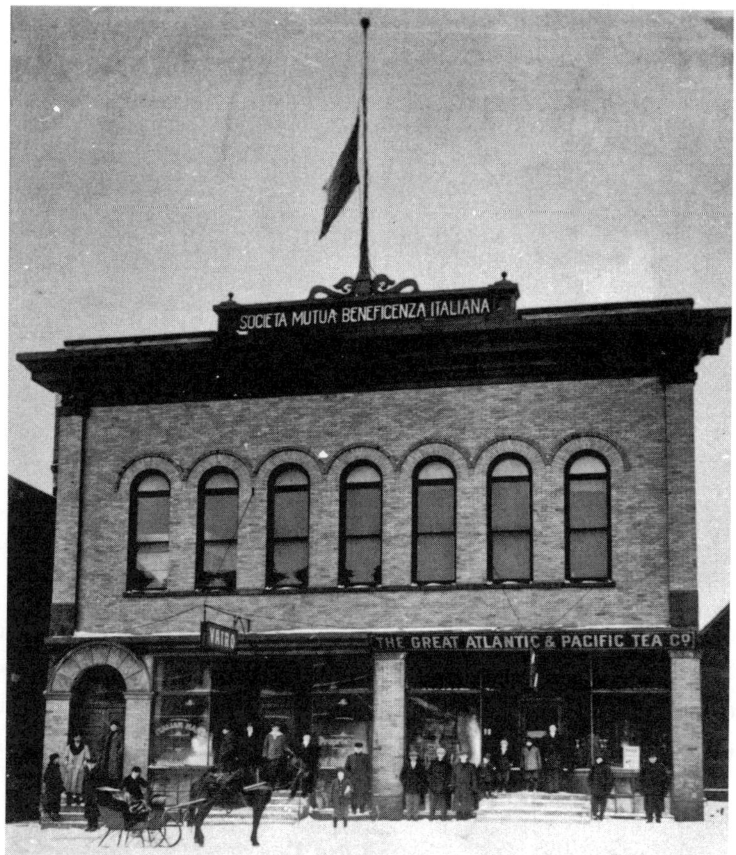

FIG. 4. The Italian Hall housed a bar and grocery store on the first floor and a meeting hall on the second. The archway on the left, which gave access to the second-floor stairway, was salvaged for the memorial. (Quincy Mining Company Collection, Box 1 F. 9 [Donor: Louis Koepel], Michigan Technological University Archives and Copper Country Historical Collections)

having inward-opening doors. On January 1, 1908, the hall burned to the ground; the Italian Hall in which the tragedy occurred was its replacement.[12]

The Società's new brick building of 1908, designed by architect Paul H. Macneil, measured 58 feet across and 100 feet deep (fig. 4). At ground level, the Great Atlantic and Pacific Tea Company and Vairo's saloon occupied two storefronts with recessed entries. In the southernmost bay of the front, double doors in a large round arch led to the stairway to the second floor. Seven round-arched windows on the second-floor façade illuminated the meeting hall. A handsome cornice, topped by the society's name, crowned the building. The second floor contained a well-equipped meeting hall, with a stage, balcony, ticket window, men's and women's toilets, barroom, and kitchen. The doorway from the street opened into a foyer that measured 6 feet wide by 8 feet deep. To the right off the foyer, a door led directly into the saloon. Two feet from the foot of the stairs, double doors separated the stairway from the foyer. The stairway was 5 feet 9 inches wide. A newspaper article written at the time of its dedication mentioned safety features such as "the ample main stairway" and two fire escapes and noted, "all doors open outward."[13]

The belief that the doors opened inward may have derived from a misleading stereoview published soon after the tragedy (fig. 5). The foreshortened view shows two sets of doors, one opening outward and one inward, apparently from the same door jamb. But this is impossible, because the foyer between the two doorways was deep enough to contain a door off to the right to Vairo's saloon. Part of the popularity of the inward-opening-door theory is due to the fact that it explains, logically, how so many could have died in the stairway. But the same situation, of sheer numbers of people preventing egress, occurred in February 2003 in a second-floor nightclub in Chicago. There, twenty-one people died in a stampede to the exits. The main exit door was apparently operable, but the capacity of the nightclub was more than the stairway could handle. The club's owners were convicted of criminal contempt and sentenced to two years in prison, but that conviction was later overturned.[14]

Commemoration

The Italian Hall tragedy was commemorated in a variety of ways, tangible and ephemeral, interpretive and documentary, by outsiders and residents. Immediately afterward, the incident received nationwide attention, appearing in the *New York Times* and other newspapers. Photographer John W. Nara documented the hall right after the tragedy. Some of these images were distributed in a set of stereoviews, along with other strike scenes, captioned in English and Finnish (fig. 6). Some were also made into postcards. The funerals of the victims, which attracted thousands of mourners who lined the route of the funeral processions, received extensive coverage. Newsreel footage of the funerals played in Chicago;

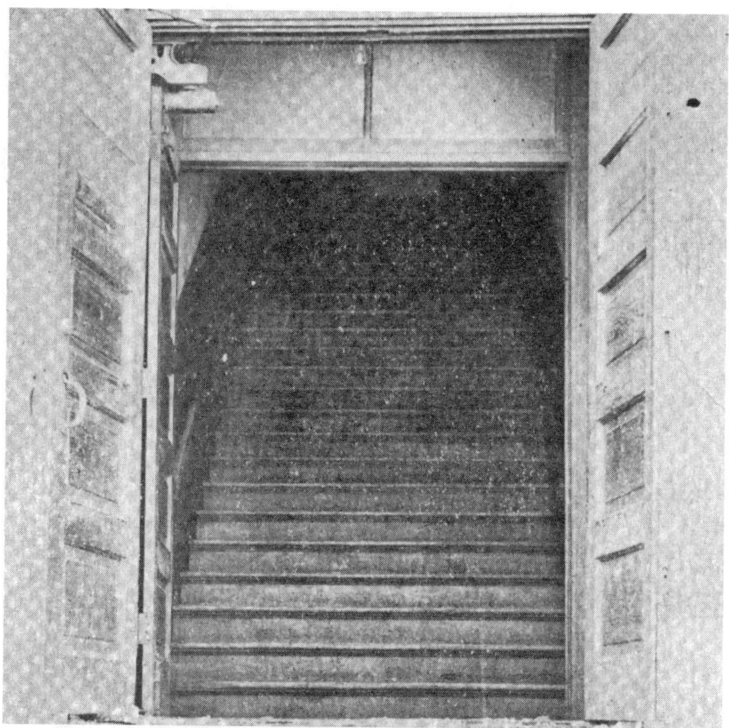

FIG. 5. The foreshortening in this photograph of the stairway seems to indicate inward-opening doors; J. W. Nara stereoview. (Quincy Mining Company Collection, Neg. #4197 [Donor: Louis Koepel], Michigan Technological University Archives and Copper Country Historical Collections)

the Western Federation of Miners used the showing as a fund-raiser. Even the film was contested; the union alleged that someone attempted to steal the film footage in Calumet, but the photographer had put a dummy in its place. The union also charged that the companies had tried to buy the film to prevent its being shown.[15]

Inevitably, though, the furor died down. In April 1914 strikers surrendered their union cards and returned to work, or left the area. There is no doubt that the tragedy cast a pall over the region. For people who lost family members and friends, it was a personal loss. For people who had been there, it was a searing experience. Ted Taipalus, who survived the tragedy as a boy although two of his sisters died in it, never spoke to his surviving sister about these events and vowed never to enter the building again.[16]

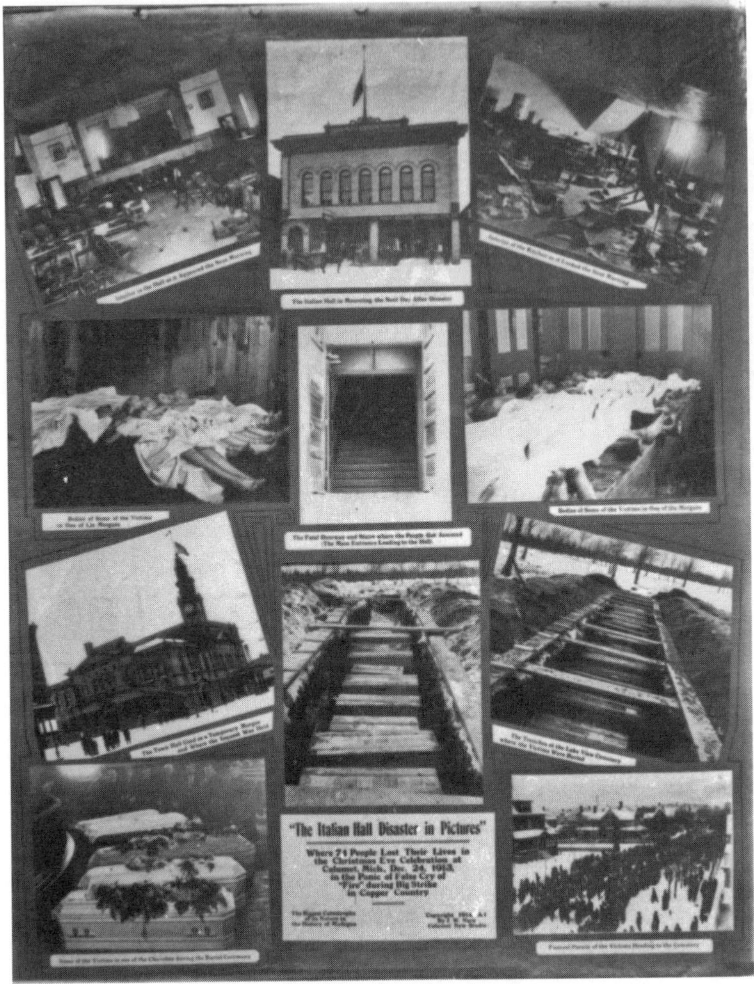

FIG. 6. Photographer John W. Nara compiled this collage of photographs, which depicted the hall after the tragedy, the victims, and their funerals. (Michigan Technological University Archives and Copper Country Historical Collections)

For decades there was no physical memorial to the tragedy. The most famous commemoration of the Italian Hall tragedy was by Woody Guthrie, who wrote a song about the incident in 1946. Guthrie never visited Calumet, but became aware of the tragedy by reading the autobiography of a labor organizer, Ella Reeve Bloor, who had been present that day. Guthrie's song had an unequivocal take on the event, as reflected in its title, "The 1913 Massacre." Guthrie blamed the event on "copper boss' thugs" who had yelled "Fire!" and then held the doors shut. He wrote, "The parents they cried and the miners they moaned, / 'See what your greed for money has done.'" Asch Records first released Guthrie's song on an album called "Struggle: Documentary #1." The other songs on the album related aspects of American history and workers' lives, including one called "Ludlow Massacre." Guthrie's song remains popular, giving the Italian Hall tragedy nationwide exposure, and guaranteeing Woody's son, Arlo, sold-out audiences when he plays Calumet.[17]

Although the Woody Guthrie song is by far the most enduring and far-reaching public commemoration of the Italian Hall tragedy, a number of other artistic renditions have attempted to tell the tale.[18] One major, recent event was an opera, commissioned by a local music festival and funded by a Michigan bank and the National Endowment for the Arts. *The Children of the Keweenaw* by composer Paul Seitz opened in the Calumet Theatre in 2001. Librettist Kathleen Masterson noted that she wanted to honor different points of view. Recognizing the complexity of the Italian Hall incident, Seitz and Masterson commented on the "unresolved nature of the event." In the last scene, a funeral, members of the chorus sing the name and age of each of the dead. But the last lines are given to the narrator, who repeats his first lines, which include a reference to Anna Clemenc:

> I do not claim
> That all I have told
> Of this, of her
> Is strictly true.
> What's true for me
> May not be true for you.[19]

Like the opera, a recently produced film does not attempt to provide a definitive explanation. Titled *1913 Massacre,* the film directed by Ken Ross and Louis V. Galdieri used the Woody Guthrie song as a departure point, but examined the memory of the event more than the event itself.

Outsiders from beyond the Copper Country developed all of these recountings and observances. Locally, as long as there was a significant number of people around who remembered the Italian Hall and the strike, this history received very little public discussion. Residents recall that the tragedy was not taught in local schools or discussed in homes. One resident remarked that it was "too emotional" a subject to discuss casually and also pointed to a lingering fear of speaking out against the company, even though the company is long gone. One reporter called the strike and the Italian Hall tragedy "an open wound in the memory of the community."[20] The unresolved nature of the tragedy — the fact that no perpetrator could be identified or punished — contributes to the raw feelings. But also the fact that this was a strike-related incident, the epitome of a divisive event, prevented open commemoration for several decades. To those who were present in 1913–14, the strike tore apart the community like nothing had before, or would since. The strikers were a minority, and a foreign-speaking one at that. Although the tragedy garnered the sympathy of the community, the strikers did not, contributing to the mixed emotions that resulted in the memorial. The residue of that divisiveness persists even today.

Renewed interest in the event derived from threats to the Italian Hall and its ultimate demolition. In 1980 the village threatened to condemn the building as unsafe; its owner, Helen Smith, was unable to maintain the building. A Friends group formed to preserve the building, but when the cost of doing so was put at $500,000, even the Friends agreed that preservation was not possible. The negative feelings associated with the Italian Hall — as a site of tragic deaths and community strife — also contributed to its demise. The Calumet Township supervisor recalled, years later, that "A lot of people did want it torn down, because they didn't want to look at it. They wanted it to go away."[21]

The Friends proposed that a memorial be made out of the doorway behind which so many died. The Italian Hall was demolished in 1984 and the archway set aside. Nothing happened for several years but the seventy-fifth anniversary of the tragedy in 1988 sparked some action and the next year the Friends completed and dedicated the park. Unionists, under the aegis of the Northwest Upper Peninsula Labor Council, provided volunteer labor. Further plans for buildings at the site to house a museum and theater to properly interpret the event have gone nowhere.[22]

Locally, commemoration also appeared in the format of privately published books around the time of the building's demolition, such as Peggy Germain's *Tinsel and Tears* and Wilbert B. Maki's poem *Stairway to Tragedy*. A video created in 2003 by a sixth-grade class at the Calumet school provided some sign that, after ninety years, this is finally a fully open and acceptable topic for discussion. In 2004 Larry Molloy produced a transcript of the coroner's inquest, with a close analysis of the text. In 2005 Peggy Germain reproduced every death certificate in another book. The next year Steve Lehto published *Death's Door: The Truth behind Michigan's Largest Mass Murder,* a highly partisan account, as its title would suggest.[23]

Historians have also related the story of the Italian Hall tragedy. Angus Murdoch published a popular history of the Copper Country in 1943, in which he painted a rosy picture of management-labor relations and blamed the union for making wild accusations about the tragedy. C. Harry Benedict, in the company-authorized history of Calumet & Hecla, called the incident an "inexplicable tragic panic," and gave the management point of view. In 1984, Arthur Thurner, a Calumet native who became a professor of history, published a history of the strike called *Rebels on the Range.* In his two chapters on the tragedy, Thurner recounted the controversy and divisiveness, but ultimately supported the companies' claims of innocence. In the most authoritative history of the region, historian Larry Lankton cast the tragedy in political terms, characterizing the conflict as one that both sides attempted to use to advantage. Even the Historical Society of Michigan's magazine entered into the controversy, publishing a photographic essay and the text of Woody Guthrie's song shortly before the building's demolition. The magazine then published an exchange of letters that demonstrated that the history of this event was not resolved. Burton H. Boyum, an iron-mining company executive, charged that Woody Guthrie, "in his haste to inflame hostilities, abandoned all truth and common sense." In response, John P. Beck, a labor historian, pointed out that the hostilities did not need inflaming; oppressive paternalism in the Copper Country had produced a large number of dissatisfied workers.[24]

Recently, a piece of public art stirred up old animosities. In the summer of 2000, the Copper Country Community Arts Council commissioned three works of art that reflected aspects of local life or history. Ed Andrzejewski's 12 × 6–foot mural depicting the screaming faces at the Italian Hall tragedy hung on an abandoned church in Calumet — but only for a few days. The board of the nonprofit organization administering the church building objected, ostensibly because of its size, perhaps because of its seemingly flippant attitude toward its subject matter — even the artist conceded that he had a "somewhat cartoonish style"— but even more likely because of the still-divisive nature of the event.[25] The mural was moved to a nearby town, where it was displayed for several months.

These various attempts at commemoration omit some of the more compelling aspects of the Italian Hall story. The memorial, however, permits a variety of interpretations. Due to the memorial's lack of didacticism, it provides a window into the community and its history. The park, almost indistinguishable from the vacant lot next door, could be a metaphor for the poverty of the community in which it sits. In 1913, Calumet, then called Village of Red Jacket, had more than 4,000 people and was the center of a copper-mining region with a population close to 100,000. Although most of the surrounding land was controlled by the powerful Calumet & Hecla, Red Jacket Village was platted as private land, accommodating bars and commercial enterprises, largely free from C&H's supervision. After the strike, the Michigan copper industry declined, outpaced by newer regions such as Butte and the American Southwest, and eventually South America. After Calumet & Hecla closed in 1968, Calumet Village's population dropped below 1,000, less than one-quarter of the numbers at its height. The Copper Country's population peaked in 1910 and is now considerably less than half of what it was then. No industry has come in to replace copper. The village of Calumet, like this lot, is depopulated and impoverished.[26]

The Italian Hall tragedy was the most galvanizing incident of a bitter strike that lasted nearly nine months and is commemorated nowhere else. The strike is an important reminder that the Copper Country was not the harmonious work setting promoted by some observers. The memorial remains a unionist construction, the clearest rallying point for labor. Plaques on the arch, placed there by organizations that helped fund the reconstruction, include a bold statement by the Northwest Upper Peninsula Labor Council: "Mourn the Dead, Fight for the Living."[27] But after the collapse of the WFM local following the strike, the copper companies managed to keep unions out until the 1940s, when the copper industry was well into decline.

The history of company paternalism also still creates divisions in the community. Ken Ross and Louis Galdieri, while developing their film, showed a portion of their work in progress to the community in July 2004 and asked for discussion. Those present clearly disagreed on the company's effect on the community; some argued that Calumet & Hecla's influence was beneficial, others that it was sinister. C&H's paternalism was evident even in the Italian Hall itself, a privately constructed building on private land. At the building's dedication on Columbus Day, 1908, James MacNaughton, the general manager of C&H, was invited to speak but was unable to do so due to a death in his family; in his absence his speech was read by someone else. He wrote, "The hall stands as a monument to the intelligence, the thrift, and the good citizenship of the Italian population of

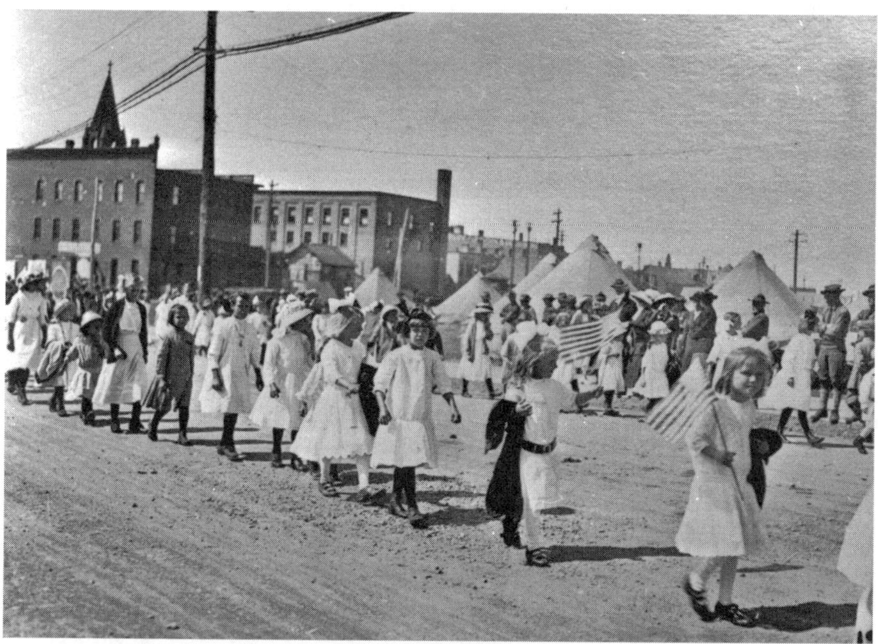

FIG. 7. Children paraded on behalf of the strikers. In the background of this photograph are tents pitched by National Guard soldiers, who look on. (Quincy Mining Company Collection, Neg. #5201-1 [Donor: Louis Koepel], Michigan Technological University Archives and Copper Country Historical Collections)

Calumet."[28] The Italians' desire for the imprimatur of the general manager and the condescending nature of his remarks indicate a complex relationship.

One of the more poignant plaques on the memorial arch reads, "In Loving Memory of Mary"; Mary Krainatz was eleven years old when she died. A tragic aspect of this event was that so many children lost their lives. Sixty-nine of the victims were women and children. The fact that these were not striking men, but, rather, women and children, enabled the community at large to unite in sympathy for the victims. Often overlooked in the historical record, however, is the role that women and children played during the strike. Striking women paraded through the streets frequently, often led by dynamic Croatian Anna Clemenc, known as Big Annie. There was also at least one children's parade; a stereoview of it was captioned in English and Finnish, "Parading children. (Several of these met their death in the disaster)" (fig. 7). Women rallied to the companies' side, too; thousands of petitions from "mothers" of the Copper Country sought the release of deputies who had been convicted of killing unarmed strikers.[29] The commemoration of the strike, in the form of the Italian Hall tragedy, focuses attention on women and children, not for their activism during the strike (aside from Anna Clemenc, whose popularization merits a study of its own) but for their passive deaths. Nonetheless, it reinforces the idea that the strike, working conditions, and management-worker relations had an impact not only on employees but also on their families and the community. The disproportionate suffering of women and children in this tragedy broadens the strike story to include everyone.

Another aspect of the resonance of this tragedy is that it was not confined to one ethnic group but, rather, like the strike itself, stretched across ethnic lines. Forty-nine of the victims were Finnish, fourteen Croatian, six Slovenian, three Italian, and one Swedish. These numbers reflect the ethnic variety of the strikers. Noticeably absent were Americans and English, who tended toward management and more secure, skilled jobs. In 1913, the Copper Country was populated largely by immigrants; nearly 90 percent of the population were foreign-born or the children of foreign-born parents. Although immigrants socialized in their own churches and fraternal organizations, they engaged in some cross-cultural contact. Six or seven different organizations met regularly in the Italian Hall and the Croatian Printing Company had occupied space in the previous building.[30] One triumph of the union was its uniting of so many ethnic groups under one banner.

In commemorating this tragedy, the lives of workers in the copper mines — lives that are not portrayed anywhere else — are also commemorated. Despite the creation in 1992 of Keweenaw National Historical Park, dedicated to interpreting the copper-mining past, and several former mines that are open to the public, a coherent interpretation of workers' lives remains to be effected. While miles of underground shafts and drifts and tons of mined-out rock might represent work lives, and rows of company houses might show their home lives, the workers themselves are harder to recall. The Italian Hall disaster catches them in their most vulnerable and self-righteous moment.

The local population still struggles with ways to understand the event and all it stood for, ninety-nine years later. The sheer variety of commemorations — postcards and photographs, films and videos, songs and poems, plays and operas, murals and histories — indicates an enduring interest in the event, a repeated delving into the past to obtain greater meaning. But the most permanent and significant memorial is the fragment of the Italian Hall that survives. The memorial succeeds because it avoids resolution; it offers the community an opportunity to unite behind an inconclusive interpretation of the Italian Hall tragedy. As it stands, the stone archway provides a focal point for various acknowledgments of the dead, the strike, the mine workers, and even the now-defunct industry itself.

Notes

My thanks to Bill Gale, Larry Lankton, Erik Nordberg, and Sue Cone for help with various aspects of this essay.

1. "Verdict Is In," *Daily Mining Gazette,* January 1, 1914. The standard history of the Copper Country is Lankton, *Cradle to Grave.* The standard history of the strike is Thurner, *Rebels on the Range.*

2. Lankton, *Cradle to Grave,* 206–8, 219–24.

3. Hoagland, "The Boardinghouse Murders," 1–18.

4. Foner, *History of the Labor Movement in the United States,* 198; Wolff, *Industrializing the Rockies,* 236–37.

5. Luke Grant to W. Jett Lauck, March 2 and 3, 1914, U.S. Commission on Industrial Relations, "Daily Reports on Congressional Hearings, Copper Strike, Hancock, Michigan, February–March 1914," in John R. Commons Papers, microfilm edition, Wisconsin State Historical Society.

6. Molloy, "Italian Hall," 146.

7. Ibid., 142, 146; "A Harvest of Death," *Miner's Bulletin,* December 28, 1913.

8. Thurner, *Rebels on the Range,* 151; R. C. Peterson and Carl Peterson, "Italian Hall Confession," *Daily Mining Gazette,* March 16, 1982.

9. Molloy, "Italian Hall," 81, 95, 28–29; "A Harvest of Death," *Miner's Bulletin,* December 28, 1913.

10. "Eighty-Three Murdered!" *Tyomies (The Workman),* December 26, 1913, typescript translation, Record Group 46, Box 2, Folder 2, State Archives of Michigan. See also "Tyomies Office Raided," *Daily Mining Gazette,* December 28, 1913; "A Harvest of Death," *Miner's Bulletin,* December 28, 1913; J. E. Ballinger, "Christmas Festivities End in Carnage of Death," *The Miners Magazine,* January 1, 1914; Molloy, "Italian Hall," 142.

11. "80 Perish in Christmas Eve Tragedy at Calumet," *Daily Mining Gazette,* December 25, 1913.

12. "The Italian Hall," *Calumet and Red Jacket News,* September 4, 1891; *Daily Mining Gazette,* March 3, 1904, p. 6; "Italian Hall a Mass of Ruins," *Calumet News,* January 2, 1908.

13. Measurement of foyer from Taipalus, who measured the space in 1980; Ted Taipalus, "Memories of the Italian Hall," *Copper Miner's Journal* 7, no. 41 (October 11, 1984): B–1, B–8. Measurement of stairs from U.S. House, Subcommittee of the Committee on Mines and Mining, *Conditions in the Copper Mines of Michigan,* 63rd Cong., 2d sess. (Washington: GPO, 1914), 2098. Other descriptive material in Harrington, "Italian Hall." See also "The Italian Benevolent Society's New Home," *Calumet News,* October 13, 1908. The exterior set of doors is on exhibit at the Coppertown Museum in Calumet. The five-panel doors, although evidencing alterations to the locking mechanism, open outward.

14. Mike Robinson, "Chicago Nightclub Owners Could Face Criminal Charges in Stampede Deaths," *Daily Mining Gazette,* February 18, 2003. See http://www.en.wikipedia.org/wiki/2003_E2_nightclub_stampede; http://www.huffingtonpost.com/2011/11/18/e2-nightclub-stampede-wit_n_1102038.html.

15. "Xmas Tree Panic Costs 80 Lives," *New York Times,* December 25, 1913. It is worth noting that these stereoviews bore the "union label" of the Allied Printing Trades Council of Houghton. Postcard collection in Michigan Technological University Archives, Accession No. 400. See also *The Miners Magazine,* January 8, 1914; Lankton, *Cradle to Grave,* 238.

16. Taipalus, "Memories of Italian Hall."

17. Bloor, *We Are Many.* Lyric from liner notes in Woody Guthrie, *Struggle,* Smithsonian/Folkways SF 40025, released 1976. Arlo Guthrie's concert at the Calumet Theatre on September 24, 2004, sold out immediately, enabling organizers to schedule an additional concert.

18. A radio program discussing the event aired in 1975; "1913 Calumet Disaster to Be Recalled," *Tech Topics,* December 18, 1975. John Beem wrote a play called *The Mother Lode,* which opened in Detroit in 1980; Barbara Hoover, "Playwright Explores the 1913 Calumet Tragedy," *Daily Mining Gazette,* June 9, 1980, reprinted from *Detroit News,* May 29, 1980. A song by Larry Penn called "Frozen in Time" argues that Italian Hall may be gone, but it lives on in Woody Guthrie's song; Thomas James Katona, "Another Song about the Italian Hall," *1913,* n.d., http://www.angelfire.com/mi2/1913/1913T.html. Bob Dylan performed Guthrie's song in Carnegie Hall in 1961, according to Louis V. Galdieri and Ken Ross, *1913 Massacre,* n.d., http://www.1913massacre.com.

19. Seitz and Masterson quoted in Scott R. Zerbel, producer, *An American Opera: The Children of the Keweenaw,* Six Productions video (2001). See also *The Children of the Keweenaw: An American Opera,* music by Paul Seitz, libretto by Kathleen Masterson (2001), 83–90, 11; http://www.mininggazette.com/page/content.detail/id/527055/–1913-Massa.

20. Maurice Halbwachs distinguishes between collective memory and history, the latter beginning when the former ends. Collective memory is personal and experiential, while history is intellectual and rationalizing; Halbwachs, *The Collective Memory,* 52, 78. Perhaps the memorial marks the evolution from collective memory into history.

See also Norkunas, *Monuments and Memory,* 43–44; Sue Cone, Clerk of Calumet Village, interview by the author, August 15, 2002; Peggy Germain, Friends of the Italian Hall, Inc., telephone interview by the author, November 10, 2002; Robert Pieti, "C&H's Paternalism a Simmering Cauldron," *L'Anse Sentinel,* December 20, 1989.

21. Jane Nordberg, "Meeting Held to Plan Strike Centennial," *Daily Mining Gazette,* January 30, 2008.

22. "Save Italian Hall Organization Forms," *Daily Mining Gazette,* June 25, 1980; "Friends Seeking Deadline Extension," *Daily Mining Gazette,* July 16, 1980; "Italian Hall," *Daily Mining Gazette,* April 6, 1983; Peggy Germain, "Italian Hall Is Destroyed," *Daily Mining Gazette,* October 8, 1984; "Park Work Begins," *Daily Mining Gazette,* July 21, 1988; "Razing of Italian Hall Is Advised," *Daily Mining Gazette,* July 21, 1988; "Italian Hall Project," *Daily Mining Gazette,* September 19, 1989; Germain interview. The Coppertown Museum in Calumet, which displays the doors, also interprets the event in a small exhibit.

23. Germain, *Tinsel and Tears;* Maki, *Stairway to Tragedy;* "Tragedy on Seventh Street," directed by Michael Edwards, Washington Middle School Sixth-Grade North Team Reading Classes, 2003; Molloy, "Italian Hall"; Germain, *False Alarm;* Lehto, *Death's Door.*

24. Murdoch, *Boom Copper,* 225–26; Benedict, *Red Metal,* 229; Thurner, *Rebels on the Range,* 138–74; Lankton, *Cradle to Grave,* 236–39; Munch, "1913 Massacre at Italian Hall," 20–21; Letters to the Editor, *Chronicle* 20, no. 2 (Summer 1984) and 20, no. 4 (Winter 1984–85). There were also more literal depictions of the event. Photographer Eric Munch documented the building before its demolition. These photographs appeared in the *Chronicle* and again in an exhibit, *Italian Hall: Beyond the Bricks,* at the Omphale Gallery, Calumet, August 2004. Also see Wendland, "The Calumet Tragedy," 39–48.

25. Dan Roblee, "Italian Hall Disaster," *Daily Mining Gazette,* August 5, 2000. The mural is pictured in Hoagland, *Mine Towns,* 231. I sat on the board of the Keweenaw Heritage Center, the organization that asked that the mural be removed, and although I was not privy to discussions at the time, I did hear later that the objections were due to the artwork's irreverence toward its subject matter. Board members cited the feelings of people who had survived the tragedy and were still alive.

26. Calumet's population was 1,007 in 1970; Thurner, *Calumet Copper and People,* 106. Its population was 726 in 2010. The median income of $16,473 in 2009 was less than half that of Michigan's as a whole. See http://www.city-data.com/city/Calumet-Michigan.html.

27. Milder statements include the Houghton County Board of Commissioners' "In memory of the people who perished in the Italian Hall Disaster, December 24, 1913" and the Calumet Women's Club's "In Memory of the Italian Hall: Gone but not forgotten."

28. Jane Nordberg, "Italian Hall Filmmakers Preview Work," *Daily Mining Gazette,*

July 9, 2004; "Beautiful New Italian Building Is Dedicated," *Daily Mining Gazette,* October 11, 1908; "Hall Dedication Brilliant Event," *Calumet News,* October 12, 1908.

29. Record Group 46, Box 4, Folder 12, and Box 5, Folders 2 and 3, State Archives of Michigan.

30. Population statistics at the time of the 1910 census, according to Thurner, *Rebels on the Range,* 21. Organizations meeting in Italian Hall mentioned in U.S. House, *Conditions in the Copper Mines,* 2098. See also "Italian Hall a Mass of Ruins," *Calumet News,* January 2, 1908.

SALLY GREENE

Judge Thomas Ruffin and the Shadows of Southern History

Historical criticism of the American South has become deepened and enriched by a movement, long established in other fields, to study the central role of collective memory in shaping received notions of the past. The work of interrogating the nature and sources of cultural authority has proven especially fruitful in Southern studies, perhaps because of the sheer tenacity with which the dominant interpretations of the past have managed to persist. In the decades following the Civil War, through Reconstruction and into the twentieth century, the ranks of memory were closed. The broken South sought valiantly to grieve its dead, heal its wounds, reaffirm its cherished sense of honor and duty, and return, as best it could, to life as it used to be. Faced with military defeat and the specter of four million former slaves, leaders and foot soldiers of the old Confederacy put their energies toward nothing less than writing the history of the war on their own terms, terms that led to reconciliation and reunion with their foes, rather than engaging in the project of doing justice for the newly free. With the complicity of the Northern establishment, this effort largely succeeded. As David Blight has written, "the forces of reconciliation overwhelmed the emancipationist vision in the national culture," with the result that "the inexorable drive for reunion both used and trumped race."[1]

The rhetoric of the "Lost Cause," as it came to be known as early as 1866, sought fundamentally to deny the centrality of slavery to the outbreak of the war. The trouble, Southerners insisted, stemmed from the federal government's failure to recognize the rights of the sovereign states: a culture that saw itself as "a glorious, organic civilization," as Blight puts it, came to believe that it had been "destroyed by an avaricious 'industrial society' determined to wipe out its cultural foes." Although Jefferson Davis, president of the Confederate States, laid the groundwork for the Lost Cause narrative with his "fierce defense of state rights doctrine and secession, his incessant pleas for 'Southern honor,' and his mystical conception of the Confederacy," it was General Robert E. Lee, commanding officer of the Confederate Army, who ultimately embodied the full-blown myth.[2] The theme of reconciliation was well served by an emphasis on a military leader, especially one not from the deep South (as Davis was) but from Virginia, birthplace of George Washington, the nation's first commander-in-chief: focusing on the common nobility of such courageous Americans helped to channel the postwar narrative away from the new responsibilities implied by emancipation and into safer regions. Through the hard years of Reconstruction and into the twentieth century, the Lost Cause "came to represent a mood, or an attitude toward the past," for Southerners "a natural extension of evangelical piety, a civil religion that helped them link their sense of loss to a Christian conception of history." The historical accounts that emerged from the postwar South shared with other disaster narratives, such as those of the great Chicago fire and the San Francisco earthquake, the providential theme of adversity overcome. Thus the official story of the Lost Cause, striking in its coherence, found its place within what Michael Kammen has called the "rhetorical panorama of Progress" that was unfolding across the country.[3] Look away, indeed.

Look no farther, in fact, than Richmond's Monument Avenue, with its equestrian statue of General Lee, or the central square of virtually any Southern city to find tangible evidence of a story that, if unable to claim victory, at least holds out for redemption. As Kirk Savage writes in an insightful study of the great period of memorialization after the Civil War, the "ideological crisis" posed by abolition — the "momentous struggle over the idea of race and the terms of citizenship in a nation supposedly dedicated to equality"— reached, in the South, a particularly satisfying resolution in the form of public monuments. To commemorate with marker or statue "is to seek historical closure, to draw together the various strands of meaning in a historical event or personage and condense its significance," he writes. Across the Southern landscape, the Lost Cause found a powerful form of legitimation that persists into the present time. In its service, in repositories of granite, marble, and bronze, the past is solidified and celebrated in a distinctly regional vernacular. The topic of slavery is absent from these monuments (the black body not to be found, except rarely as "faithful slave").[4] Rather, they tell a lofty tale of pride and patriotism and loyalty to abiding principles. In keeping with the myth of national unity, heroes of the Civil War stand alongside the legendary figures of the American Revolution — all, in turn, imbued with the virtues of classical republican democracy: future generations are advised to take heed. The valorous history articulated in monuments in the heart of Southern cities and towns is as sure, as immutable as solid stone itself.

The Southern Civil War monuments stood largely unchallenged — unremarkable, even, in their familiarity — through two world wars. Meanwhile the emancipation narrative, for so long eclipsed, had never entirely disappeared. As the civil rights revolution forced a change in the cultural landscape, the very presence of these monuments began to suggest muted stories. Today they are more likely to be viewed as sites of clashing memories, of what Southern historian Fitzhugh Brundage describes as "a dialectic . . . between the willfully recalled and [the] deliberately forgotten." The Raleigh statue of Thomas Ruffin (1787–1870), the most highly acclaimed judge of nineteenth-century North Carolina, is a product of the rhetorical excesses of the champions of the Lost Cause (fig. 1). For almost a century it has quietly presided over anxious lawyers as they come to plead their causes to the highest tribunals in the state. Like most monuments of its period, it does not readily yield its secrets. A glimpse into how it was conceived, created, and for many years interpreted — and what crucial facts were excluded in the process — offers an instructive lesson in the tangled politics of race and memory.[5]

A single opinion Judge Ruffin wrote early in his career on the North Carolina Supreme Court gave masters almost unbridled physical power over their slaves, in language so candidly descriptive of the brutal reality of the lives of the enslaved that it became the most talked about opinion in the public discourse on the law of slavery. A slender body of criticism that began with the abolitionists has been fully embraced, more than a century later, by contemporary legal historians, for whom Ruffin has become emblematic of all that was wrong with the antebellum South. Yet, at least formally, none of this criticism has had a measurable impact on Ruffin's reputation in the halls of power in North Carolina.[6]

In considering the history of his statue, my intent is not so much to upset its foundation as to enlarge our understanding of what it represents. It marks one brief chapter in the history of the reassertion of white dominance in the South after the Civil War — a story of national reunification that, through the strength of its imagery, rendered the call for racial justice almost incomprehensible. Even

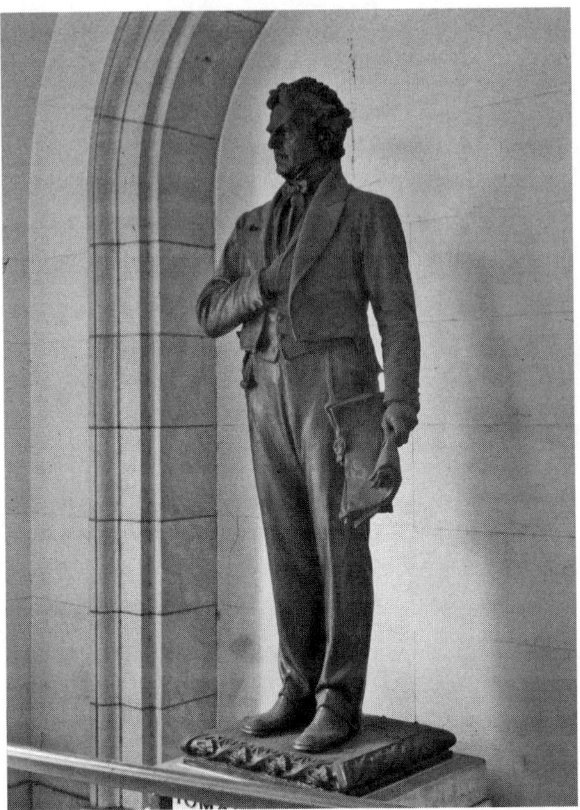

FIG. 1. *Thomas Ruffin* by Francis H. Packer, Raleigh, Court of Appeals Building, 1915. (Courtesy of the North Carolina Office of Archives and History, Raleigh, North Carolina)

so, within the contours of this narrative of Anglo-Saxon triumph can be found another one of resistance and refusal. The emancipationist counternarrative, which never conceded its own irrelevance, remains as a testament to the strength and resilience of generations of Americans committed to equal justice under the Constitution. A recognition of this counternarrative has the potential to change the way we view Ruffin's statue: the statement of the fixed and irrefutable power of law that it was no doubt intended to make unfolds into a conversation about the uses of law by the powerful. Such a shift of perspective, in turn, invites us into a broader reconsideration of our ways of navigating the contested terrain of public commemorative art.

A VISITOR TO THE North Carolina Court of Appeals could be forgiven for failing to notice Judge Ruffin's statue in an alcove in the building's foyer. Obstructed by a latter-day handicap access ramp, the larger-than-life bronze figure nevertheless stolidly presides. From its opening in 1914 until 1940, this building was the home of the North Carolina Supreme Court, of which Ruffin was chief justice from 1833 to 1852. After 1940, when the Supreme Court moved next door to a building constructed with partial funding from the federal Public Works Administration, the building became known as the Library Building; in 1967 it became home to the newly established Court of Appeals.

Ruffin's statue was created by Francis H. Packer, a New York artist of some renown who had studied with Saint-Gaudens. One of his statues already graced Union Square, as the lawn of the capitol is called. It depicts Worth Bagley, son of prominent North Carolinians and the first American officer killed in the Spanish-American War. This war, as Gaines Foster has persuasively written, served as a powerful sectional unifier. Bagley's death, Catherine Bishir notes, "was hailed in the national press as sealing the 'covenant of brotherhood between north and south.'" The monument's inscription, "First Fallen, 1898," echoed that of the nearby Confederate monument, "First at Bethel, Last at Appomattox." The threads of American history thus were brought together in these monuments, as well as others near the capitol, to be joined, only a few years later, by the statue of Ruffin, the state's most distinguished jurist.[7]

The appearance of all of these monuments in Raleigh around the turn of the twentieth century reflected a local response to a phenomenon sweeping the North as well as the South. "[T]he decades between 1870 and 1910 comprised the most notable period in all of American history for erecting monuments in honor of mighty warriors, groups of unsung heroes, and great deeds," writes Kammen in *Mystic Chords of Memory*. "The movement carried with it a kind of 'contagion' that spilled from Civil War saints to battles and martyrs of other wars."[8] Though the poverty of the South after the war meant that the monuments there were slow in coming, the political elite throughout the region poured substantial resources into the business of memorialization.

In North Carolina, the creation of what Bishir aptly calls "landmarks of power" took place in two phases. From the 1880s to the early 1890s, the focus of the memorial movement shifted from cemeteries, where statues of fallen soldiers spoke a language of grief that transcended sectional loyalties, to public spaces, as dutiful citizens heeded a more partisan call. This period culminated in 1895, in the erection on Union Square of the 75-foot monument to the state's Confederate dead. The second phase came in reaction to an unexpected political development: in 1894 and 1896, the Democrats lost control of the legislature and the governorship to a "Fusion" ticket backed by Populists and Republicans. The response to this embarrassment was swift and sharp. In 1898, the Democrats rushed backed into power on a platform of white supremacy, leaving a trail of violence, most notably the deadly coup d'état in Wilmington. In 1900 the party reclaimed the governorship and enlisted Jim Crow to seal the victory.[9]

Against this backdrop, the second phase of monument-building reflected a "remarkable sense of shared purpose," Bishir observes. "With competing visions of the state's past, present, and future all but silenced in official discourse," she continues, "leaders shared a powerful sense that both in politics and in the culture at large, matters had been returned to their correct alignment." The state's history was reinterpreted as a tapestry of "old family heritage, Anglo-Saxon supremacy, and military and political heroism"; these were the fundamentals that would inspire "a rebirth of southern progress and leadership in the nation." Civil War governor Zebulon B. Vance was honored in 1900 with a statue placed high on a pedestal at the east entrance of the capitol (a project delayed by the recent political upheavals in the state). Worth Bagley's widely celebrated memorial took its place on the square in 1907. In 1912, on a nearby spot, the United Daughters of the Confederacy placed a statue created by Gutzon Borglum (the artist of Mount Rushmore) of Henry Lawson Wyatt, the "First Confederate Soldier to Fall in the Battle of the War Between the States." Confederate veteran Ashley Horne's memorial to the North Carolina Women of the Confederacy, which faced outward from the square toward the Supreme Court building, was unveiled in June 1914.[10]

The idea of a statue honoring Judge Ruffin came out of this context of renewed pride and reflection. Like virtually all memorials of the period, it was promoted and funded not by the state but by the honoree's family and members of the political elite, in this case the North Carolina Bar Association. The reigning fiction, according to Savage, was that these "volunteer enterprises sponsored by associations of 'public-spirited' citizens" reflected the genuine voice of "the people"— that those who brought such projects forward "were merely agents of a more universal collective whose shared memory the project embodied." The reality was that the process of commemoration was guided by the self-interest of the dominant class. Even Packer, the statue's northern artisan, may have felt his work constrained, to an extent, by "hav[ing] to satisfy a committee of elite citizens who were themselves competing for popular approval with other philanthropic projects and even other monument proposals." Correspondence between Packer and members of the placement and presentation committee, however, reveals no competition or controversy over the design of the statue. Rather, the most contentious issue turned out to be its location. Though it was originally intended to join the others somewhere on Union Square, its siting became an issue after Colonel Horne managed to "preempt" what was thought the best choice. If the monument to North Carolina's preeminent judge could not face the court building, its backers finally concluded after considering other locations on the square, then the court building itself—just opened for business in 1914—would make a fine showcase. Meanwhile Packer continued to fashion the work in bronze, following the original plan for an outdoor location.[11]

At the dedication ceremony on February 1, 1915, J. Crawford Biggs, president of the bar association, emphasized the importance of placing the likenesses of the state's great historical figures on public display:

> We have not exerted ourselves to stimulate a healthy State pride, by preserving in marble and bronze the records of the past, by erecting statues and suitable memorials to commemorate the name and fame of the great men whose services have enriched and glorified the traditions of our Commonwealth. It is from the experience of the past that we draw inspiration for the future, and any act which emblazons in imperishable form the great deeds of our ancestors should be regarded with favor.[12]

Henry G. Connor, federal judge for the eastern district of North Carolina and chairman of the placement and presentation committee, similarly stressed the importance of keeping memory alive through physical likenesses:

> Inspiration to higher and nobler lives, we are taught, is imparted not alone by the story of the life and work of the great and good, but in the preservation of their form and feature by the art of the painter and the sculptor.[13]

Accepting the statue for the state, Governor Locke Craig mixed colonialist and Enlightenment rhetoric to underscore the broad reach of Ruffin's reputation:

> He is recognized everywhere as one of the greatest judges that our race has produced. In the uttermost parts of the earth, where the English juris-

> prudence exercises its beneficent rule, he speaks and will speak to legislatures, to courts, and to executives, directing and enlightening them in the way of truth and in the conception and the administration of justice.[14]

The statue, of heroic scale on a pedestal of polished white marble, makes a commanding presence, even from the alcove of the court building. Working from photographs provided by the Ruffin family, Packer rendered the judge's "form and feature" in an iconography well suited to a man born, as Ruffin himself once famously noted, "before the Constitution was adopted." Dressed in swallowtail coat and cravat, just as Episcopal bishop Joseph Cheshire remembered him as an old man at St. Matthew's Church in nearby Hillsborough, North Carolina, he stands erect, with the "air of power and of elevation" that Cheshire recalled. His squarely frontal yet unguarded position invokes a classical style of "ideal masculinity" that was refined in the eighteenth century, extending back to the *Apollo Belvedere.* Discussing this iconic tradition as it evolved through the period of J. A. Houdon's statue of George Washington (a bronze casting of which was the first statue to be erected on Union Square, in 1857), artist and critic Anthea Callen writes that the pose "communicates an expansive openness; but it is not open in the sense of receptive, rather of complacent self-assurance." Consistent with this tradition, Ruffin's eyes are cast downward in such a way as to suggest not only "introspection" but, further, an aura of "knowledge" and "authority"—intimations of "man's enlightened state."[15]

In Judge Ruffin's left hand is the symbol of his office, sealed legal papers secured with a clasp imprinted with the scales of justice. His right hand is tucked inside his waistcoat, a gesture resembling Napoleon in his study; but that would not be the proper association for a man of Ruffin's principles. More likely, this pose invokes a longer tradition of which David's portrait of Napoleon offers only one example. The hand-in-waistcoat pose was common among men of high social status in eighteenth-century English portraiture. Over the course of the century, this pose, which ultimately derived from within the tradition of classical sculpture, came to be "considered eminently suited to the taste of 'persons of quality and worth,'" according to art historian Arline Meyer. Its use became widespread "at the critical juncture when England was emerging as a national power" through a series of wars with France; in fact, the gesture contributed to what evolved as the English national style: "manly boldness tempered with modesty."[16]

In a post–Civil War context, the iconography of classical sculpture was freighted with racial implications. In support of an argument for the hierarchy of the races, a popular "scientific" treatise by Josiah Nott and George R. Gliddon, *Types of Mankind* (1854), included an illustration with a bust of Apollo on top, an exaggerated "Negro" head in the middle, and that of a chimpanzee on the bottom. The Apollo was taken from the *Apollo Belvedere.* "More than any of the other arts," writes Savage, "sculpture was embedded in the theoretical foundation of racism that supported American slavery and survived long after its demise." In conforming to the norms of classical sculpture, the statue of Judge Ruffin reinforced the assumption of the day that culture and education were associated with whiteness alone.[17]

The keynote address for the statue's dedication was given by Chief Justice Walter Clark. In rhetoric as lofty as the occasion demanded, Clark sang the manifold accomplishments of one whose "fame as a Judge is established wherever the English law is known." As he wound to his conclusion, he invited the audience to "[l]ook at his tall, sinewy figure as you shall soon see it, in monumental bronze; his firm mouth; his nose like an eagle's beak, his flashing eyes. He was a man of iron will, a man of determination, a man who would not be denied. He was every inch a man among men." Francis Packer had translated Ruffin the man into the classical language of patriarchal authority, skillfully communicating a lasting image of "elevated power and civic *gravitas*" that well suited the temper of the time.[18]

On into the first half of the twentieth century, Clark's pronouncement that Ruffin was "the ablest Judge who has ever presided in this State" was echoed widely. Writing in 1919 on the hundredth anniversary of the North Carolina Supreme Court, prominent attorney Robert W. Winston called him "the stern and clear-minded prophet." Ruffin's decisions on economic development issues, especially on eminent domain in support of the railroads, earned lasting praise for helping North Carolina shed its reputation as "the Rip Van Winkle of the States." In an important history of antebellum North Carolina published in 1937, Guion Johnson considered Ruffin's strong presence as chief justice to be instrumental to the survival of the independent judiciary against pressures of democratic reform. His contributions to the law of equity—which is fairness itself—were celebrated. Nationally, Ruffin joined the ranks of John Marshall, Joseph Story, James Kent, and other distinguished jurists as authors of the American constitutional tradition.[19]

Perhaps most significant, in 1938 eminent legal scholar Roscoe Pound elevated Ruffin to the pantheon of judges whose faithful adherence to the common-law tradition instituted the "formative era" of American law. Acknowledging that the distinctly American "natural law" jurisprudence that prevailed in the early days of the Republic was no longer dominant — indeed, Pound's critique of the 1905 *Lochner* decision was among the most compelling articulations of the Progressive revolt against a legal system that still presumed to be detached from politics and policy — he nonetheless praised Ruffin and other influential early judges for their consistent application of "a reasoned canon of values." Pound's renewed appreciation for common-law "reason" in the 1930s was part of a surprising shift toward conservatism: with the ascendancy of the New Deal he became a vocal critic of key elements of the Progressive movement he had helped to create. The Depression led Pound to identify with the business establishment, now chafing under the rules of the new regulatory state. He saw the recent move toward particularized, agency-specific administrative procedures for managing conflict — a development he had once championed — as a reflection of a dangerous slide toward totalitarianism. In *The Formative Era of American Law,* published the same year as his frontal assault on administrative legal practice, Pound puts Ruffin in the service of a reactionary argument that, in the end, resulted in a substantial victory. The passage of the Administrative Procedure Act of 1946, which wrapped a mantle of judicial consistency around federal-agency decision making, marked "the triumph," according to Morton Horwitz, of a "legalist mindset" that the New Dealers had strenuously opposed.[20]

Underwritten by Pound's assessment, then, Ruffin's reputation largely withstood the ideological challenges of the mid-twentieth century. But by the end of the 1960s, as the civil rights movement and the war in Vietnam confronted legal scholars with perplexing questions about the intersection of law and morality, "the tragic depth of the history of the law of slavery" began to reveal itself, recalls Stanley Katz. At the University of Chicago in 1974, Katz had played host to the first academic conference on the law of slavery. At the center of it all, he remembered some twenty years later, lay an opinion written by Thomas Ruffin:

> It was as though a group of people who had never seen one another before discovered that they had all been raised in the same little village. This village was intensely remembered although differently understood. It was named *State v. Mann,* which nearly all of us identified as the central text in

> the field, for the incredible manner in which Judge Thomas Ruffin, one of the great (and otherwise admirable) state judges of the nineteenth century, laid out the logic of slave law as coolly as a surgeon slicing open the belly of a patient on the operating table.[21]

Katz was then speaking at a 1996 conference on slavery law, where Sanford Levinson wondered whether Ruffin's "egregious" opinion should deprive him of such a reverential honor as, for example, having his portrait displayed in an American law school "as a presumed inspiration."[22] Although more recent scholarship has broadened the discussion of the jurisprudence of slavery to show that what transpired in the highest courts was only part of the picture — that the law itself was shaped from the bottom up by distinctly local concerns — *State v. Mann* continues to hold a singular pride of place.

In this appeal from a trial in Edenton in 1829, the North Carolina Supreme Court reversed a jury's conviction of a slave's hirer for shooting the slave as she fled to avoid his whipping. Writing for the court, Ruffin declared that John Mann, the hirer, commanded mastery over Lydia, the slave, with "absolute" powers of discipline. Short of acting with intent to kill, this case appeared to say, the master would not incur criminal liability for any degree of correction. What gives readers pause is the stark reasoning that Ruffin employs to describe the workings of slavery. In the lower court, the jury's finding of guilt had not been altogether surprising: an assault upon a slave owned by someone else was a serious criminal offense. Ruffin, however, applied a rigorously structural understanding of the power relations involved. Mann may not have owned Lydia, but he owned the right to use her for the term of his contract. During that time, Ruffin reasoned, Mann had acquired all of the rights and privileges (such as they were) of the owner. Though professing anguish that this case had come to court, Ruffin presented the law as if it were unyielding. "The power of the master must be absolute," he insisted, "to render the submission of the slave perfect." Neither duty nor pleasure compels a slave to remain a slave, he observed: the slave's loyalty "is the consequence only of uncontrolled authority over the body." Unfettered power in the hands of the master — even a temporary master — was in Ruffin's view a necessary rule of law.[23]

In its own time, *State v. Mann* became widely known, and not always for the strict proposition of its holding. Abolitionists took Ruffin's unflinching description of the power dynamics of slavery as certain proof of its immorality. Harriet

Beecher Stowe was so bewildered by the opinion that, after trying to come to grips with it in her *Key to Uncle Tom's Cabin,* she incorporated it into a novel, *Dred: A Tale of the Great Dismal Swamp.* Published in 1856, four years after *Uncle Tom's Cabin,* it is a much more searing critique of the chattel slave system. If, in the earlier novel, Stowe is content to imply that getting past slavery is just a matter of getting one's heart in the right place, this time she squarely confronts the social structure. She blames judges, lawyers, politicians, and ministers for standing in the way of reform. In her rewriting of *State v. Mann* as it plays out on appeal, the prosecutor whose trial-court victory is overturned is the judge's own son, who responds by renouncing the bar and taking his slaves to Canada. Consistent with her ideological project of advocating a "higher law" theory of racial justice, Stowe's thinly fictionalized Judge Ruffin is an essentially just man compelled by the immutable logic of an imperfect legal system to reach a heinous conclusion. As thus reinterpreted by the most popular American writer of her time, *State v. Mann* found an expanded and highly critical audience.[24]

Into the early twentieth century, when North Carolina's elite was doing its best to recast its legal history in an unbroken celebration of political freedom from the colonial period forward, *State v. Mann* figured usefully in the alternative histories of black Americans. Speaking on the topic of Reconstruction, W. E. B. Du Bois began an address before the American Historical Association in 1909 with an ironic reference to Ruffin's opinion (and perhaps Stowe's novel as well). Life in the South after the devastation of the war would have been hard enough even "if there had not been a single freedman left," Du Bois said; but given the reality of four million freedmen, each of them — here he quoted from *State v. Mann* —"'doomed in his own person, and his posterity, to live without knowledge, and without the capacity to make anything his own, and to toil that another may reap the fruits,'" each one "is bound, on sudden emancipation, to loom like a great dread on the horizon." In an essay published the same year, Booker T. Washington criticizes the emphasis that Ruffin places on "the profit of the master, his security, and the public safety" as the proper end of the master-slave relationship. With such reasoning, writes Washington, "[t]his opinion brings out into plain view an idea that was always somewhere at the bottom of slavery — the idea, namely, that one man's evil is another man's good." But the truth about slavery, he counters, is "just the opposite . . . namely, that evil breeds evil, just as disease breeds disease, and that a wrong committed upon one portion of a community will, in the long run, surely react upon the other portion of that community."[25]

And yet, despite the persistent criticism that ran from the literature of the abolitionists through the later discourse of African American letters, Judge Ruffin continued to stand tall in Raleigh well into the 1960s — even against the backdrop of the Greensboro sit-ins and the tumultuous events that followed. In fact, the court building where the statue is housed was officially named the Ruffin Building in 1969. Within months after the new name went up on the building, a class of Raleigh junior high students noticed the statue of this great man with the very scales of justice weighing in his hands. They wanted it taken out of the shadows and moved across the street, and they managed to persuade the state legislature to pass a resolution asking that it be done. This they took to the Capital Planning Commission, which appeared sympathetic until learning of the $15,000 cost, which prompted it to seek a higher authority. In February 1970, the state Supreme Court rendered its decision: it preferred not to.[26]

Though the court's reasoning was opaque, a Raleigh *News and Observer* editorial suggests that some kind of public debate did take place. Titled "Pandora's Buildings," it notes certain "real questions as to where the statue of the great Thomas Ruffin should stand or whether the building in which it stands is properly and legally to be called the Ruffin Building." Though it might be an acceptable practice to "purchase a sort of immortality by philanthropy as is the case with the Reynolds Coliseum and the Carter Stadium"— or all of Duke University — the editorialist worried that among public buildings "the competition for structural immortality might get out of bounds."[27] At some point, the name Ruffin disappeared. The brass plaque bearing the name was long ago replaced by another, marking it simply as the Court of Appeals Building, though lawyers of a certain age still call it the Ruffin Building. A logical reading between the lines of the story as reported might be that, given the tenor of the times, the Supreme Court wished to save itself and the state the embarrassment of calling attention to the author of the most strident, most telling justification of slavery in the entire body of antebellum American law. But it was not that way at all.

Raymond Taylor, Supreme Court marshal and librarian from 1964 to 1977, recalls that the idea of moving Ruffin out of the Court of Appeals building emerged from the internal politics of the Supreme Court, which had called the Ruffin Building home until 1940, and the fledgling Court of Appeals, only two years old in 1969. Former chief justice Emery B. Denny, retired by that time "but still very much on the scene," according to Taylor, was troubled by some unfinished business. Upon his appointment to that court in the early 1940s, one of his assignments had been to ensure that the court's artwork — portraits and sculpture memorializing former judges — was relocated in the new building. He succeeded with the portraits and busts, but more than twenty years later he was disappointed that Judge Ruffin remained in the old court building. He wanted the statue relocated to a site on Union Square directly facing the modern Supreme Court building. "There was not and still is not a jurist, a representative of the judicial branch, on the square," Taylor said. "Judge Denny wanted that done."[28]

A local architect confirmed that the statue could withstand the elements. The setting he then designed for the proposed location positioned the judge's statue within a low circular wall, perhaps with a sitting space, with room for the names of all of the chief justices. "But a strange thing happened," Taylor said. "Mysteriously, almost under cover of darkness," in February 1969 "a sign appeared on the Court of Appeals [building], and it said the Ruffin Building."[29] A state official called the new name part of a "program of building identification" initiated by the governor.[30] But only one building was identified by the name of a person. In Taylor's opinion, "the Court of Appeals wanted to keep the Ruffin statue," and its members felt the chances were improved if the building bore his name. Taylor searched in vain to discover how the decision was made. "I was never able to find any documentation of any decision that was made by anybody in authority to designate that as the Ruffin Building," he said. "So it was a matter of sheer political power that got that done."

Ann Kennedy's seventh-grade history students from LeRoy Martin Junior High were studying Thomas Ruffin when they began to read about Justice Denny's proposal to move the statue outside, Taylor recalled. After their enthusiastic support translated to success with the legislature, they made a field trip to the Supreme Court, where they presented Chief Justice R. Hunt Parker with a jar of money for the relocation fund. Caught off guard, he accepted the money but later asked Taylor to return it. "The children's hearts were broken," Taylor remembered. Whatever went into Chief Justice Parker's reasoning, it surely did not involve anxiety about Ruffin's emerging academic reputation as the father of the law of slavery. I asked Taylor pointedly whether in these discussions any concern had arisen that calling attention to Judge Ruffin might be politically unwise in

1968. "Absolutely not," he responded, offering in support the following passage from Parker's annual report to the state bar that year:

> The world is traveling under formidable omens into a new era, an era no man can foresee, no man can foretell. The country is undergoing more crime and violence than ever before in our history. The worst of our youngsters are growing up to become booted, sideburned, duck-tailed, unwashed, leather-jacketed beatniks and hippies; a large number of the best of our youth are coming into maturity for all the world like young people fresh from a dizzying roller-coaster ride with everything blurred, nothing clear, with no positive standards, with everything in doubt. An example of that is the turmoil and unrest in our colleges and universities wherein men with long hair and looking like women, and women with short hair dressed in pants looking like men are in the forefront of this unrest. . . . Frequently, the news media and college professors and other adults with no practical experience in the hard, concrete facts of life are encouraging this disorder. In my opinion, and in the opinion of many others, all of this disorder is created and inspired by hard core Communists.[31]

"I think that that well illustrates that the sentiment of the chief justice was not in sympathy with anybody who would have objected to Thomas Ruffin," Taylor concluded.

Fifteen years later, in 1984, another campaign sought to bring the statue outdoors, this time to the nearby Fayetteville Street Mall. Even then, no discussion appears to have taken place about Ruffin's role in the history of slavery. Rather, this second effort, led by Labor Commissioner John C. Brooks, quickly devolved into another turf war, this one with battle lines clearly visible. Brooks pressed the issue with the city's Downtown Advisory Committee. But he overplayed his hand. The committee responded by taking the curious position that the pedestrian mall, "with its flowers, trees and grass," was "inappropriate for a statue."[32] Again, nothing was done.

So there he stands, in the building that is, and is not, the Ruffin Building: the man who would not be moved. Hurried lawyers scarcely notice Judge Ruffin as they file in and out of the Court of Appeals Building—so indelibly and for so long a fixture, he is simply ignored. Yet still he remains, an iconic presence, just as the statue's first promoters intended, however they might have quibbled over the location. In an Episcopal churchyard in Hillsborough, Judge Ruffin's gravestone makes its own contribution to the cause of national reunification that the statue, taking its place near the others on Union Square, was designed to promote. Inscribed on his classical obelisk is this couplet: "A man resolved, and steady to his trust, / Inflexible to ill, and obstinately just." Ruffin's early-twentieth-century memorializers recognized how perfectly this verse, from Addison's translation of a Horatian ode, suited the man (there was talk of repeating it on the statue). But it happens that the same words once described George Washington.[33]

FOR ALL HIS ideological investment in the slaveholding world of the nineteenth century, Thomas Ruffin is fundamentally a child of Washington's time. Born in the eighteenth century, he gave his life to the law, to a particular kind of law in which rigorous discipline was bound up with equally uncompromising notions of habit and duty, honor and piety. For those classical virtues, right remembering was essential. Somewhere between his well-ordered world and ours, the ground shifted. With the rise of romanticism and modernism, the idea of memory itself became problematic. Questions that Wordsworth and Coleridge posed about the nature of memory were intensified by Bergson and Proust, who spurned the kind of memory that was synonymous with habitual behavior — what Bergson called a "closed system of automatic movements"— and sought, rather, to encourage subjective engagement with memory.[34]

Even Freud contended that forgetting the past was sometimes advisable. "[W]hat should we think," he asked,

> of a Londoner who paused today in deep melancholy before the memorial of Queen Eleanor's funeral instead of going about his business . . . ? Or again, what should we think of a Londoner who shed tears before the Monument that commemorates the reduction of his beloved metropolis to ashes, although it has long since risen again in far greater brilliance? . . . Not only do they remember painful experiences of the remote past, but they still cling to them emotionally; they cannot get free of the past and for its sake they neglect what is real and immediate.[35]

In this speech before an American audience Freud echoes Hawthorne, who, on seeing the Elgin Marbles, concluded that "[t]he present is burdened too much with the past. We have not time . . . to appreciate what is warm with life, and immediately around us." From the beginnings of the American experiment in democracy, as Kammen has amply demonstrated, the question of how to put the past in perspective — of whether it is even possible to honor the past without being bound to it — has persisted. "Democracy has no monuments," wrote John Quincy Adams. "It strikes no medals. It bears the head of no man on a coin." Although such radical idealism was never strictly put into practice in a country whose pioneers, after all, came from lands steeped in history and remembrance, it took the ordeal of the Civil War, as Kammen further notes, "to minimize genuinely revolutionary aspects of the American Revolution" and to usher in "a conservative, organic view of society."[36] In the North and throughout the vanquished South, the ravages of war provoked a longing for the stability offered by a sense of shared tradition.

This is the context in which the rhetoric of the Lost Cause gained its hold. Across the former Confederacy, by the early twentieth century "a narrative of loss had become a narrative of order, revival, and triumph," to return to Blight's analysis. "For those who needed it, the Lost Cause became a tonic against fear of social change." More than that: it "armed those determined to control, if not destroy, the rise of black people in the social order."[37] Ultimately the social cohesion that came out of these common tropes of memory could no longer hold — undone by the insistence of racial politics and the forces of modernity. In turn, a rhetorical practice grounded in longing was subjected to the peculiarly modern practice of historical criticism. Virginia Woolf, for example, teaches us how to cast a wary gaze. While "walking down Whitehall," she suggests, a woman might confront "a sudden splitting off of consciousness, . . . when from being the natural inheritor of that civilisation, she becomes, on the contrary, outside of it, alien and critical." With Bergson and Proust, Woolf resists the automatic assent that a public monument is meant to compel. "Walk through the Admiralty Arch . . . , or any other avenue given up to trophies and cannon," she advises, "and reflect upon the kind of glory celebrated there." Consider why the monuments were erected, she urges, and at what cost.[38]

If a campaign to bring Judge Ruffin out of the shadows and onto a more favorable site were to succeed today, the move would not pose a daunting logistical problem. The problem would be how to return his steady gaze. We might want to ask, as Harriet Beecher Stowe did, why he was content to be "merely an *expositor,* and not a *reformer* of law."[39] Although he never sanctioned a violent response to the crisis of race — with relentless logic and fidelity to law he condemned the Ku Klux Klan for undertaking "an attempt to do good by wrong means"[40]— we might be tempted to lay more than a century of bloodshed before him as a rational consequence of his work to strengthen a system of human bondage. We might ask him to consider the continuum of history that links his part in securing "the power of the master" to the powerful witness of artifacts from the lunch counter sit-ins of the 1960s that are found in the nearby North Carolina Museum of History.

In fact, it would be a pleasure to help Judge Ruffin down from his pedestal and take him on a walk, a short walk, past the museum, up Wilmington Street to the corner of East Lane Street. On that site, now a parking lot situated behind the state archives and across the street from the Legislative Building, a new historical monument is planned. Years in the making and still in the fund-raising stage, the North Carolina Freedom Monument promises to be a space for reflection suited to our own time — responsive to the regrets and sorrows, the hopes and longings that filter our thoughts about the ways in which race continues to shape our history. The word "monument" deceives, for what is contemplated is not a single statue or form designed to convey one message. The statues of Ruffin, Confederate soldier Worth Bagley, and others near the capitol are figures of outsize proportion that ask us to "accept the memory of [the state] as our own," as Howard Zinn put it, "conceal[ing] fierce conflicts of interest (sometimes exploding, most often repressed) between conquerors and conquered, masters and slaves, capitalists and workers, dominators and dominated in race and sex." The Freedom Monument, in contrast, is envisioned as "a series of engaging sculptural experiences seamlessly integrated with the landscape." Multiple elements will represent three broad themes of the African American freedom struggle: ingenuity and resilience, tension, and hope.[41]

Visitors will find their own paths through an intriguing landscape that features informal clusters of shade trees, evoking the "freedom groves" where slaves would gather to learn from each other. Comfortable reading benches will be situated under the trees, while in the open plaza jagged benches will suggest memories of turbulent times. Children will play hopscotch on pavers etched with the words "Not Every Step Is Sure." Vistas will be deliberately obscured by the Jim Crow Wall, which, like the system it represents, will require careful negotiation. Eastern North Carolina, where most of the state's slaves lived, will be remembered in the Serpentine Wall, its undulating lines evoking the ocean shores where their ancestors first arrived. Perhaps Judge Thomas Ruffin would join us in the clearing of the Freedom Ground as we observe others making their way down the spiraling walkways, or reacting to the provocative setting, or paused in quiet contemplation.[42] We will do our best to take it all in, knowing that though we can never rise above our history, some vantage points yield clearer views than others — knowing too that no matter how many views we can claim, no matter how expansive, another prospect always beckons.

Notes

The author would like to thank John Sanders for research assistance on Packer and the Ruffin statue's creation and Tom Davis of the North Carolina Supreme Court Library for further research assistance, and Catherine Bishir for careful editorial advice. A version of this essay appeared in *Southern Cultures* 17, no. 3 (Fall 2011): 66–89.

1. Blight, *Race and Reunion,* 2. For a helpful introduction to the contemporary study of collective memory in the American South, see, in addition to Blight, Brundage, "Introduction: No Deed but Memory," in *Where These Memories Grow,* ed. Brundage, 1–28, and, more generally, Brundage, *The Southern Past.*

2. Blight, *Race and Reunion,* 257. On Davis, see Blight, *Race and Reunion,* 259. On Lee, see Savage, *Standing Soldiers, Kneeling Slaves,* chap. 5. See also Gallagher, *Lee and His Generals.* On the history of the "Lost Cause," see Pollard, *The Lost Cause.*

3. Blight, *Race and Reunion,* 258. On nineteenth-century disasters, see Rozario, "Making Progress," in *The Resilient City,* ed. Vale and Campanella, 27–54. See also Kammen, *Mystic Chords of Memory,* 137.

4. Savage, *Standing Soldiers, Kneeling Slaves,* 3–4. The earliest of the monuments to "faithful slaves" that Savage notes, at 157, dates from 1896, after "the urgent need . . . to dissociate the Southern cause from slavery" had passed.

5. Brundage, *Where These Memories Grow,* 6; see also Brundage, *The Southern Past,* 5.

6. Yet at the University of North Carolina at Chapel Hill, where Ruffin served as trustee for many years, and where a dormitory bears his name, a recent effort has been made to reassess his historical legacy. A symposium entitled "The Perils of Public Homage: Thomas Ruffin and *State v. Mann*" was held on the UNC campus in November 2007. Proceedings from the symposium are published in the *North Carolina Law Review* 87, no. 3 (March 2009) and University of North Carolina, *Thomas Ruffin.*

7. Sanders, "Francis Herman Packer," *Dictionary of North Carolina Biography,* ed. William S. Powell (Chapel Hill: University of North Carolina Press, 1994), 5:1. Packer's work also includes the statue of George Davis, attorney general of the Confederacy, in Wilmington; and the equestrian statue of Nathaniel Greene is at the Guilford County Courthouse, Greensboro. See also Foster, *Ghosts of the Confederacy,* 145; Bishir, "Landmarks of Power," 150–51.

8. Kammen, *Mystic Chords of Memory,* 115.

9. Bishir, "Landmarks of Power," 143, 147; Bishir, "'A Strong Force of Ladies,'" 455–91. On the shift from cemeteries to public spaces, see Montagna, "A Monument for a New Century," 42–47. The work of the Wilmington Race Riot Commission, produced at the direction of the North Carolina legislature, demonstrates conclusively that the events of 1898 were indeed no "riot," as it has traditionally been called, but a "planned insurrection" intended to usher in "the resurgence of white rule of the city and state for a handful of men through whatever means necessary." See "Introduction," "1898 Wilmington Race Riot Report," final report, May 31, 2006, http://www.ah.dcr.state.nc.us/1898-wrrc/report/report.htm.

10. Bishir, "Landmarks of Power," 148–54.

11. See contract for Ruffin Memorial, Dec. 20, 1912, in Thomas Ruffin Papers, PC 896, North Carolina State Archives, Raleigh. See also Savage, *Standing Soldiers, Kneeling Slaves,* 6–7; letter, Walter Clark to Bennehan Cameron, June 16, 1913, in Walter Clark Papers, PC 8.12, North Carolina State Archives, Raleigh; letter, Judge Henry G. Connor to Walter Clark, Oct. 18, 1913, in Henry G. Connor Papers, Box 14, Folder 220, Southern Historical Collection, University of North Carolina at Chapel Hill.

12. J. Crawford Biggs, "Presentation," in *Addresses at the Unveiling,* 24–25.

13. H. G. Connor, "Opening Remarks," in *Addresses at the Unveiling,* 5–6.

14. Locke Craig, "Acceptance," in *Addresses at the Unveiling,* 26.

15. The statue is seven feet tall on a plinth of four inches. See letter, F. H. Packer to Walter Clark, Jan. 11, 1914, in Walter Clark Papers, PC 8.12, North Carolina State Archives, Raleigh. "I was born before the Constitution was adopted. May God grant that I do not outlive it," Ruffin reportedly said at the unsuccessful Peace Conference held in Washington in February 1861. A staunch Unionist, he nevertheless supported the Confederacy enthusiastically once North Carolina chose to secede. See Huebner, *The Southern Judicial Tradition,* 155–56. See also Cheshire, *Nonnulla,* 121; Callen, "Ideal Masculinities," 611–12.

16. Meyer, "Re-dressing Classical Statuary," 49, 53.

17. Savage, *Standing Soldiers, Kneeling Slaves,* 8–11.

18. Walter Clark, "Thomas Ruffin," in *Addresses at the Unveiling,* 17, 22; Callen, "Ideal Masculinities," 613.

19. Clark, "Thomas Ruffin," 15. See also Robert W. Winston, "A Century of Law in North Carolina," from the "Proceedings of the North Carolina Bar Association in the Supreme Court Room, Raleigh, 4 January 1919, on the Occasion of the Centennial Celebration of the One Hundredth Anniversary of the Establishment of the Supreme Court of North Carolina," 176 N.C. 763, 786, 789 (1919); J. G. de Roulhac Hamilton, *Party Politics in North Carolina,* 26. In *Raleigh and Gaston Railroad Co. v. Davis,* 19 N.C. 451 (1837), Ruffin settled the constitutionality in North Carolina of a taking, with compensation, of private property for a public purpose, even though no such right was articulated in the state constitution. See Johnson, *Ante-Bellum North Carolina,*

642–43. For further discussion of this period, see Pratt, "The Struggle for Judicial Independence," 129–59. See also Samuel A. Ashe, "Thomas Ruffin," *Biographical History of North Carolina from Colonial Times to the Present,* ed. Samuel A. Ashe (Greensboro, N.C.: Charles L. Van Noppen, 1906), 5:350–59, at 352–53 ("[h]is decisions illumined the annals of jurisprudence"); Carpenter, "The Influence of Justice Thomas Ruffin," 9, citing Hurst, "Who Is the 'Great' Appellate Judge?" 97.

20. Pound, *The Formative Era of American Law,* 4, 28–29, 84–86. In *Lochner v. New York,* 198 U.S. 45 (1905), the Supreme Court struck down, on the basis of freedom of contract, a federal law setting maximum hours for bakers — thus provoking a thorough reconsideration of the relationship of constitutional law to public policy. Pound's role in the Progressive legal discourse of the early twentieth century is discussed by Horwitz in *The Transformation of American Law,* 34. For the American Bar Association in 1938, Pound wrote a report on administrative law in which he "denounc[ed] the dangers flowing from 'administrative absolutism.'" See Horwitz, *The Transformation of American Law,* 219–20, 230–31.

21. Katz, "Bondage, Freedom, and the Constitution," 1690.

22. Levinson, "Allocating Honor and Acting Honorably," 1969. Continuing, he asks, "By what criteria do we decide whom to build statues of — or whose statues to leave up through time?" Levinson pursues this question with regard to Ruffin again in "Thomas Ruffin and the Politics of Public Honor," 673–700.

23. *State v. Mann,* 13 N.C. 263 (1829). For a full discussion of *State v. Mann,* arguing that Ruffin's reversal of Mann's conviction was not required by law or precedent, see Greene, "*State v. Mann* Exhumed," 701–55.

24. Stowe, *A Key to Uncle Tom's Cabin;* Stowe, *Dred.* For a helpful discussion of Stowe's influence on the popular interpretation of *State v. Mann,* see Korobkin, "Appropriating Law," 380–406.

25. Reprinted in Du Bois, "Reconstruction," 781; Washington, "The Negro's Life in Slavery," 10:163–64.

26. Jack Childs, "Will Thomas Ruffin Stay Inside?" [Raleigh] *News & Observer,* Jan. 11, 1970, I5; Rod Cockshutt, "State Supreme Court Says Ruffin Should Stay in Place," [Raleigh] *News & Observer,* Feb. 5, 1970, 44.

27. "Pandora's Buildings," editorial, [Raleigh] *News & Observer,* Jan. 18, 1970, IV4. Though the statue was not moved, it did get better lighting. See Jack Childs, "Ruffin Will Stay Inside — But He'll Have Light," [Raleigh] *News & Observer,* March 7, 1970, 3.

28. Raymond Taylor, interview by the author, April 7, 2003.

29. Ibid.; see also Childs, "Will Thomas Ruffin Stay Inside?" 62.

30. "Building Gets a New Name," [Raleigh] *News & Observer,* Feb. 21, 1969, A12.

31. Taylor, interview by the author. See also "Remarks of Chief Justice R. Hunt Parker," *The North Carolina Bar* 15, no. 4 (1968): 27.

32. Kathy Tyndall, "Panel Delays Vote on Moving Ex-justice's Statue," [Raleigh] *News*

& Observer, Feb. 2, 1984, C2. Brooks "needlessly irritates the already chafed relations between the state and the city," said an editorial in the [Raleigh] *News & Observer,* "A Turf War without a Cause," Feb. 7, 1984, A4. See also John Drescher Jr., "Statue Called Out of Step for Mall," [Raleigh] *News & Observer,* Feb. 21, 1984, C1.

33. Joseph Addison's translation of Horace, Ode 3.3, is in *Miscellaneous Work in Verse and Prose of the Late Right Honourable Joseph Addison: With Some Account of the Life and Writings of the Author by Mr. Tickell* (London: Jacob Tonson, 1726), 142–47. For the debate about the wording to be on the statue, see a letter from historian R. D. W. Connor to Frank Nash, July 8, 1914; and letter to Connor from his father, Henry G. Connor, July 17, 1914, both in R. D. W. Connor Papers, Box 2, Folder 182, Southern Historical Collection, University of North Carolina at Chapel Hill. See also Gaston, *Address Delivered,* 7.

34. See Gross, *Lost Time,* 30–35. See also Henri Bergson, *Matter and Memory* (1896), quoted in Gross, *Lost Time,* 42. See generally, Terdiman, *Present Past.*

35. This passage from Freud's 1909 Clark University Lectures is quoted in Roth, *The Ironist's Cage,* 188. See also Terdiman, *Present Past,* 259–61.

36. Kammen, *Mystic Chords of Memory,* 89.

37. Blight, *Race and Reunion,* 266.

38. Woolf, *A Room of One's Own,* 97, 38. See also Fernald, "The Memory Palace of Virginia Woolf," 110.

39. Stowe, *A Key to Uncle Tom's Cabin,* 79.

40. Ruffin, letter to son John K. Ruffin, July 8, 1869, in *The Papers of Thomas Ruffin,* ed. J. G. de Roulhac Hamilton (Raleigh: North Carolina Historical Commission, 1920), 4:226.

41. Zinn, *A People's History,* 10. See Juan Logan, multimedia artist, with Lyneise Williams, art historian, and David Swanson, landscape architect, "North Carolina Freedom Monument Design Statement," 2009, n.p.

42. Logan et al., "North Carolina Freedom Monument Design Statement," n.p. See also Janet Kagan, "The North Carolina Freedom Monument Project: A Freedom Grove for All," *Independent Weekly,* April 18, 2006, 47.

GLENN T. ESKEW

Commemorating the Civil Rights Movement with Monuments in the Urban South

❧

THE LAST decade of the twentieth century witnessed a groundswell of city support for monuments to the civil rights movement best characterized by the exhibitory one often finds on display: that of life-size monochromatic mannequins marching to freedom, riding on the bus, or sitting-in at the lunch counter. As ubiquitous to these institutions as the stone sentinels guarding courthouses across the country that in the aftermath of the Civil War represented white supremacy, these civil rights figures commemorate America's new civic religion of tolerance. Whether in Atlanta, Memphis, Birmingham, or Montgomery, an evolving collective memory of triumphant toleration rises above a localized narrative often framed within the life and work of Dr. Martin Luther King Jr. Indigenous groups have reclaimed sites of memory, renovated historic buildings, and constructed shrines to the struggle for racial equality. As expressed through architecture, art, and museum artifact, these civil rights memorials take regionally distinct memories and interpret them through exhibitory that announces an inevitable victory over oppression. Urban leaders embrace these memorials which first used private donations but increasingly turned to public money made available by black political empowerment to finance their operations. Local, state, and federal employees of the heritage tourism industry greet pilgrims who visit these sites to absorb a standardized message promoting toleration. Today cities celebrate diversity through the memorialization of the movement.[1]

A wave of civil rights memorials opened during the 1990s, although the commemoration process began within weeks of the assassination of the Reverend Dr. Martin Luther King Jr. His widow, Coretta Scott King, had wanted a "living memorial" to be organized around historic sites in Atlanta related to the life of the human rights advocate that would enable disciples to continue preaching his message of nonviolence. In communities elsewhere with civil rights legacies, others adopted her vision as they implemented their own commemorations. Twenty years passed before the first new major civil rights monument appeared on the Southern landscape. In Montgomery, the founder of the Southern Poverty Law Center commissioned the Civil Rights Memorial that, once installed in 1989, kicked off a decade of dedications. In 1992, memorialists in Memphis opened the National Civil Rights Museum in the old Lorraine Motel. The next year local leaders dedicated the Birmingham Civil Rights Institute adjacent to Kelly Ingram Park. A wave of commemorations swept the region, for in Southern towns such as Selma, Alabama, and Albany, Georgia, museums opened, while in Oxford, Mississippi, and Greensboro, North Carolina, museum plans stalled. With the 1996 Summer Olympics in Atlanta, the National Park Service intervened in the King Historic District to construct an interpretative center. Closing out the decade in 2001, the Rosa Parks Museum provided Montgomery with a new civil rights destination, while the SPLC publicized America's new ideology of tolerance by opening a memorial to Maya Lin's decade-old Civil Rights Memorial.[2]

The spontaneous and independent effort to memorialize the movement in these different communities has resulted in similar outcomes. City governments and urban reformers assisted movement veterans and scholars in developing the memorials. In some instances, national museum consultants and the federal government participated in the planning. All reinterpreted sites of memory, while some engaged historic preservation. The goal of heritage tourism became a driving force as chambers of commerce advertised the racist past for tourist dollars. Indeed, black political empowerment made possible significant public monies for the various enterprises. Through an analysis of the process in Atlanta, Memphis, Birmingham, and Montgomery, one can see how urban leaders have joined civil rights activists and veterans of the movement in promulgating a new collective memory centered in the cities. The emerging civic religion of toleration points to the centrality of cities in the memorialization of the movement. Indeed, all of the museums put local spins on a standardized Montgomery to Memphis refrain that underscores the triumph of nonviolence.[3]

Within months of King's assassination in 1968, his heirs joined the City of Atlanta in proposing a "living permanent" memorial district anchored around the historic birth home and Ebenezer Baptist Church on Auburn Avenue. With plans to add a library containing King's personal papers, and a fitting "entombment" for King's remains, the advocates promoted the creation of a "King Shrine Area" that would potentially revitalize Atlanta's old black business district. At its heart sat the Martin Luther King, Jr., Center for Nonviolent Social Change, Inc., created by King's widow to memorialize the man through the built environment. The heirs selected J. Max Bond Jr. of the minority architectural firm Bond Ryder and Associates of New York City to design the proposed King Center. Then Coretta Scott King appealed to the Johnson and Nixon administrations for financial assistance, but at first received no public money. By 1975 she had raised $6 million in private funds to pay for the Interfaith Peace Chapel, reflection pool, and marble sarcophagus containing King's body. Jesse Hill of the Atlanta Life Insurance Company headed the building committee that launched a $10 million capital campaign to pay for the offices. As part of its 1978 January King Day Celebration, the King family broke ground for the proposed complex. Shortly thereafter, the U.S. Department of the Interior announced the listing of the King birth home on the National Register of Historic Places, signifying federal interest in the area.[4]

Although the City of Atlanta vocally supported Coretta Scott King's memorial, not until black political empowerment did the government provide funding to help make the vision a reality. In September 1975 the city revealed plans to construct a community center located across Auburn Avenue from King's crypt. Coretta Scott King joined Atlanta's first black mayor, Maynard Jackson, in announcing the $2.8 million facility funded with federal grants and a $1 million donation from an anonymous Atlantan believed to be Robert Woodruff of the Coca-Cola Company. Once completed the building housed offices for Atlanta Legal Aid, a branch of the Atlanta Public Library, a gymnasium and recreation room staffed by the city's parks department, and a childcare program managed by King Center staff.[5]

Suddenly the abstract commemoration appeared real. On the birth anniversary in January 1977, the King Center dedicated the Interfaith Peace Chapel that flanked the "permanent entombment of Dr. King." With the reflection pool and perpetual flame, King's crypt became one of Atlanta's top tourist attractions. Stretching alongside Auburn Avenue stood the administrative building and archive. Four months later the King Estate completed its restoration of the birth home, giving the house the appearance of when King had lived there from 1929 to 1941. The process of historic preservation pleased family members, who arranged for the King Center staff to conduct interpretative tours of the site.[6]

President and Mrs. Jimmy Carter kicked off a fund-raising campaign to finance the Freedom Hall centerpiece of the Bond Ryder and Associates' King Center Complex. Industrialist Henry Ford II headed the campaign to raise the $8 million needed to construct the auditorium, gift shop, and classrooms in the building that anchored the corner of Boulevard and Auburn Avenue in Atlanta's Old Fourth Ward. The Ford Motor Company pledged $1 million, while the United Auto Workers gave $600,000 from its strike fund. Ford joined Vice President Walter Mondale, former United Nations ambassador Andrew Young, and members of the King family at the groundbreaking in October 1979 as the King Center implemented the final phase of J. Max Bond Jr.'s original construction plans. By then the memorial listed resources worth $1.8 million including rental property and other real estate in Atlanta. That year alone it received $218,000 in mailed donations and an additional $50,000 from the Bee Gees. It sold $175,000 in souvenirs and made $5,000 on one-dollar tours of the King Birth Home, but the King Center used this money to help cover daily expenses. In 1982 the family dedicated the final component of the King Center, the Freedom Hall complex. Then in 1984 the family retired the $10 million debt on the buildings by using donations from IBM, Coca-Cola, Disney, Southern Bell, Xerox, and Ford, but also labor unions, the National Education Association, and the kingdoms of Kuwait and Saudi Arabia. It also received a $4 million grant for the facility from the U.S. government. As Dexter Scott King later recalled, "We watched it all come up out of nothing—the reflecting pool and arched, covered walkway known as 'Freedom Walkway.' Next the administration building went up, then adjacent to it, Freedom Hall. . . . The construction of the center was rewarding to Mother, because it was her insurance that her husband's message and spirit would endure." With donations, souvenir sales, and gate receipts, the King heirs operated the memorial; but expenses outpaced revenues, again forcing Coretta Scott King to request the intervention of the federal government.[7]

Coretta Scott King wanted to recognize her martyred husband's life with a national holiday established in his honor that would promote his philosophy of nonviolence. Beginning in 1968 with the introduction of the first bill, great effort went into convincing Congress to adopt the January commemoration that culminated in the 1984 ratification of a law that went into effect in 1986. While federal and most state offices close on the Monday closest to January 15, King's birthday, many people observe King Day in a variety of ways, often seeing it as an opportunity to assist the less fortunate in society. In an elaborate ceremony, Coretta Scott King gave a "State of the Dream" address from historic Ebenezer Baptist Church that allowed her to comment on world events in a fashion similar to that of her martyred husband. Having created a successful civil rights memorial out of the King Center and having convinced Congress to set aside a day in January for an annual observance of nonviolence and civil rights, Coretta Scott King put in place the pieces necessary for the memorialization of the movement.[8]

Others followed her example by proposing civil rights memorials in their own cities that advanced King's philosophy, so that a series of shrines developed that promulgated an emerging ideology of tolerance. Private contributions funded the monument that the Southern Poverty Law Center erected in Montgomery in 1989. Its founder, attorney Morris Dees, after giving a lecture to black students on victims of race hatred and discovering that many of them knew nothing about these civil rights martyrs, commissioned Maya Lin to design a memorial to forty of the victims killed for advocating race reform between 1954 and 1968. Like her Vietnam Veterans' Memorial in Washington, D.C., the Civil Rights Memorial is deceptively simple in its juxtaposition of black against white granite, a conical shape against arches and angles, and smooth stone against cool water. In explaining the "dissimilar elements maintaining equilibrium," Lin suggested, "things can look different . . . but still be the same." The contrasts pull at the senses just as the names, dates, and brief descriptors tear at the emotions. No other memorial provides quite the same impact. At the dedication, the mother of Andrew Goodman recalled his murder and that of others sacrificed during 1964's Mississippi Freedom Summer as "part of the consciousness of the nation." Having successfully broken the Ku Klux Klan through a series of celebrated court cases, Dees wanted to influence the nation's consciousness, so he shifted the attentions of the Southern Poverty Law Center to fund-raising for pedagogical purposes. In addition to increasing the SPLC endowment to $25 million, Dees raised an additional $650,000 in 1989 to pay for the sculpture.[9]

Raising money proved to be the problem for D'Army Bailey, an African American native of Memphis and Yale Law School graduate, who organized the effort to save the historic black-owned Lorraine Motel and turn it into a civil rights shrine. From the start Bailey had to overcome opposition from black and white people in Memphis who opposed a memorial at the site of King's assassination.

Yet others believed in his vision, and with radio disc jockey Charles "Chuck" Scruggs, the two men launched a fund-raising campaign to purchase the facility for $144,000 during foreclosure proceedings in 1982. Having organized the nonprofit Martin Luther King Memphis Memorial Foundation with himself as president, Bailey appealed for financial support. While his calls to the corporate sector fell on deaf ears, he received donations from black schoolchildren, union members, and small business owners. Because of opposition from Coretta Scott King, who feared the museum would focus on King's death and not his life, the board changed its name to the Lorraine Civil Rights Museum Foundation and set about mothballing the structure and planning a civil rights museum that told the story of the struggle for back equality.[10]

Owning a building in terrible need of repair with no resources proved difficult, but Bailey met the challenge with creativity and commitment. Embracing historic preservation, he turned to the Memphis Design Center and recruited its architectural students to reinterpret the motel space as a museum. He enlisted black entertainers James Earl Jones and Robert Guillaume to appear in a video pitching the project. Only after having a conceptual model and a promotional video did D'Army Bailey convince regional commissions to contribute $45,000 in planning grants. With the seed money, Bailey hired as a consultant Benjamin Lawless, who brought to bear on the project his thirty years of experience in the Smithsonian Institute's Museum of American History. Bailey and Lawless saw the Lorraine as an opportunity to teach black history, so they began their story in Africa and carried it through the successes of the civil rights movement. In 1986 Lawless presented his report, "A National Civil Rights Center: Technical Proposal," and estimated it would cost $8.8 million to complete.[11]

Black political empowerment provided the money necessary to turn the old motel into the country's first museum devoted to civil rights exhibitory. Bailey and the Lorraine Foundation board convinced A. W. Willis Jr., the first African American elected to the Tennessee General Assembly since Reconstruction, to take on the project. He convinced the state government to earmark $4.4 million for the project, money matched by the City of Memphis with $2.2 million and Shelby County with $2.2 million, so that the estimated $8.8 million might be on hand to turn the vision into a reality. The agreement required the Lorraine Foundation to relinquish title of the property to the state, although the nonprofit board continued to manage the site. With such public buy-in, the private sector willingly contributed an additional $2 million. Having continued to rent out motel rooms to raise revenue, the Lorraine Foundation voted in 1986 to end the policy, but its last tenant, Jacqueline Smith, refused to leave, so the board had her evicted, setting the stage for her vigil outside the structure protesting that King would have preferred to house the homeless rather than see the facility turned into a civil rights shrine.[12]

Recognizing the power of the modern look of the motor court with its landmark neon sign, the designers retained the original Lorraine Motel façade and added exhibit space in the rear accessed through the back walls of the rooms. The state building commission assumed responsibility of the project and the state architect, Mike Fitts, hired the contractors to restore and renovate the building. Taking the proposal of Lawless as a starting point, the state brought in the Missouri firm of Eisterholdllewellyn Exhibit Services to develop the programmatic component of the museum. The firm later split up so that Eisterhold and Associates actually completed the work. A design company from Virginia used the monochromatic life-cast mannequins produced by Studio EIS out of Brooklyn to strengthen the exhibits. Tableaus centered around a Montgomery bus from the boycott era, a lunch counter like the one in the Greensboro Woolworth's, and a replica of the Birmingham jail, while the back of a Memphis garbage truck provided the major installation and Room 306, kept as it looked when King stayed there, remained the concluding destination of the tour. The final $9.25 million project set the tone of the civil rights memorials that followed, as its visual story of human actors displayed in the exhibits recounted the standard Montgomery to Memphis refrain of the civil rights struggle.[13]

As with other civil rights commemorations, controversy swirled around the Memphis memorial. Critics complained about cost overruns marked up by the construction crews. Local governments feared the facility could not be self-sustaining and would require public subsidy to remain open. Persistent criticism from the King Center in Atlanta marred the Memphis effort. A changing board of directors involved corporate executives who bristled at the social consciousness of the museum's subject matter. In particular J. R. "Pitt" Hyde III, owner of AutoZone, Inc., contributed $300,000 from the family Hyde Foundation and began exercising influence over the board. In March 1991 the museum hired an executive director, Juanita Moore, to daily manage the site and oversee its educational work. On August 31, 1991, the newly named National Civil Rights Museum opened to the public. While many visitors praised the facility, *Time* magazine ridiculed what it described as "a classic jumble of laudable intentions

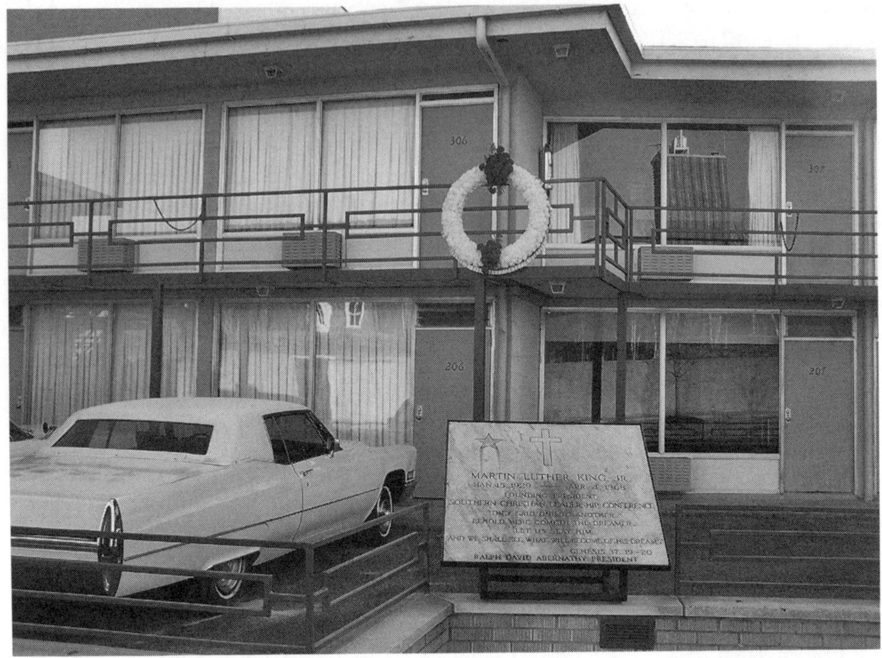

FIG. 1. Parking lot at Lorraine Motel, National Civil Rights Museum, Memphis, Tennessee. (Courtesy of the National Civil Rights Museum at the Lorraine Motel)

and bad taste." In particular it disliked the motionless monochromatic life-cast mannequins that it saw as "a parody of Disney style." Certainly the overview of black history expressed in the opening sections of the museum burden the viewer with too much information, but the dioramas depicting sites of civil rights conflict and the shrine of King's motel room drive home the drama of the story (fig. 1).[14]

D'Army Bailey envisioned the museum engaging community concerns of racial injustice and inequality that built on the message of the museum exhibitory, but the board shifted the focus away from issues of reform and towards questions concerning King's death. A recommendation by Lawless that a laser beam shot towards the balcony following the path of the assassin's bullet and then bouncing up into the heavens received a warm reception from the board and joined the content of the museum despite criticism in the media. Then, in June 1992, the board voted to remove D'Army Bailey as president and install in his place the former executive director of the National Association for the Advancement of Colored People, Benjamin Hooks, who had retired to Memphis. Hooks worked with Pitts and the remaining board members to shift the focus of the museum away from the black struggle for civil rights and towards conspiracy theories regarding King's death. The effort won the praise of Dexter Scott King, who, as the new president of the King Center, henceforth supported the Memphis memorial because it generated controversy over the assassination. In 1993 the Hyde Foundation bought for $125,000 the boardinghouse with the room in which James Earl Ray fired the fatal shot and donated it to the museum, thereby enabling Pitt Hyde to successfully redirect the focus of the museum. Meanwhile revenues failed to keep up with expenses. The museum collected $289,427 in ticket sales for 1992–93 and increased that figure to $326,912 in 1994–95, while the gift shop saw its revenues grow from $74,509 to $120,928 and donations increased from $196,768 to $440,127 over the same period. Nevertheless, expenses devoured revenues as self-sufficiency proved elusive. By 1998 calls to rejuvenate the surrounding area as a destination had turned the museum into a leading tourist attraction for Memphis.[15]

In Birmingham, advocates for a civil rights memorial used the promise of increased tourist dollars as a rationale for a museum that showcased the fire hoses and police dogs of the spring 1963 demonstrations. Beginning around the same time as D'Army Bailey's effort in Memphis but taking a year longer to complete, the Birmingham Civil Rights Institute accomplished many of the same objectives. A former mayor of the city — white attorney David Vann, who had helped negotiate with King and the Reverend Fred L. Shuttlesworth over the movement's demands — dreamed up the idea of commemorating the racial crisis as a way to move ahead in race relations. While still in office he had toured a Holocaust museum in Israel and concluded "the best way to put your bad images to rest is to declare them history and put them in a museum." The emergence of a majority black electorate resulted in Vann being defeated by the city's first black mayor, Richard Arrington, who several years later accepted the city council's endorsement of Vann's proposal and appointed the Birmingham Civil Rights Museum Study Committee to explore how such a facility might promote tourism and urban renewal in the old black business district. The committee recommended in 1981 the purchase of land near Sixteenth Street Baptist Church and Kelly Ingram Park on which to build "an educational and research center" that would include "exhibitions . . . and archives." Using $3 million in his second term, Mayor Arrington tapped local scholars, social reformers, and urban planners as a biracial Task Force to assist the African American architectural firm of Bond Ryder and Associates in its architectural design for the civil rights museum.[16]

Tourism provided the justification for the mayor's support of the project, although the members of the Task Force envisioned a chance to present Birmingham's rich albeit troubled past in a broader context, and the architects at first saw a profitable commission that simply replicated other jobs. When Arrington turned the project over to Bond Ryder and Associates, the Task Force grew anxious. As a leading architectural firm, Bond Ryder and Associates had already completed several significant buildings in America including the King Center in Atlanta and the Schomburg Library in Harlem. Initially the firm pitched a typical museum format of lobby and exhibit halls that it offered to fill with standard historical content following a master narrative of African American history. In response, Arrington's executive secretary, Dr. Edward S. LaMonte, intervened to put interpretative influence in the hands of the Task Force. The mayor's staff issued a statement, "Tourism is a major concern of the city and should be considered in relation to the museum's development." But the Task Force had concluded that "the script for the exhibitory needs to be controlled locally." With LaMonte's intervention, Arrington also recognized the need to coordinate the work of the architectural firm "with the ongoing work of the Task Force." Henceforth local people helped make the big decisions along with national consultants regarding the use of space, the development of themes, and the display of content. In September 1986, the architects proposed an estimated $12 million museum that left unanswered questions for the Task Force to resolve: how to achieve the proper balance between being a tourist attraction and an educational facility, and how best to promote the institute as a destination while supporting a larger historic district.[17]

To conceptualize the exhibits for the proposed Birmingham Civil Rights Institute, Bond Ryder and Associates and the Task Force hired museum consultant Richard Rabinowitz and his American History Workshop. Having earned his degrees from Harvard University, Rabinowitz had worked in a variety of settings including the hands-on Old Sturbridge Village and the bureaucratic National Endowment for the Humanities, as well as on more than a hundred projects including the United States Holocaust Memorial and the Center for Southern Folklore in Memphis. Immediately the Task Force got his ear and laid out for him frameworks for understanding Birmingham's racist past. Several months of meetings resulted in a rough conceptual design that the Task Force members reviewed and Rabinowitz revised before presenting to the mayor and city council. His layout became the contextual map followed in the creation of exhibits. Rabinowitz proposed a series of themes: Threshold, Barriers, Movement, Milestones, and Human Rights. While rooted in the local racial conflict, the narrative followed the Montgomery to Memphis refrain of King's life while using a Whiggish approach to history that championed progress. He called his proposal, "Walking to Freedom: The Museum of America's Civil Rights Revolution."[18]

In January 1988, the mayor and city council received the schematic design for the building from Bond Ryder and Associates, the thematic proposal from Richard Rabinowitz, and the reports on potential artifacts from the Task Force. Arrington's office responded by endorsing the Birmingham Civil Rights Institute as crucial for the success of Birmingham's Black Heritage Tourism Program. Yet no funding existed to turn the vision into a reality. Twice the mayor rolled the costs into larger bond issues that the majority black citizens of Birmingham rejected at the polls. By the fall of 1989, the mayor determined to see the project through by having the city hire the minority firm Diversified Project Management that black contractor H. R. Russell had created in Atlanta. It brought on board an exhibit design team out of Boston called Joseph A. Wetzel and Associates to turn the Rabinowitz narrative into museum displays. In the spring of 1990, Arrington arranged the sale of surplus property for $7.2 million and the city council used the proceeds to pay for construction contracts that it awarded in July. Controversies over payoffs to political cronies plagued the project that nonetheless proceeded.[19]

In November 1992, the Birmingham Civil Rights Institute opened to great acclaim in a ceremony used by Mayor Arrington to unify the black electorate behind his administration. It had taken thirteen years to go from idea to reality, but the $12 million memorial became an instant success, for in its first two weeks more than 25,000 tourists visited. In addition to the new museum, Arrington had tapped federal funds through a Street Improvements Warrant Program to turn Kelly Ingram Park into "a Place of Revolution that has given way to Reconciliation" with five outdoor sculptures that dramatically interpreted the events of 1963. Taken together, the park and museum expressed America's new ideology of toleration.[20]

Bond Ryder and Associates designed a striking building situated within a sympathetic understanding of its historic setting. With brick that recalled the building materials in nearby black churches and a domed center that echoed the twin towers of neighboring Sixteenth Street Baptist Church, the building complemented its surroundings adjacent to Kelly Ingram Park (fig. 2). The structure itself reinforced the programmatic needs of Rabinowitz's proposal. After buying a ticket at the kiosk facing Sixteenth Street, the visitor enters a courtyard and ascends a flight of steps similar to those that civil rights volunteers walked up to reach the sanctuary of the nearby church. Doors open into an entryway of arches and the space under a central dome, all of which signify a "threshold" crossed over to reach the dramatic story yet to unfold. A brief film tells of Birmingham's postbellum founding as an industrial complex in the middle of the plantation South and then explains the racial conflict bred by capitalists expropriating wealth from the region's soils. The film ends on an iconic photograph of racial segregation, the dual water fountains marked "white" and "colored." Then the screen rises to reveal the naked discrimination in actuality as the audience moves into the first of several exhibits displaying monochromatic life-cast mannequins demonstrating separate and unequal public accommodations, schools, churches, and businesses. Rabinowitz used "key spaces in the lives of black people" to provide "a multiplicity of levels of interpretation." Setting these black efforts against those of the white community revealed the inequality inherent in segregation while providing a potential yardstick against which to measure the successes of integration. These institutional "barriers" contrast with personal "barriers" as images of white authority figures reproduced on plexiglass block the now-darkened walkway that Bond Ryder and Associates gradually sloped upwards. Underscoring the complicated choreography of segregation, Rabinowitz wanted no "defined single pathway" in this dim section to emphasize the dangers and frustrations caused by white supremacy.[21]

The story shifts to the standard narrative of the civil rights struggle with a time line that runs from the *Brown* decision to King's assassination. A prologue begins with the Montgomery Bus Boycott. Act one introduces the student movement with sit-ins and the Freedom Rides. Act two looks at community organizing in Georgia, Alabama, and Mississippi. Act three focuses on the climax of the civil rights struggle in Birmingham. An epilogue picks up the story in Selma and carries it through the rest of the decade. Displays feature artifacts such as the Greyhound Bus burned outside Anniston, period televisions broadcasting a loop of black and white film footage from 1963, the jail cell that once housed King, and the speeches delivered at the March on Washington. The steady upwards climb through the Montgomery to Memphis master narrative ends in brightness with

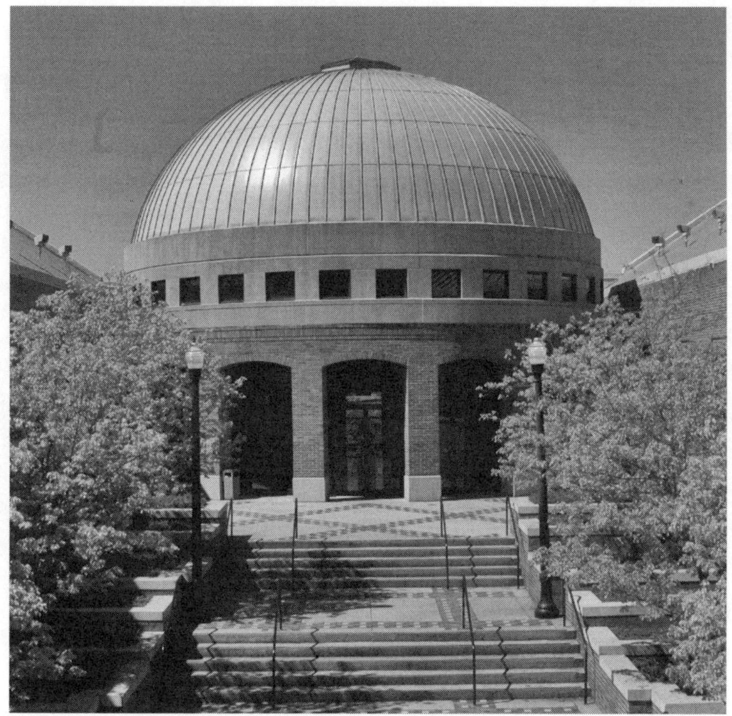

FIG. 2. Birmingham Civil Rights Institute dome. (Photo by Carol Highsmith; Courtesy of the Birmingham Civil Rights Institute)

the victory won. Like streams joining a river, the various paths merge into a wide, well-lighted opening of a parade of monochromatic life-cast mannequins marching alongside the famous photograph by James H. Karales used in the opening credits to *Eyes on the Prize* (fig. 3). This culminating section, called Milestones, intersperses alongside the representational figure placards listing African American advances since the 1964 Civil Rights and 1965 Voting Rights Acts. As these focus on political gains because of the social and economic shortcomings, the exhibitory turns to human rights in a bid to place Birmingham within an international context that makes the ambiguous outcomes more palatable. Using the United Nation's Declaration of Human Rights as a model, the institute invites visitors to take the "Birmingham Pledge" and embrace toleration.[22]

With flashy facilities having opened in Memphis and Birmingham, the Atlanta attraction put together by Coretta Scott King proved incapable of meeting the needs of civil rights pilgrims, so the National Park Service intervened.

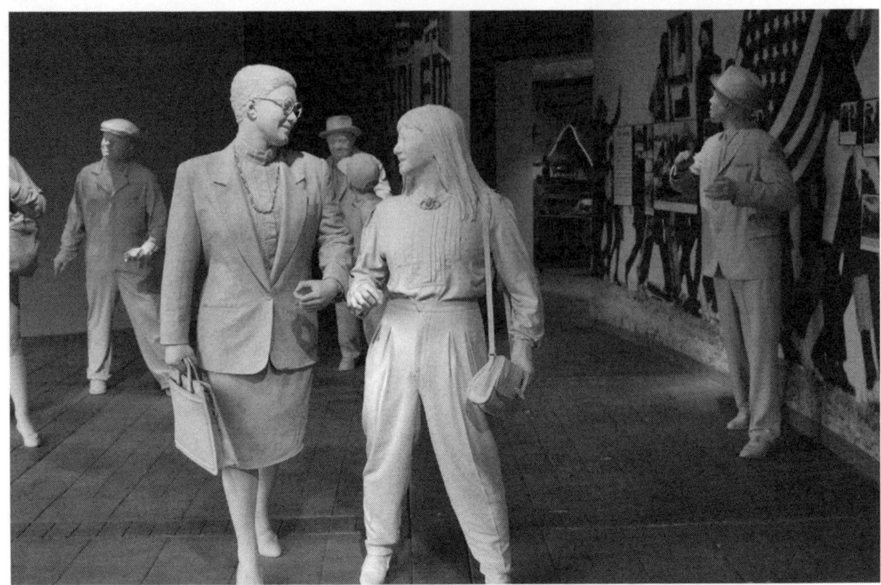

FIG. 3. "Come Walk with Me" mannequins. (Photo by Carol Highsmith; Courtesy of the Birmingham Civil Rights Institute)

Through private funding heavily subsidized by grants from the government, the corporate structure, and nonprofit agencies, the King heirs had created the King Center with its gravesite and gift shop but little else to entertain visitors. Few events occurred in the auditorium of Freedom Hall. The archives and library attracted only a limited scholarly audience. A failure to construct interpretative displays or to showcase the remarkable holdings of the collections prevented the King Center from achieving its potential. Instead it provided Coretta Scott King with office space and a staff to assist her in meeting the demands placed on her time. Originally intended to assist her efforts, the creation by Congress of the Martin Luther King Jr. National Historic Site and Preservation District in October 1980 ultimately resulted in the federal government exerting control over the civil rights commemoration. The legislation that Jimmy Carter had endorsed as one of his last acts as president introduced the National Park Service into the King Shrine Area. The federal legislation authorized the NPS to develop historic preservation plans and to purchase property to protect the look of the neighborhood. The City of Atlanta welcomed Washington as a partner in helping to stabilize the "stricken area" along Auburn Avenue. Once actively involved on the site, the NPS responded to the shortcomings of the King Center by recommending in 1986 that the government provide more services for the 350,000 tourists who visited annually. As an NPS report made clear, "visitors currently are limited in what they can see and learn about Dr. King and the Sweet Auburn community. Visitor services and facilities are lacking. In addition, current visitor use places a severe strain on the limited resources of the King Center." To protect the built environment, the government spent nearly $5 million to restore a fire station and a row of shotgun houses and other tenements near the King birth home, landscape the community center plaza, create visitor parking, and staff an information kiosk. The report fell short of advocating a "major visitor center."[23]

The September 1990 announcement that Atlanta would host the 1996 Olympics created an opportunity for the Park Service to dominate the city's King shrine. Within months Park Service officials had proposed a visitor center with restrooms and interactive exhibits, off-street parking for buses, and a new landscape for a total bill of $11 million. More than two million tourists visited the site in 1991 and the Park Service estimated 100,000 a day would attend during the Olympics for a total of five million people in 1996. Local rangers recognized an "unprecedented opportunity to provide additional facilities for visitors" and held to "a tenacious belief that it was now or never for the site to be developed." Site superintendent Troy Lissimore explained, "The Olympics were not the reason that improvements were needed . . . but the Olympics were the reason it had to be done now." The proposal involved swapping land among the Park Service, Ebenezer Baptist Church, and the City of Atlanta. It called for demolishing the city-owned Martin Luther King Community Center and splitting the site between an interpretative center and a new sanctuary for Ebenezer Baptist Church that would then turn its old sanctuary over to rangers for restoration, maintenance, and regular tours. The federal government lined up black political support with Mayor Maynard Jackson, city councilman Bill Campbell, and U.S. representative John L. Lewis of the Fifth Congressional District that included the site, while white U.S. senators from Georgia Sam Nunn and Paul Coverdell endorsed the measure, as did Ebenezer's clergy. Although in 1992 the George H. W. Bush administration had funded $2.2 million for Park Service restoration work in the King Shrine Area, the election of President William J. Clinton secured the necessary millions that the federal government appropriated in November 1993. As the new head of the King Center, Dexter Scott King opposed the NPS plan, arguing that the government should not offer an interpretation of events. He proposed

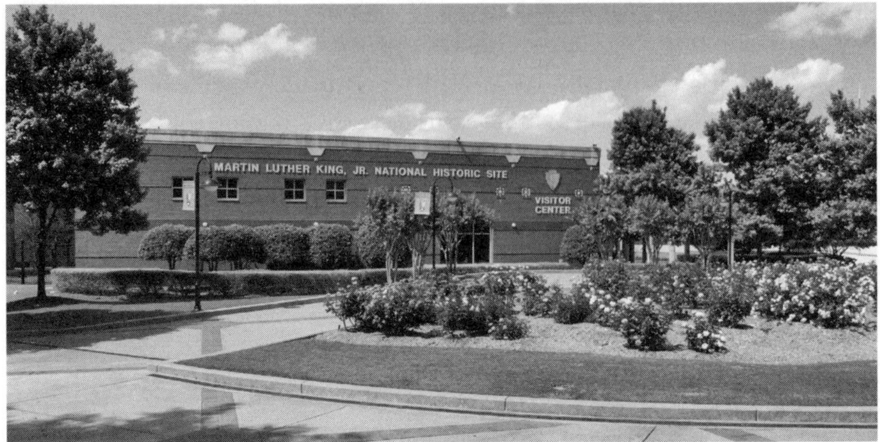

FIG. 4. Martin Luther King Jr. National Historic Site Visitor Center and "I Have a Dream" World Peace Rose Garden, Atlanta, Georgia. (Gary Tarleton, NPS Photographer)

instead an alternative multimillion-dollar "King Dream Machine." Protests by the King family failed to halt the proposal as the land swap went through and construction began in 1994.[24]

By opening its Martin Luther King Jr. National Historic Site Visitor Center in June 1996, the National Park Service just made the Olympics. In addition to the bathrooms, bookstore, large lobby, offices for staff, and galleries for traveling exhibits, the center contains an interactive display on the civil rights movement (fig. 4). Six pods use King's life as a common thread to explain the system of segregation, the emergence of "Sweet Auburn" as a thriving black neighborhood, the Montgomery Bus Boycott with its call for King's leadership, his role in the civil rights movement, his advocacy of sweeping reforms and nonviolence, and his assassination in Memphis. Rising up in the middle with three pods on either side appears Freedom Road, on which monochromatic life-cast mannequins march up an incline towards a picture window that looks out to the King gravesite across the street. Firmly grounded in a master narrative of progressive race reform, the exhibitory reiterates the message of toleration expressed at other civil rights venues across the urban South.[25]

Just as Congressman Lewis helped direct federal money into his home district of Atlanta to assist the NPS with the King historic site, so too did he secure millions in tax dollars for his natal state of Alabama to help develop the route from Selma to Montgomery for tourism purposes. As a veteran of "Bloody Sunday," when in March 1965 in Selma the voting rights advocates who had crossed the Edmund Pettus Bridge confronted brutality at the hands of state and county officials, Lewis saw an opportunity to emphasize the importance of the franchise through a federally supported commemoration of the famous march. He joined proponents of the effort in the late 1980s that led in 1990 to his convincing the National Park Service to undertake an exploration of the feasibility of the route. In the public hearings that followed, many movement veterans went on record endorsing the proposal such as Johnnie Mae Carr, a stalwart from the bus boycott days who — as head of the Montgomery Improvement Association — promoted civil rights tourism as a growth industry. By 1995 the State of Alabama gave its imprimatur, identifying the historic section of Highway 80 a National Scenic Byway. This marked Alabama's third designation for the same stretch of blacktop that had previously received regional recognition as the Jefferson Davis Memorial Highway in memory of the Confederate president and statewide recognition as the Walter C. Givhan Memorial Highway in memory of a long-standing member of the Alabama legislature from Dallas County who just also happened to be head of the state's white supremacist Citizens Council during Massive Resistance. Representative John Lewis convinced the U.S. Congress to designate the same fifty-four miles a National Historic Trail in 1996. With President Bill Clinton in the White House, the funds appeared in the budget to pay for the necessary planning, and Alabama set aside its shares of money from the federal Inter-modal Surface Transportation Efficiency Act (ISTEA) as its contribution towards the building of civil rights trailheads in Selma, Whitehall, and Montgomery.[26]

Other federal dollars found their way into civil rights projects in Montgomery. A $50 million addition on the city's historic federal courthouse, where Judge Frank M. Johnson Jr. handed down numerous landmark decisions in civil rights cases, encroached on the site of the Freedom Ride riot that took place outside the Court Street Greyhound Bus Station. To compensate, federal authorities set aside $325,000 to pay for interpretation of the landscape. The Alabama Historical Commission assisted by Johnnie Mae Carr and movement veterans created the Greyhound Bus Station Restoration Committee and hired Main Street Designs of Boston for plans. Then the funding stopped and the project stalled. By the end of the 1990s, Montgomery had yet to open an interpretative memorial, although the sale of land for the expanded federal courthouse ultimately resulted in such a civil rights attraction.[27]

Given Montgomery's role as the "Birthplace of the Modern Civil Rights Movement" and the popularity of Maya Lin's moving memorial, city boosters determined to develop a museum that might tap the pilgrimage trade. In the 1980s, state officials had assisted the congregation in restoring the exterior to Dexter Avenue King Memorial Baptist Church, while on the interior an art teacher from Alabama State University executed an elaborate mural depicting scenes and people from the struggle. Yet years of slow tourist traffic had left the church staff less concerned with capturing the occasional dollar so that regular access to the building proved difficult. Often locked out of the church, those same civil rights pilgrims wandered down to the Empire Theater to find the corner on Montgomery Street where police had arrested Rosa Parks in 1955. Only a state historical marker — one of several planned in the 1980s and erected across Montgomery by the Alabama Historical Commission in the first serious effort to document for visitors the city's civil rights legacy — explained the significance of the site. Watching from nearby office windows, administrators at Troy State University's branch campus in Montgomery realized the value of the theater property that it owned and the potential of developing the site as a civil rights attraction.[28]

College plans called for the demolition of the Empire Theater — the first air-conditioned theater in the South and the stage upon which famed country singer Hank Williams got his start — but historic preservationists protested, so the administrators hit on the idea of constructing into the proposed new library a museum about the bus boycott. With the main campus of the school in nearby Troy, Alabama, and with its own history of being the segregated branch for urban white kids, but now being just one branch of a state institution that partnered with the military and the Internet to open campuses across the country, Troy University wanted a new image that a proposed Rosa Parks museum could provide. Administrators had bought several blocks of downtown buildings, one of which the federal government wanted for its courthouse expansion, so the school sold it at an inflated price that resulted in the $5 million necessary to bulldoze the Empire Theater and build the Troy University Rosa Parks Library and Museum.[29]

As a purely public relations ploy, Troy University joined the civil rights commemoration business. The school's majority white administration required it to create a museum board with credibility in the movement community, so it recruited Johnnie Mae Carr and attorney Fred Gray, and then in 1997 convinced Rosa Parks to support the school's museum. By 1998 an architectural design by Sherlock, Smith and Adams called for a three-story building on the old theater site with the museum located on the first floor. Troy University hired the Kansas City firm of Eisterhold and Associates to develop the thematic program that used scholar recommendations, while Superior Exhibits and Design, Inc., executed the plans. On the forty-fifth anniversary of Rosa Parks's arrest, December 1, 2000, Troy administrators dedicated the $10 million facility in a program subsidized by State Farm Insurance. More than a thousand people came to see such dignitaries as Rosa Parks and Coretta Scott King, while hearing words from Alabama senator Jeff Sessions and Governor Don Siegelman. Over the weekend, seven thousand people walked through the facility.[30]

Patrons who visit the museum enter a lobby space dominated by a huge painting of Rosa Parks donated by Disney World. The interpretation begins in a theater space where three screens broadcast videos setting the stage for the historic arrest. Then folding doors like those on a period bus open, inviting the audience to witness a dramatization of the event that uses film shown against the windows of a historic vehicle, although not the one she was riding that December day. Afterwards more doors open to usher the crowd into a standard museum exhibit with displays of artifacts recounting the yearlong boycott. Again, dioramas stage moments in the movement. Monochromatic life-cast mannequins appear climbing into a Holt Street Baptist Church "taxi," one of the 1955 Chevy Bel Air Station Wagons purchased by the Montgomery Improvement Association to transport supporters. Mannequins of King and other leaders riding a bus in a desegregated fashion appear at the end of the exhibit. The artifacts and similarities of design make the Rosa Parks Museum like all the others, although the narrow focus on the boycott leaves much to be said about the context of the times.[31]

A few blocks away, the Southern Poverty Law Center makes up for the lack of ideological content in the Rosa Parks Museum with its Civil Rights Memorial and its Teaching Tolerance materials. Attorney Morris Dees had watched tourists experience the sculpture and take pictures without having an opportunity to ask questions, buy souvenirs, or make a donation. Over the past decade an estimated 250,000 people have stopped by the memorial. Reaching the same conclusion as the Troy administrators, Dees moved his staff into a new steel-encased structure across Washington Avenue and hired Eisterhold and Associates to renovate his original bombproof SPLC building, which architect Robert Cole had designed in 1983, into a memorial out front. Not only would this allow Dees to explain the names of the forty civil rights martyrs chiseled into the black granite, but he could also showcase the work of the SPLC and make a pitch for a donation. As a nonprofit, the SPLC used some of the revenue derived from its growing endowment to publish such reports as its 1982 study *The Ku Klux Klan, A History of Racism and Violence* and the biographies of the forty movement martyrs in *Free At Last* in 1990. Beginning in 1991, the SPLC developed pedagogical materials for schoolteachers that it distributed for free. Within fifteen years the SPLC had mailed out a slick magazine called *Teaching Tolerance* to more than a half a million people twice annually. Dees intended the SPLC museum to the memorial to have at its exit a gift shop selling t-shirts and postcards but also handing out his publications for free.[32]

Opening in 2005, the museum boasts no monochromatic life-cast mannequins and few artifacts, but its film, *Faces in the Water,* connects the viewer with the forty stories of the civil rights victims whose names are engraved on the stone out front, through the personal experience of seeing one's reflection in the mirror-like surface of the polished black cone. The film loosely follows the Montgomery to Memphis refrain just as the monument begins with Emmett Till and ends with King. In the hall outside the auditorium, posters complicate the once-simple theme of African American civil rights by introducing issues of discrimination rooted in ethnicity, gender, and sexuality. In conclusion, the tour invites the viewer to embrace human rights by typing a name into a database that then projects the letters onto a sheet of water that runs down a large "Wall of Tolerance" and appears to join the fountain out front. All one needs to do is promise "to work in their daily lives for justice, equality and human rights." Like at an old-time revival, the altar call generates new converts who surrender their names and mailing addresses to the SPLC. Having become a multimillionaire by selling cookbooks through mail solicitations, Dees now made a pitch for tolerance that successfully raised the SPLC endowment to $175 million by 2006. He spent a share of the proceeds from the interest blanketing the nation's educational system with Teaching Tolerance materials distributed for free to schoolteachers.[33]

Through the work of the SPLC, the annual observance of the King national holiday, and civil rights museums in Atlanta, Memphis, Birmingham, Montgomery, as well as sites not explored here such as in Little Rock, Greensboro,

Albany, Selma, and most recently the Martin Luther King Jr. Memorial on the National Mall in Washington, D.C., a civic religion promoting a new ideology of tolerance has emerged in America. Private contributions and public investments at the local, state, and federal levels have subsidized the construction of monuments to the movement that provide a tangible shape to an otherwise ambiguous message. What veterans of the struggle began through historic preservation at sites of memory has developed into a civil rights industry created for the tourism trade. Once-localized messages now appear standardized around a Montgomery to Memphis time frame. Confronted by the complicated pluralism of the body politic, municipal leaders have distanced themselves from the old ceremonies of white supremacy at Confederate monuments and instead play a central role in creating the new commemorations. Consequently, civil rights monuments have become temples where devotees of human rights visit and reflect as Deep South cities celebrate the triumph of toleration.

Notes

1. Scholars of French history have led the way in relating memory to the construction of national ideology in a fashion that relates to civil rights memorialization. See Nora, dir., *Rethinking France;* and Nora, dir., *Realms of Memory,* vol. 3: *Symbols;* as for the marketing of the movement, my thinking has been influenced by Finkelstein, *The Holocaust Industry.* A similar analysis on a national scale used to defend white supremacy is offered by Blight, *Race and Reunion;* and in Savage, *Standing Soldiers, Kneeling Slaves,* while a nuanced critique that explores similar questions from a regional perspective is offered by Brundage, *The Southern Past.* On the use of a historic site of memory for ideological and commercial purposes in America, see Weeks, *Gettysburg;* the difficulties of commemorating negative sites are addressed in Foote, *Shadowed Ground.* The similarities between memorializing the movement and the Lost Cause cannot be overlooked. For analyses of the earlier ideology of white supremacy and the Confederacy, see Wilson, *Baptized in Blood;* and Foster, *Ghosts of the Confederacy.* For an informed exploration of the relationships between monuments, heritage, and ideology, see Gillis, ed., *Commemoration.*

2. Until the 1970s there were few indigenous African American museums. See Crew, "African Americans, History and Museums"; for an earlier expression of some of these ideas, see Eskew, "Memorializing the Movement," 357–79; and Eskew, "From Civil War to Civil Rights," 201–14.

3. The commercial appeal of these memorials marks a significant departure from earlier expressions of Southern collective memory. See Brundage, ed., *Where These Memories Grow.* In a perceptive essay, Alon Confino evaluates the history of memory and warns of topical approaches that offer little analysis but simply "describe in a predictable

way how people construct the past." He suggests defining the construction of collective memory, its transmission through acts of commemoration, and its reception by the larger community. See Confino, "Collective Memory and Cultural History," 1386–1403, quotation on 1387. The controversial politics involved in commemorating the civil rights movement appear clearly in the renaming of streets after King. See Alderman, "Creating a New Geography of Memory in the South," 51–69; see also Alderman, "New Memorial Landscapes in the American South"; and Dwyer, "Interpreting the Civil Rights Movement." Unlike Dwyer's work, which suggests the civil rights memorials ignore contemporary racial issues, the argument presented here builds on ideas of Antonio Gramsci by suggesting that a kind of cultural hegemony is created through civil rights sites that promote America's new civic religion of toleration.

4. *Atlanta Journal,* June 4, 10, 1968; *Atlanta Constitution,* January 15, September 28, 1969, May 20, 1973; *Atlanta Constitution,* January 16, 1975, 1-AF.

5. For background material on King's widow, see Coretta Scott King, *My Life with Martin Luther King, Jr.; Atlanta Journal-Constitution,* January 17, 1993; and *Atlanta Constitution,* September 17, 1975.

6. *Atlanta Constitution,* April 4, 1977, 3-A, October 4, 1978, 2B. By 1976 the King Center had moved into temporary headquarters on the corner of Auburn Avenue and Boulevard, but left the papers at the Interdenominational Theological Center. See Durett and White, *An-Other Atlanta.*

7. A federal grant of $660,000 supported the running of the King Community Center. See *Atlanta Journal-Constitution,* January 8, 1984; see also *Atlanta Constitution,* December 9, 1977, 30-A, January 14, October 17, 18, 1979. Some $4 million of the $10 million construction cost for the King Center Complex came from federal grants. See Dexter Scott King, *Growing Up King,* 113.

8. *Atlanta Journal-Constitution,* January 18, 2003. Like Emancipation Day and Independence Day celebrations, King Day became another commemoration. On black collective memory, see Geneviève Fabre, "African-American Commemorative Celebrations in the Nineteenth Century," in Fabre and O'Meally, eds., *History and Memory in African-American Culture.*

9. Dees with Fiffer, *A Season for Justice,* 51–103, 332–33. Dees revised the epilogue in a reprinting of the book entitled *A Lawyer's Journey: The Morris Dees Story.* See *Atlanta Journal Constitution,* October 26, November 6, 1989; "Civil Rights Memorial Dedication Ceremony," November 5, 1989, program filed in the "Civil Rights Memorial" vertical file, Montgomery Public Library; *Time* magazine, November 6, 1989; *Free At Last;* and mission quotation from *Teaching Tolerance* magazine (Montgomery, Ala.: Southern Poverty Law Center, 2000). Since the dedication of the Civil Rights Memorial, the Law Center has distributed a number of brochures such as *Forty Lives for Freedom.*

10. *Memphis Commercial Appeal,* June 30, 1991; *Chicago Tribune,* December 12, 1982; *Memphis Commercial Appeal,* January 21, 1986, June 30, 1991.

11. *Memphis Commercial Appeal,* March 13, 1984, January 21, 1986, June 30, 1991; *Atlanta Journal Constitution,* November 30, 1986; "A National Civil Rights Center: Technical Proposal by Benjamin Lawless, April 23, 1986," in the D'Army Bailey Papers, Mississippi Valley Collection, University of Memphis.

12. House Bill 1949 passed the Tennessee General Assembly April 9, 1986, a copy of which is in the D'Army Bailey Papers; see also *Memphis Commercial Appeal,* March 13, 1984, April 8, 1986. For opposition to the state support, see the lead story in the *Weekly Memphis Advertisor,* May 21, 1986.

13. *Memphis Commercial Appeal,* June 30, 1991.

14. Ibid., March 12, 26, 1991; Duncan, *The National Civil Rights Museum Celebrates Everyday People,* 9; "The Glory and the Glitz," *Time,* July 1991.

15. *Memphis Commercial Appeal,* January 8, 1994, June 12, 1995, September 26, 1996, April 3, 1998. An effort by D'Army Bailey a decade later to re-exert influence over the state-controlled board failed.

16. See Eskew, "The Birmingham Civil Rights Institute and the New Ideology of Tolerance"; Franklin, *Back to Birmingham,* 92–133, 297–305; and *Birmingham Post-Herald,* November 19, 1992. The city council resolution of July 29, 1980, endorsed Vann's idea. See also Richard Arrington to ______ [blank form letter with addressee name to be filled in], June 16, 1981; Vann, "Memorandum To Civil Rights Museum Committee: Concepts for Consideration," n.d., attached to "Report of Civil Rights Museum Study Committee" October 7, 1981; Mayor's Office to Birmingham City Council, May 5, 1986; J. Max Bond Jr. to Edward LaMonte, June 12, 1986; James K. Baker to LaMonte June 17, 1986; and Ann Kaufman, Minutes of Birmingham Civil Rights Museum Meeting, June 21, 1986, all in the Birmingham Civil Rights Institute Collection, Birmingham Public Library Department of Archives and Manuscripts, Birmingham, Alabama.

17. J. Max Bond Jr. to Edward LaMonte, June 12, 1986; Richard Arrington to J. Max Bond Jr., June 25, 1986; Meeting summary, September 3, 1986; Summary Report of the Building Committee to the Civil Rights Museum Task Force, October 13, 1986, all in the Birmingham Civil Rights Institute Collection.

18. Richard Rabinowitz to Ann Kaufman, October 31, November 13, 1986; American History Workshop "Preliminary Exhibit Plan for the Birmingham Civil Rights Institute," April 1, 1987; "Walking to Freedom: The Museum of America's Civil Rights Revolution," June 1987, all in the Birmingham Civil Rights Institute Collection.

19. Richard Rabinowitz to Odessa Woolfolk, December 2, 1987; Diversified Project Management, November 21, 1989; minutes of Steering Committee meeting held on November 9, 1989; Brenda G. Burrell of DPM to Howard Litwak of Wetzel, January 9, 1990; Birmingham Civil Rights Institute memo #1 from Woolfolk to Board of Directors, March 6, 1990, all in the Birmingham Civil Rights Institute Collection.

20. On groundbreaking ceremonies, see *Birmingham News,* February 22, 23, 1991; on the grand opening, see November 14, 1992; and on Arrington's political ploy, see

the *Birmingham Post-Herald,* January 21, 1992, and *Time* February 3, 1992. See also the Birmingham Civil Rights Institute attendance totals, November 1992 through March 1993, in the Birmingham Civil Rights Institute Collection.

21. American History Workshop, "Walking to Freedom," Birmingham Civil Rights Institute Collection.

22. Diversified Project Management, meeting summary of April 3, 1990; BCRI exhibitory presentation, March 22, 1990; Copy of the "Birmingham Pledge," all in the Birmingham Civil Rights Institute Collection.

23. Public Law 96–428 adopted by the 96th Congress on October 10, 1980; National Park Service, *General Management Plan & Development Concept Plan,* February 21, 1986.

24. National Park Service, *Martin Luther King, Jr., National Historic Site Land Protection Plan; Atlanta Constitution,* August 11, 16, 1994; Dexter Scott King, *Growing Up King,* 207–9.

25. National Park Service, *A Grand Endeavor.*

26. *Montgomery Advertiser,* August 30, 1991; United States Department of the Interior, National Park Service, *Long-Range Interpretive Plan.*

27. *Montgomery Advertiser,* June 14, 1999, February 18, 2000, September 30, 2000.

28. *Dexter Avenue King Memorial Baptist Church: Reverend Dr. Martin Luther King, Jr. From Montgomery to Memphis, 1955–1968,* brochure (Montgomery: State of Alabama Bureau of Tourism and Travel," 1996). For a detailed analysis of civil rights commemoration in Montgomery, see Eskew, "Selling the Civil Rights Movement," 175–201.

29. *Montgomery Advertiser,* December 10, 2000; Greenhaw and Holland, *Montgomery,* 41, 47, 55, 66.

30. Troy State University Montgomery, "Rosa Parks Library and Museum Dedication Program," December 1, 2000, Davis Theatre for the Performing Arts, located in the vertical files of the Montgomery Public Library; other civil rights celebrities in attendance included Ambassador Andrew Young, the Reverend Jesse Jackson, Martin Luther King III, Maya Angelou, and Juanita Abernathy. See the *Montgomery Advertiser,* November 17 and December 2, 2000.

31. *Montgomery Advertiser,* October 20, December 10, 2000.

32. Morris Dees, interview by the author, October 9, 2006, author's possession. The Southern Poverty Law Center paid Eisterhold and Associates $556,010 for its museum design services. See the Southern Poverty Law Center IRS Form 990 for 2004.

33. See the center's website, http://www.SPLCenter.org, as well as the *Civil Rights Memorial Center & Wall of Tolerance* brochure produced by the Southern Poverty Law Center prior to the October 23, 2005, "dedication and grand opening." The Southern Poverty Law Center distributes the booklets *Ten Ways to Fight Hate: A Community Response Guide* and *101 Tools for Tolerance* in English and Spanish. Investigative journal-

ists have criticized Dees and the Southern Poverty Law Center in part over the endowment. See Ken Silverstein, "The Church of Morris Dees," *Harper's Magazine* 301, no. 1806 (November 2000): 56–57. On its IRS Form 990, the Southern Poverty Law Center explains its activities as "educating the general public, public officials, teachers, students and law enforcement agencies and officers with respect to issues of hate and intolerance and promoting tolerance of differences through the schools."

LYNNE HORIUCHI

Inventing Homelands in Japanese American Concentration Camps

Japanese and Japanese Americans used commemorative spaces and rituals to display their national loyalties and representations of their homelands within Japanese American concentration camps during World War II.[1] In these exceptional settings, acts of inventing homelands required negotiating suspicions of their loyalty to the United States and characterizations of their potential for sabotage — presumptions that had served as fundamental rationales for their imprisonment without formal charges or due process of law. The U.S. government and the prisoners themselves envisioned the concentration camps as cities with concomitant civic participation. In their expressions of national belonging, the prisoner-residents of the concentration camps adapted to governmental coercion and control through different modes of cultural material expression in envisioning their national homelands in ephemeral displays of American patriotism, such as "Keep the Home Fires Burning." With few exceptions, the War Relocation Authority (WRA), the federal agency with jurisdiction over the camps, regulated and directed these displays of national belonging.

The practice of re-visioning Japanese and Japanese American national belonging in the concentration camps must be understood within the historical context of the Japanese attack on Pearl Harbor on December 7, 1941, that triggered the United States' entry into World War II. The destruction at Pearl Harbor not only provoked anger against Japanese immigrants and Japanese Americans but also fueled calls for their removal from the West Coast of the United States and their subsequent imprisonment. Numerous politicians and alarmist media reports conflated Japanese residents in the United States and Japanese American populations, labeling them all as "treacherous Japanese."[2] The rhetoric contributed to support for the mass incarceration of entire Japanese American communities — men, women, children, the elderly, the disabled, and the sick. President Franklin Delano Roosevelt issued Executive Order 9066 on February 19, 1942, empowering the U.S. Army to remove people to secure designated military areas. The military then implemented a mass removal of 117,000 "persons of Japanese ancestry" from the West Coast, Alaska, and parts of Arizona; the U.S. Army subsequently moved approximately 110,000 people into concentration camps that the government euphemistically named "Assembly Centers" and "Relocation Centers." As part of the rationale to justify their actions, the U.S. Army described the typical Japanese American community as a "large, unassimilated, tightly knit racial group, bound to an enemy nation by strong ties of race, culture, custom and religion along a frontier vulnerable to attack."[3]

These actions and narratives reformulated discriminatory historical and racial ordering, stereotyping Japanese Americans as Orientals and foreigners capable of great cunning and deceit. Military, WRA, and other agency personnel persistently used the term "Japanese" to refer to all residents of the concentration camps, whether the prisoners were of Japanese or American citizenship. The U.S. government thereby overrode their prisoners' nationality and undermined any expressions of loyalty to the United States made on the part of their prisoners.[4]

How, then, did the incarcerated communities envision national belonging and citizenship in these camps? How did they commemorate their national belonging and loyalty to America or Japan in public and private spaces under the close surveillance and control of the U.S. government? What strategies and processes did they use to express their homelands in their building projects?

This essay explores the efforts of Japanese and Japanese Americans to commemorate their homelands and national loyalties while under surveillance, suspicion, and imprisonment in American concentration camps. Herein I elucidate the tensions of national belonging and ancestral homelands in the camps as the prisoner-residents resolved them in cultural material production. Several modes of material production are discussed: ephemeral displays; the artful transformations of barrack living spaces; cooperative building projects and community claims to space through organized events such as sumo wrestling, martial arts, dancing, and music.

Contested National Loyalties and Invented Traditions

The residents' daily experiences informed their expressions of national identity within the camps, as they drew from Japanese and American cultural traditions to invent visions that reclaimed and honored their places of birth. Eric Hobsbawm's concept of invented traditions helps to frame the production of ephemeral spaces and national identities within the camps and explain their conflicting ideological and often contradictory nature. He identified invented traditions as the ritual commemorations of nationalism associated with claims to the immemorial past that served nationalist formations when older traditions no longer fit their purposes.[5] Within Japanese American concentration camps, the act of proclaiming one's national loyalties raised basic questions about one's citizenship, group affiliations, and generational cultural interests that could be judged too Japanese or not American enough. Inventing new commemorative practices from older traditions was a daily practice involving not only the negotiation of national loyalties but also the acquisition of the means and material for building and construction. While the prisoners faced the prospect of refashioning their sense of national belonging in the wake of these challenges to their American or Japanese citizenship, their immediate needs were the adaptation and refitting of the inadequate shelter and infrastructure provided for them in their residential areas. Representations of homelands were predicated on material conditions within the camps, where the boundaries of the sites were generally delineated by barbed wire and guard towers, and where materials were limited and often recycled.

Conflicting national ideologies and loyalties were often exacerbated by a generational split between Japanese immigrants and Japanese Americans that was unique to Japanese American immigrant communities and began decades earlier. First tallied in the 1890s, Japanese immigration supplied labor to compensate for the 1882 exclusion of Chinese as laborers in the United States; Japanese immigration peaked between 1900 and 1924. The Immigration Act of 1924, levied through the lobbying of anti-Asian interests, excluded persons as ineligible for citizenship under the rule of racial unassimilability. Because Japanese were legally considered racially unassimilable into American society and therefore ineligible to naturalize as American citizens, the act resulted in a nearly complete ban of Japanese immigration. In 1942, Japanese American communities were largely composed of resident aliens, those ineligible for citizenship who had immigrated prior to 1924; the majority of their American children were born between 1915 and 1930. The first-generation Japanese immigrants, self-identified as Issei, comprised approximately one-third of the incarcerated population, while the second-generation Americans, or Nisei, comprised the other two-thirds.

National loyalties and decisions to conform to or resist U.S. government orders were the subject of the camps' daily discourses that evolved through the need to understand the long- and short-term practical decisions the prisoners would have to make regarding their basic survival needs. In the short term, they had to choose whether to try to remain in the concentration camps or attempt to resettle; those who were considered to be loyal to Japan had to contend with their forced removal to Tule Lake Segregation Center and their possible repatriation to Japan.[6] The prisoners' decisions regarding national loyalties overlapped the long-term consequences of other choices, such as military service in racially segregated units, enrollment in college, or other types of incarceration for resisting government orders, that split up family units and fragmented community support.

Aligning American Loyalties

The Nisei, first-generation Americans, struggled to declare loyalty to a government that had so decisively disenfranchised them, and they could not easily align their faith in the fundamental fairness of American civil processes associated with the everyday environments of their imprisonment. Educated in American schools, they desired nothing more than fair and equal treatment under the law and the preservation of their basic civil rights as American citizens. Mary Tsukamoto, for example, recalled producing a Fourth of July program in 1942 in the Fresno Assembly Center, one of the temporary confinement sites:

> Because we couldn't think of anything to do, we decided to recite the Gettysburg Address as a verse choir. We had an artist draw a big picture of Abraham Lincoln with an American flag behind him. Some people had tears in their eyes; some people shook their heads and said it was so ridiculous to have that kind of thing recited in the camp.[7]

Such projects as "Keep the Home Fires Burning" expressed narratives of American patriotism and nationalism officially sanctioned by the WRA (fig. 1).[8] Patriotism dominated news media in the United States during World War II, so it is not surprising that genuine expressions of patriotism were normalized in these Christmas mess hall decorations at the Minidoka Relocation Center in 1943. In an unapologetically yet carefully simulated living room scene with a fireplace, the decorations symbolically represented home, hearth, and homelands, prominently displaying photos of family members serving in the U.S. military. The geographic boundaries of the Relocation Center were clearly visible in the painted landscape in the background. The camp residents displayed family photographs to demonstrate the sacrifices of cherished and beloved Japanese American family members in the armed services and to signify national loyalty. This competition of mess hall Christmas decorations reinforced the ritual enactment of American patriotism that WRA programs prioritized in their efforts to produce model citizens for assimilation and resettlement into "American" society — a process that could only be normalized outside of the concentration camps and with official WRA approbation in each individual case as prisoners were "paroled." The irony of such determined demonstrations of national belonging forced the Nisei to acknowledge their special status as perpetual foreigners in the country of their birth.[9]

Acutely aware of the ironies of the social functions of such WRA programs, the Nisei participated in them as contributors to a major U.S. government project in social engineering and assimilation. WRA administrators espoused the democratic values of civic involvement that appeared in sharp contrast to American disciplinary control of the "Japanese" as a nonwhite population. Reflecting this consciousness, the names of their local newspapers signaled the prisoners' dilemma and the unique locales of their incarceration. For example, school papers at the Colorado River Relocation Center in Poston, Arizona, were named *The Petrified, School Daze,* and *El Bullador.*

Japanese National Belonging in American Concentration Camps

The choices the Issei made in representing their Japanese homelands within American concentration camps reveal radically different contexts of national belonging. The Issei had to consider whether to declare loyalty to a nation at war with the country of their birth and citizenship — in circumstances extremely different from those for Italian or German aliens in the United States. If the mission of the WRA was to protect Americans from the Issei incarcerated as

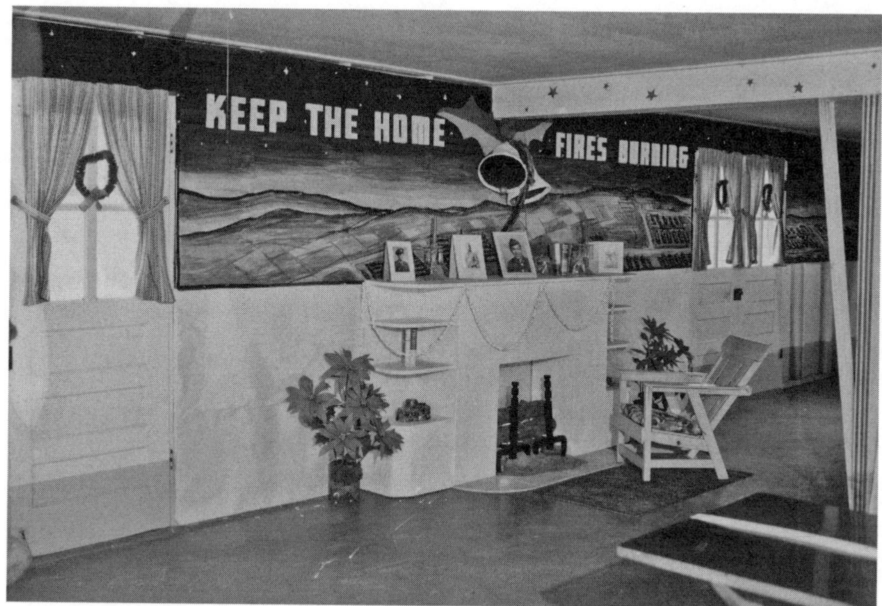

FIG. 1. "Keep the Home Fires Burning," Christmas, 1943, Minidoka Relocation Center, Hunt, Idaho. (Courtesy of the Bancroft Library, University of California, Berkeley)

enemy aliens and potential subversives, displays of Japanese culture by the Issei were contraventions of the WRA's policies of assimilation into American life as the ideal. The Issei must have anticipated that the WRA would seek to control and suppress expressions of national Japanese homelands.

Through a mandatory registration process, the WRA asked all the camp prisoners, including the Issei, to foreswear allegiance to the Japanese emperor and swear allegiance to the United States or face relocation to the Tule Lake Segregation Center and possible repatriation to Japan. Legally barred from naturalization as American citizens and uncertain of their fate after the war, the Issei, as Japanese citizens, worried about the possible repercussions of their declarations of loyalty. Most worrisome were their relationships with their American children. On the one hand, if the Issei swore allegiance to the United States, they could be tried for treason in Japan; on the other hand, if they refused to swear allegiance to the United States, their postwar status in their children's place of birth would be jeopardized. The Issei also knew that they would have to contend with continued discrimination, regardless of who won the war.

The Raw Materials for Refitting Personal Spaces

In spite of the starkness of the surroundings and meagerness of the available materials, vernacular art and architecture flourished in the domestic spaces of the camps. Reproductions of Japanese American homelands proliferated vigorously in all aspects of camp community life at both the Assembly Centers and Relocation Centers.

The U.S. government moved most of the prisoners into Relocation Centers or semipermanent concentration camps in remote locations, bleak, desert-like landscapes in the western United States with the exception of two camps in Arkansas that were located in swampy areas along the Mississippi River.[10] Designed to house populations of approximately 10,000 people each, the Relocation Centers were also new cities for which the U.S. Army provided Theater of Operation cantonment barracks for housing according to 1938 standard plans.[11] Originally designed for the temporary occupancy of military troops, the residential units in rows and rows of barracks were practically indistinguishable from one another, except for their organization into blocks with communal facilities in the middle with ten to sixteen barracks aligned on either side of them. With these repeating structures laid out on a grid, the Relocation Centers were functionally similar to military encampments but with no community facilities or schools, which the army purposefully claimed to omit in their *Final Report* at the end of 1942.[12] The electrical grid reached the barracks, but the water and sewage lines were laid down the middle of the blocks with no connections to the barracks.

For both public community facilities and personal spaces, the prisoners' primary raw materials were the barracks, generally 20 feet in width and 100 feet in length. In the U.S. War Department euphemisms, they provided five 20 × 20–foot "apartments" or "homes" in each barrack, which contained no kitchen, bathroom facilities, sources of water, or privacy.[13] With communal facilities for food preparation and hygiene at a considerable distance from the sleeping quarters, the residents' first priorities in refitting the rough barracks were acquiring furniture and establishing food preparation areas, storage, privacy, and basic shelter from the dust, the heat, and the cold.

The prisoners used scrap lumber left by construction crews and even raided contractors' supplies for raw material for furniture, shelves, and other amenities; mail-order catalogues such as Montgomery Wards or Sears and Roebuck supplied manufactured goods and fabric for interior decorating. In addition, the residents were permitted to organize and run community cooperatives with WRA approval, programs perhaps modeled on the Farm Security Administration's greenbelt towns or migrant labor camps created with the New Deal during Roosevelt's administration. The cooperatives managed stores and services and assisted the prisoners in acquiring materials for refitting their inadequate housing and ingeniously converting or subverting WRA power to ameliorate living conditions.[14]

Commemorating Ancestral Homelands

For Japanese immigrants and Japanese Americans, the Japanese environments they constructed in the concentration camp spaces remained encoded with significance that commemorated ancestral homelands. Expressions of national belonging were surprisingly and pleasantly well represented in building projects and ephemeral spaces within the camps, although not necessarily with explicit references to national politics. The prisoners' personal tastes included a great deal of hybridity, sometimes reflecting generational differences in Japanese or American tastes.

The WRA officially permitted displays of Japanese culture that were also used to demonstrate the internees' ingenuity, contentment, and innocent folkways. Aware that tensions between American and Japanese homelands could be extreme and intense, the War Relocation Authority strove to direct activities that could be considered "oriental" cultural arts — activities such as Japanese painting, caligraphy, theater, music, dancing, tea ceremonies, and interior decoration, even as the prisoners controlled a great deal of the production of recreational events. The WRA could then represent these activities as expressions of an imaginary oriental aesthetic.

The Oriental Charm of Mr. Imafuji's Barrack Home

A photograph of barrack interior redesigned by one Japanese or Japanese American man, M. Imafuji, illustrates the ways the WRA represented the prisoners' invented Japanese homelands. WRA photographer Tom Parker documented Imafuji's efforts in re-creating a room from his childhood memories in his 20 × 20–foot barrack "apartment" in a photograph taken in the Heart Mountain Relocation Center in Wyoming on January 7, 1943 (fig. 2). The WRA narrative on a photograph label described the interior:

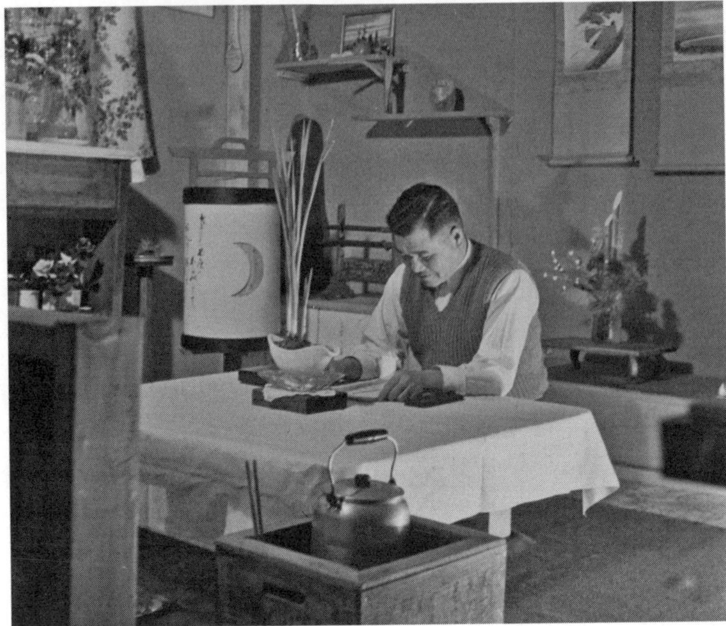

FIG. 2. Mr. M. Imafuji in the room he re-created based on his childhood memories, January 7, 1943, Heart Mountain Relocation Center, Wyoming. (Courtesy of the Bancroft Library, University of California, Berkeley)

> Out of small bits of scrap lumber and wallboard, M. Imafuji has created in his barracks home, an atmosphere of oriental charm. The low table, standing lantern, the screen and the scroll serve a double purpose of carrying out a theme remembered from childhood days in the orient. M. Imafuji, though he likes his oriental decorations, is a member of the American Legion and served in the A.E.F.[15]

The WRA's orientalist narratives functioned as a Western cultural lens representing an imaginary place, as in Edward Said's concept of orientalism and in Eurocentric inventions of exotic places: essentialized, objectified, and absent agency.[16] Mr. Imafuji's work was not identified as Japanese. Additionally, in the WRA's account, these proud displays of Japanese art and interior decoration were balanced with testimonies about Imafuji's American military service record and membership in the American Legion. While the writer may have been a WRA staff person or a Japanese American or Japanese resident employed by the WRA, the determined effort to strip the photograph of any sign of loyalty to Japan through its interpretive label is noteworthy.

Mr. Imafuji's room is evocative of a Japanese interior with many authentic and classical elements of a room in a late-nineteenth-century Japanese residence that has been influenced, in turn, by elements in the audience halls of imperial Japanese residences of the Muromachi period (1333–1567). Imafuji fashioned a display area that approximates a *tokonoma,* or alcove, that is raised slightly above the floor in which he displayed a Japanese flower arrangement with painted scrolls hanging on what should have been its back wall. To the left are staggered shelves on which art objects are displayed. These are two elements identified as part of the mature *shoin* style of Japanese feudal residential architecture; they signify important ritual areas for display within the room. A painted screen (shown in another photograph), the lantern, the hibachi warming tea, and the low table lend authenticity to Mr. Imafuji's re-creation of a Japanese room.[17]

The WRA photograph label strove to present a carefully crafted environment — a charming, innocent, and nonthreatening expression of a childhood memory that could not be easily confused with political or military national loyalties. The subject, M. Imafuji, appears preoccupied with his domestic life and carefully set table, and it would be difficult to imagine him posing a threat to national security. Yet, we know little about his efforts, or why and how he re-created a Japanese room to such a degree of authenticity as a person imprisoned for his potentially subversive loyalties to Japan.

Community Performances

Within the concentration camps, commemorative community activities abounded and the WRA found them challenging to control. In spite of the WRA's desire to maintain control over the minutiae of prisoners' everyday lives, the prisoners initiated the production of Japanese environments from the first days of their residency, presumably with little abeyance. Charles Kikuchi, observing community activities in his diary entry for Sunday, August 16, 1942, noted the construction of sumo wrestling pits in the Tanforan Assembly Center in San Bruno, California, among numerous recreational sites such as baseball diamonds, basketball courts, and places to play horseshoes.[18] To program the recreational activities and to construct facilities, the Japanese and Japanese Americans used the WRA administrative structure and their community councils to ac-

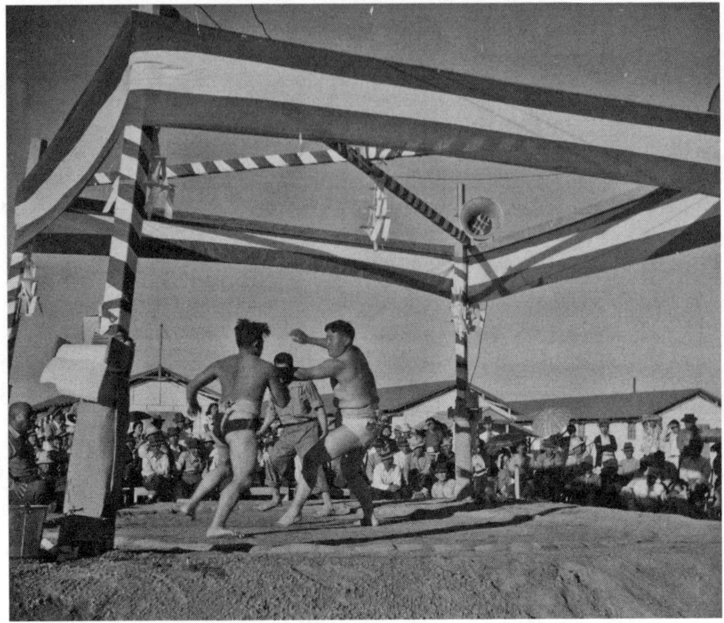

FIG. 3. Sumo wrestling competition, Thanksgiving Day, November 26, 1942, Gila River Relocation Center, Rivers, Arizona. (Courtesy of the Bancroft Library, University of California, Berkeley)

quire authority and materials. For example, sumo wrestling was part of the events organized to celebrate Thanksgiving Day in the Gila River Relocation Center at Rivers, Arizona, on November 26, 1942 (fig. 3).[19] At the Manzanar Relocation Center north of Lone Pine, California, the internees practiced kendo and judo in facilities the community built. The appearance of these activities within the camps is surprising considering that the U.S. Army had claimed as part of the rationale for imprisoning Japanese American communities that martial arts programs were used for training youth in kendo, judo, and sumo, presumably for military service, by organizations such as the Hokubei Butoku Kai, or Military Virtue Society, organized in 1931 at Alvarado, California, near San Jose.[20] Their existence was used as proof of the prewar collusion between Japanese American communities and the enemy Japanese government.

When the WRA moved internees considered disloyal into the renamed Tule Lake Segregation Center, groups such as the Hokoku Seinen-dan and Kikoku Hoshi-dan used military and physical discipline, including kendo, as part of their protests against the U.S. government and the WRA. These groups regularly conducted military and martial arts exercises at the Tule Lake Relocation Center — as part of their stated goals "to increase the appreciation of our racial heritage by a study of the incomparable culture of our mother country."[21] Such organized pro-Japanese resistance and eventual violence provoked a U.S. Army takeover of the center from November 4, 1943, through January 15, 1944, followed by the building of stockades and jails within the Tule Lake Segregation Center to hold those resisting and renouncing the assimilation programs of the WRA — prisons within a prison.[22] Nonetheless, the WRA permitted sumo wrestling at Tule Lake in 1944, presumably as a recreational activity.[23]

Some incarcerated camp residents, primarily the Nisei, demonstrated their support for the U.S. government and the war effort by building monuments to honor Japanese Americans who had volunteered for military service from the concentration camps, service that the WRA actively promoted. These monuments were among the most prominent commemorative and public landmarks built in the Relocation Centers. For example, the internees constructed a permanent monument to Nisei servicemen on a hill overlooking Butte Camp, one of the two camps at the Gila River Relocation Center (fig. 4).[24] Sited on a hilltop overlooking a broad desert vista, the Servicemen's Monument consisted of a monumental structure displaying an honor roll of the names of servicemen from Gila and an open post-and-lintel concrete structure that encircled a flagpole; both the monument and the flagpole rested on a concrete pad paved with stones.[25] At the Gila River Relocation Center, civic participation in American life was denied through incarceration and reinvented as American patriotism, as the monument testifies.

One of the primary ways prisoners maintained some independence from the WRA was through the development of community enterprise cooperatives that provided community infrastructure in services and recreation that the government failed to provide.[26] These projects were integrated into WRA programs, although the internees were responsible for paying for the use of materials, tools, or equipment and even for paying rent for space they used for cooperative activities.[27] Yet, through their community cooperative profits, the internees were able to create a great deal of independence from the WRA and to improve the quality of life within the camps.

The *shibai,* or theater, at the Colorado River Relocation Center at Poston, Arizona, is one example of numerous projects that were completed through the

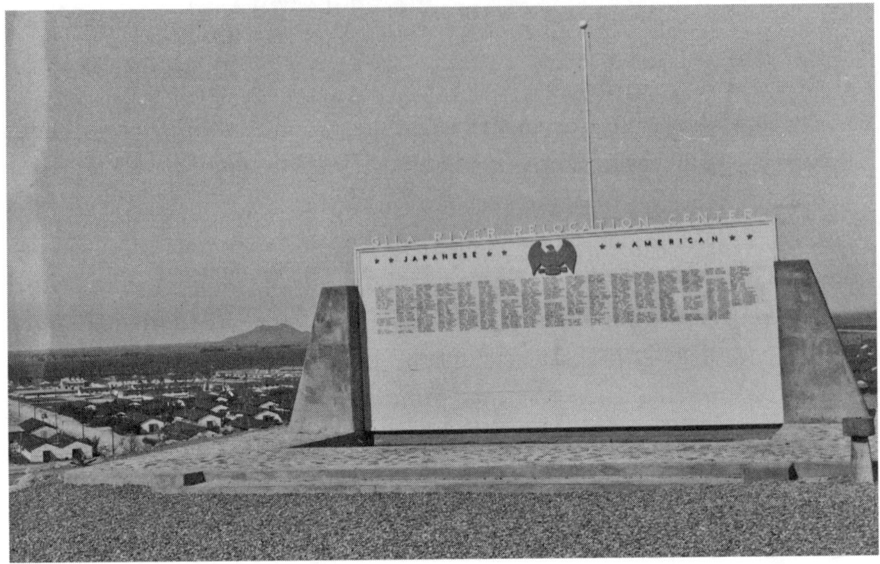

FIG. 4. Servicemen's monument, overlooking Butte Camp, April 10, 1944, Gila River Relocation Center, Rivers, Arizona. (Courtesy of the Bancroft Library, University of California, Berkeley)

community cooperative enterprises (fig. 5).[28] It was one of three theaters that the cooperative enterprises constructed at Poston, one for each unit or separate camp of 5,000 to 10,000 people within the Colorado River Relocation Center. It was not only one of the most imposing projects that the residents carried out, it unequivocally pronounced its Japanese character. The theater resembles Japanese *kabuki* theaters in some ways, particularly the two long side aisles. The main stage measured 38 × 32 feet and the left and right stage wings angled out from the main stage, at 46 feet and 41 feet in length. The storage room and dressing rooms measured 49 × 23 feet. The seating arena was a semi-oval that gradually sloped upward for 212 feet from the main stage. To carry out such projects as the *shibai* in the camps, Japanese Americans no doubt drew from their experiences prior to World War II.[29]

Invented Homelands

These ephemeral spaces, refitted personal spaces, rituals, building projects, and community performances were nostalgic and conflicted attempts to portray na-

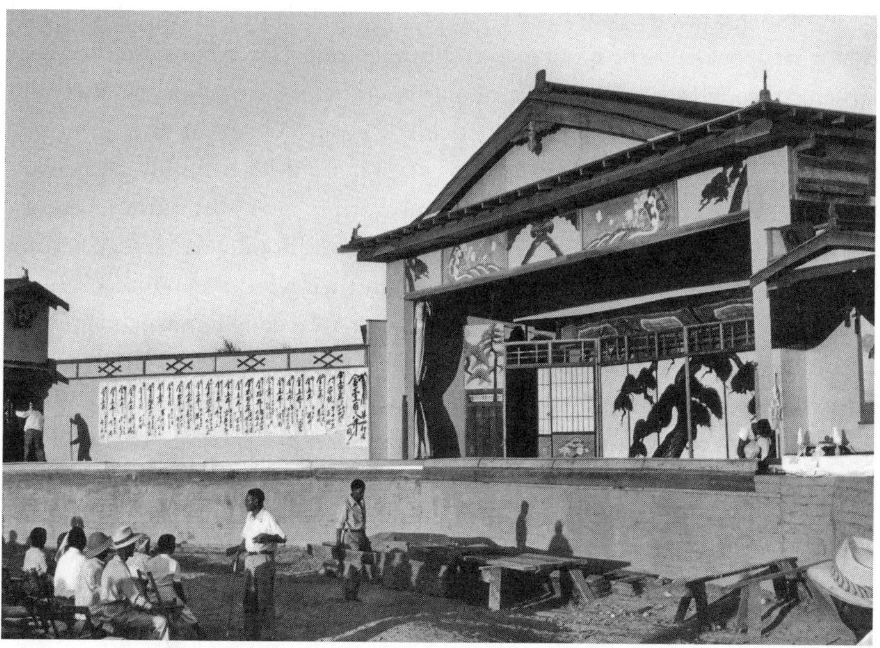

FIG. 5. The Japanese *shibai,* or theater, Colorado River Relocation Center, Poston, Arizona. (Arizona State Museum, University of Arizona, photographer unknown)

tional belonging while under WRA surveillance and within barbed wire fences. The concept of invented homelands helps to explain the conflicting and often contradictory representations in the prisoners' ephemeral spaces and building projects as part of the process of inventing traditions. As noted earlier, Eric Hobsbawm has identified invented traditions as these types of ritual commemorations associated with claims to the immemorial past that served new formations when older traditions no longer fit their purposes. While Hobsbawm and Terence Ranger have demonstrated the creation of Anglo-Saxon historical authenticity and representational values through commemorative rituals and paraphernalia that naturalized cultural authority, the objective of this essay has been to elucidate ways, often unacknowledged or signed discretely, in which Japanese and Japanese Americans addressed the problematic conditions of dominance within the camps through invented traditions.[30]

Different types of building practices in the camps, particularly the community efforts, demonstrate the flexible character of Hobsbawm's concept of invented traditions. In acknowledging Hobsbawm's observations in his study of prewar Nisei Week festivals in Los Angeles's Little Tokyo, Lon Kurashige noted that what appeared to be spontaneous cultural products were mediated and constructed through the reinscription of norms and values, repetition, practice, and experience in the articulation and rearticulation of Japanese American identity.[31] According to Kurashige, the prewar articulation of the Japanese American community's identity projected to an outsider an exotic image as well as the image of a community committed to the normative values of the dominant white American society, much in line with the WRA's vision for their relocation projects.[32] As an example, Kurashige hypothesized that *ondo,* or folk dancing, which appeared exotic to non-Japanese as part of Nisei Week's orientalized street displays, also strengthened ties among the Issei and Nisei as a cooperative community activity, solidifying ethnic pride through the association of dancing with important religious and cultural rituals in Japan.[33]

Kurashige's observations point to a powerful and sometimes overlooked aspect of cultural identity within the prison camps that was articulated through community activities in spite of the U.S. government's divisive and oppressive forces that exacerbated differences between the Issei and Nisei generations. Arriving in the concentration camps from different economic, social, and cultural conditions in the western United States, the prisoners' membership in an ethnic group had been determined by the government through ancestral bloodlines for the purposes of identifying a racialized enemy. To counteract such splintering, strong community structures lessened the tensions of strangers living in communal facilities and enabled their cooperative efforts to create community facilities not provided by the U.S. government.

The mobilizing character of this community spirit may be seen in the photographs of a traditional summertime Buddhist festival, the *o-bon odori,* honoring the corporate Japanese family, or *ie,* that extended historically to past generations and forward to future generations and was linked to Japanese nationalist rhetoric.[34] As an adaptive practice, *ondo* dancing had been incorporated historically into Japanese American summer celebrations and festivals such as Nisei Week in Los Angeles. The reenactment of the midsummer *o-bon odori* celebration during which the Japanese visit ancestral cemetery sites was an appropriate commemorative activity for the WRA and residents alike. At the Manzanar Relocation Center, the residents built a monument in an obelisk shape as a site for the commemoration of the dead that was recorded by Ansel Adams in 1943.[35] While many of these festivals were held in the concentration camps, photogra-

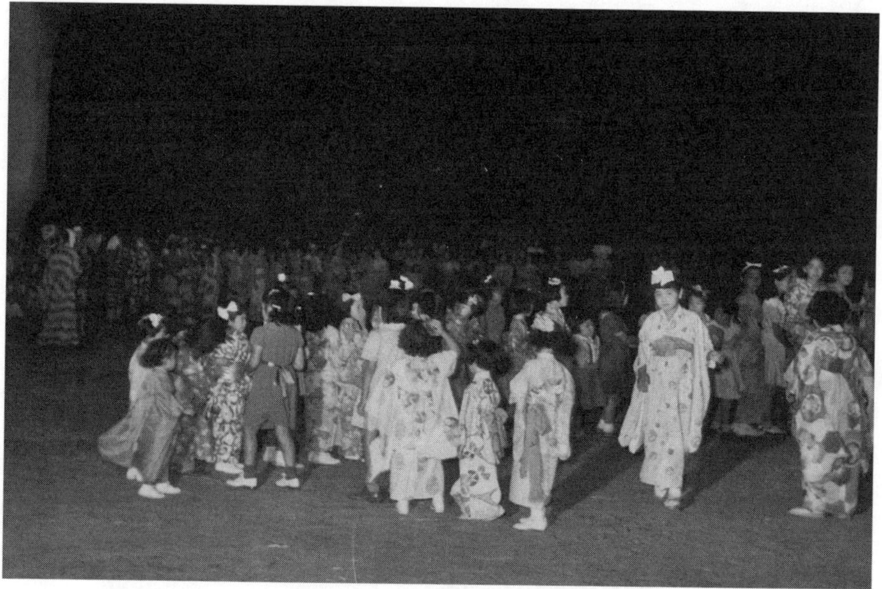

FIG. 6. Young *o-bon odori* dancers line up for refreshments during intermission, August 14, 1943, Granada Relocation Center, Amache, Colorado. (Courtesy of the Bancroft Library, University of California, Berkeley)

pher Joe McClelland extensively documented the *o-bon odori* that took place in the Granada Relocation Center on August 14, 1943 (fig. 6).[36] The musical instruments the internees played and the Japanese kimonos they wore testify to their ingenuity in securing them, since they were most likely not included in their bundles and suitcases at the time of their evacuation.[37]

Expressions of loyalty, homelands, and patriotic sentiment, whether Japanese or American, were constant reminders of the injustice of their incarceration. The internees achieved some comfort from the reenactment of their Japanese rituals, and the production of Japanese cuisine that also provided a quiet resistance and insularity from the pain of exclusion and incarceration in hostile environments. The internees set up tofu, miso, and soy sauce (*shoyu*) factories in nearly all the concentration camps, often as community cooperative enterprises.

Celebrations like the sumo wrestling at the Gila River and Tule Lake Relocation Centers, the *o-bon odori* at the Granada Relocation Center, and *kabuki* plays at the Colorado River Relocation Center *shibai* symbolically reinforced the cultural identity of the prisoners' Japanese homelands with a sense of continuity with Japanese culture and the prewar communities that they considered their homes. These cultural productions demonstrated a transfer of community organization, skills, cultural material, and commercial networks from prewar communities that were then used to maintain and invent Japanese homelands within the spatial confinement of the concentration camps while living under government domination.

Hybrid Traditions within Japanese American Concentration Camps

Invented traditions also embodied hybrid American and Japanese values such as those expressed by the Norakuro Band in the Minidoka Relocation Center. *Norakuro* may be translated as a wild cat leading an indolent life; it appears to have been a reference to both a Japanese version of Mickey Mouse and Borrah Minivitch's Harmonica Rascals—a popular contemporary harmonica band (fig. 7). The photograph label explains:

> This is called a harmonica band although harmonicas are augmented by an equal number of other instruments. The organization, including the name, is patterned after Borrah Minnevitch's [*sic*] Harmonica Rascals. This band plays for center dances and is very popular. They play both American and Japanese music, often putting Japanese lyrics to American music. Roy Matsunaga, right, with baton, formerly of Portland, Oregon, is leader.[38]

Such a happy musical note is a reminder that these recreational activities counteracted the coercion and control that ruled commemoration and representation within the Japanese American concentration camps of World War II. Tensions between American and Japanese homelands could be extreme and even violent in the camps. The U.S. government supplied only the minimal necessities for the prisoners' maintenance, barely sufficient for survival, much less comfort, shelter, recreation, and beauty.

Conclusion

The internees' ephemeral spaces and utopian building projects commemorating Japanese and American homelands may be viewed as complex forms of resistance

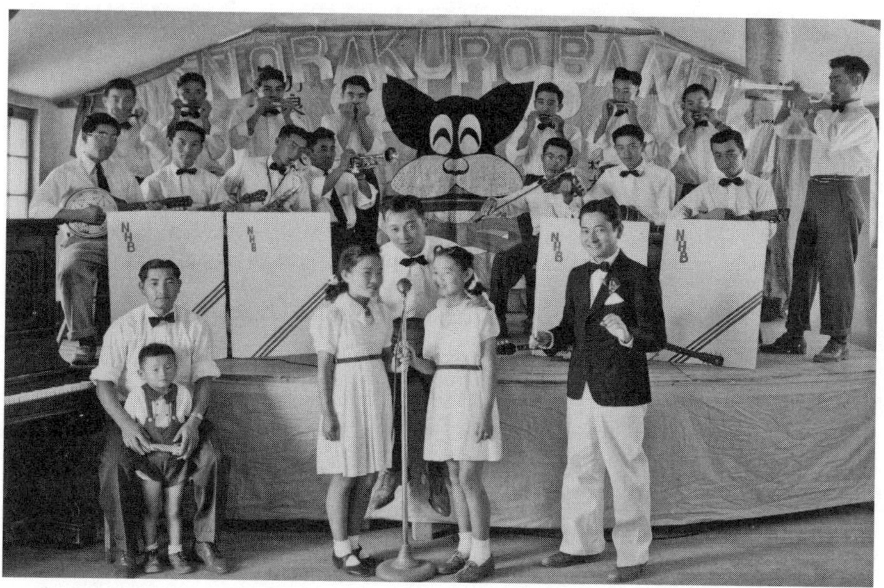

FIG. 7. The Norakuro Band, August 20, 1943, Minidoka Relocation Center, Hunt, Idaho. (Courtesy of the Bancroft Library, University of California, Berkeley)

against the racism and government policies they encountered. For the prisoners, resistance through the appropriation of authority and materials for the invention of national homelands had to be balanced with state-run forces. Their citizenship and national identities had been transformed in ways that would haunt their civic participation in American society. Yet, their invented homelands within the concentration camps were vibrant, expressive, and flexible — sustaining the commemorative practices of prewar Japanese American communities and demonstrating an independent community life quite separate from and resistant against the policies, programs, and surveillance of the War Relocation Authority and dominant society.

Notes

For their review of this work, I wish to thank Tanu Sankalia, Roger Daniels, Greg Robinson, Dell Upton, Greg Crysler, Tryphenia Peele-Eady, Carolina Serna, Ellen Fernandez-Sacco, and Blanca Gordo. Susan Snyder and Theresa Salazar of The Bancroft Library provided me with important assistance, as did Alan Ferg and Jannelle Weakly of the

Arizona State Museum. My research was funded in part by a 1997–1998 Civil Liberties Public Education Fund Fellowship; The Bancroft Library Study Award at the University of California, Berkeley, in 2000; and an American Fellowship from the American Association of University Women in 2001–2002.

1. The term "concentration camp" has been a topic of ongoing scholarly dialogue. For this essay, I use *Merriam-Webster's* definition of the term, "a camp where (prisoners of war, political prisoners, refugees, or foreign nationals) are detained or confined and sometimes subjected to physical and mental abuse and indignity." For a discussion of place-naming terminology, see Daniels, "Words Do Matter." As Tetsuden Kashima has noted in *Judgment without Trial,* 9, "internment" applies to civilian enemy nationals that during World War II included Germans and Italians. The War Relocation Authority (WRA) also referred to the prisoners as "evacuees," "colonists," and "internees." With the shift in recent scholarship to focus on the camps as a form of incarceration, I often use the terms "prisoners" to refer to incarcerated people or, as a form of counterpoint, "residents" when discussing modes of civic participation and urbanism.

2. Robinson, *By Order of the President,* 74.

3. United States Department of War, *Final Report,* vii, 8, 9, 17, 25. In addition to the mass incarceration, there were as many as 125 prison sites maintained by the Federal Bureau of Investigation, the Department of Justice, the Immigration and Naturalization Service, and other agencies that held as hostages Japanese aliens, some Japanese Americans, and Japanese civilians sent from Central and South American countries to the United States. See Kashima, *Judgment without Trial,* 10–11.

4. Horiuchi, "Dislocations," in *Guilt by Association,* ed. Mackey, 263–65.

5. Hobsbawm, "Introduction: Inventing Traditions," in *The Invention of Tradition,* ed. Eric Hobsbawm and Terence Ranger, 1–14.

6. Kashima, *Judgment without Trial,* 160–65; Weglyn, *Years of Infamy,* 156–58.

7. Tateishi, *And Justice for All,* 14.

8. The annotation reads: "Block 36 saw favor in the judges' eyes for fifth place in the Christmas dining hall decorations contest, by its homey atmosphere and clever decorations made out of waste material." Volume 25, Section C, War Relocation Authority no. G–408, Minidoka Relocation Center (Hunt, Idaho), 12/?/43 [*sic*], War Relocation Authority Photographs of Japanese-American Evacuation and Resettlement, BANC PIC 1967.014 — PIC, The Bancroft Library, University of California, Berkeley.

9. Lowe, *Immigrant Acts,* 4–31.

10. The two exceptions were in Jerome and Rohwer, Arkansas, located in the Mississippi River Delta.

11. U.S. Department of Defense and the United States Department of Interior, *World War II and the U.S. Army Mobilization Program,* 11–13, 81. See also Burton et al., *Con-*

finement and Ethnicity, 41–44. The exceptions were the Colorado River Relocation Center, which had three camps: Poston I, II, and III, and the Gila River Relocation Center, which had two camps: Butte and Canal.

12. United States Department of War, *Final Report,* 266.

13. The standard unit was 20 × 20 feet, although variations were soon introduced. See Horiuchi, "Dislocations," in *Guilt by Association,* ed. Mackey, 260.

14. Horiuchi, "Dislocations and Relocations, 206.

15. Volume 12, Section B, War Relocation Authority no. E–620, Heart Mountain Relocation Center (Wyoming), 1/7/1943, War Relocation Authority Photographs of Japanese-American Evacuation and Resettlement, BANC PIC 1967.014—PIC, The Bancroft Library, University of California, Berkeley.

16. Said, *Orientalism,* 2.

17. Hashimoto, *Architecture in the Shoin Style,* 21–22. The four prescriptive elements of a Muromachi audience hall, the *tokonoma;* the staggered shelves; the *chodaigamae,* or painted decorative doors; and the *tsukeshoin,* or desk alcove, could be found in numerous variations and adaptations in nineteenth-century Japanese residences.

18. Kikuchi, *The Kikuchi Diary,* 53.

19. The label reads: "Two of the residents at this relocation center who participated in the wrestling tournament Thanksgiving day." Volume 5, Section A, War Relocation Authority no. D–671, photographer Francis Stewart. Series 2, Gila River Relocation Center (Rivers, Arizona), 11/26/42, War Relocation Authority Photographs of Japanese-American Evacuation and Resettlement, BANC PIC 1967.014—PIC, The Bancroft Library, University of California, Berkeley.

20. United States Department of War, *Final Report,* 10–11.

21. Thomas, Thomas, and Nishimoto, *The Spoilage,* 312–20; Kashima, *Judgment without Trial,* 171.

22. Commission on Wartime Relocation and Internment of Civilians, *Personal Justice Denied,* 210–11.

23. "Scene at the Sumo tournament held at the Tule Lake Center, October, 1944," Volume 34, Section D, WRA no. G–754 and 755, War Relocation Authority Photographs of Japanese-American Evacuation and Resettlement, Vol. 12, Section B, BANC PIC 1967.014—PIC, The Bancroft Library, University of California, Berkeley.

24. Servicemen's Monument, Volume 5, Section A, War Relocation Authority no. G–587, Gila Relocation Center (Rivers, Arizona), 4/10/44, War Relocation Authority Photographs of Japanese-American Evacuation and Resettlement, BANC PIC 1967.014—PIC, The Bancroft Library, University of California, Berkeley.

25. See Volume 81, Section S, WRA no. 505, 506, and 507, War Relocation Authority Photographs of Japanese-American Evacuation and Resettlement, BANC PIC 1967.014—PIC, The Bancroft Library, University of California, Berkeley.

26. As part of their goal to create model American citizens, the War Relocation Authority permitted community cooperatives within each of the Relocation Centers modeled after New Deal cooperative projects.

27. United States Department of Interior, War Relocation Authority, Washington, D.C., *Administrative Instruction No. 26,* August 25, 1942, and Supplements 1–9.

28. "Photograph of W.R.A. subjects," Edward H. Spicer Papers, MS 5, Accession #90–116, Arizona State Museum Archives, University of Arizona.

29. For a study of prewar Japanese American building projects and types, see Dubrow and Graves, *Sento at Sixth and Main.*

30. Hobsbawm, "Introduction: Inventing Traditions," in *The Invention of Tradition,* ed. Eric Hobsbawm and Terence Ranger, 1–14.

31. Kurashige, *Japanese American Celebration and Conflict,* 9.

32. Ibid., 10.

33. Ibid., 47, 50.

34. Smith, *Ancestor Worship,* 99; Robertson, *Takarazuka,* 63–73, 89–101; Dower, *Japan in War and Peace,* 271–79.

35. Armor and Wright, *Manzanar,* xiv–xv.

36. Volume 7, Section A, War Relocation Authority no. B–894, photographer Joe McClelland. Sponsored by the Granada Buddhist Church, Amache, Colorado, 8/14/43, BANC PIC 1967.014—PIC, The Bancroft Library, University of California, Berkeley.

37. The internees acquired such Japanese goods and materials through community enterprise cooperative stores, their prewar distributors, mail-order catalogues, or requests to friends and family. See Business Enterprise folder, Reel 33, The National Archives: Records of the War Relocation Authority 1942–1946, Basic Field Documentation on microfilm, BANC FILM 1932, The Bancroft Library, University of California, Berkeley.

38. Volume 78, Section G, War Relocation Authority no. 241, Minidoka Relocation Center (Hunt, Idaho), 8/20/43, War Relocation Authority Photographs of Japanese-American Evacuation and Resettlement, BANC PIC 1967.014—PIC. The Bancroft Library, University of California, Berkeley.

FORGOING MEMORY

DAVID LOWENTHAL

Adorning Damnable Cities

Pro Urbis Amore and *Damnatio Memoriae*

Civics as an art, a policy, has to do not with U-topia but with Eu-topia; not with imagining an impossible no-place where all is well, but with making the most and the best of each and every place, and especially of the city in which we live. — Patrick Geddes

Cities, like dreams, are made of desires and fears, even if the thread of their discourse is secret, their rules are absurd, their perspectives deceitful, and everything conceals something else. — Italo Calvino

We don't need a monument. You see a monument and you don't think of anything. — Joel Shapiro (U.S. Holocaust Memorial Museum sculptor)

COMMEMORATION and the city — what an unlikely conjunction, especially in America! The American city is more usually recalled in sorrow, deplored, even reviled. Not the city but the country is nostalgically remembered. Historic houses *in the country,* parish churches *in the country,* picture-book villages *in the country* — these are the prime foci of protective care in England.[1] Recent London commemorative projects — the accident-prone Princess Diana fountain in Hyde Park, Marc Quinn's limbless *Alison Lapper Pregnant* that from 2005 to 2006 adorned the fourth plinth in Trafalgar Square,[2] the Animals at War monument at Park Lane to the dogs, horses, elephants, and carrier pigeons that served and died alongside British forces — are camp or kitsch. In France, for all the primacy of Parisian *lieux de mémoire,* the grandest monuments to ancient Gaul are in remote rural locales — Napoleon III's bronze Vercingetorix at Alesia, Pétain's at Gergovia, Mitterand's at Bibracte.[3]

Principled denigration of monuments dates at least to Athens's Pericles, who insisted that durable memories be "planted in the heart rather than graven on stone." American legacies of Puritan iconoclasm, antimonarchical republicanism, and future-oriented enlightenment confirmed antagonism to ostentatious commemorative statuary and architecture that festooned Old World cities.[4] By the nineteenth century "a thickening forest of monuments" to past national glories "almost threatened to choke the city squares and picturesque sites of Europe" in self-parodying surfeit.[5] "Every tacky little fourth-rate déclassé European country has monuments all over the place and one cannot turn a corner without banging into an eighteen-foot bronze of Lebrouche Tickling the Chambermaids at Vache while Planning the Battle of Bledsoe, or some such," grumbled an American. By contrast, his own countrymen "tend to pile up a few green cannon balls next to a broken-down mortar and forget about it."[6] (Latterly Americans have become less casual; the entire Washington Mall is now saturated with commemoration, the Lincoln and Jefferson memorials framing sites of mourning for the victims of every American war and wronged ethnicity.)[7]

In colonial New England, the "City [set] on a hill" (Matthew 5:14) was John Winthrop's godly ascription not to the city of Boston but to an archetypal Puritan village. Modern memorials abound to rural haunts, battlefields, buildings, great men, nation-states; relatively few are made, and fewer endure, for or in urban scenes. Famed exceptions, like Maya Lin's Vietnam Veterans Memorial in Washington, are more apt to be testaments to tragedy than to triumph. The typical American memorial scene is the small-town statue–cannon–historical marker set (fig. 1).

"The common image of the country is now an image of the past," noted Raymond Williams a generation ago, "and the common image of the city an image of the future."[8] Today's futurists focus less on urban prospects, but they still disdain the past, demanding like Marinetti's Futurists of a century ago that the old be swept away. If some city worthies exalt their town's origins and intone civic continuities, urban tradition normally plays second fiddle to commercial novelty.

Novelty became the guiding principle of nineteenth-century American city builders. "Overturn, overturn, overturn! is the maxim of New York," remarked former mayor Philip Hone in 1845; each "generation of men seems anxious to remove all relics of those which preceded them."[9] Antiquity *had* to be annihilated, explained Henry James; "to let any tenderness of association once accumulate, or any 'love of the old' once pass unsnubbed," would bring progress to a standstill.[10]

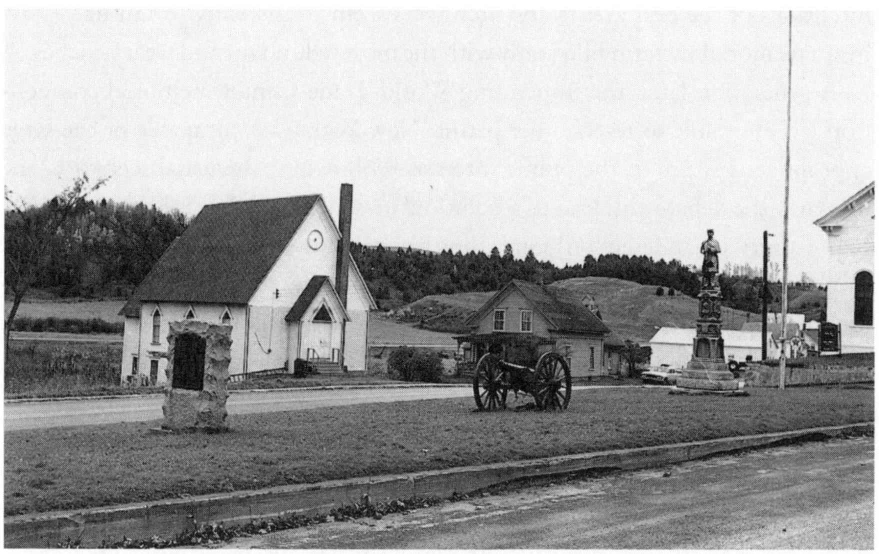

Fig. 1. Commemorative array: churches, memorial plaque, Civil War cannon, soldier atop plinth, and flagpole in unidentified northern New England village, mid–1960s. (Photo by the author)

Single-minded devotion to commerce made New York the acme of evanescence, built up "just to be torn down"; "nothing more than a provisional city . . . that will be replaced by another city," Le Corbusier echoed James forty years later.[11] But urban provisionality is now global. City dwellers the world over reject the weight of the past and resent commemorative relics: when in 1980 plans were announced to conserve the historic fabric of Dijon, that indigent city's outraged mayor derided the proposed "legacy of stones" as a mausoleum that would bury all hope of advance for the city's inhabitants.[12] In the wake of Hitler, Mussolini, and Stalin, legacies of monumental excess nowadays seem particularly retrograde.

In American cities, to celebrate the past seems especially passé. "We have trouble justifying traditional structures . . . for commemorative purposes," because they "don't foster meditation on forward looking social ideas," writes an architectural historian.[13] "Where in New York is there left a public building or monument of historic value?" was a fin-de-siècle worthy's purely rhetorical query.[14] It was the utter absence of "convincing or moving" urban monuments that struck architectural critic Ada Louise Huxtable at a 1967 New York show. In a vast array of portable, temporary, and disposable projects, "even the best intentions of the best artists and architects seem consistently to fall flat, [leaving] a memorial vacuum filled only with the most redundant and weary clichés."[15]

A generation later, the impending World Trade Center memorial competition led Huxtable to re-echo her plaint. New York was "incapable of the large appropriate gesture in the public interest. [Following] the usual scenario," she foresaw, "the debate will lead to a 'solution' in which principle is lost and an epic opportunity squandered [on] something financially inoffensive." Or as a less kind English critic wrote, "a forest of cheaply built, mediocre office skyscrapers overlooking a cheesy, morbid tourist trap."[16] The greed-and-glory hybrid master plan of 2003 was, indeed, "essentially New York — fast, vital, vain, and not too hung up on the past."[17] And two years on, security concerns forced a redesign of Daniel Libeskind's planned Freedom Tower that another critic termed so "somber, oppressive, and clumsily conceived" as to evoke only "a world shaped by fear."[18]

Commemorative city features often end up as superficial pastiche, at odds both with the actuality of the past and with the present-day scene. To honor native son Jack Kerouac, the city of Lowell tidily beautified a vacant lot; Kerouac would have been more aptly recalled by leaving the lot as it was, littered with broken glass, rusting beer cans, old tires, spent crack needles. Nostalgia marketeers' invented pasts render lifeless the vernacular present. Ubiquitous reminders of olden times strip downtown Riverside, California, of all but pedestrian malls peddling bygones and of the incongruous garaging indispensable to the heritage industry. Indeed, the multitier parking structure that half a century ago replaced Savannah's historic Old City Market was, in 2003, touted to this writer as itself heritage-worthy.

One reason for the ill-repute of urban memorials in America is the neglect that soon afflicts them; who does not deplore Grant's Tomb? Except in Washington, they are neither visited by day nor floodlit by night.[19] And even in Washington, British visitors a century ago lamented the lack of inscriptions on statues; it then emerged that even natives could scarcely tell one ossified American hero from another. Changing taste and morals outdate much public sculpture. Once popular backdrops for presidential inaugurals, Luigi Persico's blatantly racist *Discovery of America* (1844) and Horatio Greenough's *The Rescue* (1853) by the mid-twentieth century were seen as so offensive to Native Americans and African Americans they had to be removed from Washington's Capitol Rotunda and put in storage.[20] Frederick MacMonnies's 1922 statue *Civic Virtue, Triumphant over the Siren of Temptation,* was banished from New York's City Hall to the boondocks (next to Queens Borough Hall), when the classical motif failed to convey its allegorical meaning to unschooled modern viewers, who were simply offended to see a man trampling a woman. Unloved in Queens, too, "Rough Boy" has been offered a haven in Brooklyn's Greenwood Cemetery.[21]

New orthodoxies everywhere jettison previous favorites. In Russia "Bolsheviks topple czar monuments, Stalin erases old Bolsheviks, Khrushchev tears down Stalin, Brezhnev tears down Khrushchev; [we] either worship or destroy."[22] Or rehabilitate, as with recurrent proposals to return to its pedestal in Lubyanka Square the 1958 statue of Feliks Dzerzhinski, godfather of the Soviet secret police [OGPU], pulled down in 1991. "Some associate this man with the K.G.B.," argued the mayor of Moscow, but "others with the crackdown on child neglect and railroad restoration."[23] Monuments have outlived both their initial aims and their later infamy at least since Roman antiquity, when statues and commemorative inscriptions, like texts and portraits, were ceaselessly "corrected"— altered and emended — in line with whatever was politically correct.[24]

In what follows I use imagined city images, notably from Italo Calvino's *Invisible Cities,* to underline attitudes that variously inhibit, thwart, or facilitate commemoration in physical form.

Negative Stereotypes

A prime reason that, at least since classical times, cities have been relatively little glorified with monumental memories is that they are so habitually maligned. Western literature is one long recitation setting rural virtue against urban evil. "God first the garden made, and the first city Cain," intoned seventeenth-century poet Abraham Cowley ("The Garden"); Byron lauded high mountains and found "the hum of human cities torture" (*Childe Harold's Pilgrimage,* 1812); Shelley thought "Hell is a city much like London," smoky and crowded (*Peter Bell the Third,* 1819, part 3); Wordsworth's Luke "in the dissolute city / gave himself to evil courses" (*Michael,* l.442). Imagined urban splendor is apt to be overtaken and obscured by accretions of squalor. The alabaster gates, coral columns, and serpentine-encrusted pediments of Calvino's Moriana are blighted by "rusting sheet metal, sackcloth, planks bristling with spikes, pipes black with soot, . . . blind walls with fading signs, . . . ropes good only for hanging oneself from a rotten beam."[25] The Celestial City of John Bunyan's *Pilgrim's Progress* (1678) is reachable only through the cities of Stupidity and Destruction. Spared all urban defilement was the pearly-gated golden city of St. John the Divine (Revelation 21:10–27), because, of course, it was not of this world.

Afflicted by such odious milieus, it is no wonder that urbanites are so often underground (Léon Groc's *Cité des ténèbres* [1926]), afflicted by blindness (José Saramago's *Ensaio sobre a cegueira* [1995]), or asleep (Maurice Barrère's *Cité du sommeil* [1929], Kipling's "City of Sleep"). The antithesis of the fruitful countryside, the city betokens the barren desolation of death — the River of Suicide girds James Thomson's ruin-haunted "City of Dreadful Night" (1874), the City of the Dead dominates Karl Friedrich May's *Ardistan* (1909); no living soul is permitted entry to the Dead's Town of Amos Tutuola's *Palm-Wine Drinkard* (1952). Some such locales, like Byron's "silent cities of the dead" ("On the Star of 'The Legion of Honour'"), are mute and voiceless; others, like Fritz Lang's film *Metropolis* (1926), are infamously cacophonous. Actual nineteenth-century industrial cities were comparably vile, hundreds of thousands in Britain's dark Satanic mills dwelling underground amid incessant din and stench, chaotic Chicago termed by John Dewey "all hell turned loose."[26] Mike Davis's fearsome depictions of modern Los Angeles echo such desolating motifs.[27]

Cities have commonly gripped memory mainly as sites of horror and ruin, the very names of Carthage and Hiroshima connoting the cataclysms that annihilated them. Piranesi's *Vedute di Roma* and Thomas Cole's *Course of Empire* immortalized city decay and dissolution. Indeed, "The only modern monuments of any measurable impact," Huxtable concluded, "are those devoted to . . . memorials to twentieth-century group massacre."[28] Modern cities brazenly market their past adversities: the moment I landed in Perth, Western Australia, I was handed *A Good Place to Die In,* a searing saga of Perth's famines and epidemics, and made to tour the city's cemeteries. One critic of the proposed Ground Zero 9/11 memorial found it no surprise that "a tragedy of global proportions has given birth to an occasion for civic self-regard; . . . that is how cities have been responding to acts of terror for at least 4,000 years."[29] The movie *28 Days Later* (2002) follows countless others, from *Godzilla* through *On the Beach,* that depict The End as urban nightmare.

Sources of Anti-Urban Prejudice

Cities have not always suffered so unremitting disrepute. Old World metropolitan centers were seen as seats of both corruption *and* redemption, and their positive features often predominated. They were touted as the peaks of civilization, fonts of civic freedom, prime loci of progress, *la ville lumière* that was Paris. From the City of God to the Renaissance city-state, the citadel was fortress and refuge against the mundane, the trivial, the ignorant, the savage hordes and rural idiots beyond the walled sanctuary.[30]

But grim reality came to mock fair urbane promise. From St. Augustine's celestial vision, the City of God degenerated into the scruffy Brazilian shantytown of Paulo Lins's book (1997) and Fernando Meirelles's film (2002) *City of God.* Planners' visions and citizens' hopes are regularly blasted by autocracy and greed, vitiated by social and physical blight. Cities came to be seen as seats of tyranny, sources of subversion, their populace alien, their pursuits parasitical. Sodom and Gomorrah were archetypes of urban evil, Rome notorious for self-indulgence and an epitome for corruption that pauperized far-flung colonies. Roman ill-repute inflated from ancient secular to later imperial and then sacred tyrants; to mid-nineteenth-century pleas for reform, Pope Pius IX's Cardinal Antonelli rejoined that the notion of cleansing Rome was as ridiculous as scrubbing the pyramids with a toothbrush.[31]

By then, Britain's urban heartland had become a Dickensian byword for infernal depravity — Ruskin's "growling, smoking, stinking, ghastly heap of fermenting brickwork, pouring out poison at every pore, the furnaces of the city foaming forth perpetual plague of sulphurous darkness."[32] "God made the country, and man made the town," William Cowper had written in 1783.[33] He was manifestly mistaken; indeed, the lineaments of his own village had just been transformed by a parliamentary enclosure. But Cowper's aim was to glorify the country and defame the town, and his countrymen ever since have followed suit. "The English are town-birds through and through," as D. H. Lawrence declared. "Yet they don't know how to build a city, how to think of one, or how to live in one."[34] Instead, they learned with William Morris to "forget the spreading of the hideous town"[35] and to perfect visions of *rus in urbe.*[36]

American Archetypes of Evil

City infamy escalated across the Atlantic. "The country life is to be preferred, for there we see the works of God," preached William Penn, "but in cities little else but the works of men."[37] Penn's City of Brotherly Love was an etymologically precise but highly ironical nickname for Philadelphia, the first U.S. capital. Its successor, Washington, long infamous for pestilential Foggy Bottom, became "The City of Magnificent Distances"— scenic vistas of grandiose structures too far away for comfort.

In the new democratic republic anti-urban bias waxed pervasive. Americans found civic merit not in urban grandeur but in rural seemliness; they linked virtue with farming and village community, villainy with cities and commerce. All over America, from Ivy League to Arcana Siwash, boarding-school and college education became quintessentially rural and small-town, not big-city.[38] So corrupting were cities —"gangrenes on the body politic," "greenhouse[s] of crime," Thomas Jefferson's "pestilential sores"[39] — that most states sited their capitals in small towns, lest legislators fall prey to metropolitan vice. Gubernatorial functions located in Albany and Augusta, Dover and Springfield, Jefferson City and Harrisburg, Columbia and Madison reflected mistrust of New York City and Portland, Wilmington and Chicago, St. Louis and Philadelphia, Charleston and Milwaukee. In Vermont, despite an isolation so inconvenient that "if the State House had not been here," railed a mid-nineteenth-century delegate, "no man who was not fit for a place in the insane asylum, would believe that its location in Montpelier could be thought of." Yet to avert rule from roisterous Rutland or boozy Burlington, "most peculiar" Montpelier was and still is Vermont's capital.[40]

Jeffersonian rural ideals remained canonical in politics and popular culture even when family farms had become little more than quaint relics in the depopulated countryside. As late as the 1960s, U.S. Information Agency familiarization tours for visiting foreign staff began with a compulsory week in rural central Nebraska, the last refuge of frugal, God-fearing, Currier & Ives–cum–Norman Rockwell America. Today, family farms survive mainly in cinematic imagery and in such fiction, set in somewhat less forbidding Iowa, as Robert James Waller's saccharine *Bridges of Madison County* (1992) and Jane Smiley's whimsical *Moo* (1995), or in Garrison Keillor's endearing Minnesotan Lake Wobegon. Hence the Ground Zero milk-farm memorial imagined by artists Vitaly Komar and Alex Melamid seems supremely apt. "We need something pastoral here, real cows, a smell of manure, and, of course, everything organically fed and grown and so forth. In the middle of hell."[41]

Transatlantic urban antipathy became notably virulent because American cities served few of the functions that had redeemed their European prototypes.

Not ceremonial sites, not seats of high culture, not sanctuaries of freedom, cities in the United States were raw and hustling commercial emporia, built with small regard for aesthetic or cultural comity. In steeply hierarchical Old World society, few but urban merchants and artisans had enjoyed citizens' rights; in the democratic, egalitarian New World the rural yeoman was sovereign. Europe's *Stadtluft macht Frei* tradition was an obsolete irrelevance across the Atlantic: it was ownership of land and freedom of labor that secured liberty for most Americans. There were black slaves, but few white serfs, no "peasants."[42]

Two dynamic processes formed the distinctive character of American cities and at the same time intensified urban antipathy: immigration and the automobile. Newcomers entered through city ports; most stayed on in urban centers. Ever fewer of Anglo-Saxon stock, immigrant urbanites were a polyglot lot foreign to old-time rural America in language, culture, and religion. Censured as crowded and unhealthy, cities incurred further onus for harboring unassimilable hordes whose alien ways threatened domestic American values. Cities were sinks of iniquity, cancers on the body politic. Demonized in best-sellers like Josiah Strong's *Our Country* (1885), Joaquin Miller's *Destruction of Gotham* (1886), and Edward Bellamy's *Looking Backward* (1888), immigrant-infested cities long continued to exhibit every evil spawned, as a patrician New Yorker put it in 1936, by the "influx of foreign ideas utterly at variance with those" of the Founding Fathers.[43] Antebellum nativists blamed Irish Catholics for municipal blight; fin-de-siècle WASPs shuddered at Jewish and Sicilian ghettoes; twentieth-century whites saw slums and crime spawned by black and Hispanic social pathology.

The automobile exacerbated urban degradation. Car culture distanced workplace from residence, rendered existing city centers vacuous or lethal, begot new cities all but devoid of any center at all. "How many visitors to Las Vegas," asks Joel Garreau, "discover that downtown even exists?"[44] No amount of faux–Olde Worlde pastiche can create a Campo dei Fiori in Las Vegas, nor does London Bridge transplanted to Havasu a Thames-side ambience in Arizona make. Anciently compact and coherent, modern cities decenter into amorphous sprawl. As in Calvino's Penthesilea,

> you advance for hours and it is not clear whether you are already in the city's midst or still outside it. . . . Every now and then . . . a cluster of constructions with shallow facades, very tall or very low, like a snaggle-toothed

> comb, seems to indicate that from there the city's texture will thicken. But . . . you find instead other vague spaces, then a rusty suburb, . . . a street of scrawny shops which fades amid patches of leprous countryside.

Today's archetypal city has become "only the outskirts of itself."[45]

Urban sprawl is now common the world over. And "decay metastasizes," in Eugen Weber's phrase. "In the suburban badlands, ageing garden cities turn to crabgrass slums. Mouldering centres [feature] their own feral life and riot tectonics."[46] Urban degradation is global, megalopolis the haunt of the impoverished. By 2011 there were twenty-six megacities with more than ten million people, the great majority in woefully indigent lands. The modern city is less like Chicago than Cairo or Calcutta. Even in Europe's gracious old capitals, rampant crime and runaway mobility make cities the template of today's worst ills.[47]

These trends speed city abandonment by elites, first into green and spacious suburbs, then into gated simulacra of nostalgized village communities, at length into the remoter scenes vacated by the rural poor. Breton folklorist Pierre-Jakez Hélias projects the ironic end result of French agricultural decline and rural depopulation:

> After the peasants abandoned the countryside, all fell into ruins. But the new masters began living there. The richest acquired entire farms and villages. . . . Their country homes became their only homes. Protected from the common people now locked up in the cities, the former bourgeoisie became professional peasants, while children of the former peasants consoled themselves with electronic toys in the city.[48]

The quintessential parable of urban degeneration is Los Angeles, once the garden-city dream, "the New Eden, Nature's Town, the *un*-city city of pure air and sun and sea and fertile soil." By the 1960s nature's dream was a nightmare, the air polluted, the sky blackened, the beaches fouled, the river paved; by the 1990s the drumbeat of disasters had turned Los Angeles "from the American city that destroyed nature into the apocalyptic city where Nature came back for revenge."[49] And who but an Old Testament Jeremiah would want to commemorate *that*?

Three endemic maladies further frustrate urban memory. City scenes are fleeting and transitory; those who live there see little of what is around them; and what they do see they soon forget. Each of these conditions is vividly depicted in literature.

URBAN EVANESCENCE

Urban fabric tends to be short-lived, erased from the scene not only soon but with pride in the erasure. When the wrecker's "work of demolition is accomplished," grieved an early-twentieth-century preservationist, "he surveys the scene of ruin and devastation he had wrought with as much pride and complacency as the builder before him."[50] As the demolition team began to raze the Singer Building, a New York City Beaux-Arts landmark, the foreman proudly said, "This is the tallest building to come down yet, anywhere in the world."[51] Shortly before 9/11, the Big Apple's penchant for pulling down was seen to exemplify what economist Joseph Schumpeter (following Marx's *Communist Manifesto*) termed the "creative destruction" of capitalist urbanization.[52] Profit makes buildings ever sooner obsolete, their destruction a surety of progress. As Las Vegas supplants hoary 1980s hotels with postmodern replicas of ancient Rome, a local demolition firm's reductions to rubble become popular spectacles.[53] The urban fabric's leitmotif is not the rooted tree; it is the roving bulldozer.

Speed of renovation embodies many virtues. It attests a city's prosperity and affirms its devotion to progress. "New buildings are scarcely occupied before they are torn down to make ways for better ones," noted an architectural booster in 1920s New York; he wrote not to deplore but to applaud the dizzying pace of change. Swift replacement guarantees a spanking clean and sparkling newness — that "desperate clean freshness" reproved by Henry James.[54] Older buildings "will never disintegrate from rust — they are scrapped before rust can start."[55] Material evanescence also reflected moral improvement, implying a healthy preference for the future as opposed to the past. So Hawthorne's Holgrave preached that "Our public edifices — our capitols, state-houses, court-houses, city-halls, and churches — ought [not] to be built of such permanent materials as stone or brick. It were better that they should crumble to ruin once in twenty years, . . . as a hint to the people to examine into and reform the institutions which they symbolize."[56] Half a century later, James Huneker lauded New York for leaving "no room for ghosts or landmarks. . . . In our town memories like rats are chased away by the ever-rising flood of progress."[57] Developers equated personal profit with social, moral, and aesthetic betterment, "not only by constructing new buildings but by destroying, at the same time, whole areas of disgraceful and disgusting sores."[58]

Yet this metamorphic fury also engenders angst. The energetic buzz of urban change, averse to anything stable or permanent, often gives rise to Herculean maintenance to conceal, if not to stave off, decay and dissolution. A carapace of care encases buildings, routes, and subterranean channels; from sewers to streets to skyscrapers, canonical city structures are perpetually being patched up. Omnipresent are the adjuncts of repair on landmark buildings — the Coliseum, the Eiffel Tower, the Houses of Parliament, the Empire State Building. Indeed, so much year-round mending do such icons need that they are often invisible; "when a man is tired of London," as one wit paraphrased Samuel Johnson, "he must be tired of scaffolding." As in Calvino's Thekla, "one can see little of the city, beyond the plank fences, the sackcloth screens, the scaffoldings, the metal armatures, the wooden catwalks hanging from ropes or supported by sawhorses, the ladders, the trestles." Underlying the frenzy of renovation lurks a deep anxiety about urban fragility — a "fear that, once the scaffoldings are removed, the city may begin to crumble and fall to pieces."[59]

We demand the new yet at the same time dread to lose the old, all the more so because we disparaged it when it was new. Thus natives of Calvino's Maurilia fondly show visitors postcards of the city as it used to be: the "square with a hen in the place of the bus station, a bandstand in the place of the overpass, two young ladies with white parasols in the place of the munitions factory." But Maurilia's lost grace "can be appreciated only now in the old post cards," while back then "one saw absolutely nothing graceful and would see it even less today, if Maurilia had remained unchanged."[60]

URBAN BLINDNESS

Indeed, habituation increasingly blinds city dwellers to what surrounds them. The vivid diversity of Calvino's Phyllis at first enchants the newcomer: "What a variety of windows looks down on the streets: mullioned, Moorish, lancet, pointed, surmounted by lunettes or stained-glass roses." But the longer you stay, "the more the city fades before your eyes, the rose windows are expunged, the domes" pale into lackluster vacancy. Eventually only utility counts; you follow the shortest route, noting "a bench where you can put down your basket, a hole where your foot stumbles if you are not careful. All the rest of the city is invisible. . . . Millions of eyes look up at windows . . . and they might be scanning a blank page."[61]

The same familiarity dims novelist Norman Juster's Reality, which had at one time been

> a beautiful city of fine houses and inviting spaces. . . . The streets were full of wonderful things and people would often stop to look at them. . . . Then one day someone discovered that if you walked as fast as possible and looked at nothing but your shoes you would arrive at your destination much more quickly. Soon everyone was doing it. They all rushed down the avenues and hurried along the boulevards seeing nothing. . . . No one paid any attention to how things looked, and as they moved faster and faster everything grew uglier and dirtier. . . . Because nobody cared, the city slowly began to disappear. . . . The buildings grew fainter and fainter, and the streets faded away, until at last it was entirely invisible.

Inhabitants of Reality now darted through nonexistent streets and in and out of missing buildings with their heads down, seeing nothing, "but it hardly matters, for they don't miss it at all." And even if they did by chance see something, they would anyway find it harder and harder to remember.[62]

URBAN OBLIVION

"The great city is the best organ of memory man has yet created," wrote Lewis Mumford half a century ago; "the historic city retains . . . a larger and more various collection of cultural specimens than can be found elsewhere," with a fabulous "capacity for making available layer upon layer of human history and biography." But when the urban fabric swells into "a colossal, clotted, self-defeating" megalopolis, clutter and disorganization frustrate memory.[63] Hence Sam Bass Warner Jr.'s bleak remark that "Americans have no urban history. They live in one of the world's most urbanized countries as if it were a wilderness in both time and space. Beyond some civic and ethnic myths and a few family and neighborhood memories, Americans are not conscious that they have a past."[64]

To the eyes of antiquaries and archaeologists, urban remnants can yield manifold clues. But cities' hurly-burly evanescence deprives their chroniclers of the palimpsest so often clearly laid out for the rural historian. Compare the lucidity of W. G. Hoskins's agrarian English sequence with the incongruity of Freud's successive Romes. Remnants of a Saxon boundary bank, of tenures recorded in Domesday Book, of thirteenth-century fiefdoms, of Georgian cultivation and Victorian sheep grazing enabled Hoskins to trace the "immense unbroken stream that has flowed over this scene for more than a thousand years."[65] In contrast to Hoskins's "unbroken stream," Freud's Rome was a tangle of juxtaposed fragments, later structures each effacing their precursors. If architecture were like memory, he mused, the palaces of the Caesars would still survive on the Palatine.

> Where the Palazzo Caffarelli stands, there would also be . . . the Temple of Jupiter Capitolinus, not merely in its latest form, . . . but also in its earliest shape, when it still wore an Etruscan design. . . . Where the Coliseum stands now we could at the same time admire Nero's Golden House; on the Piazza of the Pantheon we should find not only the Pantheon of today as bequeathed to us by Hadrian, but . . . also Agrippa's original edifice; indeed, the same ground would support the church of Santa Maria sopra Minerva and the old temple over which it was built.[66]

Merely to limn this supposition proved it the fantasy Freud intended as a lesson; unlike the human mind's retention of ancient memories, modern Rome's obdurate presence ceaselessly expunges its physical past.

As with Freud's Rome, amnesia afflicts Calvino's Clarice despite its inhabitants' strenuous efforts to conserve a memorable past. The city repeatedly decays and thrives again. During centuries of decadence, residents "grabbed everything that could be taken . . . and put it in another place to serve a different use: brocade curtains ended up as sheets; in marble funerary urns they planted basil; wrought-iron gratings torn from the harem windows were used for roasting cat-meat on fires of inlaid wood." With each renewal of prosperity, conservators of memory went to work, "The shards of the original splendor . . . were now preserved under glass bells, locked in display cases, set on velvet cushions, . . . because people wanted to reconstruct through them a city of which no one knew anything now." Thus "each new Clarice [exhibited] what remains of the ancient Clarices." But in this incessant turmoil no one could recall which embodiment of Clarice came first and which next; "the order of the eras' successions has been lost; . . . the capitals could have been in the chicken runs before they were in the temples, the marble urns could have been planted with basil before they were filled with dead bones."

Continually shuffled and reassembled, what remained of the past city was "only a confusion of chipped gimcracks, ill-assorted, obsolete."[67]

In literary accounts, urban memorial efforts typically succumb to amnesia. Inscribed on great stone blocks, the names of the "Virtuous Women" in Christine de Pisan's *Cité des dames* (1405) endure, but their virtuous deeds are forgotten. To stave off rampant memory loss — first of their childhood, then of the names and uses of things, at length of their very identities — the inhabitants of Gabriel García Márquez's Macondo label objects "pail," "table," "cow," and the like, together with instructions for how to make use of them; but no effort can prevent final oblivion, the past wholly wiped out of everyone's existence.[68]

Are we then doomed to evanescence, blindness, and amnesia? Not always; some urban memorials, though not necessarily those that are adjudged most worthwhile, occasionally endure. I end by briefly noting a range of commemorative devices that have proved durable under various circumstances.

Modes of Urban Commemoration

Some memorialize by protecting past city remains. Others restore what they have lost, as Poles did with Old Warsaw, purposely annihilated by Nazis to break their spirit. Still others recall their past through nomenclature, imagery, pictorial display. Streets and lanes in the City of London, extensively rebuilt after wartime bombing, now carry both their present and previous names, in some temporal confusion — the historical marker on what is now "Old Fleet Lane" says "Formerly Fleet Lane." Turin's main pedestrian arcade features photo-posters of a century and a half of the city's history. Memorial displays on former immigrant sites and streets bring ethnic history in Los Angeles to life. Just as photos on mantelpieces and bureau tops help bring to mind recollections of our childhood and our forebears, so do memory displays in public urban spaces enlarge and enhance collective identities.[69]

Urban continuity is often fabricated when needed: much as invented charters shore up ancestral credentials of shaky regimes, so do plaques and pageants tangibly certify fabulous origins, heroes, and epochal events. Borrowed antiquity succors urbanites who have been expelled from their own familial memories. Like Old Warsaw, Wrocław's medieval quarter was lovingly rebuilt after the Second World War. I wondered what memorial purpose Wrocław's restoration served, for the city's former Silesian German inhabitants were gone; those who lived there in 1974 were exiles from eastern Polish lands annexed by the Soviet Union. These newcomers would not "remember" the city as it had been. True, planners told me, but their *children* would so recall it; for succeeding generations, rebuilt Wrocław would be the "ancient" city the younger generation had always known.

Visual concealment is another way of dealing with memories that are hard to bear, yet cannot be jettisoned; hiding a trauma reminds us of it more than ever. After laying waste to the island of Rhodes and killing its leaders, Queen Artemisia of Halicarnassus "put up in the city a trophy of her victory, including a bronze statue of herself," recounted Vitruvius. Yet when the Rhodians regained their autonomy, the hated statue stayed put. "Laboring under a religious scruple which makes it a sin to remove trophies once they are dedicated, they [instead] constructed a building to surround the place, and thus . . . covered it so that nobody could see it."[70]

Romans, whose rulers from the early Republic on were given to self-glorification, improved upon the Rhodian strategy. When famed figures fell out of favor their statues were not removed or expunged but transformed, new heads replacing old ones on the same bodies. Caligula's portrait was recut as his uncle Claudius who succeeded him, or turned into his ancestor Augustus. Friezes and arches and inscriptions likewise were not wholly but partially erased or overwritten: the newly infamous were not consigned to oblivion but remembered by defamation.[71] *Damnatio memoriae* worked "to *dishonor* memory, not to destroy it," etching recall into stone as eternal punishment. Or even to confirm the existence of a previous set of memories.[72]

Modern Germans, like ancient Rhodians, conserve monumental remains of the Nazi past because it would be wrong to get rid of them. Counter-monuments (*Gegendenkmale*) — memorial shafts sunk slowly into the ground until no trace of them is visible — are ceremonially shut out of sight but not out of mind. Antiquarian masochism prevails — a habit of keeping atrocious relics as "historical documents" on which Germans should meditate. They have become accustomed to historical hair shirts, clinging to what is aesthetically ugly as reminders of what was morally offensive and politically repugnant.[73]

Repellent or attractive, art of every kind is indispensable in reanimating urban pasts. Antiquity glimpsed through Piranesi's engravings, "a part of the lens of every cultivated eye," has primed countless tourists. On arrival in Rome, travelers screen out noxious modern vistas and noisy Vespas, the better to savor vestiges of imperial, Renaissance, and neoclassical Rome. (They do not always succeed; William Hazlitt complained of Rome's "vulgar looking streets where the smell of garlick prevails over the odour of antiquity.") But centuries of "visitors to Rome remarked upon finding a city that they already knew" through Piranesi, "in which the greatest pleasure lay not in discovery of the new, but recognition of the familiar."[74] Saturated with pictorial impressions of Roman antiquity, tourists conflate their own experiences with countless memories of how Rome has been portrayed over time.

Eschewing such portrayals, the Chinese by contrast bypass most pitfalls of material memory. They memorialize cities not by conserving or even literally depicting them but by celebrating them in poetic metaphor. "China has no ruins comparable to the Roman Forum, or even to Angkor Wat, . . . because of a different attitude about how to achieve an enduring monument." Ancient cities commemorate "a past of words, not of stones." The sacred city of Soochow's famed Maple Bridge is recalled as an icon but not as an image: "no single poem refers to its physical presence." What mattered "was not the stones forming the span" but verbal allusions that exalted enduring memories.[75] Indeed, the absence of the actual bridge might, as with German *Gegendenkmale,* more truly spur memorial imaginations.

When consummated in a single blinding instant, such absences shock us into eidetic recall. It is not the bulldozer but the bomb that makes modern cities unforgettable. From Dresden and Hiroshima, to the Pruitt-Igoe St. Louis slums imploded in 1972, to 9/11 in New York, obliteration transforms buildings into memorial sites.[76] Previously "something of an anti-place, . . . with its demise, the World Trade Center became a place like no other."[77] Only their sudden *disappearance* made the unloved towers "the city's most conspicuous and symbolically freighted civic monument. . . . They now stand among the great and vanished monuments of the past. Like the Seven Wonders of the Ancient World . . . they have reached their apotheosis through destruction."[78]

Telling City Stories

Cities are best celebrated by storytelling. And one potent stimulus to memorable fables is urban rivalry. The aging king of Norman Juster's City of Wisdom commands his two sons to "found new cities in the wilderness." One goes south to the Foothills of Confusion to build Dictionopolis, the city of words; the other goes north to the Mountains of Ignorance to build Digitopolis, the city of numbers. Ancient Wisdom falls into grave disrepair because the two sons quarrel incessantly over the relative importance of words and numbers. But enlivened by their feud, both Dictionopolis and Digitopolis flourish mightily.[79]

The real-life urban counterparts of Juster's fictions are Britain's Leeds and Bradford, whose rivalry has generated tales strikingly at odds, one based on buildings, the other on texts. These twin Yorkshire towns were both enriched by nineteenth-century cloth manufacture. But by the mid-twentieth century both were bankrupt, their great factories idle, their grandiose civic buildings moribund. War-battered Leeds rebuilt in modern style in the 1960s; Bradford languished derelict until it embraced heritage tourism in the 1980s. The neoclassical relics of Bradford's Victorian magnates became museums of technology, eloquent witnesses to bygone industrial advance and civic progress. Appalled by this seemingly sanitized whitewash of the Industrial Revolution's evils, Leeds unleashed a stream of pamphlets, laced with lurid quotes from parliamentary inquiries and court records, on child labor, starvation wages, pestilential tenements, tuberculosis, prostitution in dark Satanic mills. Architectural relics and archival remains thus gave rise to opposing narratives, each true in part, that engaged residents and visitors alike, illumining awareness of both cities' pasts.

Monuments that trigger opposing versions of the past can inspire new historical insight. Oral history revealingly clashed with written record in Karen Fields's efforts to verify her grandmother's account of growing up in post–Civil War Charleston, South Carolina—most notably in a tale about the statue of Confederate leader John C. Calhoun. Blacks like Mamie Garvin Fields "hated all that Calhoun stood for."

> [But] our white city fathers wanted to keep what he stood for alive. . . . They put up a life-size figure of John C. Calhoun. . . . As you passed by, there was Calhoun looking you in the face and telling you, "Nigger, you may not be a slave, but I am back to see you stay in your place." . . . We used to carry something with us . . . to deface that statue—scratch up the coat, break the watch chain, try to knock off the nose. [We] beat up John C. Calhoun so badly that the whites had to come back and put him up high, so we couldn't get to him. That's where he stands today, on a tall pedestal. He is so far away now that you can hardly tell what he looks like.[80]

But when Mamie Fields's granddaughter-memoirist checked local newspapers of the time, no reports of "rowdy" black misbehavior surfaced. Instead, she found something "much more interesting [that] opened out instead of pinning down Gram's story": a bizarre saga of the bronze statue the Ladies' Calhoun Memorial Association had erected only in 1879. Alongside Calhoun the sculptor put an allegorical female (to Truth, Justice, the Constitution or History) "in such a state of disrobement that some of the ladies are said to have fainted at the unveiling. . . . Black Charlestonians figured in the city-wide uproar [for] the public work of art began to be called, in Gullah syntax, 'Calhoun and he wife.'" Owing to "the female figure's state of disattire," it was said, "the nickname greatly distressed the ladies of Charleston and Mrs. Calhoun, who was still alive." At last in 1895 the *Charleston Post* reported that "the old statue which has so long been a thorn in the flesh of the ladies of the Calhoun Monument Association . . . to say nothing of the general public will be taken down and consigned to oblivion."[81]

Like Mamie Fields's battered Calhoun and the statue that shocked the ladies, an earlier monument had come to grief. En route from Italy, a Calhoun statue by Florence-based sculptor Hiram Powers had sunk off Long Island in 1850. Raised and repaired in 1857, Powers's Calhoun was sent to South Carolina and set on a pedestal in Charleston city hall. For some viewers "the statue transcended art and became a political symbol." But most "scoffed at it as showing the great statesman barefooted and wrapped in a wet sheet, just as if he had momentarily emerged from his bath, while the discolored tip of his nose, caused by submersion in sea water, indicated Calhoun's addiction to cigars." Perhaps it was well that the statue was taken to Columbia for safekeeping in 1861 and destroyed with that city by Sherman in 1865.[82] It is doubly ironic that Calhoun's sculptor was Powers, whose famed *Greek Slave* made his antislavery bias so patent that his *America,* commissioned long before the Civil War to adorn the U.S. Capitol, never got presidential approval.[83] The saga of all these failed commemorations shines more light on Calhoun's posthumous repute than any extant monument.

Five of Calvino's *Invisible Cities* are what he calls cities of memory. But memorial efforts in each are thwarted by the passage of time, the pace of change, delusions of permanence, or a nostalgic mirage. In his Zaira, it is pointless to try to remember the city's streets, arcades, rooflines, bastions. It is not these physical features that demand and deserve to be recalled, but what has happened in and around them. Zaira is made up of the entwined events that have connected the city's structures and street furniture: the hanging of a usurper from a lamppost, a cat on a gutter, a gunboat's bomb that destroys the guttering, "three old men seated on the dock mending nets and telling each other for the hundredth time the story of the gunboat of the usurper." In soaking up this wave of memories the city expands like a sponge, not only telling its past but embedding and embellishing it "like the lines of a hand, with scratches, indentations, scrolls" marking street corners, window gratings, banisters, flagpoles.[84]

It is not self-conscious commemoration so much as the slow quotidian scratches of time — injuries, erosions, accretions, encrustations — that engrave the residues of memory. The millions of souvenirs left by visitors at the Vietnam Memorial in Washington — army dog tags, medals, gum wrappers, wedding rings, beer bottles — are no mere footnotes to Maya Lin's trench but codicils, corollaries, epitaphs that accrete continuing memory.[85] Collective memories need time to consolidate, and commemoration should respect that deliberate pace. "The significance of [Ground Zero] now is that we don't know what its significance is; we'll know in fifteen or twenty years," said Jane Jacobs in 2004.[86] The right thing to do is to do nothing right away, and hope that the soaring towers of one artist's vision of "New Manhattan City 3021" no longer look like such targets for terrorists.[87]

It is by virtue of the towers' very absence that Ground Zero now resonates, for so many, more like ancient monumental inscriptions than modern commemorative structures. For the holes and scratches left behind evoke a *former* presence, attest what was once there, recall the trauma of its departure. The vanished towers' explicit forms are themselves unmemorable. Save as Godzillan horrors, they will in time be less depicted than the Seven Ancient Wonders, which were famed for their beauty. Ground Zero's present remnants —"this mark here, on the stone before me now"— remind us that *something* was here and significantly lost, even if we do not and care not to remember precisely what. "This vague sense" of monumental aura, Charles W. Hedrick Jr. maintains, this quasi-Freudian impression of palimpsest, is the foundation of historical awareness.[88] As in Calvino's cities, monumental residues, whether in the mind or in the town, endure and can accrete meaning even when only casually and intermittently attended to.

Notes

1. Lowenthal, "Conserving the Heritage," 225–27.

2. Marc Quinn, "Putting the Future on a Pedestal," *The Times* (London), Sept. 7, 2005, 2:28.

3. Dietler, "'Our Ancestors the Gauls'"; Dietler, "A Tale of Three Sites," 72–89.

4. Savage, *Monument Wars,* 1–2.

5. Ariès, *The Hour of Our Death,* 215, 230, 235; Trachtenberg, *The Statue of Liberty,* 100.

6. Barthelme, "Monumental Folly," 33.

7. Savage, *Monument Wars,* 2–7, 257–59, 309–10; Doss, *Monumental Mania.*

8. Williams, *The Country and the City,* 297.

9. Hone, *The Diary of Philip Hone,* 730.

10. James, *The American Scene,* 112.

11. Ibid., 112; Le Corbusier, *When the Cathedrals Were White,* 45.

12. R. Poujade (1980), quoted in Guillaume, *La Politique du Patrimoine,* 167–70.

13. Shanken, "Planning Memory," 130–47; Andrew Shanken quoted in "For the Sake of the Dead, or the Living?" *Berkeleyan* (University of California, Berkeley), Nov. 18, 2004, 8.

14. Andrew Haswell Green (1893), quoted in Page, *The Creative Destruction of Manhattan,* 129.

15. Huxtable, "Monumental Questions," 188–90.

16. Ada Louise Huxtable quoted in Martin Filler, "Filling the Hole," *New York Review of Books,* Feb. 24, 2005, 7; Nicholas Wapshott, "Mistrust and Muddle Aggravate Twin Towers' Desecration," *The Times* (London), June 28, 2004, 14.

17. Philip Nobel, *Sixteen Acres: Architecture and the Outrageous Struggle for the Future of Ground Zero* (2005), quoted in Michiko Kakutani, "After a Day of Terror, a Long Architectural Tug of War," *New York Times,* Jan. 18, 2005.

18. Nicolai Ouroussoff, "A Tower Shaped by Fear," *International Herald Tribune,* June 30, 2005, 1, 8.

19. Kenneth Anderson, "Expanded Horizons: Memory, Memorials and Manhattan's Living Skyline," *Times Literary Supplement,* Sept. 6, 2002, 4–5.

20. Kammen, *Mystic Chords of Memory,* 140–41; Glassberg, "Monuments and Memories," 146.

21. Bogart, *Public Sculpture and the Civic Ideal,* 266–68; Jay Maeder, "For Unloved Queens Statue, Brooklyn Cemetery May Be the Last Stop," *New York Times,* March 7, 2011, A3.

22. Vitaly Komar quoted in Lawrence Weschler, "Slight Modifications," *The New Yorker,* July 12, 1993, 59–65, quotation on 59.

23. Yuri M. Luzhov quoted in Steven Lee Myers, "Moscow: A Call to Restore a Soviet 'Knight,'" *International Herald Tribune,* Sept. 14, 2002; Paul Gobel, "Duma Deputies Applaud Proposal to Restore Dzerzhinsky Statue to Lubyanka Square," *Polish News,* Sept. 22, 2008.

24. Hedrick, *History and Silence,* 238, 243.

25. Calvino, *Invisible Cities,* 105.

26. John Dewey to his family, Aug. 25–26, 1895, quoted in Menand, *The Metaphysical Club,* 319; Mumford, *The City in History,* 461–62, 479–81.

27. Davis, *Ecology of Fear.*

28. Huxtable, "Monumental Questions."

29. Herbert Muschamp, "Balancing Reason and Emotion in Twin Towers Void," *New York Times,* Feb. 6, 2003, B1.

30. Mumford, "City: Forms and Functions."

31. Coppa, *Cardinal Giacomo Antonelli,* 39–49, 68–71, 125–26.

32. John Ruskin (1864; *The Crown of Wild Olive,* 1866), quoted in Lees, *Cities Perceived,* 38; Ruskin, "Rochdale and Pisa" (1859), in Clayre, ed., *Nature and Industrialization,* 137.

33. William Cowper, *The Task,* Book 1, line 749, in his *Poems,* 2 vols. (London, 1814), 2:40.

34. D. H. Lawrence quoted in Briggs, *Victorian Cities,* 8.

35. Morris, "Prologue: The Wanderers," 1:69.

36. Lowenthal and Prince, "English Landscape Tastes."

37. William Penn, *Reflexions and Maxims relating to the Conduct of Human Life* (Philadelphia, 1792), pt. i, no. 220.

38. Fitch, *At Good Old Siwash;* Le Duc, "Arcana Siwash."

39. John Todd, *The Moral Influence: Dangers and Duties Connected with Great Cities* (1841), and Thomas Jefferson, both quoted in Lees, *Cities Perceived,* 91–96.

40. George F. Edmunds (1855), quoted in Lowenthal, *George Perkins Marsh,* 43, see also 186.

41. Alex Melamid quoted in Calvin Tomkins, "After the Towers," *The New Yorker,* July 15, 2002, 59.

42. See Lowenthal, "Visible Cities."

43. Page, *The Creative Destruction of Manhattan,* 79, and (quoting W. T. H. Halsey), 163.

44. Garreau, *Edge City,* 430.

45. Calvino, *Invisible Cities,* 156–58.

46. Eugen Weber, "The Last Days of Los Angeles: Apocalypse in the City of Fallen Angels," *Times Literary Supplement,* July 9, 1999, 5–6.

47. Norbert Gansel (mayor of Kiel, Germany), cited in *International Herald Tribune,* April 8, 2000, 5.

48. Hélias, *The Horse of Pride,* 335–36.

49. Price, "Thirteen Ways of Seeing Nature in LA," 242.

50. William Loring Andrews (1913), quoted in Page, *The Creative Destruction of Manhattan,* 38.

51. Lowenthal, "The American Scene," 76.

52. Schumpeter, *Capitalism, Socialism, and Democracy,* 81–86.

53. Karen Voss, "Venerating Las Vegas: Nostalgia and National Identity," paper presented at the Western Humanities conference, "Cities on the Edge," Oct. 23, 1998. See Rothman, *Neon Metropolis.*

54. "The Building of New York," *Architecture* 56 (Dec. 1927): 324, quoted in Page, *The Creative Destruction of Manhattan,* 5; James, *The American Scene,* 268.

55. "The Building of New York," 324, quoted in Page, *The Creative Destruction of Manhattan,* 5.

56. Hawthorne, *The House of the Seven Gables,* 2:183–84.

57. Huneker, *The Pathos of Distance,* 189.

58. Fred F. French, "Housing in Lower Manhattan" (Address, Princeton University, April 24, 1934), quoted in Page, *The Creative Destruction of Manhattan,* 101.

59. Calvino, *Invisible Cities,* 127.

60. Ibid., 30.

61. Ibid., 90–91.

62. Juster, *The Phantom Tollbooth,* 117–18.

63. Mumford, *The City in History,* 562.

64. Warner, *The Urban Wilderness,* 4.

65. Hoskins, *Provincial England,* 228.

66. Freud, *Civilization and Its Discontents,* 17–18.

67. Calvino, *Invisible Cities,* 106–8.

68. García Márquez, *One Hundred Years of Solitude,* 46.

69. Hayden, *The Power of Place.*

70. Vitruvius, *De architectura,* Book II, chap. 8, and Book VI (New York: Dover, 1960), 56, 167.

71. Holliday, *The Origin of Roman Historical Commemoration,* 203–21; Jan Elsner, "Iconoclasm and the Preservation of Memory," in Nelson and Olin, *Monuments and Memory,* 209–31.

72. Hedrick, *History and Silence,* xii, 242.

73. Stubblefield, "Do Disappearing Monuments Simply Disappear?" 1–11; Perry Anderson, "The German Question," *London Review of Books,* Jan. 7, 1999, 10–16.

74. A. Hyatt Mayor (on Piranesi), quoted in Huxtable, "On Piranesi" (1972), in her *Kicked a Building Lately?* 197–98; Cooper, "Forgetting Rome and the Voice of Piranesi's 'Speaking Ruins,'" 107–8, 114; Hazlitt, "Notes of a Journey through France and Italy" (1826), *Complete Works,* X, 232, quoted in Bromwich, *Hazlitt: The Mind of a Critic,* 16.

75. Mote, "A Millennium of Chinese Urban History," 49–53.

76. Robert S. Nelson and Margaret Olin, "Epilogue: The Rhetoric of Monument Making: The World Trade Center," in Nelson and Olin, *Monuments and Memory,* 305–23.

77. Verlyn Klinkenborg, "The Complex Art of Honoring Memory," *International Herald Tribune,* July 23, 2002, 7.

78. Michael J. Lewis, "In a Changing Skyline, a Sudden, Glaring Void," *New York Times,* Sept. 16, 2001.

79. Juster, *The Phantom Tollbooth,* 73–77.

80. Fields with Fields, *Lemon Swamp and Other Places,* 57.

81. Karen E. Fields, "What One Cannot Remember Mistakenly," 93, 96–98.

82. Wunder, *Hiram Powers,* 1:194–205, 2:115–16.

83. Lowenthal, "'Flesh Warm & Nobly Human!: The Impassioned Purity of Hiram Powers."

84. Calvino, *Invisible Cities,* 10–11.

85. Hass, *Carried to the Wall.*

86. Jane Jacobs quoted in Adam Gopnik, "Cities and Songs," *The New Yorker,* May 14, 2004, 30–31.

87. See Frank Rich, "Culture in the Crossfire after 9/11," *International Herald Tribune,* July 12–13, 2003, 18, on Bodys Isek Kingelez's sculpture at The American Effect exhibition at the Whitney Museum, New York.

88. Hedrick, *History and Silence,* 242, 246.

Bibliography

Adams, Nehemiah. *Boston Common, or Rural Walks in Cities.* Bostonian Society edition. Boston: George H. Light, 1838.

Adams, Zabdiel. *The Evil Designs of Men Made Subservient to the Public Good, . . . A Sermon Preached at Lexington, on the Nineteenth of April, 1783.* Boston: Benjamin Edes and Sons, 1783.

Addresses at the Unveiling and Presentation to the State of the Statue of Thomas Ruffin by the North Carolina Bar Association: Delivered in the Hall of the House of Representatives, 1 February, 1915. Raleigh, N.C.: Edwards & Broughton Printing Co., 1915.

Alderman, Derek H. "Creating A New Geography of Memory in the South: (Re) Naming of Streets in Honor of Martin Luther King, Jr." *Southeastern Geographer* 36, no. 1 (May 1996): 51–69.

———. "New Memorial Landscapes in the American South: An Introduction." *Professional Geographer* 52, no. 4 (November 2000): 658–60.

Allard, Joseph. "The Painted Sermon: The Self-Portrait of Thomas Smith." *Journal of American Studies* 10, no. 3 (December 1976): 341–48.

American Heritage Foundation. "Conference at the White House: For the Purpose of Organizing The American Heritage Program and Inaugurating the Freedom Train, May 22, 1947." N.p.: American Heritage Foundation, 1947.

———. *Good Citizen: The Rights and Duties of an American.* N.p.: American Heritage Foundation, 1948.

Anderson, Benedict. *The Spectre of Comparisons: Nationalism, Southeast Asia and the World.* New York: Verso, 1998.

Anderson, Robert Charles. *The Great Migration Begins: Immigrants to New England, 1620–1633.* 3 vols. Boston: New England Historic Genealogical Society, 1995.

Anderson, Virginia DeJohn. *New England's Generation: The Great Migration and the Formation of Society and Culture in the Seventeenth Century.* Cambridge: Cambridge University Press, 1991.

Ariès, Philippe. *The Hour of Our Death.* New York: Knopf, 1981.

Armor, John, and Peter Wright. *Manzanar,* commentary John Hersey, photographs Ansel Adams. New York: Times Books Division of Random House, Inc., 1988.

Association of American Railroads. *An Outline of Activities of the Association of American Railroads for the Year 1939*. Washington, D.C.: The Association, 1939.

Aston, Margaret. *England's Iconoclasts*. Oxford: Clarendon Press, 1988.

Ayers, Edward L. *The Promise of the New South: Life after Reconstruction*. New York: Oxford University Press, 1992.

Baltzell, E. Digby. *The Protestant Establishment: Aristocracy and Caste in America*. New York: Random House, 1964.

Barthelme, David. "Monumental Folly." *Atlantic Monthly* 237, no. 2 (February 1976): 33–40.

Bassett, John Spencer. *Slavery in the State of North Carolina*. Baltimore: Johns Hopkins University Press, 1899.

Batchelder, Samuel Francis. "The Washington Elm Tradition." *Proceedings of the Cambridge Historical Society* 18 (1926): 46–75.

———. "The Washington Elm Tradition — Is It True?" *Proceedings of the Cambridge Historical Society* 17 (1925).

Benedict, C. Harry. *Red Metal: The Calumet and Hecla Story*. Ann Arbor: University of Michigan Press, 1952.

Benes, Peter. *The Masks of Orthodoxy: Folk Gravestone Carvings in Plymouth County, Massachusetts, 1689–1805*. Amherst: University of Massachusetts Press, 1977.

———. "Night Processings: Celebrating the Gunpowder Plot in England and New England." In *New England Celebrates: Spectacle, Commemoration, and Festivity*, ed. Peter Benes, 9–28. Dublin Seminar for New England Folklife Annual Proceedings, 2000. Boston: Boston University Press, 2002.

Bennett, Tony. *The Birth of the Museum: History, Theory, Politics*. London: Routledge, 1995.

Bercovitch, Sacvan. *The Puritan Origins of the American Self*. New Haven: Yale University Press, 1975.

Bernays, Edward L. *Crystallizing Public Opinion*. New York: Liveright Publishing Corporation, 1996.

Bishir, Catherine. "'A Strong Force of Ladies': Women, Politics, and Confederate Memorial Associations in Nineteenth-Century Raleigh." *North Carolina History Review* 77, no. 4 (October 2000): 455–91. Republished in *Monuments to the Lost Cause: Women, Art, and the Landscapes of Southern Memory*, ed. Cynthia Mills and Pamela H. Simpson. Knoxville: University of Tennessee Press, 2003.

———. "Landmarks of Power: Building a Southern Past, 1885–1915." *Southern Cultures* Inaugural Issue (1993): 5–46.

———. "Landmarks of Power: Building a Southern Past in Raleigh and Wilmington, North Carolina, 1885–1915." In *Where These Memories Grow: History, Memory, and Southern Identity*, ed. W. Fitzhugh Brundage, 139–68. Chapel Hill: University of North Carolina Press, 2000.

Blight, David W. *Race and Reunion: The Civil War in American Memory.* Cambridge, Mass.: Harvard University Press, 2001.

Bloor, Ella Reeve. *We Are Many: An Autobiography of Ella Reeve Bloor.* New York: International Publishers, 1940.

Bogart, Michele H. *Public Sculpture and the Civic Ideal in New York City, 1890–1930.* Chicago: University of Chicago Press, 1989.

Bourdieu, Pierre. *The Field of Cultural Production: Essays on Art and Literature,* ed. Randal Johnson. New York: Columbia University Press, 1993.

Bowen, Daniel. *A History of Philadelphia, Up to the Year 1839.* Philadelphia: Daniel Bowen, 1839.

Boyer, Paul. *Urban Masses and Moral Order in America, 1820–1920.* Cambridge: Harvard University Press, 1978.

Bradsher, James Gregory. "Taking America's Heritage to the People: The Freedom Train Story." *Prologue* 7, no. 4 (Winter 1985): 229.

Brandon, Edgar Ewing. *Lafayette, Guest of the Nation: A Contemporary Account of the Triumphal Tour of General Lafayette.* Oxford, Ohio: Oxford Historical Press, 1954.

Briggs, Asa. *Victorian Cities.* London: Odham's, 1963.

Bromwich, David. *Hazlitt: The Mind of a Critic.* New Haven: Yale University Press, 1999.

Brophy, Alfred L. "Humanity, Utility, and Logic in Southern Legal Thought: Harriet Beecher Stowe's Vision in *Dred: A Tale of the Great Dismal Swamp.*" *Boston University Law Review* 78, no. 4 (October 1998): 1113–62.

Brown, Matthew P. "'BOSTON/SOB NOT': Elegiac Performance in Early New England and Materialist Studies of the Book." *American Quarterly* 50, no. 2 (June 1998): 306–39.

Brownlee, David Bruce. *Building the City Beautiful: The Benjamin Franklin Parkway and the Philadelphia Museum of Art.* Philadelphia: University of Pennsylvania Press, 1989.

Brundage, William Fitzhugh. *The Southern Past: A Clash of Race and Memory.* Cambridge, Mass.: Harvard University Press, 2005.

———, ed. *Where These Memories Grow: History, Memory, and Southern Identity.* Chapel Hill: University of North Carolina Press, 2000.

Burton, Jeffrey F., Mary M. Farrell, Florence B. Lord, and Richard W. Lord. *Confinement and Ethnicity: An Overview of World War II Japanese American Relocation Sites.* Seattle: University of Washington Press, 2002.

Callen, Anthea. "Ideal Masculinities: An Anatomy of Power." In *The Visual Culture Reader,* ed. Nicholas Mirzoeff, 603–16. 2d ed. New York: Routledge, 2002.

Calvino, Italo. *Invisible Cities,* trans. William Weaver. New York: Harcourt Brace, 1974.

Campanella, Thomas J. *Republic of Shade: New England and the American Elm.* New Haven: Yale University Press, 2003.

Carpenter, Channing C. "The Influence of Justice Thomas Ruffin on American Constitutional Law." Ph.D. diss. University of Nebraska, Lincoln, 1972.

Cheah, Pheng. *Spectral Nationality: Passages of Freedom from Kant to Postcolonial Literatures of Liberation.* New York: Columbia University Press, 2003.

Cheshire, Joseph Blount. *Nonnulla: Memories, Stories, Traditions, More or Less Authentic.* Chapel Hill: University of North Carolina Press, 1930.

The Chicago Clubs Illustrated. Chicago: Lanward Publishing Co., 1888.

Chuh, Kandice. *Imagine Otherwise: On Asian Americanist Critique.* Durham: Duke University Press, 2003.

Chuman, Frank. *The Bamboo People: The Law and Japanese-Americans.* Chicago: Japanese American Research Project, 1981.

Clayre, Alasdair, ed. *Nature and Industrialization.* Oxford: Oxford University Press, 1977.

Commission on the Wartime Relocation and Internment of Civilians. *Personal Justice Denied: Report of the Commission on Wartime Relocation and Internment of Civilians,* foreword Tetsuden Kashima. 1982. Reprint. Seattle: University of Washington Press, 1997.

Confino, Alon. "Collective Memory and Cultural History: Problems of Method." *The American Historical Review* 102, no. 5 (December 1997): 1386–1403.

Cooke, Lynne, and Michael Govan. *Dia: Beacon.* New York: Dia Art Foundation, 2003.

Cooper, Tarnya. "Forgetting Rome and the Voice of Piranesi's 'Speaking Ruins.'" In *The Art of Forgetting,* ed. Adrian Forty and Susanne Küchler, 107–25. Oxford: Berg, 1999.

Coppa, Frank J. *Cardinal Giacomo Antonelli and Papal Politics in European Affairs.* Albany: SUNY Press, 1990.

Coppini, Pompeo. *From Dawn to Sunset.* San Antonio, Tex.: Author, 1949.

Crane, Gregg D. *Race, Citizenship, and Law in American Literature.* New York: Cambridge University Press, 2002.

Craven, Wayne. *Sculpture at Gettysburg.* Durham, N.C.: Eastern Acorn Press, 1982.

Crew, Spencer R. "African Americans, History and Museums: Preserving African American History in the Public Arena." In *Making Histories in Museums,* ed. Gaynor Kavanagh, 80–91. London: Leicester University Press, 1996.

Dame, Lorin L. *Typical Elms and Other Trees of Massachusetts.* Boston: Little Brown, 1890.

Daniels, Roger. *Concentration Camps USA: Japanese Americans and World War II.* New York: Holt, Rinehart and Winston, 1971.

———. "Words Do Matter: A Note on Inappropriate Terminology and the Incarceration of the Japanese Americans Nikkei." In *Nikkei in the Pacific Northwest: Japanese*

Americans and Japanese Canadians in the Twentieth Century, ed. Louis Fiset and Gail M. Nomura, 190–214. Seattle: University of Washington Press, 2005.

Davis, Mike. *Ecology of Fear: Los Angeles and the Imagination of Disaster.* London: Picador, 1998.

Davis, Susan G. *Parades and Power: Street Theatre in Nineteenth-Century Philadelphia.* Berkeley: University of California Press, 1986.

Dees, Morris, with Steve Fiffer. *A Season for Justice: The Life and Times of Civil Rights Lawyer Morris Dees.* New York: Charles Scribner's Sons, 1991. Rev. ed., *A Lawyer's Journey: The Morris Dees Story.* Chicago: American Bar Association, 2001.

Dewey, Orville. *An Address Delivered Under the Old Elm Tree in Sheffield, With Some Remarks on the Great Political Question of the Day.* New York: C. S. Francis & Co., 1856.

Dietler, Michael. "'Our Ancestors the Gauls': Archaeology, Ethnic Nationalism, and the Manipulation of Celtic Identity in Modern Europe." *American Anthropologist* 96, no. 3 (September 1994): 584–605.

———. "A Tale of Three Sites: The Monumentalization of Celtic Oppida and the Politics of Collective Memory." *World Archaeology* 30, no. 1 (June 1998): 72–89.

Doss, Erika. *Monumental Mania: Public Feeling in America.* Chicago: University of Chicago Press, 2010.

———. *Spirit Poles and Flying Pigs: Public Art and Cultural Democracy in American Communities.* Washington, D.C.: Smithsonian Institution Press, 1995.

Douglas, George W., comp. *The American Book of Days.* New York: H. W. Wilson, 1937.

Dower, John W. *Japan in War and Peace.* New York: New Press, 1993.

Downing, Andrew Jackson. *Rural Essays,* ed. George W. Curtis. New York: George A. Leavitt, 1869.

Drake, Samuel Adams. *Historic Mansions and Highways Around Boston.* Boston: Little, Brown and Company, 1906.

Dresser, Louisa. "The Background of Colonial American Portraiture." *American Antiquarian Society Proceedings* 76, pt. 1 (1966): 19–58.

Du Bois, W. E. B. "Reconstruction and Its Benefits." *American Historical Review* 15, no. 4 (July 1910): 781–99.

Dubrow, Gail, and Donna Graves. *Sento at Sixth and Main: Preserving Landmarks of Japanese American Heritage.* Seattle: Seattle Arts Commission, 2002.

Dubuque, Robert. "The Painter and the Patriot: John Singleton Copley's Portrait of Paul Revere." *Revere House Gazette* 17 (1989): 1–5.

Dudziak, Mary L. *Cold War Civil Rights: Race and the Image of American Democracy.* Princeton, N.J.: Princeton University Press, 2001.

Duffy, Eamon. *The Stripping of the Altars: Traditional Religion in England, 1400–1580.* New Haven: Yale University Press, 1992.

Duncan, Alice Faye. *The National Civil Rights Museum Celebrates Everyday People.* Memphis: Troll Medallion, 1995.

Durett, Dan, and Dana F. White. *An-Other Atlanta: The Black Heritage.* Atlanta: The History Group, 1975.

Dwyer, Owen J. "Interpreting the Civil Rights Movement: Place, Memory, and Conflict." *Professional Geographer* 52, no. 4 (November 2000): 660–71.

Edmonds, Helen G. *The Negro and Fusion Politics in North Carolina, 1894–1901.* Chapel Hill: University of North Carolina Press, 1951.

Edwards, Laura F. "Law, Domestic Violence, and the Limits of Patriarchal Authority in the Antebellum South." *Journal of Southern History* 65, no. 4 (November 1999): 733–70.

"Eighth Annual Message." In *The State of the Union Messages of the Presidents, 1790–1966,* ed. Fred L. Israel, 2855–61. New York: Chelsea House-Robert Hector Publishers, 1966.

Emerson, B. A. C., comp. *Historic Southern Monuments: Representative Memorials of the Heroic Dead of the Southern Confederacy.* New York and Washington, D.C.: Neale Publishing Company, 1911.

Emerson, Ralph Waldo. "Concord Hymn: Sung at the Completion of the Concord Monument, April 19, 1836." In *Collected Poems and Translations,* ed. Harold Bloom and Paul Kane, 125. New York: Library of America, 1994.

———. "English Traits." In *Selected Writings of Ralph Waldo Emerson,* ed. Brooks Atkinson, 521–690. New York: Modern Library, 1950.

Eskew, Glenn T. "The Birmingham Civil Rights Institute and the New Ideology of Tolerance." In *The Civil Rights Movement in American Memory,* ed. Renee C. Romano and Leigh Raiford, 28–66. Athens, Ga.: University of Georgia Press, 2006.

———. "From Civil War to Civil Rights: Selling Alabama AS Heritage Tourism." In *Slavery, Contested Heritage, and Thanatourism,* ed. Graham M. S. Dann and A. V. Seaton, 201–14. New York: The Haworth Press, 2001.

———. "Memorializing the Movement: The Struggle to Build Civil Rights Museums in the South." In *Warm Ashes: Issues in Southern History at the Dawn of the Twenty-First Century,* ed. Winfred B. Moore Jr., Kyle S. Sinisi, and David H. White Jr., 357–79. Columbia, S.C.: University of South Carolina Press, 2003.

———. "Selling the Civil Rights Movement: Montgomery, Alabama, since the 1960s." In *Dixie Emporium: Tourism, Foodways, and Consumer Culture,* ed. Anthony J. Stanonis. Athens: University of Georgia Press, 2008.

Everett, Edward. *An Address, Delivered at Lexington, on the 19th (20th) April, 1835.* Charlestown: William W. Wheildon, 1835.

Fabre, Geneviève, and Robert O'Meally, eds. *History and Memory in African-American Culture.* New York: Oxford University Press, 1994.

Farnham, Jonathan E. "Staging the Tragedy of Time: Paul Cret and the Delaware

River Bridge." *Journal of the Society of Architectural Historians* 57, No. 3 (September 1998): 258–79.

Favro, Diane. "The Street Triumphant: The Urban Impact of Roman Triumphal Parades." In *Streets: Critical Perspectives on Public Space,* ed. Zeynep Celik, Diane Favro, and Richard Ingersoll, 151–64. Berkeley: University of California Press, 1994.

Felker, Christopher D. *Reinventing Cotton Mather in the American Renaissance:* Magnalia Christi Americana *in Hawthorne, Stowe, and Stoddard.* Boston: Northeastern University Press, 1993.

Fernald, Anne E. "The Memory Palace of Virginia Woolf." In *Virginia Woolf: Reading the Renaissance,* ed. Sally Greene, 89–114. Athens: Ohio University Press, 1999.

Fields, Karen E. "What One Cannot Remember Mistakenly." In *Memory and History: Essay on Recalling and Interpreting History,* ed. Jaclyn Jeffrey and Glenace Edwall, 89–104. Lanham, Md.: University Press of America, 1994.

Fields, Mamie Garvin, with Karen Fields. *Lemon Swamp and Other Places: A Carolina Memoir.* New York: Free Press, 1983.

Finkelstein, Norman G. *The Holocaust Industry: Reflections on the Exploitation of Jewish Suffering.* London: Verso, 2000.

Fischer, David Hackett. *Paul Revere's Ride.* New York: Oxford University Press, 1994.

Fitch, George Helgeson. *At Good Old Siwash.* Boston: Little Brown, 1911.

Flinn, John J., ed. *The Hand-Book of Chicago Biography.* Chicago: Standard Guide Co., 1893.

Foner, Philip S. *The AFL in the Progressive Era, 1910–1915.* Vol. 5 of *History of the Labor Movement in the United States.* New York: International Publishers, 1980.

Foote, Kenneth E. *Shadowed Ground: America's Landscapes of Violence and Tragedy.* Austin: University of Texas Press, 1997.

Forty, Adrian, and Susanne Küchler, eds. *The Art of Forgetting.* Oxford: Berg, 1999.

Foster, Gaines M. *Ghosts of the Confederacy: Defeat, the Lost Cause, and the Emergence of the New South 1865 to 1913.* New York: Oxford University Press, 1987.

Foxe, John. *Foxe's Book of Martyrs, or, the Acts and Monuments of the Christian Church.* Philadelphia: J. J. Woodward, 1830.

Franklin, Jimmie Lewis. *Back to Birmingham: Richard Arrington, Jr., and His Times.* Tuscaloosa: University of Alabama Press, 1989.

Free At Last: A History of the Civil Rights Movement and Those Who Died in the Struggle. Montgomery, Ala.: Civil Rights Education Project, Southern Poverty Law Center, 1989.

Freud, Sigmund. *Civilization and Its Discontents,* trans. Joan Riviere. 3rd ed. London: Hogarth Press and the Institute of Psycho-Analysis, 1946.

Gallagher, Gary W. *Lee and His Generals in War and Memory.* Baton Rouge: Louisiana State University Press, 1998.

García Márquez, Gabriel. *One Hundred Years of Solitude.* New York: Penguin, 1972.

Garreau, Joel. *Edge City: Life on the New Frontier.* New York: Doubleday, 1991.

Gaston, William. *Address Delivered before the Philanthropic and Dialectic Societies at Chapel Hill, June 20, 1832.* Raleigh: Jos. Gales & Son, 1836.

Germain, Peggy. *False Alarm: 1913 Italian Hall Disaster and Death Certificates.* N.p.: Privately printed, 2005.

———. *Tinsel and Tears.* Calumet, Mich.: Privately printed, 1984.

Gibson, Deirdre, and United States National Park Service Denver Service Center. *Cultural Landscape Report, Independence Mall: Independence National Historical Park.* Denver, Colo.: U.S. Dept. of the Interior, National Park Service, Denver Service Center, 1994.

Gilbert, James. *Perfect Cities: Chicago's Utopias of 1893.* Chicago: University of Chicago Press, 1991.

Gillis, John R., ed. *Commemoration: The Politics of National Identity.* Princeton, N.J.: Princeton University Press, 1994.

Glassberg, David. "Monuments and Memories." *American Quarterly* 43, no. 1 (March 1991): 143–56.

Goode, James M. *The Outdoor Sculpture of Washington, D.C.: A Comprehensive Historical Guide.* Washington, D.C.: Smithsonian Institution Press, 1974.

Goode, Jeanne. "Andrew Jackson Downing on Trees." *Arboricultural Journal* 12, no. 2 (May 1988): 189–94.

Greene, Jack P. *The Intellectual Construction of America; Exceptionalism and Identity from 1492 to 1800.* Chapel Hill: University of North Carolina Press, 1993.

Greene, Sally. "*State v. Mann* Exhumed." *North Carolina Law Review* 87, no. 3 (March 2009): 701–55.

Greenhaw, Wayne, and Kathy Holland. *Montgomery: Center Stage in the South.* Chatsworth, Calif.: Windsor Publications, Inc., 1990.

Greiff, Constance M. *Independence: The Creation of a National Park.* Philadelphia: University of Pennsylvania Press, 1987.

Griffith, Robert. "The Selling of America: The Advertising Council and American Politics, 1942–1960." *Business History Review* 57, no. 3 (Autumn 1983): 388–412.

Gross, Ariela J. *Double Character: Slavery and Mastery in the Antebellum Courtroom.* Princeton, N.J.: Princeton University Press, 2000.

Gross, David. *Lost Time: On Remembering and Forgetting in Late Modern Culture.* Amherst: University of Massachusetts Press, 2000.

Gross, Robert A. "Commemorating Concord." *Common-place: The Interactive Journal of Early American Life* 4, no. 1 (October 2003): n.p. http://www.common-place.org.

———. "The Most Estimable Place in All the World: A Debate on Progress in Nineteenth-Century Concord." *Studies in the American Renaissance* 2 (1978): 1–15.

Guibault, Serge. *How New York Stole the Idea of Modern Art: Abstract Expressionism, Freedom, and the Cold War.* Chicago: University of Chicago Press, 1983.

Guillaume, Marc. *La Politique du Patrimoine.* Paris: Galilée, 1980.

Gurney, George. "Sculpting the World War II Memorial: A Conversation with Raymond Kaskey." *American Art* 18, no. 2 (Summer 2004): 96–105.

Gutman, Herbert. *Work, Culture, and Society in Industrializing America.* New York: Alfred A. Knopf, 1976.

Hadden, Sally. "Judging Slavery: Thomas Ruffin and *State v. Mann.*" In *Local Matters: Race, Crime, and Justice in the Nineteenth-Century South,* ed. Christopher Waldrep and Donald G. Nieman, 1–28. Athens: University of Georgia Press, 2001.

Halbwachs, Maurice. *The Collective Memory,* trans. Francis J. Ditter Jr. and Vida Yazdi Ditter. New York: Harper and Row, 1980.

Hall, David D., ed. *Lived Religion in America: Toward a History of Practice.* Princeton, N.J.: Princeton University Press, 1997.

———. *Worlds of Wonder, Days of Judgment: Popular Religious Belief in Early New England.* New York: Alfred A. Knopf, 1989.

Hamilton, J. G. de Roulhac. *Party Politics in North Carolina, 1835–1860.* Durham, N.C.: Seeman Printery, 1916.

Hamilton, J. W. *Memorial of Jessie Lee and the Old Elm.* Boston: J. P. Magee, 1875.

Harrington, Kevin. "Italian Hall." Draft Report for the Historic American Buildings Survey. Washington, D.C.: National Park Service, 1975.

Hashimoto, Fumio. *Architecture in the Shoin Style: Japanese Feudal Residences,* trans. H. Mack Horton. New York: Kodansha International, Ltd., and Shibundo, 1981.

Hass, Kristin Ann. *Carried to the Wall: American Memory and the Vietnam Veterans Memorial.* Berkeley: University of California Press, 1998.

Hawthorne, Nathaniel. "Chippings with a Chisel." In *Tales and Sketches,* ed. Roy Harvey Pearce, 616–25. New York: Library of America, 1982.

———. "The Gray Champion." In *Tales and Sketches,* ed. Roy Harvey Pearce, 236–43. New York: Library of America, 1982.

———. *The House of the Seven Gables.* 1852. Vol. 2 of *The Centenary Edition of the Works of Nathaniel Hawthorne.* Columbus: Ohio State University Press, 1963.

Hayden, Dolores. *The Power of Place: Urban Landscapes as Public History.* Cambridge, Mass.: MIT Press, 1995.

Hedrick, Charles W., Jr. *History and Silence: Purge and Rehabilitation of Memory in Late Antiquity.* Austin: University of Texas Press, 2000.

Hélias, Pierre-Jakez. *The Horse of Pride: Life in a Breton Village.* New Haven: Yale University Press, 1978.

Helper, Hinton Rowan. *The Impending Crisis of the South: How to Meet It.* 1857. Reprint, intro. George M. Frederickson. Cambridge, Mass.: Harvard University Press, 1968.

Hemenway, Henry G. "An Analysis of Civic Education in American Secondary Schools, 1890–1916." Ph.D. diss. University of Nebraska, 1969.

Hoagland, Alison K. "The Boardinghouse Murders: Housing and American Ideals in Michigan's Copper Country in 1913." *Perspectives in Vernacular Architecture* 11 (2004): 1–18.

———. *Mine Towns: Buildings for Workers in Michigan's Copper Country.* Minneapolis: University of Minnesota Press, 2010.

Hobsbawm, Eric, and Terence Ranger, eds. *The Invention of Tradition.* 1983. Reprint. Cambridge: Cambridge University Press, 1997.

Holliday, Peter J. *The Origin of Roman Historical Commemoration in the Visual Arts.* Cambridge: Cambridge University Press, 2002.

Hone, Philip. *The Diary of Philip Hone, 1828–1851,* ed. Allan Nevins. 2d ed. New York: Dodd, Mead, 1936.

Horiuchi, Lynne. "Dislocations and Relocations: The Built Environments of Japanese American Internment." Ph.D. diss. University of California at Santa Barbara, 2005.

———. "Dislocations: The Built Environments of Japanese American Internment." In *Guilt by Association,* ed. Mike Mackey, 255–76. Powell, Wyo.: Western History Publications, 2000.

———. *Nuts and Bolts: A Guide to Researching Japanese American Internment in the Bancroft Library.* Berkeley: The Bancroft Library, 2002.

Horwitz, Morton J. *The Transformation of American Law, 1870–1960: The Crisis of Legal Orthodoxy.* New York: Oxford University Press, 1992.

Hoskins, W. G. *Provincial England: Essays in Social and Economic History.* London: Macmillan, 1963.

Howe, Henry. "New Haven's Elms and Green." In a scrapbook of his articles from the *New Haven Daily Morning Journal and Courier* (1883–1884), 6. Sterling Memorial Library, Yale University.

Huebner, Timothy S. *The Southern Judicial Tradition: State Judges and Sectional Distinctiveness, 1790–1890.* Athens: University of Georgia Press, 1999.

Huffington, Arianna. "A Monument to Distorted Priorities." June 12, 2001. *Arianna Online.* http://www.ariannaonline.huffingtonpost.com/columns.

Hughes, Langston. "Freedom Train." *New Republic.* September 5, 1947, 27.

Hull, N. E. H. *Roscoe Pound and Karl Llewellyn: Searching for an American Jurisprudence.* Chicago: University of Chicago Press, 1997.

Huneker, James. *The Pathos of Distance: A Book of a Thousand and One Moments.* London: T. Werner Laurie, 1913.

Hurst, Williard. "Who Is the 'Great' Appellate Judge?" *Indiana Law Journal* 24 (1949): 394–400.

Huxtable, Ada Louise. *Kicked a Building Lately?* New York: Quadrangle Books, 1976.

———. "Monumental Questions [1967]." In *Will They Ever Finish Bruckner Boulevard?: A Primer on Urbicide,* 188–90. New York: Macmillan, 1970.

Idzerda, Stanley J., Anne C. Loveland, and Marc C. Miller. *Lafayette, Hero of Two Worlds: The Art and Pageantry of His Farewell Tour of America, 1824–25.* Hanover N.H.: University Press of New England, 1989.

Irving, Washington. *Life of George Washington.* New York: G. P. Putnam & Co., 1855.

Jackson, Kenneth. *Crabgrass Frontier: The Suburbanization of the United States.* New York: Oxford University Press, 1985.

Jacob, Kathryn Allamong. *Testament to Union: Civil War Monuments in Washington, D.C.* Baltimore: Johns Hopkins University Press, 1998.

James, Henry. *The American Scene.* 1907. Bloomington: Indiana University Press, 1968.

Johnson, Guion Griffis. *Ante-Bellum North Carolina: A Social History.* Chapel Hill: University of North Carolina Press, 1937.

Juster, Norman. *The Phantom Tollbooth.* New York: Random House, 1961.

Kammen, Michael G. "Democratizing American Commemorative Monuments." *The Virginia Quarterly Review* 77 no. 2 (Spring 2001): 280–88.

———. *Meadows of Memory: Images of Time and Tradition in American Art and Culture.* Austin: University of Texas Press, 1992.

———. *Mystic Chords of Memory: The Transformation of Tradition in American Culture.* New York: Knopf, 1991.

———. *A Season of Youth: The American Revolution and the Historical Imagination.* New York: Alfred A. Knopf, 1978.

Kashima, Tetsuden. *Judgment without Trial: Japanese American Imprisonment during World War II.* Seattle: University of Washington Press, 2003.

Katz, Stanley N. "Bondage, Freedom, and the Constitution: New Slavery Scholarship and Its Impact on Law and Legal Historiography: Opening Address." *Cardozo Law Review* 17, no. 6 (May 1996): 1689–93.

Kauffman, Erle. "The Elm — America's Tree of Glory." *American Forests* 42, no. 5 (May 1936): 222–23.

Kazin, Alfred. *A Writer's America: Landscape in Literature.* New York: Alfred A. Knopf, 1988.

Kikuchi, Charles. *The Kikuchi Diary, Chronicle from an American Concentration Camp: The Tanforan Journals of Charles Kikuchi,* ed. John Modell. Urbana: University of Illinois Press, 1992.

King, Anthony D. *Global Cities: Post-Imperialism and the Internationalization of London.* London: Routledge, 1990.

King, Coretta Scott. *My Life with Martin Luther King, Jr.* New York: Holt, Rinehart and Winston, 1969.

King, Dexter Scott, with Ralph Wiley. *Growing Up King: An Intimate Memoir.* New York: Warner Books, 2003.

Kirker, Harold, and James Kirker. *Bulfinch's Boston, 1787–1817.* New York: Oxford University Press, 1964.

Korobkin, Laura H. "Appropriating Law in Harriet Beecher Stowe's *Dred.*" *Nineteenth-Century Literature* 62, no. 3 (December 2007): 380–406.

Kurashige, Lon. *Japanese American Celebration and Conflict: A History of Ethnic Identity and Festival in Los Angeles, 1934–1990.* Berkeley: University of California Press, 2002.

Lankton, Larry. *Cradle to Grave: Life, Work, and Death at the Lake Superior Copper Mines.* New York: Oxford, 1991.

Latrobe, Charles Joseph. *The Rambler in North America.* New York: Harper & Brothers, 1835.

Le Corbusier. *When the Cathedrals Were White, A Journey to the Country of Timid People,* trans. Francis E. Hyslop Jr. New York: Reynal and Hitchcock, 1947.

Le Duc, Thomas. "Arcana Siwash: The Function and Needs of a College Archives." *American Archivist* 9, no. 2 (April 1946): 132–35.

Lees, Andrew. *Cities Perceived: Urban Society in European and American Thought, 1820–1940.* Manchester: Manchester University Press, 1985.

Lehto, Steve. *Death's Door: The Truth behind Michigan's Largest Mass Murder.* N.p: Privately printed, 2006.

Levasseur, Auguste. *Lafayette in America in 1824 and 1825; or, Journal of a Voyage to the United States,* trans. John D. Godman. 2 vols. Philadelphia: Carey and Lea, 1829.

Levine, Lawrence W. *Highbrow Lowbrow: The Emergence of Cultural Hierarchy in America.* Cambridge: Harvard University Press, 1988.

Levinson, Sanford. "Allocating Honor and Acting Honorably: Some Reflections Provoked by the Cardozo Conference on Slavery." *Cardozo Law Review* 17, no. 6 (1996): 1969–81.

———. "Thomas Ruffin and the Politics of Public Honor: Political Change and the 'Creative Destruction' of Public Space." *North Carolina Law Review* 87, no. 3 (March 2009): 673–700.

———. *Written in Stone: Public Monuments in Changing Societies.* Durham, N.C.: Duke University Press, 1998.

Linden-Ward, Blanche. *Silent City on a Hill: Landscapes of Memory and Boston's Mount Auburn Cemetery.* Columbus: Ohio State University Press, 1989.

Litwicki, Ellen M. *America's Public Holidays, 1865–1920.* Washington, D.C.: Smithsonian Institution Press, 2000.

———. "'Our Hearts Burn with Ardent Love for Two Countries': Ethnicity and Assimilation at Chicago Holiday Celebrations, 1876–1918." *Journal of American Ethnic*

History 19, no. 3 (Spring 2000): 3–34.

Loewen, James. *Lies across America: What Our Historic Sites Get Wrong.* New York: The New Press, 1999.

Longfellow, Henry Wadsworth. "The Landlord's Tale: Paul Revere's Ride." In *The Poetical Works of Henry Wadsworth Longfellow.* Vol. 4: *Tales of a Wayside Inn,* 25–29. Boston and New York: Houghton Mifflin, 1901.

Lowe, Lisa. *Immigrant Acts.* Durham, N.C.: Duke University Press, 1996.

Lowell, James Russell. "Under the Old Elm." In *Poems,* 4:74–89. Cambridge: Riverside Press, 1890.

Lowenthal, David. "The American Scene." *Geographical Review,* 58 (1968): 61–88.

———. "Conserving the Heritage: Anglo-American Comparisons." In *The Expanding City: Essays in Honour of Professor Jean Gottmann,* ed. John Patten, 225–76. London: Academic Press, 1983.

———. "'Flesh Warm & Nobly Human!': The Impassioned Purity of Hiram Powers." In *Hiram Powers e Firenze: Atti del Convegno di Studi nel Bicentenario della Nascita (1805–2005),* ed. Caterine del Vivo. Gabinetto Vieusseux, Studi 16. Florence: L. S. Olschi, 2007.

———. *George Perkins Marsh, Prophet of Conservation.* Seattle: University of Washington Press, 2000.

———. *The Past Is a Foreign Country.* New York: Cambridge University Press, 1985.

———. *Possessed by the Past: The Heritage Crusade and the Spoils of History.* New York: Free Press, 1996.

———. "Visible Cities." *Harvard Design Magazine* No. 13 (Winter/Spring 2001): 78–81.

Lowenthal, David, and Hugh C. Prince. "English Landscape Tastes." *Geographical Review* 55, no. 2 (April 1965): 1–37.

Ludwig, Allan I. *Graven Images: New England Stonecarving and Its Symbols, 1650–1815.* Middletown, Conn.: Wesleyan University Press, 1966.

Maki, Wilbert B. *Stairway to Tragedy.* N.p.: Privately printed, 1983.

Mango, Cyril. "The Triumphal Way of Constantinople and the Golden Gate." In *Dumbarton Oaks Papers* 54, ed. Alice-Mary Talbot, 173–74. Washington, D.C.: Dumbarton Oaks Research Library and Collection, 2000.

Marshall, Anne. *Creating a Confederate Kentucky: The Lost Cause and Civil War Memory in a Border State.* Chapel Hill: University of North Carolina Press, 2010.

———. "'A Strange Conclusion to a Triumphant War': Memory, Identity, and the Creation of a Confederate Kentucky, 1865–1925." Ph.D. diss. University of Georgia, 2005.

Martin, David G. *Confederate Monuments at Gettysburg: The Gettysburg Battle Monuments.* Hightstown, N.J.: Longstreet House, 1986.

Martin, Jonathan D. *Divided Mastery: Slave Hiring in the American South.* Cambridge, Mass.: Harvard University Press, 2004.

Mather, Cotton. *Magnalia Christi Americana, or, The Ecclesiastical History of New-England.* 2 vols. Hartford: S. Andrus and Son, 1853–55.

———. *Parentator: Memoirs of Remarkables in the Life and Death of the Ever-Memorable Dr. Increase Mather.* Boston: B. Green for N. Belknap, 1724.

McCormick, Michael *Eternal Victor: Triumphal Rulership in Late Antiquity, Byzantium, and the Early Medieval West.* Cambridge: Cambridge University Press, 1990.

Menand, Louis. *The Metaphysical Club: A Story of Ideas in America.* New York: Farrar, Straus and Giroux, 2001.

Meyer, Arline. "Re-dressing Classical Statuary: The Eighteenth-Century 'Hand-in-Waistcoat' Portrait." *Art Bulletin* 77, no. 1 (March 1995): 45–63.

Meyer, James. *Minimalism: Art and Polemics in the Sixties.* New Haven: Yale University Press, 2001.

Miller, Lillian B. "The Puritan Portrait: Its Function in Old and New England." In *Seventeenth-Century New England,* ed. David D. Hall and David Grayson Allen, 153–84. Publications of the Colonial Society of Massachusetts, 63. Boston: University Press of Virginia, 1984.

Miller, Perry. *Errand into the Wilderness.* Cambridge: Belknap Press, 1964.

Mills, Cynthia, and Pamela H. Simpson, eds. *Monuments to the Lost Cause: Women, Art, and the Landscapes of Southern Memory.* Knoxville: University of Tennessee Press, 2003.

Milward, Burton. "The Unveiling of the Morgan Statue." In *Lexington — As It Was: A Memento,* 52–56. Lexington: Paddock Publishing, Inc., 1981.

Mires, Charlene. *Independence Hall in American Memory.* Philadelphia: University of Pennsylvania Press, 2002.

Molloy, Larry. "Italian Hall: The Witnesses Speak." N.p.: Privately printed, 2004.

Monaghan, Frank. *Heritage of Freedom: The History and Significance of the Basic Documents of American Liberty.* Princeton, N.J.: Princeton University Press, 1948.

Montagna, Dennis. "A Monument for a New Century." *Army* 53, no. 7 (2003): 42–47.

Morison, Samuel Eliot. *Harrison Gray Otis, 1765–1848; the Urbane Federalist.* Boston: Houghton Mifflin, 1969.

———. "Proposed Tablet Under Washington Elm." Unpublished manuscript. Cambridge Historical Commission, October 27, 1949.

Morris, Thomas D. *Southern Slavery and the Law, 1619–1816.* Chapel Hill: University of North Carolina Press, 1996.

Morris, William. "Prologue: The Wanderers." In *The Earthly Paradise: An Apology* [1868–1870], ed. Florence S. Boos. 2 vols. New York: Routledge, 2002.

Mote, F. W. "A Millennium of Chinese Urban History: Form, Time, and Space Concepts in Soochow." *Rice University Studies* 59, no. 4 (Fall 1973): 35–65.

Mouffe, Chantal. *The Democratic Paradox.* London: Verso, 2000.

Mumford, Lewis. "City: Forms and Functions." In *International Encyclopedia of the Social Sciences,* 2:447–55. New York: Macmillan/Free Press, 1968.

———. *The City in History.* New York: Harcourt, Brace & World, 1961.

———. "The Skyline: Philadelphia—II." *New Yorker.* February 9, 1957.

———. *Sticks and Stones: A Study of American Architecture and Civilization.* 1924. 2d rev. ed. New York: Dover Publications, 1955.

Munch, Eric. "1913 Massacre at Italian Hall." *Chronicle: Quarterly Magazine of the Historical Society of Michigan* 19, no. 4 (Winter 1983–84): 20–21.

Murdoch, Angus. *Boom Copper: The Story of the First U.S. Mining Boom.* 1943. Reprint. N.p.: Privately printed, 1964.

National Highway Users Conference. *Highway Transportation Re-makes America.* Washington, D.C.: National Highway Users Conference, 1939.

National Park Service. *A Grand Endeavor for a Man with a Dream: The Story of Martin Luther King, Jr.* National Historic Site and Preservation District. Washington, D.C.: Department of the Interior, 1997.

———. *Martin Luther King, Jr., National Historic Site Land Protection Plan.* Washington, D.C.: Department of the Interior, 1994.

The Nation's Birthday: Chicago's Centennial Celebration of Washington's Inauguration. April 30, 1889. Chicago: Slason Thompson & Co., 1890.

Nelson, Robert S., and Margaret Rose Olin. *Monuments and Memory, Made and Unmade.* Chicago: University of Chicago Press, 2003.

Nevins, Allan, ed. *The Diary of Philip Hone, 1828–1851.* 2d ed. New York: Dodd, Mead, 1936.

Nora, Pierre, dir. *Realms of Memory: The Construction of the French Past.* Vol. 3: *Symbols,* trans. Arthur Goldhammer, ed. Lawrence D. Kritzman. New York: Columbia University Press, 1998.

———. *Rethinking France: Les Lieux De Mémoire.* Vol. 1: *The State,* trans. Mary Trouille, trans. dir. David P. Jordan. Chicago: University of Chicago Press, 2001.

Norkunas, Martha. *Monuments and Memory: History and Representation in Lowell, Massachusetts.* Washington, D.C.: Smithsonian Institution Press, 2002.

Norton, John. *Abel Being Dead, Yet Speaketh.* London: T. Newcomb for L. Lloyd, 1658.

Okimoto, Ruth Yoshiko. *Sharing a Desert Home: Life on the Colorado River Indian Reservation, Poston, Arizona, 1942–1945.* Berkeley: Heyday Books, 2001.

O'Leary, Cecilia Elizabeth. *To Die For: The Paradox of American Patriotism.* Princeton, N.J.: Princeton University Press, 1999.

Page, Max. *The Creative Destruction of Manhattan, 1900–1940.* Chicago: University of Chicago Press, 1999.

Paige, Lucius R. *History of Cambridge.* Boston: H. O. Houghton, 1877.

Peattie, Donald Culross. *A Natural History of Trees.* New York: Bonanza Books, 1966.

Pennsylvania Hall Association. *History of Pennsylvania Hall which was Destroyed by a Mob on the 17th of May*. Philadelphia: Merrihew and Gunn, 1838.

Peterson, Mark A. "Puritanism and Refinement in Early New England: Reflections on Communion Silver." *William and Mary Quarterly* 3d ser., 58, no. 2 (April 2001): 307–46.

Phillips, John. *The Reformation of Images: Destruction of Art in England, 1535–1660*. Berkeley: University of California Press, 1973.

Pictorial Life of General Lafayette; Embracing Anecdotes Illustrative of his Character. Philadelphia: Lindsay and Blakiston, 1847.

Pollard, Edward A. *The Lost Cause: A New Southern History of the War of the Confederates: Comprising a Full and Authentic Account of the Rise and Progress of the Late Southern Confederacy — The Campaigns, Battles, Incidents, and Adventures of the Most Gigantic Struggle of the World's History*. New York: E. B. Treat, 1866.

Pound, Roscoe. *The Formative Era of American Law*. Boston: Little, Brown, 1938.

Pratt, Walter F., Jr. "The Struggle for Judicial Independence in Antebellum North Carolina: The Story of Two Judges." *Law and History Review* 4, no. 1 (Spring 1986): 129–59.

Price, Jennifer. "Thirteen Ways of Seeing Nature in LA." In *Land of Sunshine: An Environmental History of Metropolitan Los Angeles*, ed. William Deverell and Greg Hise, 220–44. Pittsburgh: University of Pittsburgh Press, 2005.

Prown, Jules David. *John Singleton Copley*. 2 vols. Cambridge: Harvard University Press, 1966.

Purcell, Sarah J. *Sealed with Blood: War, Sacrifice, and Memory in Revolutionary America*. Philadelphia: University of Pennsylvania Press, 2002.

Ramage, James A. *Rebel Raider: The Life of General John Hunt Morgan*. Lexington: University Press of Kentucky, 1995.

Rebora, Carrie, Paul Staiti, Erica E. Hirshler, Theodore E. Stebbins Jr., and Carol Troyen. *John Singleton Copley in America*. New York: Metropolitan Museum of Art, 1995.

Reps, John W. *The Making of Urban America: A History of City Planning in the United States*. Princeton, N.J.: Princeton University Press, 1992.

Robertson, Jennifer Ellen. *Takarazuka: Sexual Politics and Popular Culture in Modern Japan*. Berkeley: University of California Press, 1998.

Robinson, Greg. *By Order of the President: FDR and the Internment of Japanese Americans*. Cambridge, Mass.: Harvard University Press, 2001.

Roth, Michael S. *The Ironist's Cage: Memory, Trauma, and the Construction of History*. New York: Columbia University Press, 1995.

Rothman, Hal. *Neon Metropolis: How Las Vegas Started the Twenty-First Century*. London: Routledge, 2002.

Rozario, Kevin. "Making Progress: Disaster Narratives and the Art of Optimism in Modern America." In *The Resilient City: How Modern Cities Recover from Disaster,* ed. Lawrence J. Vale and Thomas J. Campanella, 27–54. New York: Oxford University Press, 2005.

Said, Edward. *Orientalism.* New York: Vintage Books, 1979.

Sassen, Saskia. *Losing Control? Sovereignty in an Age of Globalization.* New York: Columbia University Press, 1996.

Savage, Kirk. *Monument Wars: Washington, D.C., the National Mall, and the Transformation of the Memorial Landscape.* Berkeley: University of California Press, 2009.

———. Standing Soldiers, *Kneeling Slaves: Race, War and Monument in Nineteenth-Century America.* Princeton, N.J.: Princeton University Press, 1997.

Scharf, Thomas J., and Thompson Westcott. *History of Philadelphia.* Philadelphia: L. H. Everts & Co., 1884.

Schein, Richard H. "Normative Dimensions of Landscapes." In *Everyday America: Cultural Landscape Studies after J. B. Jackson,* ed. Chris Wilson and Paul Groth, 199–218. Berkeley: University of California Press, 2003.

Schumpeter, Joseph A. *Capitalism, Socialism, and Democracy.* 1942. 5th ed. London: George Allen & Unwin, 1976.

Schweitzer, Mary M. "The Spatial Organization of Federalist Philadelphia, 1790." *Journal of Interdisciplinary History* 24, no. 1 (Summer 1993): 45–46.

Shanken, Andrew. "Planning Memory: Living Memorials in the United States during World War II." *Art Bulletin* 84, no. 1 (March 2002): 130–47.

Simmons, James R. *The Historic Trees of Massachusetts.* Boston: Marshall Jones, 1919.

Smiley, Jane. *A Thousand Acres.* New York: Harper's, 1991.

Smith, Carl. *Urban Disorder and the Shape of Belief: The Great Chicago Fire, the Haymarket Bomb, and the Model Town of Pullman.* Chicago: University of Chicago Press, 1995.

Smith, Robert. *Ancestor Worship in Contemporary Japan.* Stanford: Stanford University Press, 1974.

Sommer, Richard M. "The Urban Design of Philadelphia: Taking the Towne for the City." In *Shaping The City: Studies in History, Theory and Urban Design,* ed. Edward Robbins and Rodolph El-Khoury, 135–76. London: Routledge, 2004.

Spicer, Edward, Asael T. Hansen, Katherine Luomala, and Marvin K. Opler. *Impounded People: Japanese-Americans in the Relocation Centers.* Tucson: University of Arizona Press, 1969.

Stein, Sally. "The President's Two Bodies: Stagings and Restagings of FDR and the New Deal Body Politic." *American Art* 18, no. 1 (Spring 2004): 32–57.

Stowe, Harriet Beecher. *Dred: A Tale of the Great Dismal Swamp.* 1856. Reprint, ed. Judie Newman. Edinburgh: Edinburgh University Press, 1999.

———. *A Key to Uncle Tom's Cabin.* 1853. Reprint. Bedford, Mass.: Applewood Books, 1998.

Stubblefield, Thomas. "Do Disappearing Monuments Simply Disappear? The Counter-Monument in Revision." *Future Anterior* 8, no. 2 (Winter 2011): 1–11.

Tateishi, John. *And Justice for All: An Oral History of the Japanese American Detention Camps.* New York: Random House, 1984.

Terdiman, Richard. *Present Past: Modernity and the Memory Crisis.* Ithaca, N.Y.: Cornell University Press, 1993.

Thomas, Dorothy, Swaine Thomas, and Richard S. Nishimoto. *The Spoilage: Japanese-American Evacuation and Resettlement during World War II.* Berkeley: University of California Press, 1946.

Thompson, Roger. *Mobility and Migration: East Anglian Founders of New England.* Amherst: University of Massachusetts Press, 1994.

Thurner, Arthur W. *Calumet Copper and People: History of a Michigan Mining Community, 1864–1970.* Hancock, Mich.: Book Concern, 1974.

———. *Rebels on the Range: The Michigan Copper Miners' Strike of 1913–14.* N.p.: Privately printed, 1984.

Trachtenberg, Marvin. *The Statue of Liberty.* New York: Penguin, 1977.

Trelease, Allen. "The Fusionist Legislatures of 1895 and 1897: A Roll-Call Analysis of the North Carolina House of Representatives." *North Carolina Historical Review* 57, no. 3 (July 1980): 280–309.

Truman, Harry S. "Special Message to the Congress on Greece and Turkey: The Truman Doctrine, March 12, 1947." In *Public Papers of the Presidents of the United States, Harry S. Truman: Containing the Public Messages, Speeches, and Statements of the President, January 1 to December 31, 1947,* 176–80. Washington, D.C.: U.S. Government Printing Office, 1963.

Tudor, William. *Letters on the Eastern States.* New York: Kirk and Mercein, 1820.

Tushnet, Mark V. *Slave Law in the American South:* State v. Mann *in History and Literature.* Lawrence: University Press of Kansas, 2003.

Union League Club. *Exercises in Commemoration of the Birthday of Washington, February 22, 1889.* Chicago: P. F. Pettibone & Co., 1889.

United States Department of Defense, Department of the Interior, National Park Service, Cultural Resources HABS/HAER section. *World War II and the U.S. Army Mobilization Program: A History of 700 and 800 Series Cantonment Construction,* research and writing Diane Shaw Wasch, Perry Bush, Keith Landreth, and James Glass; ed. Arlene R. Kriv. Washington, D.C.: Legacy Resources Management Program, 1988.

United States Department of the Interior, National Park Service. *Long-Range Interpretive Plan, Selma to Montgomery National Historic Trail.* Harpers Ferry, W.V.: Harpers Ferry Center Interpretive Planning, 2003.

United States Department of War. *Final Report: Japanese Evacuation from the West Coast 1942.* Reprint, foreword Henry L. Stimson. New York: Arno Press, 1978.

University of North Carolina at Chapel Hill School of Law. *Thomas Ruffin and the Perils of Public Homage.* Chapel Hill: North Carolina Law Review Association, 2009.

Upton, Dell. "Commemorating the Civil Rights Movement." *Design Book Review* no. 40 (Fall 1999): 22–33.

Waller, Robert James. *Bridges of Madison County.* New York: Warner Books, 1992.

War Advertising Council. *From War to Peace: The New Challenge to Business and Advertising.* New York: War Advertising Council, Inc., 1945.

Ward, William S. *A Literary History of Kentucky.* Knoxville: University of Tennessee Press, 1988.

Warner, Sam Bass, Jr. *The Urban Wilderness: A History of the American City.* New York: Harper & Row, 1972.

Warren, George Washington. *The History of the Bunker Hill Monument Association.* Boston: J. R. Osgood, 1877.

Warren, J. C. *The Great Tree on Boston Common.* Boston: John Wilson and Son, 1855.

Washington, Booker T. "The Negro's Life in Slavery." *Outlook.* September 11, 1909. Reprinted in *Papers of Booker T. Washington,* ed. Louis R. Harlan et al., 10:161–74. Urbana: University of Illinois Press, 1972–89.

"The Washington Elm, Cambridge." *Old Time New England* 14, no. 3 (January 1924): 143–46.

We Are Many: An Autobiography of Ella Reeve Bloor. New York: International Publishers, 1940.

Weeks, Jim. *Gettysburg: Memory, Market, and an American Shrine.* Princeton, N.J.: Princeton University Press, 2003.

Weglyn, Michi Nishimura. *Years of Infamy: The Untold Story of America's Concentration Camp.* Seattle: University of Washington Press, 1996.

Weinberg, Nathan. *Preservation in American Towns and Cities.* Boulder, Colo.: Westview Press, 1979.

Wells, Daniel W., and Reuben F. Wells, *A History of Hatfield.* Springfield, Mass.: F. C. H. Gibbons, 1910.

Welty, Eudora. *One Writer's Beginnings.* 1983. Reprint. New York: Warner Books, 1991.

Wendland, Michael F. "The Calumet Tragedy." *American Heritage* 37, no. 3 (April–May 1986): 39–48.

Whitehill, Walter Muir. *Boston: A Topographical History.* 2d ed. Cambridge: Harvard University Press, 1968.

Whyte, William H., Jr., and Editors of *Fortune. Is Anybody Listening? How and Why Business Fumbles When It Talks with Human Beings.* New York: Simon and Schuster, 1952.

Wigdor, David. *Roscoe Pound: Philosopher of Law.* Westwood, Conn.: Greenwood Press, 1974.

Wigglesworth, Michael. *Day of Doom, or, A Description of the Great and Last Judgment.* Cambridge, Mass.: Samuel Green and Marmaduke Johnson, 1662.

Williams, Avery. *A Discourse, Delivered at Lexington, March 31, 1813, the Day which Completed a Century from the Incorporation of the Town.* Boston: Samuel T. Armstrong, 1813.

Williams, Raymond. *The Country and the City.* London: Chato & Windus, 1973.

Wilson, Charles Reagan. *Baptized in Blood: The Religion of the Lost Cause, 1865–1920.* Athens: University of Georgia Press, 1980.

Wilson, Douglas. "Web of Secrecy: Goffe, Whalley, and the Legend of Hadley." *New England Quarterly* 60, no. 4 (December 1987): 515–48.

Wolff, David A. *Industrializing the Rockies: Growth, Competition, and Turmoil in the Coalfields of Colorado and Wyoming, 1868–1914.* Boulder: University Press of Colorado, 2003.

Woodward, C. Vann. *The Strange Career of Jim Crow.* 1955. Commemorative ed. New York: Oxford University Press, 2002.

Woolf, Virginia. *A Room of One's Own.* 1929. Reprint, foreword Mary Gordon. New York: Harcourt Brace Jovanovich, 1989.

Woolsey, Stephen. "Staging a Puritan Saint: Cotton Mather's *Magnalia Christi Americana.*" In *Puritanism and Its Discontents,* ed. Laura Lunger Knoppers, 210–30. Newark: University of Delaware Press, 2003.

Wunder, Richard P. *Hiram Powers: Vermont Sculptor, 1805–1873.* 2 vols. Newark: University of Delaware Press, 1991.

Wunsch, Aaron. "From Private Privilege to Public Place: A Brief History of Parks and Park Planning in Charlottesville." *Magazine of Albemarle County History* 56 (1998): 82–83.

Young, James E. *The Texture of Memory: Holocaust Memorials and Meaning.* New Haven: Yale University Press, 1993.

Zelizer, Barbie. "The Voice of the Visual in Memory." In *Framing Public Memory,* ed. Kendall R. Phillips, 168–70. Tuscaloosa: University of Alabama Press, 2004.

Zinn, Howard. *A People's History of the United States, 1492-Present.* Rev. ed. New York: Harper Perennial, 2005.

Contributors

JHENNIFER A. AMUNDSON is a Professor in the Department of Architecture at Judson University. Her research focuses on nineteenth-century architecture, professionalism, theory, and technology. Currently at work on a monograph of Thomas Ustick Walter, which follows her first book on his theory, *Thomas Ustick Walter: The Lectures on Architecture, 1841–1853* (2006), she has previously published and spoken at academic conferences on the topics of architectural sculpture, metallic structures, and architects' libraries and competitions.

CATHERINE W. BISHIR, a native of Lexington, Kentucky, is the author or coauthor of numerous articles and prize-winning books on North Carolina architecture and vernacular architecture, including *North Carolina Architecture* (1990); *Architects and Builders in North Carolina: A History of the Practice of Building* (1990); a three-volume series of guides to the state's architecture; and *Southern Built: American Architecture, Regional Practice* (2006). From 1971 to 2001 she served in various capacities in the North Carolina State Historic Preservation Office, and she is currently curator in architectural records special collections at the North Carolina State University Libraries. She is a founding member and former president of the Vernacular Architecture Forum, former president of the Southeast Chapter of the Society of Architectural Historians, and an honorary member of the American Institute of Architects. Her work on monuments and memory was supported by a Henry Francis duPont fellowship at the Winterthur Museum. Her most recent book is *Crafting Lives: African American Artisans in New Bern, North Carolina, 1770–1900* (2013).

THOMAS J. CAMPANELLA is Associate Professor of Urban Planning at the University of North Carolina at Chapel Hill and a Fellow of the American Academy in Rome. A recipient of Guggenheim and Fulbright fellowships, his is the author of *The Concrete Dragon: China's Urban Revolution and What It Means for the World* (2008) and *Republic of Shade: New England and the American Elm* (2003), winner of the Spiro Kostof Book Award of the Society of Architectural Historians.

GLENN T. ESKEW, Professor of History at Georgia State University in Atlanta, is a scholar of the modern American South. Among his books are a study of race reform in

Birmingham, Alabama, and a biography of the songwriter Johnny Mercer. Civil rights memorialization provides the subject for his current research project on ideology and toleration in America.

GLENN FORLEY teaches in the graduate program in the School of Constructed Environments at Parsons the New School for Design. He is a partner in Fizer Forley, a research and design office in New York City. Recent work includes the exhibits *Tailoring Form: A Brief Look at the Anonymous History of the Template* and *Artificial Memory.*

DAVID GOBEL is Professor of Architectural History at the Savannah College of Art and Design, where he teaches courses in Renaissance and Baroque Architecture, Architectural Theory, and the History of Urban Form. He has lectured and given papers on city gates in Renaissance Spain; the treatises of Philibert de l'Orme; theological perspectives on church architecture, and the architecture of the Savannah plan.

SALLY GREENE is Associate Director of the Center for the Study of the American South at the University of North Carolina at Chapel Hill. Her essays on the law, literature, and history of the American South have appeared in the *Mississippi Quarterly,* the *Southern Quarterly, Southern Cultures,* and the *North Carolina Law Review.* Essays on British and American writers have appeared in *Studies in the Novel, Studies in American Fiction,* the *Journal of Modern Literature, Mosaic,* and elsewhere. She is editor of the collection *Virginia Woolf: Reading the Renaissance* (1999).

ALISON K. HOAGLAND is Professor Emerita at Michigan Technological University, where she taught history and historic preservation for fifteen years. Her most recent book is *Mine Towns: Buildings for Workers in Michigan's Copper Country* (2010). She has also published on U.S. Army forts in the West and on Alaskan architecture.

LYNNE HORIUCHI is an architectural historian who received her Ph.D. in 2005 from the University of California at Santa Barbara. She has published articles on the art of Mine Okubo, the historic use of racial covenants in gated communities, and the movement of the Japanese Americans in and out of San Francisco. She is currently writing a book on Japanese American concentration camps with the working title, "Dislocations and Relocations: The Planning, Design, and Construction of Prison Cities for the Incarceration of Japanese Americans." She taught for two years at the University of North Carolina in the Department of Architecture and is currently a Visiting Scholar at the University of California at Berkeley.

ELLEN M. LITWICKI is a Professor of History at SUNY Fredonia. Her research centers on the history and meaning of American cultural rituals. She is the author of *America's Public Holidays, 1865–1920* (2000), and is currently working on a book on the history of domestic gift-giving in the United States.

DAVID LOWENTHAL is Professor Emeritus of Geography at University College London; the author of many works on history, heritage, landscape, and islands; and a frequent consultant for UNESCO, ICOMOS, the Council of Europe, and heritage and museum agencies from Australia to Norway. In 2010 he received the International Institute for Conservation Forbes Prize for conspicuous services to conservation. He is currently completing a revision of his 1985 book *The Past Is a Foreign Country,* to be published in 2013.

MARK A. PETERSON is a Professor of History at the University of California, Berkeley. He is the author of *The Price of Redemption: The Spiritual Economy of Puritan New England* (1997), and is completing a new book called *The City-State of Boston, 1630–1865,* to be published in 2014. He has written extensively on the relationship between words, objects, memory, and history, including "Puritanism and Refinement in Early New England: Reflections on Communion Silver," *William and Mary Quarterly* (April 2001). He is also part of the Mapping the Republic of Letters project at Stanford University, an effort to use digital technology and mapping techniques to raise new questions and avenues for exploring the intellectual world of early modernity.

DAVES ROSSELL teaches American architecture and urbanism, vernacular architecture, and cultural landscape as Professor of Architectural History at the Savannah College of Art and Design. Rossell received his B.A. and Ph.D. from the University of California, Berkeley. His research interests range from field study of the built environment of Savannah and its surrounding low country to exploration in the history of technology, as well as appreciating cross-cultural comparisons of material culture.

RICHARD M. SOMMER is an architect and Dean of the Daniels School of Architecture, Landscape and Design at the University of Toronto. Prior to 2009, he was the Director of Urban Design Programs and a member of the design faculty at Harvard Graduate School of Design for a decade. Sommer's professional and academic activities are diverse, and include recently serving for five years as the O'Hare Chair in Design and Development and Visiting American Scholar at the University of Ulster, where he has worked with government agencies, academics, and other groups to develop proposals for the design of Northern Ireland's cities and towns as they emerge from "The Troubles." Sommer's most recent publications include "Neopolitan Plan," in *Fast-Forward Urbanism: Rethinking Architecture's Engagement with the City* (2011); "Mobility. Infrastructure and Society," in *Ecological Urbanism* (2010); and "Beyond Centers, Fabric and the Culture of Congestion: Urban Design as a Metropolitan Enterprise," in *Urban Design* (2009).

DELL UPTON is a Professor of Architectural History in the Department of Art History at the University of California, Los Angeles. Upton's work focuses on the history of architecture, cities, and material culture in the United States and globally. He is the author, most recently, of *Another City: Urban Life and Urban Spaces in the New American Republic* (2008), which won the 2011 Spiro Kostof Book Award of the Society of Architectural Historians, as well as *Architecture in the United States* (1998), a volume in the Oxford History of Art series. Upton has recently completed a study of monuments memorializing civil rights and African American history and contemporary urban politics in the American South.

Index

Italicized page numbers refer to illustrations.